GW01340009

FIGURES OF LITERARY DISCOURSE

FIGURES OF LITERARY DISCOURSE

GÉRARD GENETTE

TRANSLATED BY
Alan Sheridan

INTRODUCTION BY
Marie-Rose Logan

BASIL BLACKWELL   OXFORD

© Columbia University Press 1982

In French, essays 1, 2, 3, 9, and 10 originally appeared in *Figures I*, copyright © 1966 Editions du Seuil. Essays 4, 5, 7, 8, and 11 originally appeared in *Figures II*, copyright © 1969 Editions du Seuil, and essay 6 originally appeared in *Figures III*, copyright © 1972 Editions du Seuil.

First published in Great Britain in 1982 by
Basil Blackwell Publisher
108 Cowley Road Oxford OX4 1JF England

All rights reserved. No part of this publication may be reproduced, stored in a retrieval system, or transmitted, in any form or by any means, electronic, mechanical, photocopying, recording or otherwise, without the prior permission of Basil Blackwell Publisher Limited.

British Library Cataloguing in Publication Data

Genette, Gérard
   Figures of literary discourse.
   1. French literature—History and criticism
   I. Title
   840'.9   PQ103
   ISBN 0-631-13089-6

Printed in the United States of America

CONTENTS

"Ut Figura Poiesis": The Work of Gérard Genette
by Marie-Rose Logan

Part I
1. Structuralism and Literary Criticism   3
2. The Obverse of Signs   27
3. Figures   45
4. Principles of Pure Criticism   61
5. Poetic Language, Poetics of Language   75
6. Rhetoric Restrained   103
7. Frontiers of Narrative   127

Part II
8. "Stendhal"   147
9. Flaubert's Silences   183
10. Proust Palimpsest   203
11. Proust and Indirect Language   229

    Index   297

INTRODUCTION

"UT FIGURA POIESIS":
THE WORK OF GÉRARD GENETTE

Es ist gleich tödlich für den Geist, ein System zu haben und keins zu haben. Er wird sich also wohl entschliessen müssen, beides zu verbinden.

It is just as deadly for the mind to have a system as to have none. It will thus be necessary to decide to combine both.

Friedrich Schlegel[1]

In many ways, the thrust of Gérard Genette's enterprise rests on the decision to combine a systematic approach to the study of literature with a questioning that exceeds the boundaries of a given system. Genette has, like no other critic, managed to elaborate a reflection on critical discourse which incorporates a system, i.e., structuralism, without ever becoming entirely subservient to it. Yet among the French critics whose work took shape in the sixties and whose names became associated with the structuralist endeavor, Genette is perhaps the one whose importance has been the least recognized in the English-speaking world. Except for the recently published translation of a long essay on Proust entitled *Narrative Discourse* and the forthcoming translation of the *Introduction à l'architexte,* few of Genette's studies have been made available to English readers.[2] Hence, *Figures of Literary Discourse* aims at filling a gap in our understanding of structuralist poetics and of the unfolding of an innovative project.

Introduction

The eleven essays which make up the body of *Figures of Literary Discourse* and which were selected from *Figures I* (1966), *Figures II* (1969) and *Figures III* (1972) illustrate a theoretical endeavor marked by its encounter not only with structuralism but also with historical and thematic criticism, one that progressively evolved toward a review of the boundaries of rhetoric and genre theory. The order of presentation adopted in *Figures of Literary Discourse* follows the traditional distinction between theory and practice. Part I thus consists of seven essays in which the theoretical perspective is emphasized, whereas the essays included in Part II center on the reading of specific literary texts. It should be noted, however, that a rigid distinction between theoretical and practical criticisms does not apply to Genette's work. As I hope to show in this introduction, the issue of the status of critical discourse and of its complex affinities with literary discourse appears throughout the essays. The insistence on the word "figures" in Genette's book titles deserves, in this respect, a closer examination.

What is a "figure"? In the essay entitled "Figures," he explicitly addresses the issue of what a figure stands for:

> The spirit of rhetoric is entirely contained in this awareness of a possible hiatus between real language (that of the poet) and a virtual language (that which would have been used by "simple, common expression"), which must only be reestablished by thought in order to delimit a space of figure. This space is not empty: on each occasion it contains a particular mode of eloquence or poetry. The writer's art lies in the way in which he sets out the limits of this space, which is the visible body of Literature. (p. 47)

From Quintilian on, a figure has been defined as a gap or a modification; this time-honored definition is taken up by Genette and extended to the "visible body of literature." In so doing, Genette implies that a literary work, like a figure, takes place in a space which is not empty but which in fact contains far more than a certain mode of eloquence or of rhetoric because it encompasses the very process of writing. It is precisely in connection with the process of writing that Genette in another essay establishes a relationship between the discourse of the writer and the discourse of the critic, a relationship which offers a parallel to the definition

Introduction

of a figure as "a gap between sign and meaning." In "Structuralism and Literary Criticism," he writes,

> What was a sign for the writer (the work) becomes meaning for the critic (since it is the object of critical discourse), and in another way what was meaning for the writer (his view of the world) becomes a sign for the critic, as the theme and symbol of a certain literary nature. (p. 6)

As a metalanguage, i.e., as a discourse that takes shape in the wake of a previous discourse, the critical discourse is inscribed in a trajectory similar to that which occurs when a figurative expression replaces a literal one: the critical discourse gives a form or meaning to the sign. Conversely, the discourse of the writer also operates in a gap between "real" language and "virtual" language, between sign and meaning. Such a stand implies that the language of the critic and that of the writer constitute the obverse and reverse of a same language. In "Principles of Pure Criticism," Genette states that "the frontiers between critical work and non-critical work have tended to become increasingly blurred. . . ." (p. 73)

Let us turn for a moment to the etymological and semantic substratum of the term "figure." In the *Institutio Oratoria*, Quintilian uses *figurae* as a translation of the Greek term *schemata*: "I now come to figures called schemata in Greek. . . ." There follows a description of what is to be understood by *figura*. "A figure . . . as is clear from the name itself, is the term employed when we give our language a conformation other than the obvious or the ordinary."[3] In stating, "as is clear from the name itself," Quintilian refers to the accepted meaning of *figura*, a conformation or a form. For instance, *figura* was used in the expression *formae figura*, the conformation of a mold. Hence, Quintilian operates a displacement from "virtual language" (that which would have been used as a simple or common expression) to "real language" (in this case, that of the rhetorician).

The meanings of *figura* actually parallel those of the Greek term *schema*. In Aristotle's writings, *schema* is used either to render a rhetorical notion or, simply, to designate a shape such as "the shape of the mouth," σχῆμα τοῦ στόματος.[4] *Schema, figura*: a shape, a form, as well as that particular form that one can give to language in order to move away from the common or the banal. It should be noted that the term *figura* bears etymological connotations with a representational construct. *Figura* was formed by adding the suffix *-ura* to the root *fig-*, from which *fingere*, to mold or to model soft clay and in the broader sense to imagine or to invent, derives. This detour into the historical folds of the word "figure" enables us to take measure of Genette's "figures." First of all, Genette displays a sensitivity to the concept of form as it finds its embodiment in rhetorical treatises. Moreover, the very notion of "figure" underlies a questioning of the status of representational constructs. One might suggest that the essays in the three volumes of *Figures* are an exploration of the resources implicit in the etymological substratum of the normative concept of figure.

In an incisive evaluation of the bearings of rhetoric, Valéry foresaw the turn which the study of rhetoric has taken under the aegis of a critic like Genette:

Ancient writers treated as ornaments and artifices those figures of speech and verbal relations which successive refinements of poetry have now shown to be basic to its aim and which, with the progress of analysis, will one day be regarded as the effects of fundamental properties of what might be styled "formal sensibility."[5]

The stages of rhetoric outlined by Valéry are, in one way or another, dealt with in *Figures of Literary Discourse*. In "Figures" and "Rhetoric Restrained," Genette tackles the issue of the classification of various linguistic manifestations, whereas in essays like "Proust Palimpsest" and "Proust and Indirect Language," he analyzes Proust's entanglement with language. Finally, in "Principles of Pure Criticism," "Poetic Language, Poetics of Language" and "Frontiers of Narrative," he concerns himself with an investigation of the properties of literary language in general and of representation in particular. Ever present in these essays is the notion that rhetoric is not, and cannot be, limited to a mapping out of figures of speech. For instance, in "Rhetoric Restrained," the French poetician reminds us that in antiquity a general rhetoric included style, composition, and eloquence and that Aristotle devoted only a small portion of the *Art of Rhetoric* to figures of speech and tropes. Therefore, the current emphasis on the metaphor as "the figure of figures" discloses, according to Genette, a tendency to restrain the

Introduction xi

boundaries of rhetoric. His own methodological thrust not only broadens the scope of rhetoric but also challenges a certain way of thinking about rhetoric. For instance, in "Rhetoric Restrained" he begins with an examination of the equation, rhetoric = figure = metaphor, which emerges from the Liège group's *Rhétorique générale*, Michel Deguy's *Rhétorique généralisée*, and Jacques Sojcher's *La Métaphore généralisée*; Genette proceeds to show that their mode of thinking reveals an implicit bent toward an epistemological dogmatism which is determined by a rigid use of analogies.

Such analogical patterns of thought tend, by and large, to prevail in the domain of philosophical speculation. The philosopher Chaïm Perelman calls attention to this phenomenon in his essay on "Analogie et Métaphore": "Let us note . . . that analogy quite often leads, not to an empirically verifiable theoretical hypothesis, but to a rule of conduct."[6] Perelman goes on to quote a well-known aphorism of Epictetus on the necessity of curbing one's desires. Perelman's observation could, however, be extended from the realm of ethics to that of epistemology. It is evident that Aristotle, explicity or implicitly, sets up analogical correlations among the various areas of knowledge he takes into consideration, as well as within his reflection on literary discourse. Consequently, the *Art of Rhetoric* and the *Poetics* may be viewed as illustrations of a rather dogmatic and normative mode of thinking about the bounds of literary genres. Aristotle's treatises have continued to play a determinative role in the elaboration of theoretical models, including, most recently, those of I. A. Richards, Rene Wellek, Northrop Frye, and Tzvetan Todorov. In contrast, Genette's critical strength resides in his ability to go beyond received taxonomies and to raise new issues while turning analogies into theoretical hypotheses which are empirically verifiable. A closer examination of "Poetic Language, Poetics of Language" and "Frontiers of Narrative" will help to clarify this point.

"Poetic Language, Poetics of Language" revolves around the received distinction between prose and poetry. As Genette reminds the reader, such a distinction has been based on a difference in style. For centuries, a stringent set of rules concerning rhyme and meter contributed to obliterate a semantic richness that has become more explicit in the light of the work of twentieth-century French poets who shun rhymes and metrics. Such poets not only foster our awareness of the way in which French baroque poets already exploited the graphic and phonic resources of language, but also force us to rethink the status of poetry and the related issue of poetics, i.e., of the theory of poetry. In one of his early essays on baroque poetry, Genette had written: "*To divide* (to share) *in order to unite*, this is the formula of the baroque order. Is this not the formula of language itself?"[7] This statement is in some ways put to test in "Poetic Language, Poetics of Language." Poetic language, according to Genette, by no means unfolds as the swerving from the norm embodied by prose. Prose and poetry constitute analogical modes of language. Poetry, however, stands out as a distortion of language, fostering the illusion of an idyllic stage of language where the gap between sign and meaning would be erased. In other words, what Genette terms "language in the poetic state or *the poetic state of language*" would represent a departure from a norm only insofar as it would appear to abolish the space of a figure, i.e., of "the visible body of literature." In a chapter of *Mimologiques, Voyage en Cratylie* devoted to the *rêverie mimographique* of Claudel, Genette pursues his exploration of the graphic aspect of language in general and of poetic language in particular. Broadly speaking, the underlying thesis of *Mimologiques* also illustrates his ability to turn analogies into hypotheses. Indeed, in the preface, he explains that the term *mimologie* (derived from *mimein*, to imitate) designates a special way of thinking or imagining which, rightly or wrongly, determines an analogical or mimetic relationship between the "word" and the "thing." By association, Genette forges *mimologique*, an adjectival term that renders the musings (*rêverie*) brought about by this mimetic relationship, while *mimologisme* describes the functioning of this relationship within the realm of language; Genette's *mimologismes* do not aim at establishing taxonomies but at providing an investigative mode of dealing with the powers of language.[8]

In "Frontiers of Narrative," Genette engages in a reassessment of the internal boundaries of narrative fiction. The essay centers

Introduction xiii

on an analysis of the polarities mimesis/diegesis, narration/description, narrative/discourse. Genette skillfully demonstrates that the positing of such polarities tends to obliterate the representative forcefulness of narrative. Moreover, by showing that Plato's and Aristotle's definitions of *mimesis* and *diegesis,* as well as Benveniste's acceptions of narrative and discourse overlap, Genette questions the very foundations of theoretical assumptions about the narrative mode. Viewed by Plato and Aristotle as a "weakened, attenuated mode of literary representation," narrative prose did not play a prominent role in Western criticism until the end of the nineteenth century. To a large extent, Genette's interest in prose stems from his own readings of nineteenth-century and twentieth-century novels. Two American critics, Jonathan Culler and Seymour Chatman, have successfully shown that his studies constitute major contributions to the elaboration of a sophisticated theory of narrative.[9] In this respect, Genette, like Todorov, has been able to go beyond the boundaries set by the Russian Formalists. Yet, whereas Todorov is ultimately concerned with paradigmatic models, Genette has used his involvement with narrative in order to further an open-ended interrogation of the nature of literary language.[10] Indeed, *Introduction à l'architexte* should be read as the development of the problematics in "Frontiers of Narrative." There, Genette presents an outline of literature that transcends the traditional barriers between genres. It should be kept in mind that his reflection on contemporary prose work such as that of Sollers, Thibaudeau, and Borges has been instrumental in his coming to terms with the riddle that fiction addresses to the reader. Genette's interpretation of contemporary prose revolves around the notion that literature has ceased to be an object of study but that criticism has become the object the writer's interest. Hence, in an essay on Borges, he writes:

Literature, according to Borges, does not disclose a ready-made meaning, a revelation for us to experience: it is a stock of forms which wait for their meaning, it is the imminence of a revelation which does not happen of itself and which each person must himself produce.[11]

This comment on Borges could be applied to Genette himself; it also leads to a double-edged pursuit. *Figura,* figure: the mold, the form. Literature is a stock of forms waiting to be read, forms in all the senses of the term (including that of figures of speech as set forth by Quintilian). But literature is also a production, *poiesis*,[12] and a space of representation: *figura* in the sense of writing, in whose vortex the critic, like the writer, is engulfed: "The critic cannot call himself a critic in the full sense if he, too, has not been caught up in what must be called the vertigo, or put another way, the captivating and deadly game of writing." (p. 73) Genette's endeavor thus combines the systematic approach which characterizes theoretical research with the non-systematic task of the writer. That is, the critic couples his methodological interests with an exploration of the writing process.

These two movements also take place in the work of Roland Barthes, but they do not coincide. In a forceful essay on "The Obverse of Signs," Genette takes Barthes' work into consideration. This essay, written in 1964, not only stresses Barthes' contribution to the structuralist enterprise and to the semiological project, but also detects in the folds of Barthes' discourse a longing to write, "to turn over the meaning of signs" In fact, a few years later, Barthes did engage in a self-reflexive gesture on writing. From his *The Pleasure of the Text* onward, literature was no longer perceived as an object, but became coextensive with the writing subject. The notion of text, which was previously defined in linguistic terms, came to be presented in the following manner:

Text means Tissue: but whereas hitherto we have always taken this tissue as a product, a ready-made veil, behind which lies, more or less hidden, meaning (truth), we are now emphasizing, in the tissue, the generative idea that the tissue is made, is worked out in a perpetual interweaving; lost in this tissue—this texture—the subject unmakes himself, like a spider dissolving in the constructive secretions of its web.[13]

No longer an object, a product to decipher, the text emerged as the locus where the subject puts himself in question. The project of a theory of the self and of its relationship to writing becomes increasingly molded by a confrontation, evidenced in *Barthes by Barthes* and *The Lover's Discourse*, with psychoanalysis. This gesture thus not only includes an exploration of the writing process, but also illustrates a methodological shift.

Introduction xv

In contrast, Genette has remained on the edges of the "vertigo of writing" he advocated and has resisted any sharp methodological shift. Broadly speaking, he has been faithful, perhaps more than some of his contemporaries, to the "objective" criteria characterizing the structuralist method. In "Structuralism and Literary Criticism," he praises structuralist criticism for its resistance to external ideological biases.

> Structural criticism is untainted by any of the transcendent reductions of psychoanalysis, for example, or Marxist explanation, but it exerts, in its own way, a sort of internal reduction, traversing the substance of the work in order to reach its bone-structure: certainly not a superficial examination, but a sort of radioscopic penetration, and all the more external in that it is more penetrating. (p. 13)

The "radioscopic penetration" into the literary work renders each reading by Genette—whether of Stendhal, Flaubert or Proust—an exercise in methodological rigor and a contribution to our understanding of those authors' works.

The text of Proust frequently appears in Genette's as the privileged locus where the meanings delineated by figures of speech are superimposed. To thematic analyses which grant a preponderant position either to perception or to the intention of the author, Genette opposes an analysis of transpositions which take place in language. These transpositions are a manifestation of the importance accorded by Proust himself to language in general and to metaphor in particular. Genette's approach to Proust thus illustrates two criteria that we have forever gained from the structural method. First, the text articulates its own sources. Second, the intention of the author should not be sought in the circumstances that surround the life of the author and of his entourage, for his intention too is a function of the text. A palimpsest: a manuscript which has been scratched or erased in order to write something else on the parchment. In picturing the work of Proust as a palimpsest, Genette alludes at once to Proust's reflexive writing process and to the path which the reader must follow in order to reveal the layers of meanings which cover each word. In "Principles of Pure Criticism," Genette labels a text "a woven tissue of figures in which the time (or as one says, the life) of the writing writer and the time (life) of the reading reader are tied together and twisted into the paradoxical medium of the page and the volume." The Proustian text evidences this problematic so clearly and in so many ways that, at a round-table discussion led by Serge Doubrovsky during a colloquium on Proust and New Criticism, Genette took the following stand:

> It seems to me that Proust's work, because of its scope and its complexity, and also because of its evolutionary character, of this uninterrupted succession of various states of a same text, from *Les plaisirs et les jours* up to *Le temps retrouvé* confronts criticism with a difficulty which is in my opinion also an opportunity: the opportunity to move from classical hermeneutics, which was paradigmatic (or metaphoric), to a new (or, if you wish, metonymic) hermeneutics.[14]

In spite of his plea for a new hermeneutics, Genette is probably the modern critic who displays the greatest interest in a variety of models. He has carefully read La Harpe, Charles du Bos, Albert Thibaudet, and Georges Poulet, as well as Fontanier and Dumarsais. Genette thus does not operate on the so-called epistemological break, but rather carves his own path by formulating new issues on the basis of different methodologies. For instance, in his most recent work, *Introduction à l'architexte*, he challenges the structuralist notion of the text as a closed linguistic entity from which the analytical process unfolds. In introducing the notions of *architext* and *transtext*, he carries one step further his own assumption about the text as the nodal point where the writer writing and the reader reading meet. This time the reader, i.e., the critic, not only seeks to extend the realm of the study of literary forms but also reappropriates this study within his own domain.

> It is true that *for the moment* the text interests me (only) through its textual transcendence, knowing all that puts it in relation, whether manifest or secret, with other works. This I call *transtextuality*, wherein I include *intertextuality* in the strict (and, after Julia Kristeva, "classic") sense, that is the literal presence (whether integral or not) of one text within another: the quotation, i.e., the explicit convocation of a text, both present and set apart by quotation marks, is the most evident example of the type of function which includes all others as well.[15]

The notions of transtextuality, architextuality, and more recently hypertextuality reveal Genette's will not only to dominate the en-

Introduction xvii

tire realm of literary forms but also to assert the rights of critical theory over those of literature.

In a review of *Introduction à l'architexte,* Geoff Bennington reproaches Genette for his "refusal to acknowledge deconstruction."[16] Such an assertion is perhaps too strong. Yet it is true that with the exception of a brief allusion to *Of Grammatology* in "Principles of Pure Criticism," Genette hardly refers to deconstruction. The relationship of Genette's enterprise to deconstruction nonetheless deserves a closer examination. For instance, like Jacques Derrida, Genette rereads the great philosophical works in order to disclose the equivocality of philosophical language and to rethink the presuppositions upon which our understanding of literary language rests. Genette's gesture toward the discourse of poetics is as all-encompassing as Derrida's toward philosophy. On the other hand, whereas Derrida's work has proceeded from a questioning of the underlying principles of Western metaphysics toward a *mise en effet* of philosophy into literature, Genette's work has moved from the cautious reading of so-called primary and secondary texts toward the elaboration of a new poetics.[17]

As it unfolds throughout the volumes of *Figures* as well as in *Introduction à l'architexte,* the quest of Gérard Genette ultimately challenges the reader's approach to figural modes and to the comlex intertwining of text and reader.

◆

I am much indebted to Gérard Genette, Peter Brooks, Michael Wood, and Leon Roudiez who have graciously helped at various stages of the preparation of *Figures of Literary Discourse.* I also wish to thank David Gorman and Mark Polizzotti for their insightful editorial assistance.

Marie-Rose Logan

NOTES

1. Friedrich Schlegel, Frg. 53, Athenäum, *Schriften und Fragmente* (Stuttgart: Alfred Kröner Verlag, 1956), p. 90. Translation is mine.

2. "Discours du Récit, Essai de Méthode," originally appeared in *Figures III* (Paris: Seuil, 1972) and was published in English as a book, *Narrative Discourse, An Essay in Method* (Ithaca: Cornell University Press, 1980). The English translation of *Introduction à l'architexte* (Paris: Seuil, 1979) will be published by University of California Press.

3. Quintilian, *Institutio Oratoria*, IX, 1–5 (Cambridge: Harvard University Press, Loeb edition, 1966), p. 349.

4. See Aristotle's *Poetics*, 20, 4. For the use of *schema* as a rhetorical term, see, for instance, *Art of Rhetoric*, III, 8 or *Analytica*, 2, 3, 5.

5. Paul Valéry, *Analects,* Stuart Gilbert, tr. (Princeton: Princeton University Press, 1970), p. 101.

6. Chaïm Perelman, "Analogie et Métaphore," *Revue Internationale de Philosophie* (1969), no. 87, p. 12. Translation is mine.

7. Gérard Genette, "'L'Or tombe sous le fer,'" *Figures I* (Paris: Seuil, 1966), p. 38. Translation is mine.

8. In many ways, *Mimologiques, Voyage en Cratylie* (Paris: Seuil, 1976) illustrates Genette's attempt to inscribe his views on linguistic-poetic study in a broad diachronic context. The importance of this work has been grossly underestimated by critics who have failed to relate it to the scope of Genette's approach as it unfolds in the volumes of *Figures*. In this book, Genette also explores the philosophical and literary implications of "analogy."

9. See, for instance, Jonathan Culler, *Structuralist Poetics, Structuralism, Linguistics and the Study of Literature* (Ithaca: Cornell University Press, 1976), pp. 198–99, Seymour Chatman, "Genette's Analysis of Narrative Time Relations," *L'esprit créateur* (1974), vol. 14, no. 4, pp. 353–68, and Seymour Chatman, "Towards a Theory of Narrative," *New Literary History* (1975), vol. 6, no. 2, pp. 295–318. Both authors place Genette's discussion of Benveniste's distinction between "discours" and "récit" in the broader context of the study of temporal relations in narrative. By and large, Genette's "Frontiers of Narrative" is the essay that has received the most attention in America. In a sense, the impact of Russian Formalism as well as a renewed interest in nineteenth-century fiction have contributed to the recent development of narrative theory.

10. See Gérard Genette, "Formalisme et langage poétique," *Comparative Literature* (1976), vol. 28, no. 3, pp. 233–43.

11. Gérard Genette, "La littérature selon Borges, "*L'Herne* (1964), Vol. 4, p. 327. Translation is mine.

12. The spelling "poiesis" has been adopted in order to render the Greek term "ποιησις." Derived from the verbal radical of "ποιέω" *poieo*, I do, the substantive "ποιημα," *poiesis*, designates the creation, the fabrication—hence poetry and *poésie*. In the context of this essay, I intend to stress the twofold meaning of the notion and to distinguish it from

"ποίημα," *poiema*, the object of the creation, i.e., poem. Although Genette, like most structuralist critics, views a text as an object, he also stresses the active process at play through which writing actualizes itself. The French critic Michel Charles has alluded to the paradox inherent in this gesture in *Rhétorique de la lecture* (Paris: Seuil, 1977), pp. 83-96.

13. Roland Barthes, *The Pleasure of the Text*, Richard Miller, tr. (New York: Farrar, Straus and Giroux, 1975), p. 64.

14. *Etudes proustiennes II* (Cahiers Marcel Proust, vol. 7, Paris: Gallimard, 1975), p. 91. Translation is mine.

15. Gérard Genette, *Introduction à l'architexte* (Paris: Seuil, 1979), p. 87. Translation is mine.

16. Geoff Bennington, "Genette and Deconstruction," *The Oxford Literary Review* (1980), vol. 4, no. 2, p. 86.

17. Genette's relationship to deconstructors would call for more elucidation in the light of recent publications such as Jacques Derrida, "The Law of Genre," *Glyph* (1980), vol. 7, pp. 202–32 and Paul de Man "Semiology and Rhetoric," *Allegories of Reading, Figural Language in Rousseau, Nietzsche, Rilke, and Proust* (New Haven: Yale University Press, 1979), pp. 3–19. Both authors refer to Genette's studies of figural modes in an attempt to question the epistemology of rhetoric set forth in Genette's poetics. An analysis of their insights would be beyond the scope of this introductory essay.

PART I

1

STRUCTURALISM AND LITERARY CRITICISM

In a now classic chapter of *La Pensée sauvage,* Claude Lévi-Strauss defines mythical thought as "a kind of intellectual *bricolage.*" The nature of *bricolage* is to make use of materials and tools that, unlike those of the engineer, for example, were not intended for the task in hand. The rule of *bricolage* is "always to make do with whatever is available" and to use in a new structure the remains of previous constructions or destructions, thus making the specific manufacture of materials and tools unnecessary, though at the cost of a double operation of analysis (the extraction of various elements from various already-constituted wholes) and of synthesis (the forming of these heterogeneous elements into a new whole in which none of the re-used elements will necessarily be used as originally intended).[1] It should be remembered that this typically "structuralist" operation, which makes up for a lack of production by means of an extreme ingenuity in the distribution of remnants, was discovered by an ethnologist attempting to account for the way myths are invented by so-called "primitive" civilizations. But there is another intellectual activity, peculiar to more "developed" cultures, to which this analysis might be applied almost word for word: I mean criticism, more particularly literary criticism, which distinguishes itself formally from other kinds of criticism by the fact that it uses the same materials—writing—as the works with which it is concerned; art criticism or musical criticism are obviously not expressed in sound or in color, but literary criticism speaks the same language as its object: it is a metalanguage, "discourse upon a discourse."[2] It can therefore be a metaliterature, that is to say, "a literature of which literature itself is the imposed object."[3]

If in fact one isolates the two most obvious functions of the critical activity—the "critical" function in the literal sense of the term, which consists of judging and appreciating recent works with a view to helping the public make up its mind (a function linked to the institution of journalism), and the "scientific" function (linked, generally speaking, to the institution of the university), which consists of a positive study, solely with a view to knowledge, of the conditions of existence of literary works (the materiality of the text, sources, psychological or historical origins, etc.)—there is obviously a third, which is strictly literary. A book of criticism like Sainte-Beuve's *Port-Royal* or Maurice Blanchot's *L'Espace littéraire* is among other things a book, and its author is in his own way and at least to a certain extent what Roland Barthes calls an *écrivain* (a writer, in contradistinction to the mere *écrivant*, or someone who happens to write), that is to say, the author of a message which to some extent tends to be absorbed into spectacle. This "frustration" of meaning, which is frozen and constituted in an object of esthetic consumption is no doubt the movement (or rather the *halt*) that constitutes all literature. The literary object only exists through it; on the other hand, it is dependent upon it alone and, depending on the circumstances, any text may or may not be literature, according to whether it is received (either) as spectacle or (else) as message: literary history is made up of these comings-and-goings, these fluctuations. That is, there is no literary object strictly speaking, but only a *literary function*, which can invest or abandon any object of writing in turn. Its partial, unstable, ambiguous literariness is not therefore a property of criticism: what distinguishes criticism from the other literary "genres" is its *secondary* character, and it is here that Lévi-Strauss' remarks on *bricolage* may find a somewhat unexpected application.

The instrumental universe of the *bricoleur*, says Lévi-Strauss, is a "closed" universe. Its repertoire, however extended, "remains limited." This limitation distinguishes the *bricoleur* from the engineer, who (in principle) can at any time obtain the tool specially adapted to a particular technical need. The engineer "questions the universe, while the *bricoleur* addresses himself to a collection of oddments left over from human endeavors, that is, only a subset of the culture."[4] One has only to replace in the last sentence the words "engineer" and *bricoleur* by "novelist" (for example) and "critic" respectively to define the literary status of criticism. The materials of the critical task are indeed those "oddments left over from human endeavors," which is what works of literature are once they have been reduced to themes, motifs, key-words, obsessive metaphors, quotations, index cards, and references. The initial work is a structure, like those primary wholes that the *bricoleur* dismantles in order to extract parts which may prove useful; the critic too breaks down a structure into its elements—one element per card—and the *bricoleur*'s motto, "that might always come in handy," is the very postulate that inspires the critic when he is making up his card-index, literally or figuratively, of course. His next task is to build up a new structure while "rearranging these oddments." "*Critical* thought," one might say, paraphrasing Lévi-Strauss, "builds structured sets by means of a structured set, namely, *the work*. But it is not at the structural level that it makes use of it: it builds ideological castles out of the debris of what was once a *literary* discourse."

The distinction between the critic and the writer lies not only in the secondary and limited character of the critical material (literature) as opposed to the unlimited and primary character of the poetic or fictional material (the universe); this as it were quantitative inferiority, which derives from the fact that the critic always comes after the writer and has at his disposal only materials imposed by the previous choice of the writer, is perhaps aggravated, perhaps compensated by another difference: "*The writer* works by means of concepts and *the critic* by means of signs. Within the opposition between nature and culture, there is only an imperceptible discrepancy between the sets employed by each. One way indeed in which signs can be opposed to concepts is that whereas concepts seem to be wholly transparent with respect to reality, signs allow and even require the interposing and incorporation of a certain amount of human culture into reality." If the writer questions the universe, the critic questions literature, that is to say, the universe of signs. But what was a sign for the writer (the work) becomes meaning for the critic (since it is the object of the critical discourse), and in another way what was meaning for the writer (his view of the world) becomes a sign for the critic, as the theme and symbol of a certain literary nature. This, again, is what Lévi-Strauss says of mythical thought, which, as Franz Boas remarked, constantly creates new worlds, but by reversing means and ends: "signifieds change into signifiers, and vice versa." This constant interchange, this perpetual inversion of signs and meaning is a good description of the dual function of the critic's work, which is to produce meaning with the work of others, but also to produce his own work out of this meaning. If such a thing as "critical poetry" exists, therefore, it is in the sense in which Lévi-Strauss speaks of a "poetry of *bricolage*": just as the *bricoleur* "speaks through things," the critic speaks—in the full sense, that is to say, speaks up—through books, and we will paraphrase Lévi-Strauss once more by saying that "without ever completing his project he always puts something of himself into it."

In this sense, therefore, one can regard literary criticism as a "structuralist activity"; but it is not—as is quite clear—merely an implicit, unreflective structuralism. The question posed by the present orientation of such human sciences as linguistics or anthropology is whether criticism is being called upon to organize its structuralist vocation explicitly in a structural method. My aim here is simply to elucidate the meaning and scope of this question, suggesting the principal ways in which structuralism could reach the object of criticism, and offer itself to criticism as a fruitful method.

Literature being primarily a work of language, and structuralism, for its part, being preeminently a linguistic method, the most probable encounter should obviously take place on the terrain of linguistic material: sounds, forms, words, and sentences constitute the common object of the linguist and the philologist to such an extent that it was possible, in the early enthusiasm of the Russian

Formalist movement, to define literature as a mere dialect, and to envisage its study as an annex of general dialectology.[5] Indeed, Russian Formalism, which is rightly regarded as one of the matrices of structural linguistics, was at first nothing more than a meeting of critics and linguists on the terrain of "poetic language." This assimilation of literature to a dialect raises objections that are too obvious for it to be taken literally. If literature *were* a dialect, it would be a translinguistic dialect effecting on all languages a number of transformations, different in their procedures but similar in their function, rather as the various forms of slang are parasitical in various ways on the various languages, but are similar in their parasitical function: nothing of the kind can be proposed in the case of dialects. In particular, the difference between "literary language" and ordinary language resides not so much in the means as in the ends; apart from a few inflections, the writer uses the same language as other users, but he uses it neither in the same way nor with the same intention—identical material, displaced function: this status is exactly the reverse of that of a dialect. But, like other "excesses" committed by Formalism, this particular one had cathartic value: by temporarily ignoring content, the provisional reduction of literature's "literary being"[6] to its linguistic being made it possible to revise certain traditional "verities" concerning the "truth" of literary discourse, and to study more closely the system of its conventions. Literature had long enough been regarded as a message without a code for it to become necessary to regard it for a time as a code without a message.

Structuralist method as such is constituted at the very moment when one rediscovers the message in the code, uncovered by an analysis of the immanent structures and not imposed from the outside by ideological prejudices. This moment was not to be long in coming,[7] for the existence of the sign, at every level, rests on the connection of form and meaning. Thus Roman Jakobson, in his study of Czech verse of 1923, discovered a relationship between the prosodic value of a phonic feature and its signifying value, each language tending to give the greatest prosodic importance to the system of oppositions most relevant on the semantic plane: stress or "dynamic accent" in Russian, length in Greek, pitch or "musical accent" in Serbo-Croatian.[8] This passage from the phonetic to the phonemic, that is to say, from the pure sound substance, dear to early Formalist thinking, to the organization of this substance in a signifying system (or at least one capable of signification) is of interest not only to the study of metrics, since it was rightly seen as an anticipation of the phonological method.[9] It represents rather well what the contribution of structuralism might be to the study of literary morphology as a whole: poetics, stylistics, composition. Between pure Formalism, which reduces literary "forms" to a sound material that is ultimately formless, because nonsignifying,[10] and traditional realism, which accords to each form an autonomous, substantial "expressive value," structural analysis must make it possible to uncover the connection that exists between a system of forms and a system of meanings, by replacing the search for term-by-term analogies with one for overall homologies.

A simplistic example might serve to clarify the matter: one of the traditional unsolved problems of the theory of expressivity is the question of the "color" of vowels, which was put into the forefront by Rimbaud's sonnet. The advocates of phonic expressivity, such as Otto Jespersen or Maurice Grammont, tried to attribute to each phoneme its own suggestive value, which, it was thought, governed the makeup of certain words in all languages. Others exposed the weakness of these hypotheses,[11] and, as far as the color of vowels was concerned, the comparative tables drawn up by Etiemble[12] show quite clearly that the advocates of "colored sounds" agree on none of their attributions.[13] Their adversaries naturally concluded from this that "colored sounds" were a myth—and as a fact of *nature*, they may well be nothing more. But the disparity of the individual tables does not destroy the authenticity of each of them, and structuralism can suggest an explanation here that takes account both of the arbitrariness of each vowel-color and of the very widespread sense of a vocalic chromaticism: it is true that no vowel evokes, naturally and in isolation, a particular color; but it is also true that the distribution of colors in the spectrum (which indeed is itself, as Gelb and Goldstein have shown, as much a fact of language as of vision) can find its correspondence in the distribution of vowels in a given language. Hence the idea of a table of concordance, variable in its details but constant in its function: there is a spectrum of vowels as there is a spectrum of colors; the two systems evoke and attract one another, and the overall homology creates the illusion of a term-by-term analogy, which each realizes in its own way by an act of symbolic motivation comparable to the one analyzed by Lévi-Strauss in the case of totemism. Each individual motivation, objectively arbitrary but subjectively based, can be regarded, then, as the index of a particular psychic configuration. The structural hypothesis, in this case, gives back to the stylistics of the subject what it takes from the stylistics of the object.

So structuralism is under no obligation to confine itself to "surface" analyses, quite the reverse: here as elsewhere, the horizon of its approach is the analysis of significations. "No doubt verse is primarily a recurrent 'figure of sound.' Primarily, always, but never uniquely. . . . Valéry's view of poetry as 'hesitation between the sound and the sense' is much more realistic and scientific than any bias of phonetic isolationism."[14] The importance attached by Jakobson, since his 1935 article on Pasternak, to the concepts of metaphor and metonymy, borrowed from the rhetoric of tropes, is characteristic of this orientation, especially if one remembers that one of the war-horses of early Formalism was a contempt for images, and the devaluation of tropes as marks of poetic language. Speaking of a poem by Pushkin, Jakobson himself was still insisting, in 1936, on the possibility of poetry without imagery.[15] In 1958 he took up this question with a very marked shift of emphasis: "Textbooks believe in the occurrence of poems devoid of imagery, but actually scarcity in lexical tropes is counterbalanced by gorgeous grammatical tropes and figures."[16] Tropes, as we know, are figures of signification, and in adopting metaphor and metonymy as poles of his typology of language and literature, Jakobson not only pays homage to ancient rhetoric: he places the categories of meaning at the heart of the structural method.

The structural study of "poetic language" and of the forms of literary expression in general cannot, in fact, reject the analysis of the relations between code and message. Jakobson's analysis,

"Linguistics and Poetics," in which he refers at the same time to the technicians of communication and to poets like Hopkins and Valéry or to critics like John Crowe Ransom and William Empson, shows this quite explicitly: "Ambiguity is an intrinsic, inalienable character of any self-focused message, briefly a corollary feature of poetry. Let us repeat with Empson: 'The machinations of ambiguity are among the very roots of poetry.'"[17] The ambition of structuralism is not confined to counting feet and to observing the repetitions of phonemes: it must also attack semantic phenomena which, as Mallarmé showed us, constitute the essence of poetic language, and more generally the problems of literary semiology. In this respect one of the newest and most fruitful directions that are now opening up for literary research ought to be the structural study of the "large unities" of discourse, beyond the framework—which linguistics in the strict sense cannot cross—of the sentence. The Formalist Vladimir Propp was no doubt the first to deal (in regard to a series of Russian folktales) with texts of a particular scope,[18] made up of a large number of sentences, like statements capable in turn, and on an equal footing with the traditional units of linguistics, of an analysis that could distinguish in them, by a play of superimpositions and substitutions, variable elements and constant functions, and to rediscover in them the bi-axial system, familiar to Saussurean linguistics, of syntagmatic relations (real connections of functions in the continuity of a text) and paradigmatic relations (virtual relations between similar or opposed functions, from one text to another, in the whole of the corpus considered). One would thus study systems from a much higher level of generality, such as narrative,[19] description, and the other major forms of literary expression. There would then be a linguistics of discourse that was a *translinguistics,* since the facts of language would be handled by it in great bulk, and often at one remove—to put it simply, a rhetoric, perhaps that "new rhetoric" which Francis Ponge once called for, and which we still lack.

The structural character of language at every level is sufficiently accepted by all today for the structuralist "approach" to literary expression to be adopted as it were without question. As soon as one abandons the level of linguistics (or that "bridge thrown between linguistics and literary history," as Leo Spitzer called studies of form and style) and approach the domain traditionally reserved for criticism, that of "content," the legitimacy of the structural point of view raises very serious questions of principle. *A priori*, of course, structuralism as a method is based on the study of structures wherever they occur; but to begin with, structures are not directly encountered objects—far from it; they are systems of latent relations, conceived rather than perceived, which analysis constructs as it uncovers them, and which it runs the risk of inventing while believing that it is discovering them. Furthermore, structuralism is not only a method; it is also what Ernst Cassirer calls a "general tendency of thought," or as others would say (more crudely) an ideology, the prejudice of which is precisely to value structures at the expense of substances, and which may therefore overestimate their explanatory value. Indeed, the question is not so much to know whether there is or is not a system of relations in a particular object of research, since such systems are everywhere, but to determine the relative importance of this system in relation to other elements of understanding: this importance measures the degree of validity of the structural method; but how are we to measure this importance, in turn, without recourse to this method? A circular argument.

Apparently, structuralism ought to be on its own ground whenever criticism abandons the search for the conditions of existence or the external determinations—psychological, social, or other—of the literary work, in order to concentrate its attention on that work itself, regarded no longer as an effect, but as an absolute being. In this sense, structuralism is bound up with the general movement away from positivism, "historicizing history" and the "biographical illusion," a movement represented in various ways by the critical writings of a Proust, an Eliot, a Valéry, Russian Formalism, French "thematic criticism" or Anglo-American "New Criticism."[20] In a way, the notion of structural analysis can be regarded as a simple equivalent of what Americans call "close reading" and which would be called in Europe, following Spitzer, the "immanent study" of works. It is precisely in this sense that Spitzer, retracing in 1960 the evolution that had led him from the psychologism of his first studies of style to a criticism free of any reference to the *Erlebnis*, "subordinating stylistic analysis to an explanation of the particular works as *poetic organisms in themselves*, without recourse to the psychology of the author,"[21] called this new attitude "structuralist." Any analysis that confines itself to a work without considering its sources or motives would, therefore, be implicitly structuralist, and the structural method ought to intervene in order to give to this immanent study a sort of rationality of understanding that would replace the rationality of explanation abandoned with the search for causes. A somewhat spatial determinism of structure would thus take over, but in a quite modern spirit, from the temporal determinism of genesis, each unity being defined in terms of relations, instead of filiation.[22] "Thematic" analysis, then, would tend spontaneously to culminate and to be tested in a structural synthesis in which the different themes are grouped in *networks*, in order to extract their full meaning from their place and function in the system of the work. This is the aim clearly expressed by Jean-Pierre Richard in his *Univers imaginaire de Mallarmé*, or by Jean Rousset when he writes: "There is a graspable form only when there emerges a harmony or a relation, a line of force, an obsessive figure, a texture of presences or echoes, a network of convergences; I will call 'structures' those formal constants, those links that betray a mental world and which each artist reinvents according to his own needs."[23]

Structuralism, then, would appear to be a refuge for all immanent criticism against the danger of fragmentation that threatens thematic analysis: the means of reconstituting the unity of a work, its principle of coherence, what Spitzer called its spiritual *etymon*. In fact, the question is no doubt more complex, for immanent criticism can adopt two very different and even antithetical attitudes to work, depending on whether it regards this work as an object or as a subject. The opposition between these two attitudes is brought out with great clarity by Georges Poulet in a text in which he declares himself to be an advocate of the second:

Like everybody else, I believe that the end of criticism is to arrive at an intimate knowledge of the reality criticized. Now it seems to me that such intimacy is possible only insofar as critical thought *becomes* the thought criticized, insofar as it succeeds in re-feeling, re-thinking, re-imagining that thought from the inside. Nothing could be less objective than such a movement of the mind. Contrary to common belief, criticism must avoid attending to any *object* whatever (whether it be the person of the author, considered as someone else, or his work, considered as a thing); for what must be obtained is a *subject*, that is to say, a spiritual activity that can only be understood if one puts oneself in its place and revives within us its role as subject.[24]

This intersubjective criticism, which is admirably illustrated in Poulet's own work, is related to the type of understanding that Paul Ricoeur, following Dilthey and others (including Spitzer), calls *hermeneutics*.[25] The meaning of a work is not conceived through a series of intellectual operations; it is relived, "taken up again" as a message that is both old and forever renewed. Conversely, it is clear that structural criticism is emerging from the objectivism condemned by Poulet, for structures are *experienced* neither by the creative consciousness, nor by the critical consciousness. They are at the heart of the work, no doubt, but as its latent armature, as a principle of objective intelligibility, accessible only, through analysis and substitutions, to a sort of geometrical mind that is not consciousness. Structural criticism is untainted by any of the transcendent reductions of psychoanalysis, for example, or Marxist explanation, but it exerts, in its own way, a sort of internal reduction, traversing the substance of the work in order to reach its bone-structure: certainly not a superficial examination, but a sort of radioscopic penetration, and all the more external in that it is more penetrating.

There emerges, then, a limit rather comparable to the one Ricoeur fixed on structural mythology: wherever the hermeneutic resumption of meaning is possible and desirable, in the intuitive convergence of two consciousnesses, structural analysis would (partially at least) be illegitimate and irrelevant. One might then imagine a sort of division of the literary field into two domains, that of "living" literature, that is to say, capable of being experienced by the critical consciousness, and which would have to be reserved for hermeneutic criticism, just as Ricoeur claims for hermeneutics the domain of the Judaic and Hellenic traditions, with their inexhaustible and forever indefinitely present *surplus of meaning*; and that of a literature which is not exactly "dead" but in some sense distant and difficult to decipher: its lost meaning would be perceptible only to the operations of the structural intelligence, like that of "totemic" cultures, the exclusive domain of the ethnologists. There is nothing absurd in principle about such a division of labor and it should be noted at the outset that it corresponds to the limitations of prudence that structuralism imposes on itself, tackling primarily those areas that best lend themselves, and with the least "remainder," to the application of its method;[26] it should also be recognized that such a division would leave an immense and almost virgin field for structuralist research. Indeed, the sort of literature that has "lost" its meaning is much greater than the other, and not always of less interest. There is as it were a whole ethnographic domain of literature, the exploration of which would be of great interest to structuralism: literatures distant in time and place, children's and popular literature, including such recent forms as the melodrama or serialized fiction, which criticism has always ignored, not only out of academic prejudice, but also because no intersubjective participation could animate it or guide it in its research, and which a structural criticism could treat like anthropological material and study in great bulk and in terms of their recurrent functions, following the lines laid down by such folklore specialists as Propp and Skaftymov. These works, like those of Lévi-Strauss on primitive mythologies, already show how fruitful the structural method applied to texts of this kind can be, and how much it can reveal of the hitherto unknown foundations of the canonical "literatures." Fantomas or Bluebeard may not speak to us as intimately as Swann or Hamlet; they might have as much to teach us. And certain officially consecrated works, which have in fact become largely alien to us, like those of Corneille, might speak better in that language of distance and strangeness than in that of the false proximity that we insist on imposing on them, often to no avail.

Here perhaps structuralism would begin to reconquer part of the terrain ceded to hermeneutics: for the true division between these two "methods" lies not in the object, but in the critical position. To Ricoeur, who suggested to him the division described above, alleging that "one part of civilization, precisely the part which did not produce our own culture, lends itself to the structural method better than any other," Lévi-Strauss replied by asking: "Are we dealing with an intrinsic difference between two kinds of thought and civilization, or simply with the relative position of the observer, who cannot adopt the same perspectives vis-à-vis his own civilization as would seem normal to him vis-à-vis a different civilization?"[27] The inappropriateness that Ricoeur finds in the possible application of structuralism to the Judeo-Christian mythologies, a Melanesian philosopher would no doubt find in the structural analysis of his own mythical tradition, which he *interiorizes* just as a Christian interiorizes the biblical message; but conversely this Melanesian might find a structural analysis of the Bible quite appropriate. What Merleau-Ponty wrote of ethnology as a discipline can be applied to structuralism as a method: "It is not a specialty defined by a particular object, 'primitive societies.' It is a way of thinking, the way which imposes itself when the object is different, and requires us to transform ourselves. We also become the ethnologists of our own society if we set ourselves at a distance from it."[28]

Thus the relation that binds structuralism and hermeneutics together might not be one of mechanical separation and exclusion, but of complementarity: on the subject of the same work, hermeneutic criticism might speak the language of the resumption of meaning and of internal recreation, and structural criticism that of distant speech and intelligible reconstruction. They would thus bring out complementary significations, and their dialogue would be all the more fruitful, on condition that one could never speak these two languages at once.[29] In any case, literary criticism has no reason to refuse to listen to the new significations that structuralism can obtain from the works that are apparently closest and most familiar by "distancing" their speech;[30] for one of the most profound lessons of modern anthropology is that the distant is also close to us, by virtue of its very distance.

Moreover, the effort of psychological understanding initiated by nineteenth-century criticism and continued in our own time by the various kinds of thematic criticism has perhaps concerned itself too exclusively with the psychology of the authors, and not sufficiently with that of the public, or the reader. We know for example that one of the dangers of thematic analysis lies in the difficulty it often has in distinguishing between what is properly of concern to the irreducible singularity of an individual creator and what more generally belongs to the taste, sensibility, or ideology of a period, or more generally still to the permanent conventions and traditions of a genre or literary form. The heart of this difficulty lies in a sense in the encounter between the original, "deep" thematics of the creative individual and of what ancient rhetoric called *topics,* that is to say, the treasury of subjects and forms that constitute the common wealth of tradition and culture. Personal thematics represents only a choice made between the possibilities offered by the collective topics. It is evident—to speak in a very schematic way—that the contribution of the *topos* is greater in the so-called "inferior," or as one ought rather to say *fundamental,* genres, such as the folktale or the adventure novel, and the role of the creative personality is sufficiently weakened in such works for critical investigation to turn spontaneously, when dealing with them, to the tastes, requirements, and needs that constitute what is commonly called the *expectations* of the public. But we should also be aware of what the "great works"—and even the most original of them—owe to these common dispositions. How can we appreciate, for example, the particular quality of the Stendhalian novel without considering in its historical and transhistorical generality the common thematics of the fictional imagination?[31] Spitzer recounts how the belated—and it would seem somewhat ingenuous—discovery that he made of the importance of the traditional *topos* in classical literature was one of the events that helped to "discourage" him from psychoanalytic stylistics.[32] But the passage from what one might call the psychologism of the author to an absolute anti-psychologism may not be as inevitable as it seems, for, conventional as it may be, the *topos* is not psychologically more arbitrary than the personal theme: it simply belongs to another, collective psychology, for which contemporary anthropology has done something to prepare us and the literary implications of which deserve to be explored systematically. The fault of modern criticism is perhaps not so much its psychologism as its over-individualistic conception of psychology.

Classical criticism—from Aristotle to La Harpe—was in a sense much more attentive to these anthropological aspects of literature; it knew how to measure, narrowly but precisely, the requirements of what it called *verisimilitude*, that is to say, the idea that the public has of the true or possible. The distinctions between the genres, the notions of epic, tragic, heroic, comic, fictional, corresponded to certain broad categories of mental attitudes that predispose the reader's imagination in one way or another and make him want or expect particular types of situations and actions, of psychological, moral, and esthetic values. It cannot be said that the study of these broad diatheses that divide up and inform the literary sensibility of mankind (and which Gilbert Durand has rightly called *the anthropological structures of the imaginary*) has been taken sufficiently seriously by literary criticism and theory. Gaston Bachelard gave us a typology of the "material" imagination: no doubt there also exists, for example, an imagination of behavior, situations, human relationships, a *dramatic* imagination, in the broad sense of the term, which strongly animates the production and consumption of theatrical and fictional work. The topics of this imagination, the structural laws of its functioning are obviously, and fundamentally, of importance to literary criticism: they will no doubt constitute one of the tasks of that vast axiomatics of literature that Valéry believed to be such an urgent necessity. The highest efficacy of literature rests on a subtle play between expectation and surprise "against which all the expectation in the world cannot prevail,"[33] between the "verisimilitude" expected and desired by the public and the unpredictability of creation. But does not the very unpredictability, the infinite shock of the great works, resound with all its force in the secret depths of verisimilitude? "The great poet," says Borges, "is not so much an inventor as a discoverer."

Valéry dreamed of a history of Literature understood "not so much as a history of authors and of the accidents of their careers, or that of their works, than as a History of the mind, insofar as it produces or consumes literature, and this history might even be written without the name of a single writer being mentioned." We know what echoes this idea has found in such authors as Borges or Maurice Blanchot, and Albert Thibaudet had already been pleased, by means of constant comparisons and transferences, to set up a Republic of Letters in which distinctions of person tended to be blurred. This unified view of the literary field is a very profound utopia, and one that is not unreasonably attractive, since literature is not only a collection of autonomous works, which may "influence" one another by a series of fortuitous and isolated encounters; it is a coherent whole, a homogeneous space, within which works touch and penetrate one another; it is also, in turn, a part linked to other parts in the wider space of "culture," in which its own value is a function of the whole. Thus it doubly belongs to a study of structure, internal and external.

We know that the acquisition of language by a child proceeds not by a simple extension of vocabulary, but by a series of internal divisions, without modification of the overall acquisition: at each stage, the few words at its disposal are for the child the whole of language and it uses them to designate everything, with increasing precision, but without gaps. Similarly, for a man who has read only one book, this book is for him the whole of "literature," in the primary sense of the term; when he has read two, these two books will share his entire literary field, with no gap between them, and so on; it is precisely because it has no gaps to fill that a culture may *enrich itself*: it becomes deeper and more diversified, because it does not have to extend itself.

In a way, the "literature" of mankind as a whole (that is to say, the way in which written works are organized in men's minds) can be regarded as being constituted in accordance with a similar process—bearing in mind the crude simplification that is involved here: literary "production" is a *parole*, in the Saussurian sense, a series of partially autonomous and unpredictable individual acts; but the "consumption" of this literature by society is a *langue*, that is to say, a whole the parts of which, whatever their number and nature, tend to be ordered into a coherent system. Raymond Queneau makes the amusing remark that all literature is either an *Iliad* or an *Odyssey*. This dichotomy has not always been a metaphor, and one often finds in Plato the echo of a "literature" that was almost reduced to these two poems, and which was not regarded as incomplete for that reason. Ion knew and wished to know nothing other than Homer. "That seems to be enough for me," he says, for Homer speaks sufficiently well of all things, and the competence of the bard would be encyclopedic, if poetry really proceeded from knowledge (it is this point, and not the universality of the work, that Plato challenges). Since then, literature has tended to subdivide rather than to extend, and for centuries the Homeric *oeuvre* has continued to be seen as the embryo and source of all literature. This myth is not devoid of truth, and the bookburner of Alexandria was not entirely wrong, from his point of view, to place the Koran alone in the scale against a whole library: whether it contains one book, two books, or several thousand, a library is a civilization that is always complete, because in men's minds it always forms a whole and a system.

Classical rhetoric was acutely aware of this system, which is formalized into the theory of genres. There was epic, tragedy, comedy, and so on—and all these genres shared without remainder the totality of the literary field. What was lacking in this theory was the temporal dimension, the idea that a system could evolve. Boileau himself witnessed the death of the epic and the birth of the novel without being able to integrate these modifications into his *Ars poetica*. The nineteenth century discovered history, but it forgot the coherence of the whole; the individual history of works, and of authors, effaced the table of the genres. Ferdinand Brunetière alone attempted a synthesis, but we know that this marriage of Boileau and Darwin was not a very happy one: the evolution of genres according to Brunetière is a matter of pure organicism, each genre being born, developing, and dying like a solitary species, without concern for its neighbor.

The structuralist idea, in this matter, is to follow literature in its overall evolution, while making synchronic cuts at various stages and comparing the tables one with another. Literary evolution then appears in all its richness, which derives from the fact that the system survives while constantly altering. Here, again, the Russian Formalists showed the way by paying special attention to the phenomena of structural dynamics, and by isolating the notion of *change of function*. Noting the presence or absence, in isolation, of a literary form or theme at a particular point in diachronic evolution is meaningless until the synchronic study has shown the function of this element in the system. An element can remain while changing function, or on the contrary disappear while leaving its function to another. "In this way the mechanism of literary evolution," says Boris Tomachevski, tracing the development of Formalist work on this point,

became gradually more precise: it was presented not as a succession of forms, each replacing the other, but as a continual variation of the esthetic function of literary methods. Each work finds itself oriented in relation to the literary milieu, and each element in relation to the whole work. An element that has a particular value in a certain period will completely change its function in another period. The grotesque forms, which were regarded in the period of Classicism as resources for the comic, became, in the Romantic period, one of the sources of tragedy. It is in this continual change of function that the true life of the elements of the literary work are to be found.[34]

In particular Viktor Shklovsky and Jurij Tynianov made a study, in relation to Russian literature, of those functional variations by which, for example, the same form can be transformed from a minor rank to that of a "canonical form," and which maintain a perpetual transference between popular literature and official literature, between academicism and the avant-garde, between poetry and prose, etc. Inheritance, Shklovsky was fond of saying, usually passes from the uncle to the nephew, and evolution canonizes the junior branch. Thus Pushkin imported into great poetry the effects of eighteenth-century album verse, Nekrassov borrowed from journalism and vaudeville, Blok from gypsy songs, Dostoevsky from the detective novel.[35]

In this sense literary history becomes the history of a system: it is the evolution of the functions that is significant, not that of the elements, and knowledge of the synchronic relations necessarily precedes that of the processes. But, on the other hand, as Jakobson has remarked, the literary table of a period describes not only a present of creation, but also a present of culture, and therefore a certain image of the past, "not only the literary production of any given period, but also that part of the literary tradition which for the stage in question has remained vital or has been revived. . . . The selection of a new tendency from among the classics and their reinterpretation by a novel trend is a substantial problem for synchronic literary studies,"[36] and consequently for the structural history of literature, which is simply the placing in diachronic perspective of these successive synchronic tables: in the table of French classicism, Homer and Vergil have a place, Dante and Shakespeare do not. In our present literary landscape, the discovery (or invention) of the Baroque is more important than the Romantic inheritance, and our Shakespeare is not Voltaire's Shakespeare or Hugo's: he is a contemporary of Brecht and Claudel, as Cervantes is a contemporary of Kafka. A period is manifested as much by what it reads as by what it writes, and these two aspects of its "literature" act upon one another. As Borges puts it: "If it were given to me to read any page written today—this one for example—as one will read it in the year 2000, I would know the literature of the year 2000."[37]

To this history of the *internal divisions* of the literary field, with its already very rich program (one has only to think what a universal history of the opposition between prose and poetry would be like: a fundamental, elementary, constant, immutable opposition in its function, constantly renewed in its means), one should add that of the much wider division between literature and everything that is not literature; this would be, not literary history, but the history of the relations between literature and social life as a whole: the history of the *literary function*. The Russian Formalists insisted on the *differential* character of the literary fact. Literariness is also a function of non-literariness, and no stable definition can be given of it: one is left simply with the awareness of limit. Everyone knows that the birth of the cinema altered the status of literature: by depriving it of certain of its functions, but also by giving it some of its own means. And this transformation is obviously no more than a beginning. How will literature survive the development of other media of communication? Already we no longer believe, as it was believed from Aristotle to La Harpe, that art is an imitation of nature, and where the classics sought above all a fine resemblance, we seek on the contrary a radical orginality and an absolute creation. The day when the Book ceases to be the principal vehicle of knowledge, will not literature have changed its meaning once again? Perhaps we are quite simply living through the last days of the Book. This continuing adventure ought to make us more attentive to certain episodes in the past: we cannot go on speaking of literature as if its existence were self-evident, as if its relation to the world and to men had never varied. We do not have, for example, a history of reading. Such a history would be an intellectual, social, and even physical history: if St. Augustine is to be believed,[38] his master Ambrose was the first man in Antiquity to read with his eyes, without speaking the text aloud. True history is made up of these great silent moments. And the value of the method may lie in its ability to find, beneath each silence, a question.

[1964]

NOTES

1. Claude Lévi-Strauss, *La Pensée sauvage* (Paris; Plon, 1962), p. 26; *The Savage Mind* (Chicago: University of Chicago Press, 1966), p. 17.

2. Roland Barthes, *Essais critiques* (Paris: Seuil, 1964), p. 255; *Critical Essays*, Richard Howard, tr. (Evanston, Ill.: Northwestern University Press, 1972), p. 258.

3. Paul Valéry, "Albert Thibaudet," *Nouvelle revue française* (July 1936), p. 6.

4. Lévi-Strauss, *Pensée sauvage*, p. 29; *S. M.*, p. 19.

5. Boris Tomachevski, "La nouvelle école d'histoire littéraire en Russie," *Revue des Études slaves* (1928), p. 231.

6. "The object of literary study is not literature as a whole, but its literariness (*literaturnost*), that is to say, that which makes a work literary." This sentence written by Jakobson in 1921 was one of the watchwords of Russian Formalism.

7. "In mythology, as in linguistics, formal analysis immediately raises

the question of meaning." Claude Lévi-Strauss, *Anthropologie structurale* (Paris: Plon, 1958), p. 266; *Structural Anthropology*, Claire Jacobson and Brooke Grundfest Schoepf, trs. (New York: Basic Books, 1963), p. 241.

8. Cf. Victor Erlich, *Russian Formalism* (2d. rev. ed.; The Hague: Mouton, 1969), p. 219.

9. N. S. Trubetzkoy, *The Principles of Phonology* (1939), C. A. M. Baltaxe, tr. (Berkeley: University of California Press, 1969), pp. 3–4.

10. Cf. in particular the criticism by Eichenbaum, Jakobson, and Tynianov of Sievers's methods of acoustic metrics, which tried to study the sounds of a poem as if it had been written in a totally unknown language. Erlich, *Russian Formalism*, p. 218.

11. A synthesis of these criticisms is to be found in Paul Delbouille, *Poésie et sonorités*, (Paris: Les Belles Lettres, 1961).

12. René Etiemble, *Le Mythe de Rimbaud* (Paris: Gallimard, 1952), 2:81–104.

13. "All colors have been attributed at least once to each of the vowels." Delbouille, *Poésie*, p. 248.

14. Roman Jakobson, "Closing Statement: Linguistics and Poetics," in T. A. Sebeok, ed., *Style in Language* (Cambridge, Mass: M.I.T. Press, 1960), p. 367.

15. Erlich, *Russian Formalism*, p. 175.

16. Jakobson, "Closing Statement," p. 375.

17. Jakobson, "Closing Statement," pp. 370–71.

18. Vladimir Propp, *The Morphology of the Folktale* (1928), L. Scott, tr. (Bloomington: Indiana University Press, 1958; 2d. rev. ed., Louis A. Wagner, ed.; Austin: University of Texas Press, 1968).

19. Claude Bremond, "Le message narratif," *Communications*, 4 (1964).

20. One can however find a purely methodological state of structuralism, as it were, in authors who do not claim allegiance to this "philosophy." This applies to Georges Dumézil, who puts at the service of a typically historical investigation the analysis of the *functions* that unite the elements of Indo-European mythology, these functions being regarded as more significant than the elements themselves. It also applies to Charles Mauron, whose psychocriticism interprets not isolated themes, but networks, the terms of which may vary without alteration to their structure. The study of systems does not necesarily *exclude* that of genesis or filiations: the minimum program of structuralism is that such a study should precede it and *govern* it.

21. Leo Spitzer, "Les études de style et les différents pays," *Langue et Littérature* (Paris: Les Belles Lettres, 1961).

22. "Structural linguistics, like quantum mechanics, gains in morphic determinism what it loses in temporal determinism." Roman Jakobson, Report presented to the VIIIth International Congress of Linguists, Oslo,

1957, published in *Proceedings of the VIIIth International Congress of Linguists* (Oslo, 1958).

23. Jean Rousset, *Forme et signification* (Paris: J. Corti, 1964), p. xii.

24. Georges Poulet, "Reponse de," *Les Lettres nouvelles* (June 1959), pp. 10–13.

25. Paul Ricoeur, "Structure et herméneutique," *Esprit* (November 1963); "Structuralism and Hermeneutics," Kathleen McLaughlin, tr., in Ricoeur, *The Conflict of Interpretations*, Don Ihde, ed. (Evanston, Ill: Northwestern University Press, 1974).

26. Cf. Claude Lévi-Strauss, *Esprit* (November 1963), p. 632; "A Confrontation," *New Left Review* (July-August 1970) 62:61. [This is Lévi-Strauss' paraphrase of Ricoeur's remark—M.-R. L.]

27. Lévi-Strauss, *Esprit*, p. 633; "A Confrontation" p. 61.

28. Maurice Merleau-Ponty, *Signes* (Paris: Gallimard, 1960), p. 150; *Signs*, R. C. McCleary, tr. (Evanston, Ill: Northwestern University Press, 1964), p. 120.

29. Lévi-Strauss suggests a relation of the same kind between history and ethnology: "Structures appear only to an observation practised from the outside. Conversely, this observation can never grasp the processes, which are not analytic objects, but only the particular way in which a temporality is experienced by a subject. . . . A historian can sometimes work as an ethnologist, and an ethnologist as a historian, but the methods themselves are complementary, in the sense the physicists give to this term; that is to say, one cannot, at one and the same time, rigorously define a stage A and a stage B (which is possible only from the outside and in structural terms), and reexperience empirically the passage from one to the other (which would be the only intelligible way of understanding it). Even the sciences of man have their relations of uncertainty." "Les limites de la notion de structure en ethnologie," *Sens et usage du mot structure*, R. Bastide, ed. (The Hague: Mouton, 1962), pp. 44–45.

30. A new signification is not necessarily a new *meaning*: it is a new connection between form and meaning. If literature is an art of significations, it is renewed, and with it criticism, by modifying this connection, either through the meaning or through the form. It thus happens that modern criticism is rediscovering in "themes" or "styles" what classical criticism had already found in "ideas" or "feelings." An old meaning comes back to us linked to a new form, and this "shift" displaces a whole work.

31. It is in this light that I introduce the very fine book by Gilbert Durand, *Le Décor mythique de la Chartreuse de Parme* (Paris: J. Corti, 1961).

32. Spitzer, "Les études de style," p. 27.

33. Paul Valéry, *Oeuvres*, Pléiade (Paris: Gallimard, 1960), II: 560; "Odds and Ends" in Valery, *Analects*, Stuart Gilbert, tr. (Princeton: Princeton University Press, 1970), p. 113.

34. Tomachevski, "La nouvelle ecole," pp. 238–39.

35. On the Formalist views of literary history, cf. Boris Eichenbaum, "The Theory of the Formal Method," and Jurij Tynianov, "On Literary Evolution" in *Readings in Russian Poetics*, Ladislav Matejka and Krystyna Pomorska, eds. (Cambridge, Mass: M.I.T. Press, 1970). See also Erlich, *Formalism*, pp. 254–55 and Nina Gourfinkel, "Les nouvelles methodes d'histoire litteraire en Russie," *Le Monde slave*, (February 1929).

36. Jakobson, "Closing statement," p. 352.

37. Jorge Luis Borges, *Other Inquisitions*, Ruth L. C. Simms, tr. (New York: Simon & Schuster, 1965).

38. St. Augustine, *Confessions*, Book VI. Quoted by Borges, *Other Inquisitions*, pp. 117–18.

2

THE OBVERSE OF SIGNS

The work of Roland Barthes is apparently highly varied, both in its object (literature, clothes, cinema, painting, advertising, music, news items, etc.) and in its method and ideology. *Le Degré zéro de l'Écriture* (1953) seemed to extend into the domain of "form" the reflection begun by Sartre some years earlier on the social situation of literature and the responsibility of the writer before history—a reflection on the frontiers of existentialism and Marxism. His *Michelet* (1954), though offered as a simple, "precritical" reading, borrowed from Gaston Bachelard the idea of a substantial psychoanalysis and showed what a thematic study of the material imagination could bring to the understanding of a work regarded hitherto as essentially ideological. His work for the review *Théâtre populaire* and in the struggle waged around that review to introduce the work and theories of Bertolt Brecht into France brought him a reputation, in the next few years, of being an intransigent Marxist, although official Marxists never shared his interpretation of Brecht's theory; but, at the same time, and contradictorily, two articles on *Les Gommes* and *Le Voyeur* made him the official interpreter of Robbe-Grillet and the theoretician of the *nouveau roman*, which was widely regarded as a Formalist offensive and as an attempt to "disengage" literature. In 1956, *Mythologies* revealed a sarcastic observer of the petty-bourgeois ideology concealed in the most seemingly innocuous manifestations of contemporary social life; a new "critique of everyday life," clearly Marxist in inspiration, which marked an unequivocal political attitude. In 1960, there was a new metamorphosis, a commentary on Racine for the Club français du Livre (revised in 1963 as *Sur Racine*), which seemed to effect a return to psychoanalysis, but this time closer to Freud than to Bachelard, though to the Freud of *Totem and Taboo*, an anthropologist in his own way: Racine's tragedies are interpreted in terms of the prohibition of incest and Oedipal conflict, "at the level of this ancient fable (that of the 'primal horde'), situated far beyond history or the human psyche."[1] Lastly, the latest texts collected in *Essais critiques* (1964) seem to express a decisive conversion to structuralism, understood in its strictest form, and the abandonment of any responsibility towards meaning; literature and social life are now merely languages, which should be studied as pure formal systems, not for their content, but for their structure.

This many-sided image is obviously a superficial and even, as we will see, a highly unfaithful one. Not that the scope of Barthes' reflection is actually circumscribed, open as it is in principle to the most varied tendencies of modern thought. He himself admits that he has often dreamed "of a peaceful coexistence of critical languages or, perhaps, of a 'parametric' criticism which would modify its language to suit the work proposed to it,"[2] and, speaking of the fundamental "ideological principles" of contemporary criticism (existentialism, Marxism, psychoanalysis, structuralism), he declares: "For my part, in a certain sense I subscribe to each of them *at the same time*."[3] But this apparent eclecticism conceals a constant in his thought that was already at work in *Le Degré zéro*, and which has become ever more marked, more conscious, and more systematic. If criticism can claim allegiance to several ideologies at once, it is, Barthes hastens to add, because "ideological choice does not constitute the being of criticism and because 'truth' is not its sanction": its task is not to *uncover* the secret truth of the works of which it speaks, but to *cover* their language "as completely as possible," with its own language, to *adjust* as closely as possible the language of our period to that of the works of the past, "that is to say, to the formal system of logical constraints worked out by the author in accordance with his own period."[4] This *friction* between literary language and critical language has the effect not of bringing out the "meaning" of a work, but of "reconstituting the rules and constraints governing the elaboration of this meaning," in other words, its technique of signification. If the work is a language and criticism a metalanguage, their relation is essentially formal, and criticism no longer has to concern itself with a message, but with a code, that is to say, a system the structure of which it is its task to uncover, "just as the linguist is not responsible for deciphering the sentence's meaning but for establishing the formal structure which permits this meaning to be transmitted."[5] In consideration of which, out of the varied languages that criticism can *try* on the literary works of the past (or of the present) "would appear a general form, which would be the very intelligibility our age gives to things and which critical activity helps, dialectically, both to decipher and to constitute."[6] The exemplary value of critical activity, then, derives clearly from this double semiological character: as a metalanguage (a discourse on literary language), it studies a system from the viewpoint of that metacriticism, or "criticism of criticisms," which is simply semiology in its most general form. Thus criticism helps both "to decipher and to constitute" the intelligible, since it is at the same time semantics and semanteme, subject and object, of the semiological activity.

These remarks lead us then to the central point of Barthes' thought: the problem of signification. *Homo significans*: man the sign-maker, "man's freedom to make things signify,"[7] "the strictly human process by which men give meaning to things,"[8] such is the essential object of his research. It is a traditional, even fundamental, orientation, since already *Le Degré zéro* studied the various ways in which the writer, beyond all the explicit contents of his discourse must in addition—perhaps essentially—*signify Literature*, and this book was offered as a contribution to "a history of literary expression which is neither that of a particular language, nor that of the various styles, but simply that of the Signs of Literature,"[9] that is to say, of the signs by which literature draws attention to itself as literature, and *points out its mask*. It is an old question, then, but one that has continued to reflect upon itself and to define its terms.

As we know, it was the linguist Ferdinand de Saussure who first conceived of the idea of a general science of significations, of which linguistics would be no more than a particular case, "a science that studies the life of signs within society," which would show "what constitutes signs, what laws govern them," and which he proposed to call *semiology*.[10] The natural languages (*langues*) being by far the most elaborate and best-known systems of signs, linguistics necessarily remains the irreplaceable model for all semiological research, but the domain of signs goes beyond that of articulated language. Indeed, there exist on the one hand signs outside language, which function so to speak beside it, such as those emblems or signals of all kinds that men have always used, from "primitive totemism" to the various sign-posts and symbols that modern civilization constantly proliferates before our eyes. Some of these signs have already constituted highly complex systems: one has only to think of the degree of elaboration once attained by the art of the coat-of-arms and its corresponding science of heraldry; the ability to constitute a system is precisely the characteristic of any set of signs, and it is this constitution that marks the passage from pure symbolism to the strictly semiological state, since a symbol becomes a sign only at the moment when it ceases to suggest of itself, and by virtue of an analogical or historical relationship (the Crescent, the emblem of Islam, the Cross, the symbol of Christianity) which it maintains with its "referent," in order to signify in an indirect way, mediatized by the relation of kinship and opposition that it maintains with other concurrent symbols; the Cross and the Crescent, taken in isolation, are two autonomous symbols, but the use of an Arab Red Crescent with a European Red Cross sets up a paradigmatic system in which red holds the place of a common root, and the opposition Cross/Crescent that of a distinctive inflection.[11]

What we have, then, or at least it would seem so, is a series of *extralinguistic* semiological systems; but their social importance, and still more their autonomy in relation to articulated language appear to be highly questionable: "Until now semiology has had to concern itself only with codes of little interest, such as the highway code; as soon as one passes to systems possessing real social depth, one meets language once again."[12] This is because nonlinguistic objects actually become signifiers only insofar as they are *duplicated* or *relayed* by language, as is clear enough in advertising or newspaper photography, which invariably accompany the visual image with a verbal commentary intended to confirm or to localize its virtual or floating significations, or again, in fashion writing, which gives objects (clothes, food, furniture, cars, etc.) their symbolic value by "speaking" of them, that is to say, by analyzing the signifying parts and naming the signifieds: the image might represent a man wearing a tweed jacket, standing in front of a country house, but the commentary will state more precisely "tweed jacket for the weekend," designating by name tweed as a sign and weekend as the meaning. "There is only meaning when it is named, and the world of signifieds is simply that of language." The extralinguistic domain rapidly gives way therefore (or is *absorbed* into) that other domain of semiology, which is the translinguistic, or metalinguistic order, and which embraces techniques of signification situated not beside, but above, or within, language. Semiology is thus brought back into the linguistic fold, which leads Barthes to reverse the Saussurian formula: semiology is no longer seen as an extension, but on the contrary as a specification of linguistics. However, it is not a question of assimilating the semiological fact to the linguistic fact, for language used in this way concerns semiology only as a *secondary* language, either because the verbal text is supposed to impose a signification on a nonverbal object, as in the case of the blurbs attached to press photographs or advertising images, or because it duplicates itself as it were in order to add to its own explicit, literal signification, or *denotation*, an additional power of *connotation*, which enriches it with one or several secondary meanings. Many pages of literature, as Valéry more or less remarks,[13] mean nothing more than "I am a page of literature," a sentence which, however, is nowhere to be found in them; and Sartre rightly stresses that the meaning or intrinsic quality of a text is never after all directly designated by the words of this text, and that "the literary object, though realized *through* language, is never given *in* language."[14]

This oblique language that suggests some unstated meaning is the language of *connotation*, of which literature is the domain *par excellence*, the study of which may avail itself of an illustrious, if sometimes decried precedent, that of Rhetoric. When a rhetorician of the classical period taught, for example, that the use of the word "sail" to designate a ship is a figure called synecdoche, and that this figure achieves its finest effect in an epic poem, he simply brought out, in his own way, the epic connotation implied in the use of this figure, and a treatise of rhetoric was a code of literary connotation, a collection of the means by which a poet could signify, over and above the explicit "content" of his poem, its quality of being epic, lyrical, bucolic, etc. Such is the case of those obscenities with which the prose of *Père Duchêne* is dotted, not to signify anything in the discourse, but to signal, obliquely, a whole historical situation: the precious figures of revolutionary rhetoric.[15]

In fact it is the phenomena and techniques of connotation that, since *Le Degré zéro de l'écriture*, have particularly commanded Barthes' attention. Writing, we should remember, is that *responsibility for Form* which, between the Nature represented by the horizon of the language (imposed by time and place) and that other Nature determined by the vertical thrust of style (dictated by the depths of the body and psyche), manifests the writer's choice of a particular literary attitude, and therefore indicates a particular modality of literature; the writer chooses neither his language nor his style, but he is responsible for the methods of writing that indicate whether he is a novelist or a poet, a classicist or a naturalist, bourgeois or populist, etc. All these facts of writing are means of connotation, since over and above their literal meaning, which is sometimes weak or negligible, they manifest an attitude, a choice, an intention.

This effect of super-signification may be represented by a simple schema (table 1), for which we will borrow from rhetoric once again its classic example: in the synecdoche *sail = ship*, there is a signifying word, "sail," and an object (or concept) signified, the ship: that is the denotation; but since the word "sail" has been substituted for the literal word "ship," the relation (signification) that links the signifier to the signified constitutes a figure; this figure in turn clearly designates, in the rhetorical code, a poetic state of discourse: it functions then as the signifier of a new signified, poetry, on a second semantic plane, which is that of rhe-

Table 1

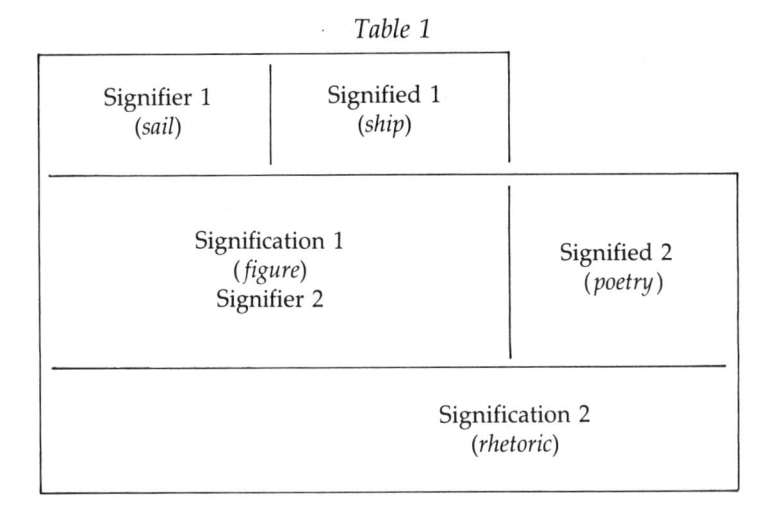

Signifier 1 (sail)	Signified 1 (ship)	
Signification 1 (*figure*) Signifier 2		Signified 2 (*poetry*)
Signification 2 (*rhetoric*)		

torical connotation; the essence of connotation is in effect to establish itself above (or below) the primary signification, but in a dislocated way, using the primary meaning as a form to designate a secondary concept; hence the schema (which might be expressed more or less in some such formula as: *the semiological system in which the word "sail" may be used to designate a ship is a figure; the secondary semiological figure in which a figure, such as the use of the word "sail" to designate a ship, may be used to signify poetry, is rhetoric*[16]).

Readers of *Mythologies* will recognize a similarity between this schema (table 1) and the one used by Barthes to represent the dislocation of myths in relation to the semiological system onto which it is grafted.[17] This is because we are dealing with an effect of the same order, and Barthes says quite rightly that *Le Degré zéro* "was, all told, nothing but a mythology of literary language" in which he defined writing "as the signifier of the literary myth, that is, as a form which is already filled with meaning and which receives from the concept of Literature a new signification."[18] From the point of view that concerns us here, what distinguishes *Mythologies* from *Le Degré zéro* is, on the one hand, an explicit recourse to the notion of semiological system and a clear view of the superimposition and dislocation of the two systems and, on the other hand, the application of this analysis to non-literary objects and even, in some cases, non-linguistic objects, such as the photograph of a black soldier saluting a French flag,[19] which adds to this uncoded and purely denoted visual message a second connoted, ideological message, which is the justification of the French empire.

Thus a whole world is opened up to semiological analysis, a much vaster world than that of literature and one that still awaits its rhetoric: the world of *communication*, of which the press, the cinema, and advertising are the most obvious and best-known forms. But the field of signification does not stop there, for the language of connotation shows that man can endow with an additional meaning any object that has previously been provided either with a primary meaning (verbal statement, graphic or photographic image, film shot or sequence, etc.) or with a non-signifying primary function, which may, for example, be some kind of use: "Food is to be eaten; but it also serves to *signify* (conditions, circumstances, tastes); food is therefore a signifying system and must one day be described as such."[20] Similarly clothes are intended to be worn, a house to provide shelter, a car to move around, but clothes, houses, and cars are also signs, indications of a condition or personality, instruments or a "showing." Semiology thus becomes coextensive with a whole civilization and the world of objects becomes a universe of signs: "In a single day, how many really non-signifying fields do we cross? Very few, sometimes none."[21] What we call history, or culture, is also that "shudder of an enormous machine which is humanity tirelessly undertaking to create meaning, without which it would no longer be human."[22]

But it has to be realized that this signifying activity is always carried out, for Barthes, an an *addition of use* imposed on things, and therefore on occasion as a distortion or an abuse. For Barthes, signs are almost never, like ships' flags, roadsigns, or any other of the clarion calls with which semiology has traditionally concerned itself, signifiers deliberately invented for explicit, limited signifieds, in short the elements of a recognized and overt code. The systems that interest him are always, as he says of literary criticism, "semiologies that dare not speak their name,"[23] ashamed or unconscious codes, always marked by a certain bad faith. To decide that a red or a green lamp will signify "stop" or "go" is not in the least equivocal: I have created a sign that could not be clearer, I have abused nothing and nobody. To decide that a leather jacket "suggests sportiness" and therefore to turn leather into a sign of "sportiness," is something quite different: for leather exists outside this imposition of meaning, as a substance that one might like for profound reasons having to do with its feel, its consistency, its color, its texture; by turning it into a signifier, I obliterate these substantial qualities and substitute for them a social concept of doubtful authenticity; but, on the other hand, I confiscate to the benefit of this signifying link the perceptible properties of leather, which are always available as a reserve of natural justification: leather *is* sporty *because* it is supple, convenient, and so forth; I wear leather *because* I am sporty: what could be more natural? The semiological link is concealed beneath an apparently causal relation, and the naturalness of the sign *exculpates* the signified.

It is clear that semiological reflection has shifted here from the level of facts to that of values. There is for Barthes an axiology of the sign, and it is doubtless not excessive to see in this system of preferences and rejections the deeper motive for his activity as a semiologist. Barthesian semiology is, both in its origin and in its active principle, that of a man fascinated by the sign, a fascination that no doubt involves, as it does for Flaubert or Baudelaire, an element of repulsion, and which has the essentially ambiguous character of a passion. Man makes rather too many signs, and these signs are not always very *healthy*. One of the texts collected in *Essais critiques* is entitled "The Diseases of Costume." It begins with this characteristic sentence: "I should like to sketch here not a history of an esthetic, but rather *a pathology or, if you prefer, an ethic* of costume. I shall propose a few very simple rules which may permit us to judge whether costume is *good or bad, healthy or sick.*"[24] The diseases of theatrical costume, which is obviously a sign, are three in number and all three turn out to be hypertrophies: hypertrophy of the historical function, archeological accuracy; hypertrophy of formal beauty, estheticism; hypertrophy of sumptuosity, money. In another text on the theater, Barthes reproaches traditional Racinian diction for its "hypertrophy of detailed significance" (signification parcellaire),[25] a plethora of details that spread over the text like a film of greasy dirt and impair the clarity of the whole; the same criticism is leveled, with more violence, at the performance of a modern actress in the *Oresteia*: "a dramatic art of the intention, of the gesture and the glance heavy with meaning, of the *signified secret*, an art suitable for any scene of conjugal discord and bourgeois adultery, but which introduces into tragedy a cunning and, in a word, a vulgarity utterly anachronistic to it."[26] It is an indiscretion comparable to that of the *rubato* dear to the romantic pianists, and which Barthes finds again in a particular interpretation of a Fauré song: "this pleonasm of intentions muffles both words and music, and chiefly their junction, which is the very object of the vocal art."[27] All these redundant, *overfed* significations, like Michelet's "lacteous and sanguine"[28] Englishwomen or the apoplectic burgomasters of Dutch painting,[29] arouse a disapproval that is indissolubly of a logical, moral, and esthetic, but perhaps above all physical, order: it is nausea, that "immediate judgment of the body" which Barthes finds so easily in his Michelet, who judges history "at the tribunal of the flesh."[30] The bad sign is bloated because it is redundant, and it is redundant because it wants to be *true*, that is, both a sign and a thing, like the costume for Chanticleer of 1910, made up of several pounds of real feathers "sewn one over the other."[31] The good sign is arbitrary: it is the common word, the name "tree" or the verb "to run," which has value only through an express convention, and does not try to deceive by adding to this conventional value the oblique power of natural evocation. It is the flag in the Chinese theater, which on its own signifies a whole regiment,[32] the masks and costumes of the *Commedia dell'arte*, or better still, the red gown of the Caliph in the *Thousand and One Nights*, which signifies "I am angry."[33] The bad sign *par excellence* is the meaning-form which serves as signifier to the mythical concept, because it uses the natural character of the meaning surreptitiously in order to justify the secondary signification. The *naturalization* of culture, and therefore of history, is in Barthes' eyes, as we know, the major sin of petty-bourgeois ideology, and its denunciation the central theme of *Mythologies*. Now the semiological instrument of this naturalization is the fraudulent motivation of the sign. When a Racinian actress utters the words "Je brûle" (I burn) in an obviously burning tone, when a singer interprets "tristesse affreuse" (terrible sadness) by terribly saddening the sounds of these two words, they commit a pleonasm and an imposture: they have to choose between the sentence and the cry, "between the intellectual sign and the visceral sign,"[34] which latter is really no longer a sign, but a direct manifestation of the signified, an *expression*, in the full sense of the term; but such effects are practically outside the reach of art, which must be accepted fully as a language. Now "if there is a 'health' of language, it is the arbitrariness of the sign which is its grounding. What is sickening in myth is its resort to a false nature, its superabundance of significant forms, as in those objects which decorate their usefulness with a natural appearance. The will to weigh the signification with the full guarantee of nature causes a kind of nausea: myth is too rich, and what is in excess is precisely its motivation."[35] The health of an art, its virtue, its elegance, lies in its strict fidelity to the system of conventions on which it rests: "The exercise of a signifying system . . . has only one requirement, which will therefore be the esthetic requirement itself: rigor":[36] this is the case of Brechtian dramaturgy, *cleansed* by the effect of distancing, which knows that "the responsibility of a dramatic art is not so much to express reality as to signify it";[37] it is the case with the sober acting of Helene Weigel, the literal performances of a Panzera or a Lipatti, the photographs of Agnès Varda, shot with "exemplary humility,"[38] the cathartic writing of Robbe-Grillet, determined *to kill the adjective* and to restore to the object its "essential thinness."[39]

Barthes does not see the semiological activity, then, as exclusively, or even essentially, belonging to the order of knowledge. For him, signs are never the neutral objects of disinterested knowledge, as Saussure conceived them when he contemplated the founding of a semiological science. The normative choice is never far behind analytical discourse, and this *ethical origin* that he recognizes in the work of the mythologist is to be found throughout his work. "Brechtian criticism will therefore be written by the spectator, the reader, the consumer, and not the exegete: it is a criticism of a *concerned* man."[40] This attitude marks all Barthes' critical activity, which is constantly underpinned by the question: in what sense does this work concern us? This criticism is and is always intended to be profoundly and aggressively subjective, because every reading, "however impersonal it forces itself to be, is a projective test"[41] into which the critic "puts all his 'profundity,' i.e., his choices, his pleasures, his resistances, his obsessions."[42] It has nothing to do, we realize, with the intersubjective participation which animates criticism like that of Georges Poulet, and which always operates to the benefit of the "thought criticized," before which critical thought stands back and falls silent, its sole *raison d'être* being to recreate a space and a language for it. Barthesian criticism is not the resumption of one subject by another, of one speech by another: it is a dialogue, and a dialogue that is "egoistically shifted toward the present." Thus, paradoxically, this notorious representation of the "newest" new criticism is alone in honoring in his work the ancient meaning of the word "criticism," which designates a militant act of assessment and challenge. His literary criticism is certainly a semiology of literature; but his semiology, in turn, is not only a study of significations, but also, in the most vivid sense of the term, a critique of signs.

Noting in the final section of *Mythologies* the imposture involved in the ambiguity of the mythical sign, "this turnstile of form and meaning,"[43] Barthes adds that one can escape this imposture, stop this turnstile, only if one focuses on form and meaning separately, that is, by applying to the mythical object a semiological *analysis*. Semiology, then, is not only a tool of knowledge and criticism: it is also, for the man besieged by signs, the only possible recourse, the only defense. To analyse the sign, to distinguish between its constitutive elements, to place on one side the signifier, on the other the signified: this activity, which, for Saussure, was a simple technique, a methodological routine, becomes for Barthes something like the instrument of an ascesis and the beginnings of a salvation. The semiological discipline stops the vertigo of meaning and authorizes a liberating choice: for it is the privilege of the semiologist to turn away from the signified in order to devote himself to the study of the signifier, and therefore to an exclusive commerce with it. He has given himself as his "moral goal," as Barthes says of the critic, "not the decipherment of the work's meaning but the reconstruction of the rules and constraints of that meaning's elaboration": thus he avoids "good conscience" and "bad faith."[44] His gaze stops at the frontier of meaning and does not cross it: like the linguist, he is concerned only with forms. But this prejudice in favor of forms is no mere methodological rule, it is an existential choice.

We have to remember that the forms in question are not sentences, words, phonemes—they are objects; and when the semiologist has operated the semiological reduction, the *epoché* of meaning on the object-form, he is presented with a matte object, cleansed of the varnish of dubious, abusive significations, with which social speech had covered it, restored to its essential freshness and solitude. Thus the formalist enterprise opens up, in an unexpected way, an adhesion to, a very profound conformity with, the reality of things. The paradox and difficulty of such a deviation have not escaped the author of *Mythologies*, who devotes the last page of that book to them: the mythologist wishes "to protect reality" against the "evaporation" with which it is threatened by the alienating speech of myth, but he fears he has himself contributed to its disappearance. The "goodness of wine" is a French myth, but at the same time wine is good and the mythologist is condemned to speak only of its mythical goodness. This abstention is regrettable, and Barthes recognizes that he has been unable to avoid it altogether: "Finding it painful constantly to work on the evaporation of reality, I have started to make it excessively dense, and to discover in it a surprising compactness which I savored with delight, and I have given a few examples of 'substantial psychoanalysis' about some mythical objects."[45] All critical irony laid aside, he gives himself up for example to praising old wooden toys, the nostalgic associations of which are characteristic: "A sign which fills one with consternation is the gradual disappearance of wood, in spite of its being an ideal material because of its firmness and its softness, and the natural warmth of its touch. . . . It is a familiar and poetic substance, which does not sever the child from close contact with the tree, the table, the floor. . . . Wood makes essential objects, objects for all time."[46] Material intimacy, access to the "essence of things" is here, as in Proust, a lost paradise, which he must try to recover, but by some indirect way. For Barthes, semiology plays the role of a *cartharsis*,[47] but this ascesis, which rejects the meaning added by history, is in its own way a return, or an attempted return, to reality. His method is almost the opposite of that of (modern) poetry, that language *without writing* by which man "confronts the world of objects without going through any of the forms of history or of social life":[48] the semiological procedure seems to consist on the contrary in accepting the deviation as inevitable, in the belief that ideology and its rhetoric overlie the entire surface of reality,[49] that the only way of obviating this is to confront them in order to traverse them, and therefore that the poetic project of an immediate speech is a sort of utopia. But the opposition of means must not conceal the kinship of ends: the semiologist as Barthes understands him is also in search of "the inalienable meaning of things,"[50] which he uncovers beneath their alienated meaning. The movement from the (ideological) signified to the (real) signifier is only apparently therefore an abandonment of meaning. It would be better to say that it leads from the ideological meaning, which is an (abusive) speech, to the poetic meaning, which is a silent presence. "Things must taste of what they are," Curnonsky demands. The rediscovery of this profound taste is perhaps the unacknowledged aim of the semiologist.

This explains the privilege accorded, and preserved throughout his work, to Literature. For Barthes, literature uses signs, following Kafka's lesson, not to name a meaning but to "deceive," that is to say, both to offer it and to suspend it. In the literary work, the transitive movement of the verbal message stops and is absorbed into a "pure spectacle."[51] To the proliferation of meaning, literature opposes a resistance that is all the more effective in that its instruments are exclusively of a semantic order, and that all its works are composed of language. Far from turning away from that rather sickening technique which Barthes calls the "cooking up of meaning," literature is wholly and entirely committed to it, but in act, in order to free itself from it, preserving the significations, but diverting them from their signifying function. The literary work tends to turn itself into a monument of reticence and ambiguity, but it constructs this silent object, so to speak, with words, and this work of abolishing meaning is a typically semiological process, liable as such to an analysis of the same order: literature is a rhetoric of silence.[52] Its *art* consists entirely in making language, a vehicle of knowledge and rather hasty opinion, a locus of uncertainty and interrogation. It suggests that the world signifies, but "without saying *what*":[53] it describes objects and people, relates events, and instead of imposing on them definite, fixed significations, as does social speech (and also, of course, "bad" literature), it leaves them, or rather restores to them, by a very subtle technique (which is still to be studied) of semantic evasion, that "shaky," ambiguous, uncertain meaning, which is their truth. Thus it *breathes new life into the world*, freeing it from the pressure of social meaning, which is a named meaning, and therefore a dead meaning,[54] maintaining as long as possible that opening, that *uncertainty of signs*, which allows one to breathe. Thus literature is for the semiologist (the critic) a permanent temptation, an endless vocation postponed until later, experienced only in this dilatory mode: like the Proustian Narrator, the semiologist is a "writer postponed";[55] he constantly intends to *write*, that is to say, to turn over the meaning of signs and to send language back to the silence that forms part of it; but the postponement is only apparent, for this intention to write, this "Moses-like gaze" on the work to come is already Literature.

[1964]

NOTES

1. Roland Barthes, *Sur Racine* (Paris: Seuil, 1963), p. 21; *On Racine*, Richard Howard, tr. (New York: Hill and Wang, 1964), p. 9.
2. Roland Barthes, *Essais critiques* (Paris: Seuil, 1964), p. 272; *Critical Essays*, Richard Howard, tr. (Evanston, Ill: Northwestern University Press, 1972), p. 275.

3. *Essais Critiques*, p. 254; *C.E.*, p. 257.
4. *Essais critiques*, p. 256; *C.E.*, p. 259.
5. *Essais critiques*, p. 257; *C.E.*, p. 260.
6. *Essais critiques*, p. 272; *C.E.*, p. 275.
7. *Essais critiques*, p. 260; *C.E.*, p. 263.
8. *Essais critiques*, p. 218; *C.E.*, p. 218.
9. Roland Barthes, *Le Degré zéro de l'écriture* (Paris: Seuil, 1953), p. 8; *Writing Degree Zero*, Annette Lavers and Colin Smith, trs. (New York: Hill and Wang, 1967), p. 8.
10. Ferdinand de Saussure, *Cours de linguistique générale* (Paris, 1916), p. 33; *Course in General Linguistics*, Wade Baskin, tr. (New York: McGraw-Hill, 1966), p. 16.
11. *Essais critiques*, p. 209; *C.E.*, p. 208.
12. *Communications* (1964), 4:2. It is evident here that for Barthes the interest of a code is to be measured not by its social utility, but by its "depth," that is to to say, its anthropological resonance.
13. Paul Valéry, *Oeuvres*, Pléiade (Paris: Gallimard, 1960), 2:696; "Rhumbs" in Valéry, *Analects*, Stuart Gilbert, tr. (Princeton: Princeton University Press, 1970), p. 259.
14. Jean-Paul Sartre, *Situations II* (Paris: Gallimard, 1948), p. 94; *What is Literature?*, Bernard Frechtman, tr. (New York: Harper, 1949), p. 38.
15. *Le Degré zéro*, p. 7; *Writing Degree Zero*, p. 7.
16. Or, more crudely, [(sail = ship) = poetry] = rhetoric.
17. Roland Barthes, *Mythologies* (Paris: Seuil, 1957), p. 222; part of this volume translated as *Mythologies*, Annette Lavers, tr. (New York: Hill and Wang, 1972), the remainder in Roland Barthes, *The Eiffel Tower and Other Mythologies*, Richard Howard, tr. (New York: Hill and Wang, 1979). *Myth.*, p. 115.
18. *Mythologies*, p. 242; *Myth.*, p. 134.
19. *Mythologies*, p. 223; *Myth.*, pp. 116–17.
20. *Essais critiques*, p. 155; *C.E.*, p. 152.
21. *Mythologies*, p. 219; *Myth.*, p. 112.
22. *Essais critiques*, p. 219; *C.E.*, p. 219.
23. *Sur Racine*, p. 160; *On Racine*, p. 165.
24. *Essais critiques*, p. 53; *C.E.*, p. 41. My italics.
25. *Sur Racine*, p. 138; *On Racine*, p. 144.
26. *Essais critiques*, p. 74; *C.E.*, pp. 62–63.
27. *Mythologies*, p. 189; *Eiffel Tower*, p. 119.
28. *Michelet par lui-même* (Paris: Seuil, 1954), p. 80.
29. *Essais critiques*, p. 25; *C.E.*, p. 9.
30. *Michelet*, p. 181.
31. *Mythologies*, p. 190; *Eiffel Tower*, p. 120.
32. *Mythologies*, p. 28; *Myth.*, p. 28.

The Obverse of Signs

33. *Essais critiques*, p. 58; *C.E.*, p. 46.
34. *Mythologies*, p. 28; *Myth.*, p. 28.
35. *Mythologies*, p. 234; *Myth.*, p. 126.
36. *Essais critiques*, p. 142; *C.E.*, p. 137.
37. *Essais critiques*, p. 87; *C.E.*, p. 74.
38. *Mythologies*, p. 25; *Eiffel Tower*, p. 22.
39. *Essais critiques*, p. 34; *C.E.*, p. 18.
40. *Essais critiques*, p. 84; *C.E.*, p. 71.
41. *Sur Racine*, p. 161; *On Racine*, p. 166.
42. *Essais critiques*, p. 257; *C.E.*, p. 260.
43. *Mythologies*, p. 231; *Myth.*, p. 124.
44. *Essais critiques*, p. 256; *C.E.*, p. 259.
45. *Mythologies*, p. 267; *Myth.*, p. 158.
46. *Mythologies*, p. 64; *Myth.*, pp. 54–55.
47. "The novelist's labor [Barthes is writing about Robbe-Grillet] is in a sense cathartic; it purges things of the *undue* meaning men ceaselessly deposit upon them." *Essais critiques*, p. 199; *C.E.*, p. 198. My italics.
48. *Le Degré zéro*, p. 76; *Writing Degree Zero*, p. 58.
49. "To the general ideology . . . correspond signifiers of connotation which are specified according to the chosen substance. These signifiers will be called *connotators* and the set of connotators a *rhetoric*, rhetoric thus appearing as the signifying aspect of ideology" ("Rhétorique de l'image," *Communications*, 4:49; "Rhetoric of the Image" in Roland Barthes, *Image-Music-Text*, Stephen Heath, tr. (New York: Hill and Wang, 1977), p. 49). This means that the raw object, as the denoted message, becomes a signifier only once it is invested, by social rhetoric, with a value of ideological connotation of which it becomes the *hostage*, that is to say, the prisoner and the guarantor, from which only semiological analysis, through criticism, can free it. While "poetic" speech, as we might call that speech which immediately names the deep meaning without having rendered the ideological meaning harmless, runs the risk in turn of being invested by social speech, and of alienating what it has taken charge of. How many poetic truths have thus become advertising myths? This is because, under the pressure of ideology, the most innocent speech is also the most exposed, and therefore the most dangerous.
50. *Mythologies*, p. 268; *Myth.*, p. 159.
51. *Essais critiques*, p. 151; *C.E.*, p. 146.
52. We know that on certain jukeboxes one can get, for the same price as the latest tune, a period of silence equal to that of a record: it may in fact be a blank record specially made for this purpose. But whatever the means, the lesson of this invention is clear, namely, that in a civilization of noise silence must also be a *product*, that it is the fruit of a technology and a commercial object. There is no question of stopping the racket,

which ought to be muffled as quickly as possible, but on occasion one is able, by paying the price, to get it to run silently. Likewise, in a civilization of meaning, though there is no longer any place for "truly insignificant objects," it is still possible to produce objects loaded with significations, but conceived in such a way that these significations cancel each other out, disperse, or are reabsorbed, like mechanical functions in Ashby's homeostat. No one is really able (or permitted) to be entirely silent, but the writer has the special, indispensable, indeed sacred function, of speaking "in order to say nothing," or to say "*What?*"

53. *Essais critiques*, p. 264; C.E., p. 267.

54. "Once [literature] turns around to look at what it loves, all that is left is a named meaning, which is a dead meaning" (*Essais critiques*, p. 265; C.E., p. 268). But "there is only meaning that is named" (*Communications*, 4:2). A whole (physical) anguish stands between these two formulas. The weight of meaning is, literally, *a dead weight*. It is the body of Eurydice, killed not by a glance, but by an indiscreet word.

55. *Essais critiques*, p. 18; C.E., p. xxi.

3

FIGURES

In his sonnet to the memory of the Duke of Osuna, Quevedo writes:

> Su Tumba son de Flandes las Campañas
> Y su Epitafio la sangrienta Luna.

What particularly strikes me in these two lines is the "sangrienta Luna," the bloodstained moon, which serves as an epitaph to the warrior; it is what in modern poetry would be called an admirable *image*. It would be better to ignore the reference to the Turkish Crescent, bloodstained by the victories of the terrible Duke, says Borges:[1] the image, the poetic vision, would vanish before so unmysterious an allegory. The same goes for the *Kenningar* of Scandinavian poetry: the "mighty bison of the seagulls' meadow" is merely a laborious "equation of the second degree." The "seagulls' meadow" is the sea, the bison of this meadow the ship. Snorri Sturluson, who in the thirteenth century drew up a complete glossary of these metaphors, committed an antipoetic act: "To reduce each Kenning to the word that it represents is not to unveil mysteries, but to abolish the poem."

Today, no doubt, approval of such a commentary would be almost unanimous. The same goes for Andre Breton's furious response to some forgotten "periphase" of Saint-Pol-Roux: "Non, Monsieur, Saint-Pol-Roux n'a pas voulu dire. S'il avait voulu dire, il l'aurait dit." (No, sir, Saint-Pol-Roux did not *mean* that. If he had meant that, he would have said that.) The literalness of language appears today as the very being of poetry, and nothing is more antipathetic to this idea than that of a possible translation, of some kind of space between the letter and the meaning. Breton writes: "La rosée à tête de chatte se berçait," by which he means that the dew (*rosée*) has the head of a cat and that it is swaying to and fro. Éluard writes: "Un soleil tournoyant ruisselle sous l'écorce," and he means that a spinning sun is streaming under the (earth's) crust.[2]

Now let us open a treatise on Rhetoric.[3] Here is a line from La Fontaine:

> Sur les ailes du temps la tristesse s'envole.
> (On the wings of time sorrow flies away.)

This line means that "sadness does not last forever" (Domairon). Here is a line from Boileau:

> Le chagrin monte en croupe et galope avec lui.
> (Sorrow mounts behind and gallops with him.)

This line means that "he rides off with his sorrow and does not forget it as he gallops away" (Fontanier). Here are four lines from Racine:

> Mon arc, mes javelots, mon char, tout m'importune;
> Je ne me souviens plus des leçons de Neptune;
> Mes seuls gémissements font retentir les bois,
> Et mes coursiers oisifs ont oublié ma voix.
> (My bow, my arrows, my chariot, everything disturbs me;
> I no longer remember Neptune's lessons;
> The woods echo only with my moans,
> And my idle steeds have forgotten my voice.)

The "translation" of these lines is to be found in Pradon, who expresses in a different way "these same thoughts and these same sentiments" (Domairon):

> Depuis que je vous vois j'abandonne la chasse.
> (Since I saw you I have given up hunting.)

"I do not think better than Pradon and Coras," says Racine, "but I write better than they." There is a "thought," that is to say, a meaning, which is common to good and bad poets, and which can be expressed by some dry, flat sentence; and there is a "way of putting it" (Domairon), which makes all the difference. We see that here, between the letter and the meaning, between what the poet has *written* and what he *thought*, there is a gap, a space, and like all space, it possesses a form. This form is called a *figure,* and there will be as many figures as one can find forms in the space that is created on each occasion between the line of the signifier ("la tristesse s'envole"—sorrow flies away) and that of the signified ("le chagrin ne dure pas"—sadness does not last), which is obviously merely another signifier offered as the literal one.

> Discourse, which is addressed only to the intelligence of the soul, is not, even considered in terms of the words that convey it to the soul through the senses, a body in the strict sense: it does not therefore possess a *figure*, in the strict sense. But, in its different ways of signifying and expressing, it does possess something similar to the differences of form and feature to be found in true bodies. . . . The figures of discourse are the features, the forms, or the turns . . . by which discourse . . . departs more or less from what had been its simple, common expression. (Fontanier)

The spirit of rhetoric is entirely contained in this awareness of a possible hiatus between real language (that of the poet) and a virtual language (that which would have been used by "simple, common expression"), which must only be reestablished by thought in order to delimit a space of a figure. This space is not empty: on each occasion it contains a particular mode of eloquence or poetry. The writer's art lies in the way in which he sets out the limits of this space, which is the visible body of Literature.

It might be objected that *figurative style* is not the only style, or even the only poetic style, and that rhetoric also takes cognizance of what is called *simple* style. But in fact this is merely a less decorated style, or rather, a style decorated more simply, and it too, like the lyric and the epic, has its own special figures. A style in which figure is strictly absent does exist, but it is what in rhetoric we would now call a *zero degree,* that is to say, a sign defined by the absence of sign, the value of which is perfectly recognized. Absolute sobriety of expression is the mark of an extreme elevation in thought: "Sublime feelings are *always* rendered by the simplest expression" (Domairon). Old Horace says, quite simply: "Would that he had died!" Médée says: "I!" Genesis says: "And there was light." Nothing is more *marked* than this simplicity: it is the very figure, indeed the perfectly obligatory figure, of the sublime. Obligatory and reserved: to use it to express less elevated sentiments or situations would show a lack of taste. We know, through the example of linguistics, that this phenomenon of the zero degree, in which an absence of signifier clearly designates a known signified, is the infallible mark of the existence of a system: an organized code of vocalic alternations is required if the absence of a vowel is to have a distinctive function. The existence of a zero figure, standing as the figure of the sublime, shows that the language of rhetoric is sufficiently saturated with figures for an empty square to designate a full meaning: rhetoric is a *system* of figures.

Yet the status of the figure has not always been clear in the rhetorical tradition. Since Antiquity rhetoric has defined figures as *ways of speaking removed from those that are natural and ordinary*, or again, as we saw in the case of Fontanier, *simple and common*; but at the same time it admits that nothing is more common and ordinary than the use of figures and, as the classic formula has it, "more figures are made in one day in the marketplace than during several days in the university." A figure is a gap in relation to usage, but a gap that is nevertheless part of usage: that is the paradox of rhetoric. César Dumarsais, who more than anyone else was aware of this difficulty, did not pursue the matter very far, but in the end fell back on a definition that is an admission of defeat: "[Figures] have first of all this general property, which is shared with all sentences and all combinations of words, and which consists of signifying something by virtue of the grammatical construction; but figurative expressions have a particular modification that is peculiar to them, and it is by virtue of this particular modification that each kind of figure is a separate species." Or again: "Figures are ways of speaking distinct from other ways by a particular modification through which each is reduced to a separate species, and which makes them either more vivid, or more noble, or more pleasing than the ways of speaking that express the same content of thought without having a particular modification." In other words: the *effect* of figures (vividness, nobility, pleasantness) is easy to describe, but their *being* can be designated only by the fact that each figure is a separate figure, and that figures in general are to be distinguished from non-figurative expressions by the fact that they have a *particular modification* which one calls figure. It is an almost tautological definition, but not quite, since it places the being of the figure in the fact of *having* a figure, that is to say, a form. Simple, common expression has no form, the figure has one: so we are brought back to the definition of the figure as a gap between sign and meaning, as the inner space of language.

Indeed, every phrase, even the simplest and most common, every word, even the most ordinary, possesses a form: sounds follow one another in a certain way (in a certain order) to form this word, words follow one another to form this sentence. But this form is purely grammatical, it concerns morphology, syntax, but not rhetoric. As far as rhetoric is concerned, the word "ship" or the proposition "I love you" have no form, involve no particular modification. The rhetorical fact begins where I am able to compare the form of this word or this sentence to that of another word or sentence that might have been used in their place and which could be regarded as standing in for them. "Sail" or "I don't hate you" do not in themselves have a rhetorical form, any more than do "ship" or "I love you." The rhetorical form—the figure—lies in the use of "sail" to designate a ship (synecdoche), or of "I don't hate you" to signify love (litotes). Thus the existence and character of the figure are absolutely determined by the existence and character of the virtual signs to which I compare the real signs when posing their semantic equivalence. Charles Bally was to say that expressiveness disturbs the linearity of language by making the reader perceive both the presence of a signifier ("sail") and the absence of another signifier ("ship").[4] Pascal had already said as much: "Figure bears absence and presence." A sign or a succession of linguistic signs form a single line, and this linear form is the concern of grammarians. Rhetorical form is a *surface*, delimited by the two lines of the present signifier and the absent signifier. This is the only way in which Dumarsais' heavy-footed definition can be interpreted: only the figurative expression is endowed with a form, because it alone encloses a space.

We see therefore that the definition of the figure as a deviation in relation to *usage* rests on a confusion between usage and literalness, a confusion that becomes very clear in the false doublet: "*simple, common* ways of speaking." The simple is not necessarily common, and vice versa; the figure may be common, but it cannot be simple, since it bears presence and absence *simultaneously*. It may very well become part of usage without losing its figurative character (that is to say, the vulgar tongue also has its rhetoric, but rhetoric itself defines a *literary usage* which resembles a language (*langue*) rather than speech (*parole*)); it disappears only when the present signifier is literalized by an anti-rhetorical, or *terrorist* awareness,[5] as in modern poetry ("When I write *sail*, I mean sail; if I had meant ship, I would have written *ship*") or when the absent signifier can no longer be found. That is why the treatises of rhetoric are collections of examples of figures followed by their translation into literal language: "The author means . . . . The author might have said. . . ." Every figure is translatable, and bears its translation, transparently visible, like a watermark, or a palimpsest, beneath its apparent text. Rhetoric is bound up with this duplicity of language.[6]

The last great French rhetorician, Pierre Fontanier, elucidated this connection in his quarrel with Dumarsais on the subject of *catachresis,* and he says himself that "[his] principles concerning catachresis serve as the foundation for the whole [of his] tropological system." After Lamy and some others, Dumarsais had, in his treatise *Des Tropes,* included catachresis among the figures, defining it as an abuse or an extension of meaning ("une feuille de papier"— a sheet, literally a *leaf*, of paper; "un pied de table"—a foot of a table). Fontanier is violently opposed to this inclusion, which seems to him to be contrary to the very principle of the theory of figures: catachresis is too *forced* a trope, imposed by necessity,[7] that is to say, by the lack of a literal word. The idea that figures are the children of scarcity and necessity goes back to Cicero and Quintilian; in the seventeenth century, René Bary explained their existence by the fact that "nature is more fertile in things than we are fertile in terms." But Dumarsais himself repudiated this explanation by pointing out that a large number of tropes *duplicate* the literal word instead of making up for its absence. "In any case," he said, "it seems to me that this is scarcely the way, so to speak, of nature; imagination has too large a part to play in language and the conduct of men to have been preceded in this matter by necessity." Nevertheless he reintroduces it by making catachresis a figure, without being aware, it would seem of the contradiction. For his part, Fontanier treats the question of origin, which so fascinated all his predecessors, with some disdain; or more exactly—and in this one might regard him as the Saussure of rhetoric—he carefully distinguishes between the search for causes and the analysis of functions. Whatever the origin of a trope, one must consider its present use, and classify it according to that use. Now catachresis is never anything more than "the *forced* use, *at least in present usage if not from the very beginning,* of one of the three great species that we have recognized (metaphor, synecdoche, metonymy)." When we say "feuille de papier" or "pied de table," we are using an obligatory metaphor, because the proper word does not exist, or no longer exists, or does not yet exist. Now "figures, however common they may be and however familiar habit has made them, can deserve and maintain their title as *figures* only insofar as they are used freely and are not in any way imposed by language. And how could one reconcile this choice, this combination of words, or this turn of thought that gives them existence, with forced usage?" Where there is choice, combination of words, turn of thought, there must be at least two terms to compare, two words to combine together, a space in which thought can operate. So the reader is able to translate implicitly one expression by another, and to assess their gap, their angle, their distance. The catachresis "pied de table" is certainly a trope because for a table it uses a word originally reserved for the human body, and diverts this word from its initial signification; and as such it is of interest to the (diachronic) history of the language. But it is not a figure-trope, since I can offer no translation of the word "pied" (foot), because no other word exists: it is of no interest therefore to the (synchronic) code of rhetoric.

The application, conscious or otherwise, of this functional criterion (every figure is translatable) might explain certain, apparently abusive, annexations and certain, apparently timid, rejections in rhetoric. Thus, during the classical period, *description* was regarded as a figure: "a figure by which we present the image of an object" (Domairon). Lamy saw it as an attenuated variant of *hypotyposis*: it speaks of absent things as absent (whereas hypotyposis pretends to bring them before us), but "in a way that makes a vivid impression on the mind." Domairon saw it as a genus of which the four species are hypotyposis, aethopoea, prosographia, and topographia. Why figure? When Théramène, in the fifth act of *Phèdre*, relates the circumstances of Hippolyte's death, he describes the "furious monster" sent by Neptune:

> Son front large est orné de cornes menaçantes;
> Tout son corps est couvert d'écailles jaunissantes;
> Indomptable taureau, dragon impérieux,
> Sa croupe se recourbe en replis tortueux.
> (His broad brow is adorned with threatening horns;
> His whole body is covered with yellowish scales;
> Untameable bull, imperious dragon,
> His croup swells out in tortuous folds.)

We can see no figure there, because we cannot imagine that Théramène would have been content to say "furious monster," and dispense with this elaboration. He says in four lines what could have been said in two words, and therefore the description replaces (that is to say, could be replaced by) a simple designation: that is the figure. In the fable *Le Loup et le Chasseur* (*The Wolf and the Huntsman*), La Fontaine gives us the following dialogue:

> Jouis. — Je le ferai. — Mais quand donc? — Dès demain.
> (Enjoy it. — I shall. — But when? —Tomorrow.)

This, says Fontanier, is a figure: for the poet has "eliminated the transitions that are usual between the parts of a dialogue . . . in order to make the exposition more animated and more interesting." And he calls this figure *abruption*. One can grasp easily enough from these two examples the way in which rhetoric produces figures: it ascertains a *quality* in the text that might not have been there—the poet describes (instead of designating with a word), the dialogue is abrupt (instead of connected); then it substantializes this quality by naming it—the text is no longer descriptive or abrupt, it *contains* a description or an abruption. It is an old scholastic habit: opium does not put one to sleep, it possesses a soporific power. There is in rhetoric a *passion to name* which is a mode of self-expansion and self-justification: it operates by increasing the number of objects in one's purview. The same result might be obtained equally well by the opposite method: the poet designates instead of describing—this is called *designation*; the dialogue is connected instead of being abrupt—this is called *connection*. Rhetorical promotions are arbitrary; the important thing is to promote and thus to found an Order of literary dignity.

But this freedom of advancement has its limits, which are those imposed by the implicit criterion (translatability). Thus, certain rhetoricians had classified among the figures of thought what they called *commination*, which is the fact of uttering threats. Stop there, says Fontanier. He examines three examples, and remarks that they contain no particular turn of language. Is it therefore the feeling that produces the figure here?

> In which case, there would be as many new figures as there are different feelings or passions, or different ways in which feelings and passions may erupt. So, I say, insult, reproach, blame, praise, flattery, advice, compliment, exhortation, offer, request, thanks, complaint, and I don't know what else, will be so many figures that will have to be classified no doubt according to their distinctive characters of malignity and violence, or gentleness and grace.

Threat, insult, reproach are contents, not modes of expression; they are not therefore translatable. One translates words, not meanings. *Commination* is therefore only a "supposed" figure. Similarly, although he accepts as a figure Dido's deliberation in Book IV of the *Aeneid* because in it Dido *pretends* to question herself about her fate, whereas she has already decided to die, Fontanier refuses this title to Hermione's *dubitation* in the fifth act of *Andromaque*, which expresses a sincere resolution. A *figure of thought* (a marginal and questionable category, for strictly speaking a figure can pertain only to expression) is such only if it is feigned or affected (a false concession, a false naivety, a false question, etc.) The subtle distinction between deliberation and dubitation rests on a very simple distinction: Hermione's dubitation means nothing more than what she says, Dido's deliberation says "What am I to do?" in order to express "I want to die." In the first, sign and meaning are contiguous, they touch without leaving a space: there is no figure. The second encloses all the space that extends between the straight line of the signified, or virtual signifier, and the curve traced by the series of false questions that constitute the real signifier: this space constitutes the figure.

The figure, then, is simply a sense of figure, and its existence depends completely on the awareness that the reader has, or does not have, of the ambiguity of the discourse that is being offered him. Sartre was to observe that the meaning of a literary object is not contained in the words, "since it is he [the reader], on the contrary, who enables the significance of each of them to be understood."[8] This hermeneutic circle also exists in rhetoric: the value of a figure is not given in the words that make it up, since it depends on the gap between these words and those that the reader perceives, mentally, beyond them, "in a perpetual supersession of the written thing." It is understandable that this essentially subjective status cannot satisfy the requirements of certainty and universality that inhabit the classical mind. Hence the need to establish a general consensus. The instrument of this consensus was to be the code of rhetoric, which consists first of all of a list, constantly revised, but always regarded as exhaustive, of the permitted figures, followed by a classification of these figures according to their form and value, it too subject to constant modifications, but also the constant object of further efforts to organize it into a coherent, functional system.

There can be no question here of tracing, from rhetorical treatise to rhetorical treatise, the development of this system. However, such a study would be well worth undertaking one day, for it would tell us a great deal about the history of representations of the world and the mind throughout the whole classical period, from Aristotle to La Harpe. The most obvious classification is based on the forms affected: figures of words regarded from the point of view of their signification, or *tropes*; figures of words regarded from the point of view of their form, or figures of *diction*; figures concerning the order and number of words in a sentence, or figures of *construction*; figures concerning "the choice and arrangement of words" (Fontanier), or figures of *elocution*; figures concerning a whole sentence, or figures of *style*; figures concerning a whole utterance, or figures of *thought*. One can then introduce subdivisions into these different groups: thus Fontanier divides the figures of elocution into figures by *extension*, like the epithet; by *deduction*, like synonymy; by *connection*, like abruption, which is a zero-connection; by *consonance*, like alliteration; the same Fontanier also divides up the metonymies, or tropes by *correspondence* (which Roman Jakobson was later to call contiguity), into metonymies of cause (*Bacchus* standing for wine), of instrument (*une bonne plume*—a fine pen—for a good writer), of effect (*revenge* for hand), of content (*Heaven* for God), of place of origin (the *Portico*, for Stoic philosophy), of the sign (*throne* for the monarchy), of the body (the *heart* for love), of patronage (*penates*, or Roman household gods, for house), of things (*wig* for the man who wears it). This type of classification is of a purely logical order; it tells us nothing about the signifying value of the figures or groups of figures under consideration. Another type, which is of more relevance to us here, is of a semiological order: it consists in distinguishing figures from one another by fixing to each of them a precise psychological value, according to the character of the divergence imposed on the expression. This value is given (to anticipate the vocabulary of modern stylistics) either as *impressive* (a particular figure is intended to arouse a particular feeling), or as *expressive* (a particular figure is dictated by a particular feeling), or, preferably, as both at once, since one likes to postulate a concordance between the state of mind of the author, or character, and that of the reader: "Since we almost never speak except to convey our affections and ideas, it is obvious that in order to make our discourse effective it must be figurative, that is to say, it must be given the characteristics of our affections" (Lamy). What we have here, then, is an unconscious or masked semiology, since it translates significations into terms of determinism, presenting meanings as causes and/or effects. Of all the French rhetoricians, the Cartesian Lamy no doubt carried the psychological (affective) interpretation of figures farthest, to the point of seeking in each of them the "character," that is to say, the mark of a particular impression: a figure for every symptom. *Ellipsis*: a violent passion speaks more quickly than words can follow it. *Repetition*: the impassioned man likes to repeat himself, just as the angry man delivers several blows. *Hypotyposis*: the obsessive presence of the loved object. *Epanorthosis*: the impassioned man constantly corrects his discourse in order to increase its force. *Hyperbaton* (inversion): emotion disturbs the order of things, and therefore the order of words. *Distribution*: one enumerates the parts of the object of one's passion. *Apostrophe*: the impassioned man turns in all directions, seeking everywhere help, etc. Other authors attribute less to affectivity, more to taste, to intellect, to imagination. The Scotsman Hugh Blair, who is very much in favor of the natural origin of figures ("They are to be accounted part of that Language which Nature dictates to men," he says and he cites as proof of this the abundance of tropes in "primitive" languages: "An Indian chief makes a harangue to his tribe, in a style full of stronger metaphors than an European would use in an epic poem"), suggests dividing figures into figures of imagination and figures of passion. Dumarsais sees the principle of all figurative meanings in taste, which carries the imagination towards details: "The name of the incidental idea is often more present to the imagination than that of the principal idea, and the incidental idea, designating the object with greater circumstantiality, depicts it with greater beauty and force." Here, too, each variant of the system implies a whole segmentation of the world and involves a whole philosophy.

There remains a fundamental question: why does the figure signify more than the literal expression? Where does its surplus of meaning come from and, for example, how can it designate not only an object, a fact, a thought, but also their affective value or their literary dignity? The technique of these impositions of meaning can be reduced to what modern semiology calls a *connotation*. When I use the word "sail" to designate a sail, this signification is arbitrary (there is no natural relation between the word and the thing, which are linked together purely by social convention), abstract (the word designates not a thing, but a concept), and univocal (this concept is designated without ambiguity): this is a simple denotation. But if I use the same word "sail" to designate, by synecdoche (the part for the whole), a ship, this signification is much richer and more complex: it is ambiguous because it is directed, at one and the same time, literally at the sail and figuratively at the ship, and therefore the whole *through* the part; it is concrete and motivated, because it chooses to designate the ship by a material detail, an "incidental idea," and not by the principal idea, and again because it uses a particular detail (the sail) rather than some other (the hull or the mast). This motivation, which is different in each type of figure (by a detail in synecdoche, by a resemblance in metaphor, by an attenuation in litotes, by an exaggeration in hyperbole, etc.) is the very soul of the figure, and its presence is a secondary signification imposed by the use of this figure. In saying "sail" for ship, I denote the ship, but at the same time I connote the motivation by the detail, the sensory deviation imprinted on the signification, and therefore a certain modality of vision or intention. This sensory modality is for rhetoric the essence of poetic expression. "Poets," says Lamy, "use expressions that form a sensory picture in the imagination, and it is for this very reason that Metaphors, which render all things sensory, are so frequent in their style." And even when a poetic figure has passed into literary usage to the point of having lost any power of concrete evocation, which is obviously the case for most of the tropes of classical poetry (sail for ship, blade for sword, flame for love, etc.), its connotative value does not disappear, for it still has the task, by its very presence and by a virtue that has become quite conventional, of signifying Poetry.

At this point there intervenes the code of rhetoric, which is entrusted with the task of enumerating the repertoire of figures and of assigning to each one its connotative value. Once it has emerged from the vivid speech of personal invention and entered the code of tradition, each figure has as its task merely to intimate in its own particular way the poetic quality of the discourse of which it is part. The "sail" of the classical ship has long since ceased to be the mark of a concrete vision; it has become, like Quevedo's "bloodstained moon" a pure emblem: a standard, above the troop of words and phrases, on which one may read not only "here, a ship," but also "here, poetry."

The ambition of the rhetoric of figures, therefore, is to draw up a code of literary connotations, or what Roland Barthes has called the "Signs of Literature." Whenever he uses a figure recognized by the code, the writer entrusts his language not only with the task of "expressing his thought," but also of intimating the quality of being epic, lyric, didactic, oratorical, and so forth, of designating itself as a literary language, and of signifying literature. Thus rhetoric concerns itself very little with the originality or novelty of figures, which are qualities of individual speech (*parole*) and which, as such, do not concern it. What does concern rhetoric is the clarity and universality of the poetic signs; its task is to rediscover at the secondary level of the system—literature—the transparency and rigor that already characterize the first—language (*langue*). Its ultimate ideal would be to organize literary language as a second language within the first, in which the evidence of signs would assert itself with as much clarity as in the dialectal system of Greek poetry, in which the use of the Dorian mode signified *lyricism* absolutely, that of the Attic mode *drama,* and that of the Ionian-Aeolian mode *epic.*

For us, today, the work of rhetoric is only of historical interest (though an underestimated one) as far as its content is concerned. The idea of reviving its code in order to apply it to our literature would be a sterile anachronism. Not that one cannot find in modern texts all the figures of ancient rhetoric; but it is the system that has broken down, and the signifying function of figures has disappeared with the network of relations that articulated them in this system. The self-signifying function of Literature is no longer conveyed through the code of figures, and modern literature has its own rhetoric, which is precisely (for the moment at least) a rejection of rhetoric, and which Jean Paulhan called Terror. What can be retained of the old rhetoric is not, therefore, its content, but its example, its form, its paradoxical idea of literature as an order based on the ambiguity of signs, on the tiny, but vertiginous space that opens up between two words having the same meaning, two meanings of the same word: two languages (*langages*) in the same language (*langage*).

[1964]

NOTES

1. Jorge Luis Borges, *Other Inquisitions*, Ruth L. C. Simms, tr. (New York: Simon & Schuster, 1965), pp. 40–41.

2. [The impossibility, strictly speaking, of "translating" this type of figure is well demonstrated here. The word *écorce* is used not only of the earth's crust, but also, more usually, means "bark" (of a tree)—Tr.]

3. The treatises of rhetoric cited here are the following: René Bary, *La Rhétorique française*, 1653; Bernard Lamy, *La Rhétorique ou l'art de parler*, 1688; César Dumarsais, *Traité des tropes*, 1730; Jean-Baptiste Crevier, *La Rhétorique française*, 1765; Hugh Blair, *Lectures on Rhetoric and Belles Lettres*, 1783; Domairon, *La Rhétorique française*, 1804; Pierre Fontanier, *Commentaire raisonné des tropes de Dumarsais*, 1818; *Manuel classique pour l'étude des tropes*, 1821, 2d. rev. ed., 1822; *Des Figures du discours autres que les tropes*, 1827.

These classical rhetorics deal essentially (and even, in the case of Dumarsais and Fontanier, exclusively) with that part of the art of speaking and writing that the ancients called *elocutio*, that is to say, the labor of style, of which figures constitute the main resource. It is this rhetoric of expression, the ancestor of modern semantics and stylistics, which is being considered here and simply called "rhetoric" for convenience. But this restriction should not let us forget the other two major parts of ancient rhetoric, *dispositio*, which is the art of combining the large unities of discourse (the rhetoric of composition), and above all *inventio*, which is the art of finding arguments (the rhetoric of content, culminating in *topics*, or the repertoire of themes).

4. Charles Bally, *Le Langage et la vie* (Paris: Payot, 1926).

5. [Genette refers here to the term "Terrorism," coined by Jean Paulhan for a doctrine which he attributed to certain modern writers: that of a general refusal to make use of the "flowers of rhetoric," and of a commitment to write without any of the traditional supports and devices of literature or *belles lettres*. *Les Fleurs de Tarbes, ou la terreur dans le lettres* (Paris: Gallimard, 1941)—M.-R. L.]

6. That is to say, if the figure must be *translatable*, it can be *translated* without losing its figurative quality. Rhetoric knows that the word "sail" designates a ship, but it also knows that it designates it quite differently from the way in which the word "ship" does: the meaning is the same, but the signification, that is to say, the relation of sign to meaning, is different, and poetry depends on significations, not on meanings. So much so that rhetoric respects in its own way Valéry's principle of the *indissoluble link of sound and sense*. In modern poetry, the word is irreplaceable *because it is literal*; in classical poetry it is irreplaceable *because it is figurative*.

7. Bary and Crevier call catechresis a forced metaphor, not in the sense of *constrained* but in the sense of *excessive*. A classical example from Theophilus: "The plough *skins* the plain." This metaphor would be regarded by classical taste as too bold, because too far-fetched. This has nothing in common, except the name, with the catechresis defined by Dumarsais and Fontanier.

8. Jean-Paul Sartre, *Situations II*, (Paris: Gallimard, 1948), p. 94; *What is Literature?*, Bernard Frechtman, tr. (New York: Harper, 1949), pp. 37-38.

4

PRINCIPLES OF PURE CRITICISM

I would like to suggest in broad outline some of the characteristics that a truly *contemporary* criticism might possess, a criticism, that is, which would correspond as precisely as possible to the needs and resources of our understanding and use of literature, at the present time.[1] But in order to confirm that the contemporary is not simply or necessarily the new, and because one would not be (however little) a critic without the habit and inclination of speaking while pretending to allow others to speak (unless the opposite is the case), I will begin with a few lines written between 1925 and 1930 by a great critic of the time, who might deserve, and for more than one reason, to be included in Georges Poulet's list of "great predecessors." I refer to Albert Thibaudet, and it goes without saying that the choice of this reference is not entirely without polemical intent, if one thinks of the exemplary antithesis that unites the type of critical intelligence represented by Thibaudet and that represented at the same time by someone like Charles du Bos—though one should not forget the deeper opposition that separated both from that type of critical unintelligence represented at that time by the name of Julien Benda.

* The title "Principles of Pure Criticism" has been chosen to render the Kantian connotations of the original French title, "Raisons de la critique pure." In the introduction to *The Critique of Pure Reason*, Kant establishes a relationship between the concept of *reason* and the ability to establish the *principles* of knowledge—M.-R. L.

In an essay published by Thibaudet in the *Nouvelle Revue Française* (April 1, 1936) and republished after his death in *Réflexions sur la critique* there is the following passage:

> The other day, in *L'Europe nouvelle*, Gabriel Marcel suggested that one of the principal qualities of a critic worthy of the name was *attention to the unique*, that is, "attention to the way in which the novelist with whom he is dealing has experienced life and felt its passing." He praised Charles du Bos for successfully posing this problem in precise terms. . . . He regretted that another critic, regarded as a Bergsonian, had not sufficiently, or rather, had less and less benefited from the lesson of Bergsonianism on this question, and he imputed this failure, this lowering of temperature, to an excess of the classificatory spirit. After all, that is quite possible. But if there is no literary criticism worthy of the name that does not attend to the unique, that has no sense of individualities and differences, is there really a criticism, apart from the Republic of Letters, understood in a certain social sense, with its feeling for resemblances and affinities, and which cannot but be expressed from time to time in classifications?[2]

It should be noted at the outset that Thibaudet has no difficulty in acknowledging "an excess of the classificatory spirit" in himself, and I would like to compare this admission with something Jules Lemaître said about Ferdinand Brunetière, which Thibaudet quoted in another article in 1922, and which would apply equally well to himself, with one possible reservation:

> Brunetière is incapable, it seems, of regarding a work, whatever it may be, great or small, other than in its relationship with a group of other works, the relationship of which with yet other groups, through time and space, is immediately apparent and so on and so forth. . . . *When he is reading a book, he thinks, it might be said, of all the books that have been written since the beginning of the world.* He touches nothing without classifying it, and for all eternity.[3]

The reservation, of course, lies in the last part of the sentence, for unlike Brunetière, Thibaudet was not one of those who think that they are working for eternity, or think that eternity is working for them. He would no doubt have been quite happy to adopt the motto of Valéry's Monsieur Teste, *Transiit classificando*, which, depending on whether one stresses the principal verb or the gerundive, signifies both "He has spent [his life] classifying," and "He classified as he went along." There is in this idea that a classification may be of value other than for all eternity, that a classification may pass with time, belong to passing time and bear its mark, something which was certainly alien to Brunetière (but not to Thibaudet), something of importance for us today, in literature and elsewhere. History also *transit classificando*. But let us not go too far from our texts, and let us rather move through the reference to Valéry toward another page of the *Réflexions sur la critique*, which dates from June 1927. There we find this lack of attention to the unique, with which Marcel reproached Thibaudet, attributed this time, even more legitimately, to the man who made his hero say: "Mind must not concern itself with persons. *De personis non curandum*." This is what Thibaudet says:

> I imagine that criticism written by a philosopher would rejuvenate our understanding of literature by thinking of worlds where classical criticism thought of the fashioners of art, working like the demiurge of the *Timaeus* on the eternal models of the genres, and where the criticism of the nineteenth century thought of men living in society. Indeed we possess a non-approximate, but paradoxically complete sample of this criticism. It is Valéry's *Léonard*. Valéry has deliberately deprived Leonardo of everything pertaining to Leonardo the man, retaining only what constituted the world Leonardo. Valéry's influence on poets is obvious enough. I can already glimpse an influence of *Monsieur Teste* on novelists. Might not an influence of *Léonard* on our young philosophical critics be reasonably desirable? In any case, they will lose nothing by reading it again.[4]

Let us politely decline the label "philosophical critics"—it is not difficult to imagine what Valéry himself would have thought of it—and set beside this quotation another, which will be the last and longest, taken this time from Thibaudet's *Physiologie de la critique*. He has just quoted and commented on a passage in Hugo's *William Shakespeare*, and adds:

> Reading these lines of Hugo and the commentary that follows them, one might have been reminded of Paul Valéry. And indeed the *Introduction à la Méthode de Léonard de Vinci* is certainly conceived in a similar way to *William Shakespeare* and has a similar aim—except that the intention is even clearer. Valéry warns his reader that his Leonardo is not Leonardo, but a certain idea of genius for which he has simply borrowed certain of Leonardo's characteristics, without confining himself to these characteristics, and combining them with others. Here, as elsewhere, Valéry is concerned with that ideal algebra, that language not common to several

orders, but rather indifferent to several orders, which might equally well be deciphered in one as in another, and which indeed resembles the power of suggestion and variation assumed by a poetry reduced to essences. The *Introduction à la méthode de Léonard*—and the same goes for other works by Valéry—might well not have been written had it not been his fate to live with a poet who had also gambled his life on that impossible algebra and that ineffable mystical theology. What was present in Valéry's and Mallarmé's meditation was also present in Hugo's. Here pure criticism is born from the same chilly spring as pure poetry. *By pure criticism I understand criticism concerned not with people, not with works, but with essences, and which sees in the vision of people and works merely a pretext for a meditation on essences.*[5]

I perceive three such essences. All three preoccupied, disturbed Hugo, Mallarmé, and Valéry, who saw them as the transcendent play of literary thought: genius, genre, and the Book.

William Shakespeare and the *Introduction* are devoted to genius. It is the highest figure of the individual, the superlative of the individual, and yet the secret of genius is to explode individuality, to be Idea, to represent, beyond invention, the current of invention.

What, in literature, represents that Idea, even above individual genius, and under it the current that bears it up, are the forms of the literary life force that we call the genres. Brunetière was right to see this as the crucial problem of great criticism, for which the theory of genres must remain its highest ambition. But he was wrong to confuse its movement with an evolution modeled on a natural evolution, the crude, arbitrary elements of which were provided by an ill-digested science. . . . But it is certain that the genres exist, live, die, are transformed, and the artists who work in the very laboratory of the genres know this even better than the critics. . . . Mallarmé wrote poetry only in order to define the essence of poetry, he went to the theater only to seek that essence of the theater that he was pleased to see in the chandelier.

Lastly, the Book. Literary criticism and literary history have often been wrong to put into the same series, to throw into the same order, what is said, what is sung, and what is read. Literature operates in terms of the Book, and yet men of books[6] think of nothing less than of the Book. . . . We know to what paradoxes Mallarmé has carried the hallucination of the Book.[7]

Let us end the quotation here and try to rediscover the movement of thought that emerges from these few texts, and which may help us to define a particular idea of criticism, for which I would be quite happy, if only for their value as provocation for simple souls, to retain the term *pure criticism* and, for that matter, the patronage of Valéry—who, one cannot remind oneself too often, and for the same reason, proposed a history of literature understood as a "history of the mind as it produces or consumes literature," which could be written "without the name of a single writer being mentioned in it." However, it should be noted that Thibaudet, less absolute than Valéry, in no way rejects attention to the unique (which, indeed, he interprets in a very characteristic way as the sense of individualities *and differences,* which is already to go beyond unicity and to enter, by the play of comparisons, what Maurice Blanchot was to call "literary infinity"), but simply sees in it, not an end, but the starting-point for a search that must ultimately concern, not individualities, but the totality of a universe of which he often dreamt of becoming the geographer (the geographer, it should be stressed—not the historian), and which he calls, here and elsewhere, the Republic of Letters. There is in this expression something rather dated, something that connotes in a rather blatant way, it seems to me, the "social," and therefore all too human, aspect of what one would now more soberly call, by a word the curious modernity of which has not yet been dissipated, Literature. We should consider above all this movement, characteristic of a still possibly "impure" criticism, which might just as well be called a *paradigmatic* criticism, since the occurences, that is to say, the authors and the works, still appear in it, but only as cases or examples of literary phenomena, which exceed them and for which they become a kind of *index*, somewhat like those eponymous poets, Hoffmann, for example, or Swinburne, to whom Gaston Bachelard entrusts the task of illustrating a complex, without letting them forget that a *complex is never very original*. To study the work of an author (Thibaudet, let us say, to take a quite imaginary example) would be to study a Thibaudet who was no more Thibaudet than Valéry's Leonardo is Leonardo, but a certain idea of genius for which one would borrow certain characteristics from Thibaudet, without confining oneself to those characteristics, and which one would combine with others. This would not be to study a person, or even a work but, through this person and this work, to pursue an *essence*.

We must now consider in more detail the three types of essences referred to by Thibaudet. The first bears a name that has virtually dropped out of use, on account of its apparent presumption, but which we have been unable to replace with any other. Genius, Thibaudet says rather enigmatically, is both the superlative of the individual and an exploding of individuality. If we want to find the most illuminating commentary on this paradox, it is perhaps to Blanchot (and Jacques Lacan) that we should turn, pursuing the idea, now familiar enough to literature, but of which criticism has been perhaps rather slow to take account, that the author, the craftsman of a book, as Valéry also called him, *is not precisely anybody*—or, again, that one of the functions of language, and of literature as language, is to destroy its user and to designate him as absent. What Thibaudet calls genius might here be the absence of the subject, that exercise of decentered language, deprived of a center, of which Blanchot speaks in relation to Kafka's experience on discovering "that he entered literature as soon as he was able to substitute the 'he' for the 'I'." "The writer," Blanchot adds, "belongs to a language that no one speaks, which is addressed to no one, which has no center, which reveals nothing."[8] The substitution of the "he" for the "I" is here obviously only a symbol, perhaps too clear a one, of which one would find a subtler, and apparently inverse, version in the way in which Proust renounces the all too well centered "he" or *Jean Santeuil* for the decentered, equivocal "I" of a Narrator who is not precisely either the author or anyone else, and who shows rather well how Proust encountered his *genius* at the moment when he found in his work the locus of language in which it would be possible to explode his individuality and become dissolved in the Idea. Thus for the critic to speak of Proust or Kafka, would perhaps be to speak of the genius of Proust or of Kafka, not of his person. It would be to speak about what Proust himself calls "the deep self," of which he said, more strongly than anyone, that it was to be seen only in his books, and of which he showed, more strongly than anyone, in his very book, that it is a self without foundation, a self without a self—that is, almost the opposite of what is usually called a "subject." And, let it be said in passing, this consideration might raise a great deal of interest in any controversy as to the objective or subjective character of criticism: the *genius* of a writer is not strictly speaking for the critic (or for the reader) either an object or a subject, and the critical relationship, the reading relationship, might equally well involve the very thing that, in literature, dissipates and dismisses this oversimplified opposition.

The second "essence" referred to by Thibaudet, in what might be thought an unhappy choice of words, concerns *genres*, which he sees as "forms of the literary life force," a rather adventurous formula in which his own Bergsonianism takes over from Brunetière's Darwinism, and which it would no doubt be better to call, to avoid any vitalist reference, the fundamental structures of literary discourse. The notion of genre is not a very popular one nowadays, perhaps indeed because of the somewhat crude organicism with which it was tinged in the late nineteenth century, but also above all perhaps because we are living through a literary age that has seen the dissolution of the genres and the advent of literature as abolition of the internal frontiers of writing. If it is true, as has already been said, that one of the tasks of criticism is to apply the literary experience of the present to the literature of the past and to read the ancients in light of the moderns, it might seem odd, even ridiculous, in a period dominated by such names as Lautréamont, Proust, Joyce, Musil, and Bataille, to try to revive, even as an act of renewal, the categories of Aristotle and Boileau. Nevertheless, it does mean something to us, something that requires a response, when Thibaudet reminds us that Mallarmé wrote poetry only in order to define the essence of poetry, that he went to the theater only in order to seek the essence of the theater. It is perhaps not true, or no longer true, that genres live, die and are transformed, but it is still true that literary discourse is produced and developed in accordance with structures that it can transgress only because it finds them, even today, in the field of its language and its writing. To take one particularly clear example, Émile Benveniste has shown, in one or two chapters of his *Problèmes de linguistique générale*,[9] how very differently the systems of *narrative* and *discourse* operate, in the very structures of language, at least of the French language, by the restricted use of certain verbal forms, certain pronouns, certain adverbs, etc. From these analyses, and from those that could follow from them, extending the example, the very least that emerges is that narrative, even in its most elementary forms, and even from the purely grammatical point of view, delineates a very particular use of language, akin to what Valéry called, in relation to poetry "language within language," and any study of the great narrative forms (epic, novel, etc.) ought at least to take this fact into account, just as any study of the great works of poetry ought to begin by considering what was recently called the "structure of poetic language." The same goes, of course, for all the other forms of literary expression and, to take an example, it is rather strange that no one has ever thought (to my knowledge at least) to study for itself, in the system of its specific resources and constraints, so fundamental a type of discourse as description. This kind of study, which has still hardly begun, and then only on the fringes of the official framework of literary teaching, might be dubbed with the very old and somewhat discredited name of rhetoric; personally, I would be quite willing to accept the fact that criticism, as we conceive it, might be something like a new rhetoric, in part at least. But I would like to add (and the reference to Benveniste was partly intended to suggest this) that such a new rhetoric would quite naturally become, as indeed Valéry predicted, part of linguistics, which is no doubt the only scientific discipline that has anything to say at present on literature *as such*, or, to resort once more to Roman Jakobson's word, on the "literariness" of literature.

The third essence named by Thibaudet—and it is certainly the highest, and the broadest—is the Book. Here there is no need to transpose, and the reference to Mallarmé would easily dispense us from any obligation to comment. But we should be grateful to Thibaudet for reminding us so firmly that *literature operates in terms of the Book,* and that criticism is wrong to think so little about the Book and to mix together in a single series "what is said, what is sung, what is read." Criticism has perhaps not, even today, sufficiently confronted an evident concept, the importance of which was taught to us by Mallarmé's meditation on the Book: literature does not consist simply of language but, more specifically and more broadly it consists of *writing*. The world stands for literature, before it and within it, as Claudel so rightly said, not as a spectacle but as a *text* which ought to be deciphered and transcribed. Against a very ancient, almost (since it goes back to Plato) foundational tradition of our culture, which saw writing as a mere auxiliary of the memory, a mere instrument for the notation and preservation of language, or more precisely of speech—living speech, regarded as irreplaceable, as the immediate presence of the speaker in his discourse—we are now beginning to discover or at least to understand better, thanks in particular to Jacques Derrida's work on "grammatology," what was already implied in the most penetrating intuitions of Saussure's linguistics, namely, that language, or to be more precise, each language, is itself primarily a *writing*, that is to say, an interplay based on pure difference and spacing, in which it is the empty relation, not the full term, that signifies. "A system of infinitely complex spatial relations," says Blanchot, "the originality of which neither ordinary geometrical space nor the space of practical life enables us to grasp."[10] The idea that the time of speech should always already be situated and, as it were, performed in the space of the language, and that the signs of writing (in the ordinary sense) are in a way, in their disposition, better suited to the structure of this space than are the sounds of speech in their temporal succession, is not irrelevant to our notion of literature. As Blanchot puts it, Mallarmé's *Coup de dés* was intended to be this space "become poem." Every book, every page, is in its own way a poem of the space of language, which is played out and performed under the reader's eye. Criticism has perhaps done nothing, can do nothing, until it has decided—with all that such a decision implies—to regard every work or every part of a literary work initially as a *text*, that is to say, as a woven tissue of figures in which the time (or, as one says, the life) of the writing writer and the time (life) of the reading reader are tied together and twisted into the paradoxical medium of the page and the volume. That is why, as Philippe Sollers has succinctly put it:

Today the fundamental question no longer concerns the *writer* and the *work*, but *writing* and *reading*, and consequently it is our task to define a new space in which these two phenomena might be understood as reciprocal and simultaneous, a curved space, a medium of exchanges and reversibility in which we would at last be on the same side as our language. . . . Writing is linked to a space in which time would have *turned* as it were, in which there would no longer be anything but that circular, operational movement.[11]

The *text* is that Moebius strip in which the inner and outer sides, the signifying and signified sides, the side of writing and the side of reading, ceaselessly turn and cross over, in which writing is constantly read, in which reading is constantly written and inscribed. The critic must also enter the interplay of this strange reversible circuit and thus become, as Proust says, and like every true reader, "one's own reader." Whoever reproves himself for this simply shows that he has never known what it is to *read*.

There is certainly a great deal more that could be said about the three themes that Thibaudet proposes for the consideration of "pure criticism," but I will have to confine myself here to the following brief commentary. Indeed it is obvious that these three essences are not the only ones that may or must concern critical reflection. It seems rather that Thibaudet is setting out for us here a number of *a priori* frameworks or categories of literary space, and that the task of pure criticism would be to try, within these frameworks, to discover more particular essences, though ones that transcend the individuality of the works. I would propose to call these particular essences quite simply *forms*—on condition that the word "form" is understood here in a rather special sense, which is roughly that given it in linguistics by the Copenhagen School. For Louis Hjelmslev, as we know, the opposite of form was not, as in the academic tradition, *content*, but *substance*, that is to say, the inert mass, either of extralinguistic reality (the substance of the content), or the means, phonic or otherwise, used by language (the substance of expression). What constitutes language as a system of signs is the way in which content and expression cut into one another and structure one another in their relation of reciprocal articulation, determining the conjoint appearance of a *form of the content* and a *form of the expression*. The advantage of this new distribution, as far as we are concerned here, is that it dispenses with the vulgar opposition between form and content, in the sense of an opposition between words and things, between "language" and "life," and insists on the contrary on the mutual involvement of signifier and signified that governs the existence of the sign. If the relevant opposition is not between form and content, but between form and substance, "formalism" will consist not in privileging forms at the expense of meanings—which is senseless—but in considering meaning itself as a form imprinted in the continuity of the real, in accordance with an overall segmentation that is the system of the language: language can "express" the real only by *articulating* it, and this articulation is a system of forms, just as much on the level of the signified as on the level of the signifier.

Now, what is true for the elementary linguistic fact may be true on another level, *mutatis mutandis*, for that "supra-linguistic" fact (to use the term that Benveniste applies to dream-language) that is literature: between the literally amorphous mass of the real and the literally amorphous mass of the means of expression, each literary "essence" interposes a system of articulation that is, inextricably, a form of experience and a form of expression. These formal "knots" might constitute the object par excellence of a type of criticism that could equally well be called formalist or thematic—if one is willing to give to the notion of *theme* an opening on the level of the signifier symmetrical with that which we have just given to the notion of form on the level of the signified.

For a formalism such as we envisage it here is not opposed to a criticism of meaning (there is no criticism without meaning), but to a criticism that would confuse meaning and substance, and neglect the role of form in the *work of meaning*. Indeed it should be noted that it would be equally opposed (as it is with certain Russian Formalists) to a criticism that would reduce expression to substance alone, whether phonic, graphic, or of any other kind. What it would prefer to seek are those theme-forms, those two-sided structures in which the concerns of language and the concerns of existence are articulated together, the connection of which composes what tradition calls, by a felicitously equivocal term, *style*. It was thus, to take an example from my own critical experience (which will at least have the advantage of not compromising others in a theoretical enterprise of uncertain outcome), that I once thought that I had found in the French Baroque, as revealed to us by Marcel Raymond and Jean Rousset, some predilection for a situation that might seem to characterize both its "world view" and, let us say, its rhetoric. This situation is the *vertigo*, or more precisely that vertigo of *symmetry*, an immobile dialectic of the same and the other, of difference and identity, which is apparent also, for example, in a certain way of organizing the world around what Bachelard was to call the "reversibility of the great spectacles of water," and in recourse to a figure of style that consisted of reconciling two supposedly antithetical terms in an alliance of paradoxical words: "birds of the waves, fish of the sky."[12] The fact of style here, of course, to resort to Proustian vocabulary, is a matter both of *technique* and *vision*: it is neither a pure "feeling" (which is "expressed" as well as possible), nor a mere "manner of speaking" (which would express nothing). It is indeed a *form*, a way that language has of at once dividing up and ordering words and things. And, of course, this form is not the exclusive privilege of the Baroque, even if one has to admit that the Baroque made a particularly immoderate use of it; it can equally well be found elsewhere, and it is no doubt more legitimate to direct one's attention to this "essence" than to the various instances through which it happened to be manifested. In order to throw more light on this notion I should like to draw on a second example, again personal and therefore in no sense an exemplary one. The form of the *palimpsest*, or superimpression, struck me as being a common characteristic of Proust's writing (it is the celebrated "metaphor"), of the structure of his work, and of his vision of things and persons, and it induced in me, if I may be permitted to use this expression, the "critical desire," only because it organized, in a single gesture, the space of the world and the space of language.[13]

To conclude, without moving too far away from our guide for the day, let me say something about a question raised by Thibaudet himself in many a page of his critical reflections, and which has been a constant source of discussion ever since. It concerns the relations between the critical activity and literature, or, to put it another way, whether the critic is or is not a writer.

To begin with it should be said that Thibaudet was the first to have given what he called the Criticism of the Masters its rightful place in the critical landscape. He is referring of course to the critical work of those who are usually regarded as creators, and one has only to mention the names of Diderot, Baudelaire, and Proust to realize that the best criticism, perhaps ever since it existed, is to be found there.

But we also know that this critical aspect of literary activity has constantly grown over the last hundred years, and that the frontiers between critical work and non-critical work have tended to become increasingly blurred—one has only to think of Borges or Blanchot to realize this. And one might equally well define modern criticism, without recourse to irony, as a criticism of creators without creation, or of creators whose creation is in some sense that central void, that profound idleness the form of which is outlined by their critical work in reverse, as in a mold or cast. As such, critical work might be regarded as a type of creation, highly characteristic of our time. But in actual fact this question is perhaps not very relevant, for the notion of creation is certainly one of the most confused in our critical tradition. The significant distinction is not between a critical literature and a "creative" literature, but between two functions of writing which also oppose one another within the same literary "genre." What for me defines the writer—the *écrivain*, as opposed to the person who happens to write, whom Roland Barthes calls the *écrivant*—is that for him literature is not a means of expression, a vehicle, an instrument, but the very locus of his thought. As has often been said, the true writer is capable of thinking only in the silence and secrecy of writing; he knows and experiences at each moment that when he writes it is not he who is thinking his language, but his language which is thinking him and thinking outside him. In this sense, it seems obvious to me that the critic cannot call himself a critic in the full sense if he, too, has not been caught up in what must be called the vertigo, or put another way, the captivating and deadly game of writing. Like the writer—*qua* writer—the critic has only two tasks, which are really one: to write and to be silent.

[1966]

NOTES

1. This essay was first read as a paper at a conference entitled "Les Chemins actuels de la critique" at Cérisy-la-Salle, in September 1966.
2. Albert Thibaudet, *Réflexions sur la critique* (Paris: Gallimard, 1939), p. 244.
3. Thibaudet, *Réflexions*, p. 136. My italics.
4. Thibaudet, *Réflexions*, p. 191.
5. My italics.
6. ["Hommes de livre"] Thibaudet is referring to the critic here.
7. Albert Thibaudet, *Physiologie de la critique* (Paris: Nouvelle Revue Critique, 1930). pp. 120–24.
8. Maurice Blanchot, *L'Espace littéraire*, (Paris: Gallimard, 1955), p. 17.
9. Émile Benveniste, *Problèmes de linguistique générale* (Paris: Gallimard, 1966), ch. 19, "Les relations de temps dans le verbe français" and ch. 21, "De la subjectivité dans le langage"; *Problems in General Linguistics*, M. E. Meek, tr. (Coral Gables, Fla.: University of Miami Press, 1971).
10. Maurice Blanchot, *Le Livre à venir* (Paris: Gallimard, 1959), p. 286.
11. Philippe Sollers, "Le roman et l'expérience des limites," *Tel Quel* conference, Dec. 8, 1965; published in *Logiques* (Paris: Seuil, 1968), pp. 237–38.
12. [Genette here alludes to "L'Univers réversible," *Figures* I (Paris: Seuil, 1966).—M.-R.L.]
13. ["Proust palimpseste," *Figures* I; included in this volume.—M.-R.L.]

5

POETIC LANGUAGE, POETICS OF LANGUAGE

There is probably no more ancient or more universal category in literature than the opposition between prose and poetry. This remarkable survival over centuries, and even over millennia, is matched by a relative stability in the fundamental distinctive criterion. We know that up to the beginning of the twentieth century, this criterion was essentially of a phonic order: it concerned, of course, that set of constraints reserved for (and therefore constitutive of) poetic expression, which can crudely be reduced to the notion of *meter*: the regulated alteration of short and long, stressed and unstressed syllables, the compulsory number of syllables and the homophony of line endings, and (in the case of so-called lyric poetry) the rules governing the construction of stanzas, that is to say, recurrent sets of lines in the course of the poem. This criterion could be called fundamental in the sense that the other, variable characteristics, whether of a dialectal order (for instance, the use of the Dorian mode for lyrics inserted into Attic tragedy, or the tradition, maintained up to the Alexandrian period, of writing epics in the Ionian dialect mixed with Aeolian, which had been that of the Homeric poems), or a grammatical one (morphological or syntactical peculiarities, called "poetic forms" in the ancient languages, inversions and other "licenses" in classical French), or strictly stylistic (special vocabularies, dominant figures), were never, in classical poetics, regarded as obligatory and determining to the same extent as metrical constraints: they were rather secondary embellishments and, for some, optional ones, of a type of discourse the relevant feature of which remained in any case respect for metrical form. The question, so embarrassing for us today, of *poetic language*, was then perfectly simple, since the presence or absence of meter constituted a decisive and unequivocal criterion.

We also know that the late nineteenth and early twentieth centuries saw, particularly in France, the gradual decline and final, no doubt irreversible, collapse of this system and the birth of a new concept, which has become familiar to us, if not entirely clear: that of a poetry freed of metrical constraints and yet distinct from prose. The reasons for so profound a mutation are far from evident, but it would seem at least that this disappearance of the metrical might be connected to a more general development, the principle of which is the continuous weakening of the auditory modes of literary consumption. It is well known that ancient poetry was essentially sung (the lyric) and recited (the epic), and that, for sufficiently obvious material reasons, the fundamental mode of literary communication, even for prose, was public reading or declamation—not to mention the preponderant role in prose of eloquence, in the strict sense. It is not quite so well known, though there is a good deal of evidence for it, that even private reading was practiced aloud: St. Augustine asserts that his master Ambrose (fourth century) was the first man of Antiquity to practice silent reading, and there is no doubt that the Middle Ages saw a return to the earlier state, and that the "oral" consumption of the written text continued long after the invention of printing and the mass distribution of books.[1] But there can also be no doubt that this distribution and that of the practice of reading and writing were in the end to weaken the auditory mode of receiving texts in favor of a visual mode,[2] and therefore their mode of phonic existence in favor of a graphic mode (we should remember that the beginnings of modern literature saw, not only the first signs of the disappearance of the system of classical versification, but also the first systematic attempts, with Mallarmé and Apollinaire, to explore the poetic resources of graphism and page setting)—and above all, and because of this, to bring out other characteristics of poetic language, which might be called *formal* in the Hjelmslevian sense, in that they concern not the mode of realization, or "substance" (phonic or graphic) of the signifier, but the very articulation of the signifier and signified considered in their ideality. Thus the semantic aspects of poetic language become increasingly important, not only in the case of modern works, written without regard to meter and rhyme, but also, necessarily, in the case of older works, which we cannot prevent ourselves today from reading and appreciating according to our current criteria—which are less sensitive, for example, to the melody or accentuated rhythm of Racinian verse than to the play of its "images," or preferring to the strict, or subtle, metrics of a Malherbe or a La Fontaine the audacious "counter-battery of words" of Baroque poetry.[3]

Such a change, which leads to nothing short of a new drawing of the boundary between prose and poetry, and therefore to a new division of the literary field, poses directly to literary semiology a task that is very different from those assumed by the poetics of the Ancients or the treatises on versification of recent centuries, a crucial and difficult task that Pierre Guiraud calls "a semiology of poetic expression."[4] Crucial, because no task corresponds more specifically to its vocation, but also difficult, because the effects of meaning that it encounters in this domain are so subtle and so complex that they could discourage analysis and, secretly reinforced by the very ancient and persistent religious taboo that weighs on the "mystery" of poetic creation, help to label anyone who ventures into this area as either sacrilegious or foolish, or both: whatever precautions it surrounds itself with in order to avoid the errors and absurdities of scientism, the "scientific" attitude is always intimidated when confronted with the means of art, which we generally tend to believe are of value only because of the "unbreakable kernel of night" that is in them, and which eludes study and knowledge.

We should be grateful to Jean Cohen for having ignored these scruples and to have entered these mysteries with a boldness that might be regarded as brutal, but which is not afraid of debate or even, on occasion, of refutation.[5]

Either poetry is a grace from on high, to be received in silence and recollection [he rightly remarks], or one decides to speak of it, in which case one has to try to do so in a positive way. . . . One has to pose the problem in such a way that solutions do turn out to be conceivable. It is quite possible that the hypotheses that I am presenting here will prove to be incorrect, but at least they will have the merit of providing the means of proving that they are so. It will then be possible to keep correcting them or replacing them until the right one has been found. There is, in any case, no guarantee that truth is accessible on this subject and scientific investigation may prove in the end to be ineffective. But how will we know this if we do not make the attempt?[6]

The major principle of poetics thus offered to discussion is that poetic language is defined, in relation to prose, as a *gap (écart)* in relation to a norm, and therefore (the gap, or deviation, being, according to Guiraud—and Paul Valéry, Leo Spitzer, and Charles Bally agree with him—the very mark of the "fact of style") that poetics can be defined as a *stylistics of genre*, studying and measuring the characteristic deviations, not of an individual, but of a *linguistic genre*,[7] that is to say, more or less what Roland Barthes proposed to call a *writing (écriture)*.[8] But one would run the risk of depriving Cohen's notion of poetic gap of any interest if one did not make it quite clear that it corresponds not so much to the concept of deviation as to that of *infraction*. Poetry does not deviate, in relation to the code of prose, like a free variant in relation to a thematic constant; it violates and transgresses it, it is its very contradiction: poetry is *antiprose*.[9] In this precise sense, one could say that the poetic gap for Cohen is an absolute gap.

A second principle, which I will call the minor principle, might meet elsewhere with the liveliest opposition, if not outright dismissal: this principle states that the diachronic development of poetry constantly moves in the direction of an ever-increasing poeticity, just as painting, from Giotto to Klee, has become more and more pictorial, "each art *involving*, in a sense, through an ever closer approach to its own pure form,"[10] or to its essence. It is clear at once how questionable in principle such a postulate of involution may be,[11] and we will see later how the choice of methods of verification stresses its gratuitousness; and when Cohen declares that "the classical esthetic is an antipoetic esthetic,"[12] such an assertion could throw some doubt on the objectivity of his enterprise. But I do not intend to pursue this discussion here, since I regard *Structure du langage poétique* as an attempt to constitute a poetics on the basis of criteria derived from the practice of "modern" poetry. Perhaps, quite simply, a clearer awareness of this initial choice would have spared it an axiom which, presented as nontemporal and objective, raises the most serious methodological difficulties, for it often seems to have been introduced solely for the purposes of demonstration—that is, to be more precise, to furnish the major principle (gap is the essence of poetry) with an objectively established evolution (poetry is increasingly a gap). In fact, the two postulates support one another rather surreptitiously in an implicit turnstile of premises and conclusions that might be explained rather like this: first syllogism, poetry is increasingly a gap, it is increasingly close to its essence, therefore its essence is gap; second syllogism, poetry is increasingly a gap, the gap is its essence, therefore it is increasingly close to its essence. But it is probably of little account if one decides to accept without demonstration (and with good reason) the minor principle as expressing the inevitable, and in a sense legitimate, anachronism of the *point of view*.

The empirical verification, which takes up the greater part of the book, is essentially concerned therefore with the fact of evolution, the decisive strategic role of which we have just noted. It is entrusted to a very simple, very revealing statistical test that consists in comparing, on certain decisive points, either among themselves or with a sample of scientific prose from the late nineteenth century (Berthelot, Claude Bernard, Pasteur), a body of poetic texts selected from three different periods: Classical (Corneille, Racine, Molière), Romantic (Lamartine, Hugo, Vigny), and Symbolist (Rimbaud, Verlaine, Mallarmé).[13] The first point to be examined, which of course can only concern the poetic texts among themselves, is that of *versification*, considered first from the angle of the relation between metrical pause (at the end of lines) and syntactical pause; the mere computation of unpunctuated line endings (those that run across the natural rhythm of a sentence therefore) reveals an average proportion of 11 percent among the Classical poets, 19 percent among the Romantics and 39 percent among the Symbolists: a gap, therefore, in relation to the prose norm of isochrony between sentence as sound and sentence as meaning. Versification is then considered from the point of view of the grammaticality of the rhymes: "non-categorial" rhymes, that is to say, those linking vocables that do not belong to the same morphological class, rise, for every hundred lines, from an average 18.6 among the Classical poets to 28.6 among the Romantics and 30.7 among the Symbolists: a gap in relation to the linguistic principle of the synonymy of the final homonyms (ess*ence*—exist*ence*, part*iront*—réuss*iront*).

The second point is that of *predication*, studied from the viewpoint of the appropriateness of the epithets. The comparison of the samples of scientific prose, fictional prose (Hugo, Balzac, Maupassant), and of Romantic poetry reveals in the nineteenth century respective averages of 0 percent, 8 percent, and 23.6 percent of "inappropriate" epithets, that is to say, ones logically unacceptable in their literal meaning, examples: "ciel *mort*" (*dead* sky), or "vent *crispé*" (*shrivelled* wind). The three poetic eras considered differ as follows: Classical, 3.6; Romantic, 23.6; Symbolist, 46.3. Again one must distinguish here between two degrees of inappropriateness: the lesser degree is reducible by simple analysis and abstraction, as in "herbe *d'émeraude*" (*emerald* grass) = *green* grass because *emerald* = (*stone* +) *green*; the greater degree is not amenable to such an analysis, and its reduction requires a more labored deviation, that of a synesthesia, as in "*bleus* angélus" (*blue* angelus) = *peaceful* angelus, by virtue of the synesthesia *blue* = *peace*.[14] If one considers from this point of view the number of inappropriate color epithets, the Classical poets have to be excluded from the table because of their very small number of color epithets, and one rises from 4.3 percent among the Romantics to 42 percent among the Symbolists, the widening gap here obviously being the inappropriateness of the predication, the semantic anomaly.

The third test concerns *determination*, that is in fact to say, the lack of determination detected by the number of *redundant* epithets, of the "*verte* émeraude" (*green* emerald) or "éléphants *rugueux*" (*rugged* elephants) kind. The notion of redundance is justified here by the principle, linguistically questionable and indeed questioned, according to which the appropriate function of an epithet is to determine a species within the genus designated by the name, as in "*white* elephants are very rare." Any descriptive epithet is, therefore, for Cohen, redundant. The proportion of these epithets in relation to the total number of appropriate epithets rises from 3.66 percent in scientific prose, to 18.4 percent in Romantic prose and 58.5 percent in nineteenth-century poetry, the poetic corpus contrasted with the other two now no longer being, as for inappropriate epithets, that of the Romantics, but that formed by Hugo, Baudelaire, and Mallarmé together (why this shift toward the modern period?). Within poetic language, the table of evolution gives 40.3 percent to the Classics, 54 percent to the Romantics, and 66 percent to the Symbolists: a weaker progression, to be corrected, according to Cohen, by the fact (alleged without statistical verification) that the redundant epithets of the Classics are "in the overwhelming majority of cases" of lesser degree, that is to say, reducible to a circumstantial value: Corneille—"Et mon amour flatteur déjà me persuade" (and my flattering love already persuades me = And my love, because it is flattering); while those of the moderns: Mallarmé—"d'azur *blue* vorace" (of voracious azure *blue*) cannot usually be interpreted in this way. There is therefore a gap, and here too, an increasing one in relation to the norm (?) of the determinative function of the epithet.[15]

Fourth point of comparison: the (increasing) inconsequence of coordinations. The progression is marked here, without any statistical apparatus, by the passage from the almost always logical coordination of Classical discourse ("Je pars, cher Théramène,/ Et quitte le séjour de l'aimable Trézène" (I go, dear Theramenes,/ and end my stay in delightful Troezene) to the sudden breaks of Romantic discourse ("Ruth songeait et Booz rêvait; l'herbe était noire" (Ruth was dreaming and Boas was dreaming; the grass was black), then on to the systematic and, one might say, continuous inconsequence initiated by Rimbaud's *Les Illuminations*, which reached its full development in Surrealist writing.

The fifth and final confrontation concerns inversion, and more specifically the anteposition of epithets. The comparative table gives here 2 percent for scientific prose, 54.3 percent to Classical poetry, 33.3 percent to Romantic poetry, and 34 percent to Symbolist poetry. The dominance of the Classical poets in a table of poetic inversions should come as no surprise in principle, but the postulate of involution dear to Cohen prevents him from accepting such a fact: so he has no regrets in being able to re-establish his norm by excluding "evaluative" epithets, which tend more to a normal anteposition (un *grand* jardin, une *jolie* femme). Thus corrected the table gives 0 percent to scientific prose, 11.9 percent to Classical poetry, 52.4 percent to Romantic poetry, and 49.5 percent to Symbolist poetry. This correction is probably justified, but it cannot conceal one well-known fact, namely, the greater relative frequency in Classical poetry of inversion in general, which cannot be reduced to the anteposition of the epithet.[16]

Similarly one might question the absence of other comparisons that might have been just as instructive: we know for example that Guiraud has drawn up,[17] on the basis of a rather curiously chosen corpus (Racine's *Phèdre*, Baudelaire's *Les Fleurs du mal*, Mallarmé, Valéry, and Claudel's *Cinq grandes odes*), a poetic vocabulary the frequency of which he has compared with that given, for normal language, by Van der Beke's table, and that this comparison reveals a very marked gap in vocabulary (of the 200 most frequent words in poetry, or *theme-words*, one finds 130 the frequency of which is abnormally high in relation to that of Van der Beke; among these 130 *key-words*, only 22 belong to the first 200 of normal language). It would be interesting to subject Cohen's samples to a similar comparison, but it is by no means certain *a priori* that the gap in vocabulary would be more marked among the Symbolists, still less among the Romantics, than among the Classics: were not the seventeenth and eighteenth centuries the period *par excellence* of the special vocabulary in poetry, with its *ondes* (instead of *vagues*, the common word for waves), its *coursiers* (steeds), its *mortels* (mortals), its *lèvres de rubis* (ruby lips), and its *seins d'albâtre* (alabaster breasts)? And was not the revolutionary gesture on which Hugo prided himself in the *Réponse à un acte d'accusation* precisely, as it happens, *a reduction of gap?*

But this objection, like several other similar ones, no doubt would probably not affect Cohen's essential thesis. According to him, indeed, the gap is not, for poetry, an end, but merely a means, which excludes from his field of interest certain of the more massive deviations of poetic language, like the effects of vocabulary mentioned just now or the dialectal privileges referred to above. The most obvious linguistic gap, that which would consist in reserving a special idiom for poetry, would not be an exemplary case, since the gap carries out its poetic function only insofar as it is the instrument of a *change of meaning*. So it must at the same time establish within natural language an anomaly or inappropriateness, and this inappropriateness must be *reducible*. The nonreducible gap, as in the Surrealist statement "l'huitre du Sénégal mangera le pain tricolore" (the oyster from Senegal will eat tricolored bread), is not poetic; the poetic gap is defined by its reducibility,[18] which necessarily implies a change of meaning, and more specifically a shift from the "denotative," (read, intellectual) meaning to the "connotative," (read, affective) meaning: the current of signification blocked at the denotative level (angélus *bleu—blue* angelus) moves on at the connotative level (angélus *paisible—peaceful* angelus), and this blockage of denotation is indispensable to the freeing of connotation. A message cannot, according to Cohen, be both denotative and connotative: "Connotation and denotation are antagonistic. An emotional response and an intellectual response cannot be produced at the same time. They are antithetical, and in order for the first to rise up, the second must disappear."[19] Furthermore, all the infractions and inappropriatenesses observed in the various domains of versification, predication, determination, coordination, and word-order are such only on the denotative plane: it is their negative moment, which abruptly terminates in a positive moment when inappropriateness and respect of the code are re-established to the advantage of the signified of connotation. Thus the denotative inappropriateness that separates the two terms of the rhyme *soeur—douceur* (sister—gentleness) in Baudelaire's "L'Invitation au voyage" fades before a connotative appropriateness: "The affective truth corrects the notional error. If 'sorority' connotes a value, felt as such, of intimacy and love, then it is true that every sister is gentle, and even vice versa, that all gentleness is 'sisterly.' The semanticism of the rhyme is metaphoric."[20]

If one wishes to apply to this book, one of the virtues of which is that on almost every page it stimulates discussion by the vigor of its approach and the clarity of its argument, the spirit of rigorous challenge that its author solicits with so much good grace, one must first note in the procedure of verification adopted three prejudices that incline reality rather too conveniently in a direction favorable to his thesis. The first concerns the choice of the three periods considered. To begin with, it goes without saying that the history of French poetry does not stop at Mallarmé, but one would accept readily enough that, at least in relation to some of the criteria selected, a sample from the poetry of the twentieth century would merely emphasize the evolution detected by Cohen in Romantic and Symbolist poetry. On the other hand, it is really too convenient to take as a point of departure the seventeenth century (and even, in fact, its second half) under the pretext that to go further back would introduce states of the language that were altogether too heterogenous.[21] A corpus from the second half of the sixteenth century, made up for example of Du Bellay, Ronsard, and d'Aubigné, would not noticeably have distorted the state of the language that we call, in what is in any case a very relative term, "modern French"—especially in an investigation that did not concern itself with lexical variations (*écarts*); on the other hand, it would probably have compromised the curve of involution on which Cohen's entire thesis rests, and one would have seen the appearance, at the beginning of the cycle, at least in terms of some of the criteria, of a "ratio of poetry,"[22] that is to say, a tendency to a higher gap, one suspects, than that of Classicism, but perhaps also to that of Romanticism. The inconvenience for the author would no doubt have been of the same order if, instead of choosing from the seventeenth century three "Classical" poets as canonical as Corneille, Racine, and Molière, he had made his selection rather from such poets as Régnier, Théophile, Saint-Amant, Martial de Brives, Tristan, Le Moyne—who are not exactly *minores*. I am well aware that Cohen justifies this choice, which is not his, but that of "posterity,"[23] on the grounds of objectivity: but the consensus of the public is simply not immutable, and there is some disparity between the choice of criteria which are modern (because essentially semantic) and that of an avowedly academic corpus. At first sight, it is a surprising disparity, and one that becomes shocking once one becomes aware of its principal effect, which is to facilitate the demonstration: Classicism, which in the history of French literature is an episode, a *reaction*, here becomes an origin, a first, still timid state of a poetry in its infancy, which will have to acquire little by little its adult characteristics. Eliminate the Pléiade, rub out the Baroque, forget mannerism and preciosity! Boileau said: "At last Malherbe came. . . ," which was at least an involuntary homage to history, the unconscious admission of a disavowed past. With Cohen, this becomes rather: in the beginning was Malherbe.

In actual fact, Malherbe is scarcely rewarded for his pains, since he does not even appear in the list of the three Classical poets: an odd enough list, which has in its favor neither (probably) the sanction of posterity, nor (certainly) methodological appropriateness. It goes without saying that, among the three greatest Classical *poets*, in an investigation concerned specifically with poetic language, Racine should almost inevitably be included; the case of Corneille is much more unsure; as for Molière. . . . To elect, or to claim to have elected by consensus, these three names to form the corpus of Classical *poetry*, and then to contrast them with the Romantics and Symbolists, is really to load the argument in one's favor and certainly not to prove that "the Classical esthetic is an anti-poetic esthetic." A list made up for example of Malherbe, Racine, and La Fontaine would have been somewhat more representative. In any case, it is not only a matter of the poetic "value" of the works considered; it is above all a matter of the balance of genres: Cohen congratulates himself on having covered "highly varied genres, lyric, tragic, epic, comic, etc." (etc. ?),[24] but how can he not see that all of the dramatic is in his Classical sample, and vice versa, and that consequently all his confrontation amounts to is a comparison of the three Classical dramatists with six essentially lyrical modern poets?[25] Now, when we realize what a difference the Classical poets recognized (for obvious reasons) between the poetic tenor required of lyric poetry and that with which a tragedy could (and should) content itself, and *a fortiori* a comedy, one becomes aware of the effects of such a choice. A single example (the least obvious) might be enough to illustrate this: Cohen observes a progression of non-categorial rhymes from 18.6 to 28.6 and to 30.7. But who does not know that the rhymes of tragedy (and, again, *a fortiori* of comedy) were as it were statutorially more *facile* (which signifies, among other things, more categorial) than those of lyric poetry? How would Cohen have argued on this point with a different sample? He quotes Banville's principle ("You will rhyme together, as far as is possible, words that are very similar in sound, and very different in meaning"), which is typically Malherbian in spirit; but Malherbe's requirements do not apply to dramatic verse, the whole merit of which lies in its simplicity and immediate intelligibility. To compare the "ratio of poetry" of Classicism and modernity in these conditions is almost like comparing the climates of Paris and Marseille by taking the December average for Paris and the July average for Marseille: it is obviously to distort the argument.

The reply will no doubt be made that these methodological accidents do not disprove the essential thesis, and that a more rigorous investigation might equally well reveal in "modern" poetry, at least on the simply semantic plane, an increase of the gap. Again we should be quite clear as to the signification and scope of this notion, which is perhaps not clear enough, nor as appropriate as might at first seem.

When Cohen characterizes as a gap the inappropriateness or the redundancy of an epithet, and when he speaks on this question of *figure*, it certainly does seem that there is a gap here in relation to a norm of literality, with a shift of meaning and a substitution of terms: it is certainly in this way that *angélus bleu* is opposed to *angélus paisible*. But when he declares that a common metaphor —say, *flamme* for *amour*) is not a gap, and, moreover, that it is not so "by definition," denying for example a value of gap to Racine's double metaphor "*flamme si noire*" for *amour coupable*, because these two tropes "are in common use in the period," adding that "if the figure is a gap, the term 'figure of usage' is a contradiction in terms, the usual being the very negation of the gap,"[26] he is no longer defining the gap, as Fontanier defined the figure, by opposition to the literal, but by opposition to usage, ignoring in doing so the cardinal truth of rhetoric that more figures occur in one day in the marketplace than in a month in the university—in other words, usage is saturated with figure-gaps and neither usage nor gap is any the worse for it, quite simply because the figure-gap is defined linguistically, as different from the *literal term*, and not, psychosociologically, as different from normal usage; it is not the fact of "falling into common usage" that invalidates a figure as such but the disappearance of the literal term. *Tête* (head) is no longer a figure, not because it has been used too much, but because *chef* (chief) in this sense, has disappeared; *gueule* (mug) or *bobine* (noggin), however commonly used, will be felt as gaps as long as they have not eliminated or replaced *tête*. And *flamme*, in classical discourse, does not cease to be a metaphor because it has become part of common usage: it would have ceased to do so only if the use of the word *amour* had been lost. If rhetoric distinguishes between figures of usage and figures of invention, it is certainly because the first remain figures from its viewpoint, and it seems to me that it is rhetoric which is right. The urchin who repeats "Faut le faire" (got to) or "Va te faire cuire un oeuf" (literally, "go and fry yourself an egg," meaning "get stuffed") is perfectly well aware that he is using clichés and even catch-phrases of the time, and his stylistic pleasure lies not in inventing an expression, but in using a *distorted* expression, a *distortion of expression* that is fashionable: the figure lies in the distortion, and fashion (usage) *does not efface the distortion*. One has to choose, therefore, between the definition of gap as infraction or as distortion, even if some of them happen to be both at once, as Archimedes is at the same time a prince and a geometrician: it is this choice that Cohen refuses to make,[27] playing sometimes on one characteristic, sometimes on the other, which enables him to welcome modern metaphor, on the ground that it is invention, and to reject Classical metaphor, because it is a matter of usage, although the "inappropriateness," and therefore, according to his own theory, the passage from the denotative to the connotative, are also present in it; it is as if the semantic criterion (gap = distortion) enabled him to found his theory of poetic language, and the psychosociological criterion (gap = invention) to reserve its benefits for modern poetry. It is certainly an involuntary equivocation, but one no doubt encouraged by the unconscious wish to increase the effect of the principle of involution.

If the notion of gap is not, therefore, exempt from all confusion, it is not, when applied to poetic language, decisively appropriate either. We have seen that it was borrowed from stylistics, and that Cohen defines poetics as a "stylistics of genre": an argument that might be justifiable, but only on condition that the difference of extension and of comprehension between the concepts of style in general and of poetic style in particular is clearly maintained. Now this is not always the case, and the last chapter opens with a very characteristic shift. Anxious to respond to the objection, "Is it enough that there is a gap for there to be poetry?", Cohen replies thus: "I believe in fact that it is not enough to violate the code in order to write a poem. Style is a mistake, but not every mistake is style."[28] This clarification may be necessary, but it turns out that it is not enough, for it leaves on one side the most important question: *is all style poetry?* Cohen sometimes seems to think that it is, as when he writes that

from the stylistic viewpoint (literary prose) differs from poetry only in terms of quantity. Literary prose is merely a moderated poetry, or to put it another way, poetry constitutes the vehement form of literature, the paroxysmic degree of style. Style is one. It includes a finite number of figures, always the same ones. From prose to poetry, and from one state of poetry to another, the difference is only in the boldness with which language uses the methods inscribed *in potentia* in its structure.[29]

This explains why Cohen adopted as his sole point of reference late nineteenth-century "scientific" prose, which is a neutral writing, purposely devoid of stylistic effects, the very writing that Bally uses to bring out by contradistinction the expressive effects of language, including those of spoken language. One might wonder what would have emerged from a systematic comparison, period by period, of Classical poetry and Classical literary prose, Romantic poetry and Romantic prose, modern poetry and modern prose. Between Racine and La Bruyère, Delille and Rousseau, Hugo and Michelet, Baudelaire and Goncourt, Mallarmé and Huysmans, the gap may have been neither so great nor so very increasing, and

Poetic Language, Poetics of Language

Cohen is really convinced of this in advance: "Style is one." The "structure" that he uncovers is perhaps not so much that of poetic language as that of style in general, emphasising certain *stylistic features* which poetry does not possess in itself, but shares with other literary species. It is hardly surprising then that he should reach a definition of poetry that is more or less the one given by Bally to expressivity in general: the substitution of affective (or emotional) language for intellectual language.

What is surprising is that Cohen should call this substitution *connotation*, insisting with some vehemence, as we have seen above, on the antagonism between the two significations, and on the need for one to disappear if the other is to appear. Indeed, even without confining oneself to the strictly linguistic definition (Hjelmslev-Barthes) of connotation as a signifying system dislocated from a primary signification, it would seem that the prefix indicates clearly enough a co-notation, that is to say, a signification that is *added* to another without eliminating it. "To say *flame* for *love* is, as far as the message is concerned, to say 'I am poetry'":[30] this is typically a connotation and it is obvious in this case that the secondary meaning (poetry) does not eliminate the "primary" meaning (love); *flame* denotes *love* and at the same time connotes "poetry." Now the effects of meaning characteristic of poetic language are certainly connotations, but not only because, as we have seen here, the presence of a figure of usage connotes for us the Classical "poetic style": for anyone who takes metaphor seriously, *flame* also connotes, and in the first instance, the divergence by perceptible analogy, the presence of the comparing element in the compared, in other words, in this case, the "fire of passion."[31] It is a strange retrospective illusion to attribute to the Classical public and poets an indifference to the sensuous connotations of figures, which would be rather the case, after three centuries of wear-and-tear and academic repetition, of the semi-skilled, spoiled, all-too-aware modern reader, who has made up his own mind in advance to find no savor, no color, no relief, in a discourse that is supposed to be "intellectual" and "abstract" throughout. The rhetoricians of the Classical period, for example, did not regard tropes as such stereotyped indications of the poeticity of style, but true sensuous images.³² Perhaps, too, we should see in Racine's "flamme noire" rather more than flame and rather more than blackness than Cohen is willing to admit if we are to recover a proper appreciation of Racinian discourse: between an "overactivating" reading and one that—on the pretext of leaving words their "period value"—systematically *reduces* the perceptible gap of the figures, the more *anachronistic* reading might not be the one we might expect.

In short, denotation and connotation are far from being as "antagonistic" as Cohen says, and it is their double, simultaneous presence that maintains the poetic ambiguity, as much in the modern *image* as in the classical figure. *Angélus bleu* does not only "signify" the peaceful angelus: even if one accepts the translation proposed by Cohen, one has to admit that the deviation through color is important to the "affective" meaning, and therefore that the connotation has not eliminated the denotation. What drives Cohen to assert that it does is his wish to transform poetic language entirely into a language of emotion: having linked the destiny of the *emotional* to connotative language and that of the *conceptual* to denotative language, it is absolutely necessary for him to expel the second to the exclusive advantage of the first. "Our code is denotative," he says somewhat hastily on the subject of natural language. "And that is why the poet is bound to force language if he wishes to stir the emotions."³³ At one and the same time, perhaps, this is to assimilate the poetic function too widely to the expressivity of the affective style (which, as we have known at least since Bally, is so consubstantial with the spoken language itself), and to cut off poetic language too sharply from the deep resources of the language. Poetry is both a more specific operation, and one more closely bound up with the intimate being of language. Poetry does not *force* language: Mallarmé said with greater moderation, and ambiguity, that it "made up for its shortcomings." This means at one and the same time that poetry corrects these shortcomings, makes up and makes use of them (by exploiting them); it replenishes, eliminates, and exalts them: it *fills* them. Far from moving away from language, poetry finds its place and its function *where language falls short*, in precisely those shortcomings that constitute it.³⁴

Poetic Language, Poetics of Language 91

By way of justifying these statements, which Cohen would no doubt reject—not without appearing to have right to some extent on his side—as "vain, because they are neither clear nor verifiable," we should consider more closely a text by Mallarmé that seems to me to touch on what is essential in the poetic function:

> Languages, imperfect in that they are several, lack the supreme: to think being to write without accessories, nor whispering but immortal speech being still unspoken, the diversity, on earth, of idioms prevents anyone from uttering the words that, otherwise would find themselves, at a stroke, materially the truth itself. . . . My meaning regrets that discourse fails to express objects by means of touches corresponding to them in coloring or tone, which exist in the instrument of the voice, among the various kinds of language and sometimes in one. Besides the opaque word *ombre, ténèbres* does not grow much darker; how disappointed one is by the perversity that confers on the word *jour* a suggestion of darkness and on *nuit,* contradictorily, a suggestion of light. The wish for a term of brilliant splendor, or, on the other hand, for one that dies out; as for the simple, luminous alternatives—*Only,* let it be known, *verse would not exist*: it philosophically makes up for the shortcomings of the languages, a superior complement.[35]

The style of this passage should not conceal the firmness of the opinions expressed, or the soundness of their linguistic foundation: the "shortcomings" of language, demonstrated for Mallarmé, as, later for Saussure, by the *diversity of idioms,* and illustrated by the disparity between sounds and significations, is obviously what Saussure was to call the arbitrariness of the sign, the conventional character of the link between signifier and signified; but these very shortcomings are the raison d'être of poetry, which exists only through them: if languages were perfect, *verse would not exist*, because all speech would be poetry and, therefore, there would be no poetry. "If I follow you," Mallarmé said to Viélé-Griffin (according to the latter), "you attribute the creative privilege of the poet to the imperfection of the instrument on which he must play; a language hypothetically adequate to convey one's thought would eliminate the writer, who, by that very fact, would be called Mr. Average."[36] For the poetic function lies precisely in this effort to "make up for," if only in an illusory way, the arbitrariness of the sign, that is to say, to motivate language. Valéry, who had thought long and deeply about the example and teaching of Mallarmé, often came back to this idea, contrasting the essentially transitive, prosaic function, in which we see the "form" eliminated in its meaning (to understand being to *translate*), with the poetic function, in which the form is united with the meaning and tends to be perpetuated indefinitely with it: we know that he compared the transitivity of prose with that of walking and the intransitivity of poetry with that of dancing. Speculation on the *sensuous properties* of speech, the indissolubility of form and meaning, the illusion of a resemblance between the "word" and the "thing" were for him, as for Mallarmé,[37] the very essence of poetic language: "The power of a line of poetry stems from an indefinable harmony between what it *says*, and what it *is*."[38] So we see the poetic activity closely bound up for certain thinkers, including Mallarmé himself (see his *Mots anglais*, and the interest he took in René Ghil's *Traité du verbe*), with a ceaseless *imagination of language* that is fundamentally a motivating daydream, a daydream of linguistic motivation, marked with a sort of semi-nostalgia for some hypothetical "primitive" state of language, when speech is supposed to have *been* what it said. "The poetic function, in the broadest sense of the term," says Barthes, "would thus be defined by a Cratylian awareness of signs, and the writer would be the reciter of that great age-old myth according to which language imitates ideas and, contrary to the lessons of linguistic science, signs are motivated."[39]

The study of poetic language thus defined ought to be based on another study, which has still not yet been systematically undertaken, and which would concern the *poetics of language* (in the sense in which Gaston Bachelard spoke, for example, of a poetics of space), that is to say, the innumerable forms of linguistic imagination. For men dream not only with words, they also dream, even the least educated among them, about words, and about all the manifestations of language: there is on this subject, since Plato's *Cratylus* itself, what Claudel calls a "considerable file"[40]—that should one day be opened. We should also analyze more closely all the methods and artifices to which poetic expression has recourse in order to motivate signs; we can do no more here than indicate its principal species.

The best-known, because the most immediately perceptible, groups together those procedures which, before tackling the "shortcomings" of language, apply themselves to reducing them, exploiting in a sense the shortcomings of the shortcomings, that is to say, the few bits of motivation, direct or indirect, which are to be found naturally in the language: onomatopoeia, forms of mimicry, imitative harmonies, effects of phonic or graphic expressivity,[41] evocations by synesthesia, lexical associations.[42] Valéry, who was as capable as anyone else of cracking his whip,[43] had little regard for this kind of effect: harmony between being and saying "must not be definable," he wrote. "When it is, it is imitative harmony, and that is not good."[44] What is certain at least is that these are the easiest means, since they are given in the language itself, and therefore are within reach of "Mr. Average," and above all that the mimicry that they set up is of the crudest kind. More subtlety is to be found in the artifices that (thus corresponding more directly to Mallarmé's statement) strive to correct the shortcomings by bringing more closely together, by adapting one to the other, the signifier and signified separated by the stern law of the arbitrary. Roughly speaking, this adaptation can be achieved in two different ways.

The first consists in bringing the signified closer to the signifier, that is to say, by bending the meaning, or, more exactly, perhaps, by choosing among the semic potentialities those that best suit the sensory form of the expression. Thus Roman Jakobson demonstrates how French poetry can exploit, and by that very fact justify, the inappropriateness noted by Mallarmé between the phonetisms of the words *jour* and *nuit*, and I have tried elsewhere to show in what way the effects of this inappropriateness and its exploitation may contribute to the particular nuance given by French poetry to the opposition of night and day;[45] this is merely one example out of thousands of possible ones: we would need innumerable prepoetic semantic studies, in every domain (and in every language) if we were so much as to begin to appreciate the effects of these phenomena and what is perhaps improperly called poetic "creation."

The second way consists, conversely, in bringing the signifier closer to the signified. This action on the signifier may be of two different kinds: of a morphological kind, if the poet, not satisfied with the expressive resources of his idiom, tries to modify the existing forms or even to forge new ones; the chapter of verbal invention has been, as we know, particularly illustrated in the twentieth century by such poets as Fargue and Michaux, but the method has remained unusual to this day, for obvious reasons. The most frequent, no doubt the most effective action on the signifier—in any case, the one most suited to the vocation of the poetic game, which is to situate oneself within natural language and not beside it—is of a semantic order: it consists not in deforming signifiers or inventing new ones, but in *displacing* them, that is to say, in substituting for the literal term another term that one diverts from its use and meaning by giving it a new use and a new meaning. This action of displacement, which Verlaine wittily called *méprise* (mistake), is obviously at the source of all those "figures of words taken outside their signification" that are the tropes of classical rhetoric. It is a function of the figure that has not been sufficiently elucidated,[46] and which is of direct concern to our subject; unlike the literal term, which is usually arbitrary, the figurative term is essentially motivated, and motivated in two senses: first, quite simply, because it is *chosen* (even if it belongs to a traditional repertoire like that of the tropes of usage) instead of being imposed by the language; second, because the substitution of term always proceeds from a certain relation between the signifieds (a relation of analogy in the case of metaphor, of inclusion in the case of synecdoche, of contiguity in the case of metonymy, etc.) that remains present (connoted) in the displaced and substituted signifier, and because this signifier, though generally just as arbitrary, in its literal meaning, as the supplanted term, becomes motivated in its figurative use. To say *flame* to designate flame, *love* to designate love is to subject oneself to the language by accepting the arbitrary and transitive words it suggests to us; to say *flame* for *love* is to motivate one's language (I say *flame* because love burns), and by that very fact to give it the density, the relief, and the weight of existence which it lacks in general, *everyday circulation*.

However, it should be made quite clear that not every kind of motivation corresponds to the deep poetic wish, which is, in

Eluard's words,[47] to speak "a sensuous language." The "relative motivations," of an essentially morphological order: *vache/vacher* (cow/cowherd), *égal/inégal* (equal/unequal), *choix/choisir* (choice/to choose), etc., of which Saussure speaks, and which he sees at work in the most "grammatical" languages,[48] are not among the more felicitous for poetic language, perhaps because their principle is too intellectual and their functioning too mechanical. The relation between *obscur* and *obscurité* is too abstract to give *obscurité* a real poetic motivation. An unanalyzable lexeme like *ombre* or *ténèbres*, with its immediate, sensory qualities and shortcomings and its network of indirect suggestions (*ombre-sombre, ténèbres-funèbre*) will no doubt give a pretext to a richer motivating action, despite its greater linguistic immotivation. And *obscurité* itself, in order to acquire some poetic density, will have to be given a sort of verbal freshness by drawing attention away from its derivation and by reactivating the sonorous and visual attributes of its lexical existence. This implies among other things that the presence of the morpheme is not stressed by a "categorial" rhyme of the *obscurité-vérité* kind, and one can imagine, let it be said in passing, that this reason, albeit unconsciously and among several others, has contributed to the proscription of grammatical rhymes. On the other hand, observe how the word becomes regenerated and more sensory in the appropriate surroundings, as in these lines by Saint-Amant:

> J'écoute, à demi transporté,
> Le bruit des ailes du silence
> Qui vole dans l'obscurité.[49]
> (I listen, half transported,
> To the sound of the wings of silence
> That beat in the darkness.)

"*Obscurité*" has found its poetic destiny here; it is no longer the abstract quality of that which is obscure or darkened, but has become a space, an element, a substance, and even (we can say, despite all logic and following the secret truth of the nocturnal) something luminous.

This digression has taken us away from the *procedures of motivation*, but it is not a matter for regret, for in fact the essence of poetic motivation is not to be found in these artifices, which perhaps serve it only as catalysts; more simply and more profoundly, it is to be found in the attitude of reading that the poem succeeds (or, more often, does not succeed) in imposing on the reader: a motivating attitude which, beyond or short of all the prosodic or semantic attributes, accords to all or part of the discourse the sort of intransitive presence and absolute existence that Eluard calls "poetic evidence."

Poetic language reveals here, it seems to me, its true "structure," which is not to be a particular *form*, defined by its specific accidents, but rather a *state*, a degree of presence and intensity to which any statement may be led, so to speak, on condition that there is established around it that *margin of silence* which isolates it from its surroundings (but not from the gap) of everyday speech.[50] It is no doubt in this way that poetry is best distinguished from all sorts of style, with which it shares only a number of means. Style is certainly a gap in the sense that it moves away from neutral language by a certain effect of difference and eccentricity; poetry does not proceed in this way: it would be more correct to say that it withdraws from common language *from the inside*, by an action—no doubt largely illusory—of deepening and reverberation comparable to those exalted perceptions gained through drugs, which, according to Baudelaire, transform "grammar, arid grammar itself" into a sort of "evocative witchcraft: the words rise up in flesh and bones, the substantive, in its substantial majesty, the adjective, a transparent garment that clothes it and colors it like a glaze, and the verb, angel of movement, which sets the sentence in motion."[51]

Of poetic language in this sense, which it might be better to call language in the poetic state, or *the poetic state of language*, one could say without pushing the metaphor too far, that it is language *in a state of dreaming*, and we know that the relation between dreaming and wakefulness is not one of gap, but on the contrary—but how can one *say* what the contrary of a gap is? In fact, what allows itself to be most accurately defined by the gap, as gap, is not poetic language, but prose, the *oratio soluta*, disjointed speech, language itself as gap and disjunction between signifiers and signifieds, signifier and signified. In which case, poetry would certainly be, as Cohen says (but in a different sense, or rather in the opposite direction), *antiprose* and *reduction of the gap*: gap from the gap, negation, rejection, oblivion, effacement of the gap, of the gap that *makes* language;[52] illusion, dream, the necessary and absurd utopia of a language without gap, without hiatus—without shortcomings.

[1967]

NOTES

1. "Information was still principally imparted by word of mouth: even the great of this world listened more than they read. They were surrounded by counsellors who spoke with them, instructed them orally, and read to them. . . . Moreover, even the enthusiastic readers, the humanists, were accustomed to doing so aloud—and *hearing* the text before them." Robert Mandrou, *Introduction à la France moderne* (Paris: Albin Michel, 1961), p. 70; *Introduction to Modern France, 1500–1640*, R. E. Hallmark, tr. (New York: Harper & Row, 1977), p. 50.

2. Valéry had already said all this, among other things, very well: "For a very long time, the human voice was the basic to all 'literature.' This presence of the voice explains the earliest literature out of which classical literature built up its form and its admirable 'temperament.' The whole human body was present *under* the voice, upholding and ensuring the equilibrium of the idea. . . . The day came when people could read with their eyes, without spelling out, without hearing, and literature was quite altered by the fact. Evolution from the articulated to the skimmed—from the rhythmic and the linked to the instantaneous—from what supports and requires an audience to what supports and borrows a rapid, avid eye, free over the page." Paul Valéry, *Oeuvres*, Pléiade (Paris: Gallimard, 1960), II:549; "Rhumbs" in Valéry, *Analects*, Stuart Gilbert, tr. (Princeton: Princeton University Press, 1970), p. 99.

3. This change of criterion does not signify, however, that the phonic, rhythmic, metrical reality of ancient poetry is entirely lost (which would be a great pity); it has rather been transposed into the visual and, by that very fact, in some sense idealized; there is a silent way of perceiving "sound" effects, a sort of silent diction, similar to the experience of a musician reading a score. All prosodic theory should be reexamined from this point of view.

4. Pierre Guiraud, "Pour une sémiologie de l'expression poétique," *Langue et littérature*, (1961).

5. Jean Cohen, *Structure du langage poétique* (Paris: Flammarion, 1966).

6. Cohen, *Structure*, p. 25.

7. Cohen, *Structure*, p. 14. A striking example of the influence of genre on style is given on p. 122 in the case of Hugo, who uses 6 percent of "inappropriate" epithets in the novel and 19 percent in poetry.

8. With the reservation, however, that according to Barthes modern poetry ignores writing as a "figure of History or of social life" and is reduced to a dust of individual styles (Roland Barthes, *Le Degré zéro de l'écriture* (Paris: Seuil, 1953), ch. 4; *Writing Degree Zero*, Annette Lavers and Colin Smith, tr. (New York: Hill and Wang, 1968), ch. 4.

9. Cohen, *Structure*, pp. 51, 97.

10. Cohen, *Structure*, p. 21.

11. Above all one might wonder whether this postulate really does claim to be applicable to "every art" in the sense of *all the arts*; in what sense can one say that the art of Messiaen is more purely musical than that of Palestrina or that of Le Corbusier more purely architectural than that of Brunelleschi? If involution is reduced, as one might believe to be the case from the example of painting and sculpture, to a gradual abandonment of the representative function, one must ask oneself more precisely what this abandonment might signify in the case of poetry.

12. Cohen, *Structure*, p. 20.

13. At the rate of 100 lines (10 series of 10) per poet.

14. This interpretation in particular, and the idea in general that all secondary inappropriatenesses are reducible to synesthesias, seem highly debatable. One might equally well read *bleus angélus* as a metonymic predication (the angelus resounding in the blue sky); the hypallage *ibant obscuri* is typically metonymic; "dark man" for "man with dark hair" is obviously synecdochic, etc. There are no doubt, to say the least, as many species of inappropriate epithets as there are species of tropes; the "synesthetic" epithet corresponding simply to the species of metaphors, the importance of which is usually overestimated by "modern" poetics.

15. The total of "abnormal" epithets (inappropriate + redundant ones) gives the following progression: 42 percent, 64.6 percent, 82 percent.

16. "Often [inversion] is, as Laharpe says, the only feature that differentiates verse from prose" (Fontanier, *Les Figures du discours*, 1827; new ed. (Paris: Flammarion, 1968), p. 288).

17. Pierre Guiraud, *Langage et versification d'après l'oeuvre de Paul Valéry: Étude sur la forme poétique dans ses rapports avec la langue* (Paris: Klincksieck, 1952).

18. But how do we know where the frontier lies? It is clear here that for Cohen *bleus angélus* constitutes a reducible gap and *huître du Sénégal* . . . an absurd gap (which is debatable). But where would he put (for example) "la mer aux entrailles de raisin" (Claudel) or "la rosée à tête de chatte" (Breton)?

19. Cohen, *Structure*, p. 214.

20. Cohen, *Structure*, p. 220.
21. Cohen, *Structure*, p. 18.
22. Cohen, *Structure*, p. 15.
23. Cohen, *Structure*, pp. 17–18.
24. Cohen, *Structure*, p. 19.
25. Even if certain items taken from *La Légende des siècles* were counted as epics, which would obviously be a matter for discussion.
26. Cohen, *Structure*, p. 114, note, and p. 46.
27. Following many others, it is true, including the rhetoricians themselves, who in their definitions so often contrast figure to "simple, common" expression, without further distinguishing between the norm of literality (*simple* expression) and the norm of usage (*common* expression), as if they necessarily coincided. Such a view is further weakened by their own observations on the current, popular, even "wild" use of figures of all sorts.
28. Cohen, *Structure*, p. 201.
29. Cohen, *Structure*, p. 149.
30. Cohen, *Structure*, p. 46.
31. The relation between the literal/figurative opposition and the denotated/connoted opposition is fairly complex, as is any adjustment between categories belonging to disparate epistemological fields. It seems to me that the best solution is to regard, in the trope, as *denoted*, although "secondary," the figurative meaning (here: *love*), and as connoted among others, the trace of the literal meaning (*fire*) and the effect of style, in the classical sense, of the very presence of the trope ("poetry").
32. "Expressions please that form in the imagination a sensible painting of the conception to be conveyed. That is why the poets, whose principle aim is to please, employ only these latter expressions. And it is for this very reason that metaphors, which make all things sensible, are so frequent in their style"—Lamy, *Rhétorique* (1688), IV, 16. One would find similar opinions expressed in later treatises on tropes, but I have purposely kept to a rhetorician from the middle of the Classical period. And, what is more, a Cartesian.
33. Cohen, *Structure*, p. 225.
34. It would be instructive to compare Cohen's book with another work, which represents one of the most interesting attempts to produce a theory of poetic language: *Les Constantes du poème*, by A. Kibédi Varga (The Hague: Van Goor Zonen, 1963). The notion of *strangeness*, which is at the heart of this "dialectical" poetics, is obviously reminiscent of the *ostranenie* of the Russian Formalists. It strikes me as being a better term than that of *gap*, insofar as it does not erect prose as a necessary reference for the definition of poetry, and is closer to the idea of poetic language as an intransitive state of language, of any text received as a "message centered

on itself" (Jakobson): which, perhaps, delivers us from M. Jourdain—I mean from the prose/poetry "turnstile."

35. Stéphane Mallarmé, *Oeuvres complètes*, Pléiade (Paris: Gallimard, 1945), p. 364.

36. "Stéphane Mallarmé, esquisse orale," *Mercure de France*, (February 1924).

37. Or for Claudel: "In ordinary life we use words not strictly insofar as they *signify* objects, but insofar as they *designate* them and insofar as, from a practical point of view, they allow us to take them and use them. They provide us with a kind of portable, crude reduction of them, a value, as banal as money. But the poet does not use words in the same way. He uses them not for their utility, but in order to constitute out of all those sonorous phantoms that the word puts at his disposal a picture that is both intelligible and pleasing" (Paul Claudel, *Oeuvres en prose*, Pléiade (Paris: Gallimard, 1965), pp. 47–48). Sartre's theory, in *What Is Literature?* and in *Saint Genet*, is not essentially different.

38. Valéry, *Oeuvres*, II:637; "Rhumbs" in Valéry, *Analects*, p. 211.

39. Roland Barthes, "Proust et les noms," *To Honor Roman Jakobson*, (The Hague: Mouton, 1967); "Proust and Names" in Barthes, *New Critical Essays*, Richard Howard, tr. (New York: Hill and Wang, 1980).

40. Claudel, *Oeuvres en prose*, p. 96.

41. The first have been well known (no doubt too well known) since Maurice Grammont and Otto Jespersen. The second have been studied much less, despite Claudel's insistence (cf. in particular *Idéogrammes occidentaux* in *Oeuvres en prose*, p. 81).

42. This term can be applied, despite some fluctuations in linguistic terminology, to the semantic contagions between words that are close in form (*frustre-rustre*); the frequent association, through rhyme for example, with *funèbre*, may thus obscure, as Mallarmé wished, the "natural" semanticism of *ténèbres*.

43. For example, "L'insecte net gratte la sécheresse" (*Le Cimetière marin*).

44. Valéry, *Oeuvres*, II:637.

45. "Le Jour, la Nuit," *Figures II* (Paris: Seuil, 1969), pp. 111–19.

46. Cf. however Charles Bally: "Hypostases are all motivated signs"— *Le Langage et la vie* (Paris: Payot, 1926) p. 95.

47. Paul Eluard, *Sans âge* (Cours naturel).

48. Ferdinand de Saussure, *Cours de linguistique générale* (Paris: Payot, 1955), pp. 180–84; *Course in General Linguistics*, Wade Baskin, tr. (New York: McGraw-Hill, 1966), pp. 131–34.

49. Saint-Amant, *Le Contemplateur*.

50. "Poems always have wide white margins, wide margins of silence" (Paul Eluard, *Donner à voir*, p. 81). It will be noted that the poetry that is freest of traditional forms has not abandoned (on the contrary) the power

of assuming the poetic condition that derives from the disposition of the poem on the *white* of the page. There is, in every sense of the term, a *poetic disposition*. Cohen shows this very well with the concocted example:

> Hier sur la Nationale sept
> Une automobile
> Roulant à cent à l'heure s'est jetée
> Sur un platane
> See quatre occupants ont été
> Tués
> (Yesterday on Highway Seven
> A car
> Driving at 70 miles per hour collided
> With a plane-tree
> Its four occupants were
> Killed.)

Arranged in this way, as he rightly says, the sentence "is already no longer prose. The words spring to life, the current flows" (p. 76). This derives not only, as he says, from the grammatically aberrant division into lines, but also and above all by a page setting that is certainly intimidating. The elimination of punctuation in a great deal of modern poetry, the importance of which Cohen quite rightly stresses (p. 62), further enhances this: an effacement of grammatical relations and a tendency to constitute the poem, in the silent space of the page, as a pure *verbal constellation* (we know how this image haunted Mallarmé).

51. Charles Baudelaire, *Le Poème du haschisch*, 4th part. The mention of grammar here does not contradict the idea, which in large measure I share with Cohen, of poetry as degrammaticalization of language, and does not support, as Jakobson would wish ("Une microscopie du dernier *Spleen*," *Tel Quel* 29 (1967)) the notion of a *poetry of grammar*. For Baudelaire, arid grammar becomes "evocative witchcraft" (a cardinal formula, as we know, which turns up again in *Fusées* and in the article on Gautier, in contexts that no longer owe anything to the use of drugs) only by losing the purely relational character that constitutes its "aridity," that is to say, by degrammaticalizing itself: the *partes orationis* come back to life covered with flesh and bones, rediscovering a *substantial* existence, words become material, colored, animated beings. Nothing is further from an exaltation of grammar as such. There may exist linguistic imaginations centered on the grammatical, and Mallarmé, at least, claimed to be a "syntaxier." But the poet who praised in Gautier "that magnificent *dictionary* whose leaves, stirred by a divine breath, open just enough to let the proper *word*, the unique word, escape," and who writes again in the article of 1861 on

Hugo: "I see in the Bible a prophet whom God orders to eat a book. I don't know in what world Victor Hugo previously ate the *dictionary* of the language that he was called upon to speak: but I see that the French *lexicon*, springing from his mouth, has become a world, a colored, melodious and moving universe" (my italics)—is not this poet on the contrary a typical example of what might be called the *lexical* imagination? Let me quote again the article of 1859 on Gautier: "I caught lexicomania while still very young."

52. This leap from stylistic *gap* (*écart*) to a *spacing* (*écartment*) that is constitutive of any language might seem sophistical. I wish simply, by means of this equivocation, to draw (or bring back) attention to the reversibility of the prose/poetry opposition, and to the essential *artifice* of "natural language." If there is a gap between poetry and language, then there is a gap between language and all things, and in particular a gap within poetry itself. De Brosses designates by this term the separation, which in his view is gradual (and unfortunate), in the history of languages, between object, idea, and signifiers (phonic and graphic): "No matter what the *gaps* in the composition of languages, no matter what part the *arbitrary* may play. . . ." "When one has penetrated this difficult mystery (of the union, in the primitive languages, of the "real being," of the idea, of the sound and of the letter), one is no longer surprised, in the course of observation, to recognize to what extent these four things, after thus coming together in a common center, *spread out* (*s'ecartent*) again through a system of derivation. . . ." (*Traité de la formation mécanique des langues* (Paris, 1765), pp. 6, 21 (my italics).

6

RHETORIC RESTRAINED

> G.C.: *Three or four years ago, journals, reviews, and essays were full of the word "metaphor." The fashion has changed. "Metonymy" is now replacing "metaphor."*
> J.L.B.: *I don't think there is much to be gained from this difference.*
> G.C.: *Certainly not.*
> Georges Charbonnier,
> Entretiens avec Jorge Luis Borges

The academic year 1969–70 saw the almost simultaneous appearance of three texts, different in scope, but bearing titles so similar as to be symptomatic: I am referring to *Rhétorique générale*, published by the Liège group,[1] the original title of which was *Rhétorique généralisée;* an article by Michel Deguy, "Pour une théorie de la figure généralisée";[2] and another by Jacques Sojcher, "La métaphore généralisée.[3] Rhetoric-figure-metaphor: under the disavowing—or compensatory—cover of a pseudo-Einsteinian generalization, we have here, outlined in its principal stages, the (approximately) historical course of a discipline that has witnessed, over the centuries, the gradual contraction of its field of competence, or at least of action. Aristotle's *Rhetoric* made no claims to be "general" (still less "generalized"): yet in its range it was so, and so much so that a theory of figures did not yet merit any particular mention in it; just a few pages on comparison and metaphor, in one Book (out of three) devoted to style and composition, a tiny territory, an out-of-the-way region, lost in the immensity of an Empire. Nowadays we call general rhetoric what is in fact a treatise on figures.[4] And if we have so much to "generalize," it is obviously because we have restricted it too much: from Corax to our own day, the history of rhetoric has been that of a *generalized restriction*.

It was in the early Middle Ages, it seems, that the balance peculiar to ancient rhetoric, as represented in the works of Aristotle and, better still, of Quintilian, began to be lost: to begin with, the balance between the genres (deliberative, judicial, epidictic), because the death of the republican institutions, which Tacitus had already seen as one of the causes of the decline of eloquence,[5] brought with it the disappearance of the deliberative genre, and also, it seems, of the epidictic, so bound up with the major events of civic life; Martianus Capella and Isidore of Seville both noted these defections: "rhetorica est bene dicendi scientia in civilibus quaestionibus";[6] next the balance between the "parts" (*inventio, dispositio, elocutio*), because the rhetoric of the *trivium*, crushed between grammar and dialectic, soon came to be confined to the study of *elocutio*, the ornaments of discourse, *colores rhetorici*. The classical period, especially in France, and even more especially in the eighteenth century, inherited this situation and carried it still further by constantly giving pride of place in its examples to the literary (and particularly poetic) corpus of oratory: Homer and Vergil (and soon Racine) supplanted Demosthenes and Cicero, and rhetoric tended to become for the most part a study of the poetic *lexis*.

What is needed, to fill out and correct this more than cavalier account,[7] is an immense historical investigation, which is well beyond my competence, but of which Roland Barthes has provided a sketch in his seminar at the École pratique des Hautes Études.[8] I would like to do no more here than to draw attention to the later stages of this movement—those marking the passage from classical rhetoric to modern neo-rhetoric—and to consider what their significance might be.

The first of these stages was the publication, in 1730, of César Dumarsais' treatise *Des Tropes*. This work did not claim of course to cover the entire field of rhetoric, and the point of view adopted by the grammarian of the *Encyclopédie* is not even exactly that of a rhetorician, but rather that of a linguist and, to be more precise, of a semantician (in the sense that Michel Bréal was later to give this term), as is made quite clear by his subtitle: ". . . or concerning the different senses in which the same word may be taken in the same language." But by its very existence and the prestige it acquired, it did much to place at the center of rhetorical studies, not so much the theory of figures in general but, in an even more specific way, that of the figures of meaning, "by which one gives a word a signification that is not exactly the literal signification of that word," and therefore to place at the center of historical thought the opposition between the *literal* and the *figurative* (which is dealt with in chapters VI and VII of the first part), and therefore to turn rhetoric into a consideration of figuration, a turnstile of the figurative defined as the other of the literal, and of the literal defined as the other of the figurative—and to enclose it for a long time to come in this meticulous vertigo.

Nothing illustrates better the influence of this *tropological reduction* on the development of French rhetoric than the work of the man who prided himself, nearly a hundred years later, not only on taking over, but also on destroying the legacy of Dumarsais by an *Aufhebung* that he first called *Commentaire raisonné des tropes* (1818), then *Traité générale des figures du discours* (1821–27). Indeed the way Pierre Fontanier "took over" from Dumarsais is, from the viewpoint that concerns us here, remarkably ambiguous: on the one hand, Fontanier once again enlarged the field of study to cover all figures, tropes and non-tropes; but, on the other hand, returning with increased vigor (by the exclusion of catachresis, as a non-figurative trope, because it is not a substitution: *feuille de papier*, for example, in which *feuille* does not replace any literal word) to the criterion of substitution that governs the tropological activity, and extending it to the figurative field as a whole (hence the exclusion of a "so-called figure of thought," on the grounds that it expresses nothing more than what it says), he tends to make of the trope the model for all figures, and therefore to stress still further, by giving it *de jure* foundation, the *de facto* restriction begun by his predecessor. Dumarsais was doing no more than offering a treatise on tropes; Fontanier imposes (by the adoption of his manual in public education) a treatise on figures, tropes, and "other than tropes" (the lameness of this terminology is eloquent enough in itself), the *object* of which is indeed all figures, but the *principle* (the criterion of admission and exclusion) of which is fundamentally and purely tropological.[9]

So the trope is installed at the paradigmatic heart of what is no longer simply a theory of figures but, through the effect of a singular and apparently universal lexical scarcity, will nevertheless continue to be called rhetoric:[10] a good example of generalizing synecdoche. But this first move by Fontanier was followed by another, which confirms him in his role as founder of modern rhetoric,[11] or rather of the modern idea of rhetoric, which is based on the classification or, in the language of the time, the *division* of the tropes.

Dumarsais had drawn up a rather chaotic and sometimes redundant list of eighteen tropes, which was duly shortened without too much trouble by reducing the doubles (irony-antiphrasis) or subspecies (antonomasis, euphemism, hypallage) and by including in other classes such "supposed tropes" as metalepsis, periphrasis, or onomatopoeia. But he had also suggested, in a special chapter,[12] which, curiously enough, had had no effect on the arrangement of his own inventory, the possibility of a "subordination of the tropes," that is to say, an indication of the "rank that they must occupy in relation to one another." Vossius had already posed such a hierarchy, in which all the tropes would be related, "like species to genera," to four principles: metaphor, metonymy, synecdoche, and irony. Dumarsais sketches a new conflation of synecdoche and metonymy, which are seen as connected since they are both based on a *relation,* or *connection* (together with "dependence" in the case of synecdoche), which is neither the relation of *resemblance* of metaphor nor the relation of *contrast* of irony: it was implicitly to "subordinate" all tropes to the free associative principles of similarity, contiguity, and opposition. Fontanier restored to the metonymy/synecdoche distinction all its hierarchical function, but on the other hand he excluded irony, on the grounds that it was a figure "of expression" (a trope in several words and therefore a pseudo-trope), and above all he was not content to "relate" all tropes to the three fundamental genera that he allowed to survive: he recognized only those three, the rest being a confused mass made up of non-figurative tropes, non-trope figures, and even non-figures and non-tropes. The only tropes worthy of the name were therefore (in order) metonymy, synecdoche, and metaphor. As one may already have realized, all that was needed now was to add up these two subtractions—Dumarsais' connection between metonymy and synecdoche and Fontainier's elimination of irony—to obtain the exemplary figurative pair, the irreplaceable bookends of our own modern rhetoric: metaphor and metonymy.

This new reduction was acquired, if I am not mistaken, in the vulgate of Russian Formalism, with Boris Eichenbaum's work on Anna Akhmatova, which dates from 1923, including the metonymy = prose, metaphor = poetry equivalences. It turns up again with the same value in 1935 in Jakobson's article on Pasternak's prose, and above all in his text of 1956, "Two Aspects of Language and Two Types of Aphasia," in which the classical opposition analogy/contiguity (which, it should be remembered, concerns the *signifieds* in a relation of substitution in metaphor and metonymy: gold and corn, iron and sword) is confirmed by a perhaps overly bold assimilation to the strictly linguistic oppositions (which concern the signifiers) between paradigm and syntagma, equivalence and succession.

This episode is too close to us and too well known to be labored. Perhaps we should, on the other hand, ask ourselves why so drastic a reduction could have been effected within the figurative domain itself. I have already remarked on the gradual displacement of the rhetorical object of eloquence toward poetry,[13] already very marked in the classical writers, which leads one's meta-rhetorical attention to be concentrated preferably on figures with a stronger semantic tenor (figures of signification in a single word) and, among these, preferably on figures of a "sensory" semanticism[14] (the spatio-temporal relation, the relation of analogy), to the exclusion of tropes with a reputedly more intellectual semanticism like antiphrasis, litotes, or hyperbole, which have been more and more firmly excluded from the poetic field or more generally from the esthetic function of language. This shift of object, of an obviously historical nature, contributes therefore to giving pride of place to the two relations of contiguity (and/or of inclusion) and of resemblance. But one could easily detect other convergent movements, like the one to be found in Freud in his analysis of the "principles of association" in *Totem and Taboo*. In his *Esquisse d'une théorie de la magie* (1902) Marcel Mauss, in line with a tradition that goes back to E. B. Tylor, defined the laws of magical association in terms of three associationist principles of contiguity, similarity, and contrast. In *Totem and Taboo* (1912), Freud, repeating on another terrain Fontanier's gesture of excluding irony from the list of tropes, keeps as principles of association only the first two, which in any case are subsumed together under the "more comprehensive" concept of *contact*, similarity being defined, somewhat amusingly as it happens, as a "contact in the metaphorical sense."[15]

The bringing together of synecdoche and metonymy had already, as we have seen, been proposed by Dumarsais, but the concept of "connection" was for him rather too broad (or too slack) to contain both the connections without "dependence" (that is to say, without inclusion) that govern metonymy and also the relations of inclusion that define synecdoche. The notion of *contiguity*, on the other hand, reveals or effects a choice in favor of "connection without dependence," and therefore a unilateral reduction of synecdoche to metonymy, which Jakobson makes explicit when he writes for example: "Uspensky had a penchant for metonymy, especially for synecdoche."[16] The justification for this gesture is given among others by Mauss in the text already mentioned: "The simplest form [of association by contiguity]," he says, "is the identification of the part with the whole."[17]

Yet it is not at all certain that one can legitimately regard inclusion, even in its most crudely spatial forms, as a particular case of contiguity. This reduction no doubt has its origin in an almost inevitable confusion between the relation of the part to the whole and the relation of this same part to the *other parts* that make up the whole: a relation, it might be said, of the part to the *remainder*. The sail is not contiguous to the ship, but it is contiguous to the mast and to the yard and, by extension, to the rest of the ship, to everything that is part of the ship except the sail itself. Most of the "dubious" cases derive from this always-open choice between considering either the relation of the part to the whole or that of the part to the remainder: hence the symbolic relation in its ancient etymon, in which one may read both a relation of contiguity between the two complementary halves of the *sumbolon,* and a relation of inclusion between each of these two halves and the whole that they constitute and reconstitute. Each demi-symbol both suggests the other and evokes their common totality. Similarly, one might read *ad libitum,* in the figure by attribute ("crown" for "monarch," for example), a metonymy or a synecdoche, depending on whether one regards the crown as simply linked to the monarch, or as forming part of him, by virtue of the implicit axiom: no monarch without a crown. One then sees that every metonymy can be converted into a synecdoche by appeal to the higher totality, and every synecdoche into a metonymy by recourse to the relations between constituent parts. The fact that each figure-event can be analysed in two ways at will certainly does not imply that these two ways are in fact one, any more than Archimedes is *in the same way* both a Prince and a geometrician, but one can see very well how in fact this kind of double membership might cause confusion.

It remains of course to explain why this confusion has operated in one way rather than in the other, to the benefit of metonymy and not of synecdoche. It may be that here the pseudo-spatial notion of contiguity has played the role of a catalyst by proposing a model of the relation that is both simpler and more material than any other. But it should be noted once again that although this notion operates in favor of metonymy, it also effects, within the field of this figure, a new reduction; for many relations covered by classical metonymy (the effect for the cause and vice versa, the sign for the thing, the instrument for the action, the physical for the moral, etc.) do not allow themselves so easily, except perhaps through metaphor, to be reduced to an effect of contact or spatial proximity: what kind of "contiguity" could be maintained by the heart and courage, the brain and intelligence, the bowels and mercy? To reduce every metonymy (*a fortiori* every synecdoche) to a pure spatial relation is obviously to restrict the play of these figures to their physical or sensory aspect alone, and here again one can see the privilege gradually acquired by poetic discourse in the field of rhetorical objects, and the displacement effected by this discourse itself, in the modern period, toward the more material forms of figuration.

To this gradual reduction of the figures of "connection" to the single model of spatial metonymy corresponds a noticeably symmetrical reduction on the other side (that of the figures of "resemblance"), which operates here to the benefit of metaphor alone. We know that the term metaphor tends increasingly to cover the whole of the analogical field: whereas the classical ethos saw in metaphor an implicit comparison,[18] modern thinking would tend to treat comparison as an explicit or motivated metaphor. The most typical example of this use is obviously to be found in Proust, who always called metaphor what in his work was generally pure comparison. Here again, the motives for the reduction appear fairly clearly in the perspective of a figuratics centered on poetic discourse or at least (as in Proust) on a poetics of discourse: we no longer have much use for Homeric comparisons, and the semantic concentration of the trope ensures its almost obvious esthetic superiority over the developed form of the figure. Mallarmé congratulated himself on having banished the words "like" and "as" from his vocabulary. Yet although explicit comparison is tending to desert poetic language, the same cannot be said, it should be remarked in passing, in literary discourse as a whole, and still less in spoken language, especially as the comparison can make up for the lack of intensity that characterizes it by an effect of semantic anomaly that metaphor can hardly allow itself under pain of remaining, in the absence of the compared, totally unintelligible. This effect in particular is what Jean Cohen calls inappropriateness.[19] There are famous examples like Eluard's line "La terre est bleue comme une orange" (the earth is blue as an orange), or Lautréamont's series of "beau comme . . ." (beautiful as . . .); one may also be reminded of the prevalence in popular language of arbitrary comparisons, "comme la lune" (like the moon), or antiphrastic ones, "aimable comme une porte de prison" (as pleasant as prison gates), "bronzé comme un cachet d'aspirine" (tanned as an aspirin tablet), "frisé comme un oeuf dur" (curly as a hard-boiled egg), or those deliciously farfetched ones, such as those to be found in Peter Cheyney, San Antonio, or Pierre Perret: "thighs open like a pious woman's missal." A theory of the figures of analogy excessively centered on the metaphoric form is doomed to neglect such effects, and others.

Lastly, it should be said that the reduction to the "metaphoric pole" of all the figures of analogy is detrimental not only to comparison, but also to several forms of figure the diversity of which does not seem to have been entirely appreciated until now. Metaphor and comparison are usually opposed in the name of the absence in one and the presence in the other of the compared term. This opposition does not seem to me to be very well formulated in these terms, for a syntagma of the type "pâtre promontoire" (promontory pasture—Hugo), or "soleil cou coupé" (sun neck cut—Aimé Césaire), which contains both a comparing and a compared element, is not regarded as a comparison, nor for that matter as a metaphor, and in the end has to be counted out for lack of a more complete analysis of the constituents of the figure of analogy. One should really consider the presence or absence not only of the comparing and compared elements ("vehicle" and "tenor," in I. A. Richards' vocabulary), also of the comparative modalizer ("like," "as," "to resemble," etc.), and of "motive" (ground) of the comparison. One then sees that what we generally call "comparison" can assume two quite different forms: an unmotivated comparison ("my love is like a flame"), and a motivated comparison ("my love burns like a flame), which is necessarily more limited in its analogical scope, since a single common seme (heat) is retained as motive, among others (light, lightness, mobility), which the unmotivated comparison might, at the very least, not exclude; one sees therefore that the distinction between these two forms is not entirely useless. It appears that the canonical comparison, under its two species, must include not only a comparing and a compared element, but also the modalizer without which one will be dealing with an *identification*,[20] motivated or not, either of the type "my love (is) a burning flame," or "my burning love (is) a

Table 2

FIGURES OF ANALOGY	Compared	Motive	Modalizer	Comparing	EXAMPLES
Motivated comparison	+	+	+	+	My love burns like flame
Unmotivated comparison	+		+	+	My love is like a flame
Motivated comparison without comparing*	+	+	+		My love burns like...
Motivated comparison without compared*		+	+	+	...burning like a flame
Unmotivated comparison without comparing*	+		+		My love is like...
Unmotivated comparison without compared*			+	+	...like a flame
Motivated identification	+	+		+	My love (is) a burning flame
Unmotivated identification	+			+	My love (is) a flame
Motivated identification without compared		+		+	My burning flame
Unmotivated identification without compared (metaphor)				+	My flame

* Elliptical states

flame" ("You are my proud and generous lion"), or of the type "my love (is) a flame" ("Achilles is a lion," "promontory pasture," already mentioned). The ellipsis of the compared element will determine two more forms of identification, one motivated, of the type "my ardent flame," and the other unmotivated, which is the metaphor in the strict sense: "my flame." Table 2 brings together these different forms, plus four elliptical, less canonical, but fairly conceivable states,[21] motivated or unmotivated comparisons with an ellipsis of the comparing element ("my love is burning like . . ." or "my love is like . . .") or the compared element (". . . like a burning flame," or ". . . like a flame"): these apparently hypothetical forms are not to be ignored, as Cohen has realized: who for example remembers the compared element of Lautréamont's "beautiful as . . ." series in which the disparity between the motive and the comparing element is obviously more important than the attribution of the total predicate to the Grand Duke of Virginia, the vulture, the beetle, Mervyn, or Maldoror himself?

This rather rough-and-ready table has no other aim than to show the extent to which metaphor is merely one form among many others,[22] and that its promotion to the rank of figure of analogy *par excellence* is the result of a sort of takeover. But we still have to consider one last reductionist movement,[23] by which again, metaphor, absorbing its ultimate adversary, turns itself into the "trope of tropes" (Sojcher), "the figure of figures" (Deguy), the kernel, the heart, and ultimately the essence and almost the whole of rhetoric.

I referred a little while ago to the way in which Proust dubbed any figure of analogy "metaphor": we should now add that he also, by a quite significant parapraxis, extended this appellation to any kind of trope, even the most typically metonymic, like the expression "to do a cattleya" (*to make love* by using as an accessory, or at least as a pretext, a bunch of cattleyas).[24] I will try elsewhere to show that many of the Proustian "metaphors" are in fact metonymies or at least metaphors based on metonymies.[25] The fact that neither Proust nor most critics have noticed the fact is characteristic, even if this confusion, or inappropriateness, proceeds from a mere terminological scarcity: at the beginning of the twentieth century, "metaphor" was one of the rare terms to survive the great shipwreck of rhetoric, and this miraculous survival is obviously neither fortuitous nor insignificant. For others the terminological alibi is less understandable, as when Gérald Antoine calls an advertising slogan like "You weigh ten years too much" a metaphor, whereas the designation of cause by effect is clear enough, or when Jean Cohen is willing to see in Mallarmé's "bleus angélus" no more than an analogical synesthesia;[26] Jacques Lacan tells how one day, looking for a "metaphor" that "would not seem to be chosen for my own purposes," he turned to Quillet's dictionary and found the well-known line of Victor Hugo: "Sa gerbe n'était point avare ni haineuse" (his sheaf was neither miserly nor spiteful).[27]

Even among rhetoricians as well informed as the members of the Liège group, one still finds an inflation of metaphor that is obviously the result neither of ignorance nor of oversight: indeed, this group chooses as its symbol the letter μ, "the initial of the word that designates, in Greek, the most prestigious of the metabola." It so happens that the same initial, and for a very good reason, also belongs to *metonumia*, but there is no possible doubt as to the identity of the prestigious metabolon, especially if one refers to another passage from the *Rhétorique générale*, where we are told that metaphor is "the *central* figure of all rhetoric."[28] "Prestigious" might seem rather juvenile an epithet, but it does reflect a widely-held opinion.[29] "Central," on the other hand, is the result of a deliberate movement of valorization, which recalls irresistibly Gaston Bachelard's remark on Buffon's animal hierarchies: "The lion is king of the animals because it suits an advocate of order that all creatures, even the animals, should have a king."[30] Similarly, no doubt, metaphor is "the central figure of all rhetoric" because it suits the mind, in its weakness, that all things, even figures, should have a center.

Thus, by virtue of an apparently universal and irrepressible *centrocentrism*, there tends to be set up, at the very heart of rhetoric—or what is left of it—not the polar opposition of metaphor and metonymy, which still left room for a little air to circulate and to blow here and there a few "débris d'un grand jeu," but metaphor alone, frozen in its useless royalty. "If poetry is a space that opens up in language," writes Sojcher, "if through it words speak again and meaning becomes significant again, it is because there is between the everyday language and rediscovered speech a shift of meaning, metaphor. Metaphor is no longer, from this point of view, *a* figure among others, but *the* figure, the trope of tropes."[31] One will notice here the implicit recourse to etymological proof, according to which all "shift of meaning" is metaphor. Do we have to point out that the same argument, if it were worth anything at all, could also be applied equally well to *metonymy, metalepsis, hypallage, antonomasis,* and several others?

More imposing (even if one ignores the poetic genius of the author) is Deguy's argument in the article, already quoted, "Pour une théorie de la figure généralisée," which might well be appropriately entitled "Métaphore généralisée": "If it is possible to subordinate one of the species to a genus, it is metaphor, or the figure of figures, that might play the role of genus. . . . There is only one supreme genus, that of the *figure* or metaphor. . . . Metaphor and metonymy belong, beneath their secondary difference, to the same dimension—for which the term metaphoricity may generally serve."[32] Deguy bases this hierarchical superiority, so vigorously asserted, on the idea that the system of classico-modern tropology (Fontanier-Jakobson), in the very division that it effects between figures, obeys a spatialized perceptual model—contiguity or proximity or juxtaposition in the case of metonymy, intersection in the case of synecdoche, resemblance, "which suggests possible superimpositions," in the case of metaphor—and is therefore already metaphoric.

This description of the tropological division is not quite correct, at least as far as the classical period is concerned. I have already said that the concept of contiguity used by the moderns reduced the various modalities of metonymic relation to a single one, while Fontanier himself left it much broader scope under the prudent term of "tropes by correspondence." The schema of intersection has never really, in any tropology, classical or modern, defined synecdoche: it concerns in fact an inclusion, or belonging (Fontanier uses the word "connection"), and of a logical rather than of spatial type: the inclusion of "sail" in "ship" might be regarded as spatial, but in no sense is that of "iron" in "sword," or "man" in "mortal." Were it so, the rhetoricians would not define the figure "to drink a glass," as they constantly do, as a *metonymy of content*, but as a synecdoche, considering that the wine is "included" in the glass—a blunder they have never committed. Similarly, the relation of superimposition, towards which Deguy pushes the relation of resemblance in the name of rhetoric, has never defined metaphor; the Liège group analyse it rather, and quite rightly, as a partial co-possession of semes, and therefore as a logical intersection: between "gold" and "corn," there is a common seme that is color, and the *substitution* of one signifier for another in the text nowhere signifies *superimposition* of the two signifieds, since in that case every kind of trope would be covered by this schema.

This distortion, which Deguy effects on the concepts of tropology with a view to isolating the essence of metaphor, also appears in his analysis of syllepsis according to Fontanier. Taking up the example from Racine, "Un père en punissant, Madame, est toujours père" (Even while punishing, Madame, a father is still a father), he accuses Fontanier of considering first as its literal meaning "the property of copulator-father," then as its figurative sense "all the rest of paternity, *including* something as *natural* as 'the feeling, the heart of a father,' "[33] and further on he designates the paternal feeling as being a *"metaphorical" addition* for Fontanier, and quite rightly rejects so crude a semantic analysis. The trouble is that this analysis is not at all Fontanier's; for him, the second father of "a father is still a father" is not a metaphorical addition but, on the contrary, the synecdochic reduction of a "primary" meaning (that of the first "father" in the sentence) that is first of all *total*. Let us read again the text from the *Figures du discours:* "A *father*, that is to say, he who has the quality, the title of father: the *literal meaning*. *Is still a father*, that is to say, always has, even at his strictest, the feelings, the heart of a father, is always kind and tender as a father: the *figurative meaning*, and more or less the same sort of *synecdoche* as above."[34] Now let us turn to the beginning of this article on the "syllepsis of synecdoche." We find this double example "The monkey is always a monkey, and the wolf always a wolf," with the following comment:

This means that nothing can change nature, the habits of the monkey and the wolf, and that these animals will always be the same in this respect. The monkey and the wolf are there, first of all, for those animals themselves, including all the ideas that each word expresses: the literal meaning; and then they are there for something specific to those animals, their habits, their naturalness: the *figurative meaning*, a *synecdoche* of the whole for the part.

The primary meaning according to Fontanier is not therefore, as it happens, either for "monkey," "wolf," or "father," that meaning reduced to the biological properties which Deguy claims to see in them, but on the contrary the meaning taken *to include all the ideas that it expresses*, and it is here the "figurative" that restricts. The "metaphorical" broadening of which Fontanier is accused does not therefore exist, and when Deguy concludes: "the polysemia is primary," he does not refute rhetoric, he *repeats* it.[35]

We see, then, that the metaphorical character attributed by Deguy to the definitions of classical rhetoric and, subsequently, of their revival by linguistics is somewhat distorted by his own reading. Furthermore, and perhaps above all, it is difficult to see how one can invalidate the tropological "divisions," especially the metaphor/metonymy opposition, in the name of the fact that they rest—on a metaphor. Why a metaphor? The articulation of the complaint presupposes acceptance of the very thing that the complaint is intended to reject. The opposition cannot at one and the same time be deconstructed and referred to one of its terms: one can say that the divisions of rhetoric are pointless, and that all figures are merely one, on condition that one does not call it "metaphor," rather than antanaclasis or polyptotis, under pain of revealing inevitably what I shall simply call, and without any polemic intention (everyone has his own), a *parti pris*. It seems to me in fact that the profound desire of a whole modern poetics is to suppress the divisions and to establish the absolute, undivided rule of metaphor. The rest is perhaps no more than *motivation*.

The age-old tendency of rhetoric to reduction seems, then, to have culminated in an absolute valorization of metaphor, bound up with the idea of the essential metaphoricity of poetic language—and of language in general.[36] Before examining the significance of this latest manifestation, it might serve some purpose to remark on two lexical characteristics that no doubt proceed from the same tendency, and which in any case cannot fail to strengthen it in return. The first is the often abusive use of the term *image* in our critical vocabulary to designate, not only figures by resemblance, but a whole kind of figure or semantic anomaly, whereas the word almost inevitably connotes by its origin an effect of analogy, if not of mimesis. In particular, there is the extraordinary success enjoyed by this term in the vocabulary of Surrealism, so much so that its use generally dispenses with any other designation of the procedures proper to Surrealist writing, and to modern poetry in general. It is by no means certain that syntagmas like "j'entends les herbes de ton rire" (I hear the grassiness of your laughter), or "les barques de tes yeux" (the boats of your eyes—Eluard), or of the non-evaporatable "rosée à tête de chatte" (cat-headed dew—Breton) can be reduced without much damage to a purely metaphorical process; this is not the place to take up a semantic analysis of these phrases, which in any case is probably outside the scope of the instruments left us by the classical tradition: it is worth noting however that the use of the word "image" acts as a screen, if not as an obstacle to analysis, and leads in an uncontrolled way to a perhaps incorrect, and in any case reductive, metaphorical interpretation.

The other convergent characteristic is, in French at least, the shift (again reductive) in the meaning of the word *symbol*. We know that the Greek *sumbolon* originally designated, as I said above, a metonymico-synecdochic relation between the parts, or between each part and the whole, of an object broken in two in order to serve later as a sign of recognition. But let us leave to one side etymology, which everyone is quite willing to invoke when it supports his thesis; the fact is that the real use of the term in the French language concerns any motivated semiotic relation (and even, in mathematics, an unmotivated one)—whether this motivation is of an analogical order or not, as is clearly shown by this sentence by Marmontel, quoted by Littré: "The sickle is the symbol of harvests, scales the symbol of justice," in which the second example is obviously metaphorical, and the first typically metonymic. But this variety in actual use in no way prevents the common "linguistic consciousness" from defining the symbol as an analogical sign—as is eloquently demonstrated by its confiscation at the hands of the Symbolist movement, whose esthetic is based as we know on the "universal analogy," and as Lalande's *Dictionaire philosophique* (quoted in the *Petit Robert*) calmly puts it, defining the symbol thus: "that which represents something else by virtue of an analogical correspondence." Here again, therefore, the analogy tends to mask—or to submerge—every kind of semantic relation.

It would be easy, not to say facile, to interpret such annexations in terms of ideology, if not theology: we know, for example, what the Baudelairian theme of the correspondence of Earth to Heaven owes to a tradition that is both Platonic and Judeo-Christian. In the metaphor-metonymy couple, it is tempting to see the opposition between the spirit of religious transcendence and the down-to-earth spirit, dedicated to the immanence of the here-below. Metonymy and Metaphor are the two sisters of the Gospel: Martha, the active one, the housewife busying herself, walking up and down, duster in hand, from one object to another, and Mary, the contemplative one, who has "chosen the better part" and will go straight to heaven. Horizontal *versus* vertical. Minds could be classified in the same way as "materialists" (the prosaic), those who—like Freud—privilege "contact"[37] and see in similarity only its pale reflection, and "spiritualists" (the poetic), driven on the contrary to elude contact, or at least to sublimate it in terms of analogy. I will not pursue this game of Manicheian extrapolation, since we know well enough where it leads. It would no doubt be better to examine here, before concluding, one of the psychological motives—perhaps the most strongly determining one—of this valorization of the analogical.

By definition, every trope consists of a substitution of terms, and consequently suggests an *equivalence* between these two terms, even if their relation is in no way analogical: to say "sail" for "ship" is to make the sail the substitute, and therefore the equivalent of the ship. Now, the semantic relation that is closest to equivalence is obviously similarity, which is spontaneously felt as a quasi-identity, even if only a partial resemblance is involved. There is, it would seem, an almost inevitable confusion, and one that it would be tempting to regard as "natural," between *standing for* and *being like*, in the name of which any trope may be *regarded* as a metaphor.[38] Any rational semiotics must be constituted in reaction against this apparently primary illusion, *a symbolic illusion*, which Bachelard might have placed among those epistemological obstacles that objective knowledge has to overcome by "psychoanalyzing" them. The illusory motivation of the sign, *par excellence*, is the analogistic motivation, and one would readily agree that the first movement of the mind, confronted by any semantic relation, is to regard it as analogical, even if it is of a quite different kind and even if it is purely "arbitrary," as generally happens in linguistic semiosis, for example: hence the spontaneous belief in the resemblance of words and things, which is illustrated by a kind of eternal Cratylism—which has always functioned as the ideology, or the "indigenous theory" of poetic language.

For two centuries (the seventeenth and eighteenth), and above all in France, this "natural" tendency to valorize (and sometimes, to overvalue) the analogical relation was repressed—which was probably not the best way to "psychoanalyze" it—by the repressive objectivism proper to the Classical ethos, which *a priori* regarded any metaphor as suspect of the excessively fantastical, and kept the "symbolic" imagination strictly on a leash.[39] We know how Romanticism and Symbolism gave it back its liberty; but Surrealism, at least in its doctrine, remained in this respect more faithful than is generally believed to the spirit of the nineteenth century, as is shown clearly enough in this statement by Breton: "[Beside metaphor and comparison] the other 'figures' that rhetoric persists in enumerating are absolutely devoid of interest. Only the analogical trigger excites us: it is only through it that we can act on the engine of the world."[40] The preference is expressed here categorically, as if by right, but for the moment it is the motivation that interests me—and, I must admit, disturbs me; for this action *by analogy* on the "engine of the world" can really have only one meaning, which is a return to magic.

It goes without saying, I hope, that it is not being suggested here that either poetry or poetics should abandon the use or theory of metaphor. What is true, on the other hand, is that a metaphorics, a tropology, a theory of figures, does not relieve us of general rhetoric, still less of that "new rhetoric" (as it might be called), which we need (among other things) if we are to "act on the engine of the world," and which would be a semiotics of discourses. Of all discourses.[41]

So, for once, and in a particular way, we might listen to the ambiguous advice of the old and young librettist of *Falstaff*: "Torniamo all' antico, sara un progresso."

[1970]

NOTES

1. Groupe μ, *Rhétorique générale* (Paris: Larousse, 1970).
2. Michel Deguy, "Pour une théorie de la figure généralisée," *Critique* (October 1969).
3. Jacques Sojcher, "La métaphore généralisée," *Revue internationale de philosophie*, no. 87, p. 1.
4. This "we" is not a polite form, used in accordance with the figure called *communication*. The reproach, if such it be, is addressed here just as much to its author, who, in the present relative abuse of the notion of *figure*, would find it difficult to maintain his complete innocence. The criticism here will take the disguised (and convenient) form of self-criticism.
5. Tacitus, *Dialogue of the Orators*, xxxvi–xxxvii.
6. Ernst Robert Curtius, *European Literature and the Latin Middle Ages*, Willard R. Trask, tr. (Princeton: Princeton University Press, 1973), p. 75.
7. A. Kibédi Varga, *Rhétorique et littérature* (Paris: Didier, 1970), pp. 16–17, challenges the notion that classical French rhetoric is, as I have said

elsewhere, "above all a rhetoric of *elocutio*," and the whole of his book demonstrates in effect the interest shown by certain seventeenth- and eighteenth-century rhetoricians in the techniques of argument and composition. This is a question of relative emphasis and proportion, and also of one's choice of references: Varga relies heavily on Barry, Legras, Crevier, and me on Lamy, Dumarsais, Fontanier. One would have to examine systematically, for example, the hundred or so titles collected by P. Kuentz (*XVIIe Siècle*, no. 80–81). It also seems to me that the part devoted to *elocutio*, even when it was not the largest, was already at that time the most vivid, the most original in relation to the ancient models and therefore the most productive (despite the new material provided by the sermon). Perhaps this is an effect of projection, but Varga himself brings grist to this mill by noting that, as early as the sixteenth century, Ramus suggested bringing *inventio* and *dispositio* under dialectics, leaving to rhetoric only the art of *elocutio*.

8. Roland Barthes, 'L'ancienne rhétorique,' *Communications* (December 1970), vol. 16.

9. I refer here to my Introduction to the new edition of Fontanier's *Figures du discours* (Paris: Flammarion, 1968).

10. We must overcome, as best we can, this scarcity: thus I will propose to call this part of rhetoric *figuratics*, which has the virtue at least of being unequivocal.

11. A symbolic role, it should be said, for if his handbook was widely used in schools throughout the nineteenth century, its later influence seems to have been almost nonexistent, until his recent resurrection.

12. César Dumarsais, *Traité des tropes* (1730), II, ch. 21.

13. Or toward written prose regarded from the point of view of its esthetic function as is the case with modern stylistics.

14. We should recall Lamy's words, "Metaphors make all things sensible."

15. "The two principles of association—similarity and contiguity—are both included in the more comprehensive concept of 'contact.' Association by contiguity is contact in the literal sense; association by similarity is contact in the metaphorical sense. The use of the same word for the two kinds of relation is no doubt accounted for by some identity in the psychical processes concerned which we have not yet grasped." Sigmund Freud, *Totem and Taboo* (1912) in *Standard Edition*, (London: Hogarth Press, 1953–56) 13:85. This dichotomy obviously revives the opposition set up by Frazer between *imitation* and *contagion*. However, from *The Interpretation of Dreams* of 1900 and *Jokes and Their Relation to the Unconscious* of 1905, we know how large a role Freud gave to "representation by the opposite" in the work of the dream and of the joke, and how the figure of antiphrasis returns later in the rhetoric of denial in the article "Negation" of 1925.

16. Roman Jakobson and Morris Halle, *Fundamentals of Language* (The Hague: Mouton, 1956), p. 80. The reduction is already apparent, incidentally, in Dumarsais, *Tropes*, II:4—"Synecdoche, then, is a species of metonymy by which . . . I take the *more* for the *less*, or the *less* for the *more*."

17. Marcel Mauss, *Sociologie et anthropologie*, (Paris: P.U.F., 1950), p. 57. See also Jakobson, "Remarques sur la prose de Pasternak," French translation in *Poétique* (1971), 7:317: "The passage from the part to the whole and from the whole to the part is only a particular case of the process [of association by contiguity]."

18. ". . . by virtue of a comparison that is in the mind" (Dumarsais, *Tropes*, II, 10).

19. Jean Cohen, "La comparaison poétique: essai de systématique," *Langages* (December 1968), vol. 12.

20. I borrowed this term from Danielle Bouverot, "Comparaison et Métaphore," *Le Français moderne* (1969). The author proposes a division of "images" (figures of analogy) into four types: *comparison* ("night thickened like a wall"), which corresponds to our motivated comparison; *attenuated identification* ("and that immense night like chaos of old"), which corresponds to our unmotivated comparison; *identification* ("night, surly hostess"), which I specify as an unmotivated identification; *metaphor* ("listen to the gentle steps of night"). The essential difference between the two classifications concerns the importance accorded to the presence or absence of the modalizer, which determines for me the distinction between comparison and identification.

21. Marked here with an asterisk.

22. In particular it neglects the role of the copula and its various forms. On this subject cf. Christine Brooke-Rose, *A Grammar of Metaphor* (London: Secker and Warburg, 1958).

23. The adjective [last] is obviously not to be taken here in a strictly chronological sense. In the movement that I am describing, certain stages overlap, and Proust for example, represents a more "advanced" stage of restriction than Jakobson.

24. "And long afterwards, when the arrangement (or, rather, the ritual pretence of an arrangement) of her cattleyas had quite fallen into desuetude, the metaphor 'Do a cattleya,' transmuted into a simple verb which they would employ without a thought of its original meaning when they wished to refer to the act of physical possession (in which, paradoxically, the possessor possesses nothing), survived to commemorate in their vocabulary the long forgotten custom from which it sprang." *À la recherche du temps perdu* Pléiade (Paris: Gallimard, 1955–56), I:234; *Remembrance of Things Past*, Scott Moncrieff, tr. (New York: Random House, 1970), 1:179.

25. "Metonymie chez Proust," *Figures III* (Paris: Seuil, 1972).

26. Gérald Antoine, "Pour une méthode d'analyse stylistique des im-

ages," *Langue et littérature*, (Paris: Les Belles Lettres, 1961), p. 154; Jean Cohen, *Structure du langage poétique* (Paris: Flammarion, 1966), pp. 128–29.

27. Jacques Lacan, *Écrits* (Paris: Seuil, 1966), p. 506; "The Agency of the letter in the unconscious" in *Écrits: A Selection*, Alan Sheridan, tr. (New York: Norton, 1977), p. 156. The confusion has been noted by J.-F. Lyotard, *Discours, Figure* (Paris: Klincksieck 1971), p. 256: "It seems to me that 'sa gerbe n'était point . . .' is a good case of metonymy, 'sa gerbe' having been taken as an emblem by Boaz." On the following page, however, Lacan proposes as a "formula" of metaphor, "one word for another," which is the definition of the trope in general. Lyotard declares that this formula is "entirely suitable," but reproaches Lacan at once for not saying what is "the essential in metaphor." How can a definition that omits the essential be "entirely suitable"? In actual fact, this essential is not for Lyotard the relation of analogy between tenor and vehicle, but (according to the prejudice of the Surrealists, erected here into a norm and criterion) the novelty, not to say the arbitrariness of their bringing together, the fact of a "substitution unauthorized by usage": "True metaphor, the trope, begins with excess in the gap, with the transgression of the field of possible substitutes sanctioned by usage" (Lyotard, pp. 254–55). Thus, according to Lacan, "sheaf" for "reaper" is a metaphor and according to Lyotard "flame" for "love," being part of "usage," is doubtless not one. The notion of usage, defined in the singular, as if there were only one, is obviously here, as elsewhere, a source of confusion, since on the contrary rhetoric lives on a plurality of usages. Yet Lyotard is no doubt not incorrect when he reproaches Jakobson for his surreptitious extension of a (rhetorical) concept of metaphor to the totality of (linguistic) relations of selection—and I would add, of the concept of metonymy to the totality of relations of combination.

28. *Rhétorique générale*, pp. 7, 91. My italics.

29. We should remember that for Tesauro metaphor was the "queen of figures" (Jean Rousset, *La Littérature de l'âge baroque* (Paris: J. Corti, 1953), p. 187), and for Vico "the most luminous of figures"; and that Aristotle himself saw it as the index of a sort of genius (euphuia), the gift of "seeing resemblances" (*Poetics*, 1459a).

30. Gaston Bachelard, *Formation de l'esprit scientifique* (Paris: Vrin, 1947), p. 45.

31. Sojcher, "La métaphore généralisée," p. 58.

32. Deguy, "Pour une théorie," pp. 841, 852, 861.

33. Deguy's italics (p. 848).

34. Fontanier, *Figures du discours*, p. 107.

35. The same deviation occurs when Deguy rejects the division of metaphors into animate/inanimate as itself metaphoric, "when the whole of the being is referred to 'like' life or breath (*spiritus, anima*) so that there

can even be a difference such as that between the *animate* and the *inanimate!*" (Deguy, "Pour une théorie," p. 847). But "breath" for "life" also proceeds from a synecdoche (as attribute) or from a metonymy (as effect and sign), and in no sense from a metaphor.

36. There is certainly no question here of denying this metaphoricity, which in any case is obvious, but simply to recall that the essential figurativeness in any language should not be *reduced* to metaphor.

37. We should really know what German word is translated here by Dr. Jankélévitch but for some reason the French word (contact) strikes me as decidedly irreplaceable. [Freud's original German word was *kontakt*, which the Standard Edition, like the French translation, renders as "contact"—Tr.]

38. This is more or less what Fontanier implies when, criticizing Dumarsais' definition of metaphor (transference of signification "by virtue of a comparison that is in the mind") he writes: "If metaphor occurs by comparison, and by a mental comparison, does it not have this in common with other tropes? Is it not by virtue of a mental comparison that one transfers the name from the cause to the effect, or from the effect to the cause? The name of the part to the whole, or of the whole to the part? Is it not in fact a sort of comparison that encompasses all the relations, of whatever kind, between objects and between ideas?" (*Commentaire*, pp. 161–62). The word *comparison* is obviously understood here in its widest sense (the perception of a relation "of any kind" between two objects or ideas), but this very extension is characteristic: to compare is to perceive (or to establish) some kind of relation and, more particularly, a relation of similarity. It is "as if" analogy were the relation *par excellence.* We should also remember that Jakobson (*Fundamentals of Language*, pp. 81–82 and *Child Language, Aphasia and Phonological Universals;* The Hague: Mouton, 1968) attributes the reduction, in literary studies, of the "actual bipolar structure" of metaphor/metonymy to an "amputated, unipolar scheme" to the fact that the relation between any theoretical metalanguage and its object-language is essentially of a metaphorical order: the theory of metaphor, that is to say, discourse on metaphor, is therefore more homogeneous with its object—more "natural"—than discourse on metonymy, or on any other trope. Or on any other object. When the "principle of equivalence" concerns the equivalence itself, *similitudo similitudinem fricat.* What could be more voluptuous for a (hypothetical) *narcissism of language*?

39. Cf. Jean Rousset, "La querelle de la métaphore," *L'Intérieur et l'extérieur*, (Paris: J. Corti, 1968). Rousset links the "relative decline" of metaphor in the seventeenth century (which is one of the forms taken by the repression of the Baroque by Classicism) to the substitution of the post-Galilean cosmology for "the ancient analogical cosmos, which provided a logical foundation for the validity of the metaphorical spirit resting

on the similitudes and correspondences between all orders of reality, from the stone to man and from man to the stars" (p. 67).

40. André Breton, *La Clé des champs* (Paris, 1953), p. 114.

41. However one should welcome certain recent exceptions to the general tendency described here to restrict the concept of rhetoric: among these, already cited, are Roland Barthes' seminar and the book by A. Kibédi Varga, in which rhetoric is treated in all its fullness.

7

FRONTIERS OF NARRATIVE

If one agrees, following convention, to confine oneself to the domain of literary expression, one will define narrative without difficulty as the representation of an event or sequence of events, real or fictitious, by means of language and, more particularly, by means of written language. This positive (and current) definition has the merit of being simple and self-evident; its principal inconvenience may be precisely that it confines itself and confines us to self-evidence, that it conceals from us what specifically, in the very being of narrative, constitutes a problem and a difficulty, by effacing as it were the frontiers of its operation, the conditions of its existence. To define the narrative positively is to give credence, perhaps dangerously, to the idea or feeling that narrative *tells itself*, that nothing is more natural than to tell a story or to put together a set of actions in a myth, a tale, an epic, or a novel. The evolution of literature and of literary consciousness in the last half century will have had, among other fortunate consequences, that of drawing our attention, on the contrary, to the singular, artificial, and problematic aspect of the narrative act. We must return once more to Valéry's amazement at a statement like "the marquise went out at five o'clock." We know how, in various and sometimes contradictory ways, modern literature has lived and illustrated this fruitful amazement, how it has striven and succeeded, in its very foundations, to be a questioning, a disturbance, a contestation of the notion of narrative. That falsely naive question "why narrative?" could at least encourage us to seek, or more simply to recognize, what might be called the negative limits of narrative, to consider the principal sets of oppositions through which narrative is defined, and constitutes itself over against the various forms of the non-narrative.

DIEGESIS AND MIMESIS

The first opposition to occur to us is that indicated by Aristotle in a few brief sentences in the *Poetics*. For Aristotle, narrative (*diegesis*) is one of the two modes of poetic imitation (*mimesis*), the other being the direct representation of events by actors speaking and moving before the public.[1] It is here that the classic distinction between narrative poetry and dramatic poetry is established. This distinction was already suggested by Plato in the third book of the *Republic*, though with two differences: first, Socrates denied to narrative the quality (that is to say, for him, the defect) of imitation and, second, he took into account aspects of direct representation (dialogues) that can be included in a non-dramatic poem like those of Homer. There are, therefore, at the origins of the classical tradition, two apparently contradictory divisions, in which narrative is opposed to imitation, either as its antithesis or as one of its modes.

For Plato, the domain of what he calls *lexis* (or way of saying, as opposed to *logos*, which designates what is said) is theoretically divided into imitation proper (*mimesis*) and simple narrative (*diegesis*). By simple narrative, Plato means whatever the poet relates "in his own person," without trying "to persuade us that the speaker is anyone but himself,"[2] as when Homer, in Book I of the *Iliad*, tells us of Chryses: "[He] had come to the Achaean ships to recover his captured daughter. He brought with him a generous ransom and carried the chaplet of the Archer God Apollo on a golden staff in his hand. He appealed to the whole Achaean army, and most of all to its two commanders, the sons of Atreus."[3] Imitation, on the other hand, begins with the next line, when Homer has Chryses himself say, or rather, according to Plato, when Homer speaks in the person of Chryses and "does his best to make us think that it is not Homer but an aging priest that is talking." This is the text of Chryses' speech: "My lords, and you Achaean men-at-arms; you hope to sack King Priam's city and get home in safety. May the gods that live on Olympus grant your wish—on this condition, that you show your reverence for the Archer-god Apollo Son of Zeus by accepting this ransom and releasing my daughter." Now, Plato adds, Homer could equally well have continued his narrative in a purely narrative form, *recounting* Chryses' words instead of quoting them, which, for the same passage, would have given, in indirect style and in prose: "The priest came and prayed that the gods would allow the Achaeans to capture Troy and return in safety, and begged the Achaeans to show their respect for the god by releasing his daughter in exchange for the ransom."[4] This theoretical division, which opposes, within poetic diction, the two pure, heterogeneous modes of narrative and imitation, brings with it and establishes a practical classification of the genres, which comprises the two pure modes (narrative, represented by the ancient dithyramb, and mimetic, represented by the theater), plus a mixed or, to be more precise, alternate mode, which is that of the epic, as we have just seen with the example from the *Iliad*.

At first sight Aristotle's classification is quite different, since it reduces all poetry to imitation, distinguishing only two imitative modes, the direct, which is the one Plato calls strict imitation, and the narrative, which he calls, as does Plato, *diegesis*. On the other hand, Aristotle seems to fully identify not only, like Plato, the dramatic genre with the imitative mode, but also, without taking into account in principle its mixed character, the epic genre with the pure narrative mode. This reduction may derive from the fact that Aristotle defines the imitative mode, more strictly than Plato, by the scenic conditions of dramatic representation. It might also be justified by the fact that the epic work, however important a part is played in it by dialogues or discourse in the direct style, and even if this part exceeds that of the narrative, remains essentially narrative, in that the dialogues are necessarily framed in it and induced by narrative parts that constitute, in the strict sense, the *basis* or, to put it another way, the web of its discourse. In any case, Aristotle recognizes Homer's superiority over all other epic poets in that he intervenes personally as little as possible in his poem, usually dramatizing his characters directly, in accordance with the role of the poet, which is to imitate as much as possible.[5] This would suggest that he implicitly recognizes the imitative character of the Homeric dialogues and therefore the mixed character of epic diction, basically narrative, but dramatic in a wider sense.

The difference between Plato's and Aristotle's classifications amounts, then, to a simple variation of terms; these two classifications certainly agree on the main point, that is to say, the opposition between the dramatic and the narrative, the first being regarded by both philosophers as more fully imitative than the second: an agreement on facts that is in a sense brought out more by the disagreement on values, since Plato condemns poets as imitators, beginning with the dramatists, and not excepting Homer, who is regarded as still being too mimetic for a narrative poet, admitting into the City only some ideal poet whose austere diction would be as little mimetic as possible; whereas Aristotle, symmetrically, places tragedy above epic, and praises in Homer whatever brings his writing closer to dramatic diction. The two systems, then, are certainly identical, except for a reversal of values: for Plato as for Aristotle, narrative is the weakened, attenuated mode of literary representation—and it is difficult, at first sight, to see how one could come to a different conclusion.

However, we must introduce here an observation which does not seem to have concerned either Plato or Aristotle, and which will restore to the narrative all its value and all its importance. Direct imitation, as it functions on the stage, consists of gestures and speech. Insofar as it consists of gestures, it can obviously represent actions, but at this point it escapes from the linguistic plane, which is that in which the specific activity of the poet is practised. Insofar as it consists of words, discourse spoken by characters (and it goes without saying that in a narrative work the role of direct imitation is reduced to that), it is not strictly speaking representative, since it is confined to reproducing a real or fictitious discourse as such. It can be said that verses 12 to 16 of the *Iliad*, quoted above, give us a verbal representation of Chryses' actions, but the same cannot be said of the next five lines; they do not *represent* Chryses' speech: if this is a speech, actually spoken, they *repeat* it, literally, and if it is fictitious speech, they *constitute* it, just as literally. In both cases, the work of representation is nil; in both cases, Homer's five lines are strictly identical with Chryses' speech: this is obviously not so in the case of the five narrative lines preceding it, which are in no way identical with Chryses' actions: "The word 'dog' does not bite," William James remarked. If we call poetic imitation the fact of representing by verbal means a non-verbal reality and, in exceptional circumstances, a verbal reality (as one calls pictorial imitation the fact of representing in pictorial means non-pictorial reality and, in exceptional circumstances, a pictorial reality), it must be admitted that imitation is to be found in the five narrative lines and not at all in the five dramatic lines, which consist simply in the interpolation, in the middle of a text representing events, of another text directly taken from those events: as if a seventeenth-century Dutch painter, anticipating certain modern methods, had placed in the middle of a still life, not the painting of an oyster shell, but a real oyster shell. I make this simplistic comparison in order to point out the profoundly heterogeneous character of a mode of expression to which we are so used that we do not perceive its most sudden changes of register. Plato's "mixed" narrative, that is to say, the most common and universal mode or relation, "imitates" alternately and in the same register ("without even seeing the difference," as Michaux would say), non-verbal material, which in fact it must represent as best it can, and verbal material that represents itself, and which it is usually content to quote. In the case of a strictly faithful historical account, the historian-narrator must certainly be aware of the change of manner when he passes from the narrative effort of relating completed actions to the mechanical transcription of spoken words, but in the case of a partially or totally fictitious narrative, fictional activity, which bears equally on the verbal and non-verbal contents, no doubt has the effect of concealing the difference that separates the two types of imitation, one of which involves, if I may so put it, direct contact, while the other introduces a rather more complex system of levels. Even if one admits (as is difficult enough) that imagining actions and imagining spoken words proceeds from the same mental operation, "telling" these actions and telling these words constitute two very different verbal operations. Or rather, only the first constitutes a true operation, an act of *diction* in the Platonic sense, involving a series of transpositions and equivalences, and a series of inevitable choices between the elements of the *story* to be retained and the elements to be left out, between the various possible points of view, and so on—all of which are operations that are obviously absent when the poet or historian confines himself to transcribing a speech. One may certainly (indeed one must) challenge this distinction between the act of mental representation and the act of verbal representation, between the *logos* and the *lexis*, but it amounts to challenging the very theory of imitation, which conceives poetic fiction as a simulacrum of reality, as transcendent to the discourse that sustains it as the historical event is external to the discourse of the historian or the landscape represented to the picture that represents it: a theory that makes no distinction between fiction and representation, the object of fiction being reduced to a feigned reality that is simply awaiting representation. Now it appears that from this point of view the very notion of imitation on the level of the *lexis* is a pure mirage, which vanishes as one approaches it; the only thing that language can imitate perfectly is language, or, to be more precise, a discourse can imitate perfectly only a perfectly identical discourse; in short, a discourse can imitate only itself. *Qua lexis*, direct imitation is simply a tautology.

So we are led to this unexpected conclusion, that the only mode that knows literature as representation is the narrative, the verbal equivalent of non-verbal events and also (as the example made up by Plato shows) of verbal events, unless it vanishes, as in the last case, before a direct quotation in which all representative function is abolished, rather as a speaker in a court of law may interrupt his speech to allow the court to scrutinize some exhibit. Literary representation, the *mimesis* of the ancients, is not, therefore, narrative plus "speeches": it is narrative, and only narrative. Plato opposed *mimesis* to *diegesis* as a perfect imitation to an imperfect imitation; but (as Plato himself showed in the *Cratylus*) perfect imitation is no longer an imitation, it is the thing itself, and, in the end, the only imitation is an imperfect one. *Mimesis* is *diegesis*.

NARRATION AND DESCRIPTION

But if literary representation defined in this way is identical with narrative (in the broad sense), it is not to be reduced to the purely narrative elements (in the narrow sense) of the narrative. We must now admit, within diegesis itself, a distinction that appears neither in Plato nor in Aristotle, and which will draw a new frontier within the domain of representation. Every narrative in fact comprises two kinds of representations, which however are closely intermingled and in variable proportions: on the one hand, those of actions and events, which constitute the narration in the strict sense and, on the other hand, those of objects or characters that are the result of what we now call *description*. The opposition between narration and description, which was so stressed by academic tradition, is one of the major features of our literary consciousness. Yet it is a relatively recent distinction, the birth and development of which in the theory and practice of literature should one day be studied. It does not seem, at first sight, that it enjoyed a very active existence before the nineteenth century, when the introduction of long descriptive passages in a typically narrative genre like the novel brought out the resources and the requirements of the method.[6]

This persistent confusion, or carelessness of distinction, which in Greek is shown very clearly by the use of the common term *diegesis*, derives perhaps above all from the very unequal literary status of the two types of representation. In principle, it is obviously possible to conceive of purely descriptive texts, the aim of which is to represent objects simply and solely in their spatial existence, outside any event and even outside any temporal dimension. It is even easier to conceive of a pure description of any narrative element than the reverse, for the most neutral designation of the elements and circumstances of a process can already be regarded as the beginnings of a description: a sentence like "The house is white, with a slate roof and green shutters," involves no element of narration, whereas a sentence like "The man went over to the table and picked up a knife," contains at least, apart from two verbs of action, three substantives which, however little qualified, can be regarded as descriptive by the very fact that they designate animate or inanimate beings; even a verb can be more or less descriptive, in the precision that it gives to the spectacle of the action (one has only to compare "grabbed a knife," for example, with "picked up a knife"), and consequently no verb is quite exempt from descriptive resonance. It may be said, then, that description is more indispensable than narration, since it is easier to describe without relating than it is to relate without describing (perhaps because objects can exist without movement, but not movement without objects). But this elementary situation already indicates, in fact, the nature of the relation that unites the two functions in the overwhelming majority of literary texts: description might be conceived independently of narration, but in fact it is never found in a so to speak free state; narration cannot exist without description, but this dependence does not prevent it from constantly playing the major role. Description is quite naturally *ancilla narrationis*, the ever-necessary, ever-submissive, never-emancipated slave. There are narrative genres, such as the epic, the tale, the novella, the novel, in which description can occupy a very large place, even in terms of sheer quantity the larger place, without ceasing to be, by its very vocation, a mere auxiliary of the narrative. On the other hand, there are no descriptive genres, and one finds it difficult to imagine, outside the didactic domain (or semi-didactic fictions such as those of Jules Verne) a work in which narrative would serve as an auxiliary to description.

The study of the relations between the narrative and the descriptive amount, then, in essence, to a consideration of the *diegetic functions* of description, that is to say, the role played by the descriptive passages or aspects in the general economy of narrative. Without attempting to go into the detail of such a study here, one could at least mention, in the "classical" literary tradition (from Homer to the end of the nineteenth century), two relatively distinct functions. The first is of what might be called a decorative kind. We know that traditional rhetoric places description, together with the other figures of style, among the ornaments of discourse: extended, detailed description appears here as a recreational pause in the narrative, carrying out a purely esthetic role, like that of sculpture in a classical building. The most famous example is perhaps the description of Achilles' shield in Book XVIII of the *Iliad*.[7] It is no doubt this decorative role that Boileau has in mind when he recommends richness and splendor in this kind of piece. The Baroque epic was noted for a sort of proliferation of the descriptive excursus, very marked for example in Saint-Amant's *Moyse sauvé*, which finally destroyed the balance of the narrative poem in its decline.

The second major function of description, and the most obvious in our own day because it was imposed, with Balzac, on the tradition of the novel, is both explanatory and symbolic: physical portraits, descriptions of dress and furniture tend, in Balzac and his realist successors, to reveal and at the same time to justify the psychology of the characters, of which they are at once the sign, the cause, and the effect. Description becomes here a major element in the exposition, which it was not in the classical period: one has only to think of the houses of Mlle Cormon in *La Vieille fille* or of Balthazar Claës in *La Recherche de l'absolu*. But all this is too well known to be labored here. I would just like to remark that, in substituting significant description for ornamental description, the evolution of narrative form has tended (at least until the early twentieth century) to reinforce the domination of the narrative element: without the slightest doubt description has lost in terms of autonomy what it has gained in dramatic importance. As for certain forms of the contemporary novel that appeared initially as attempts to free the descriptive mode from the tyranny of the narrative, it is by no means certain that the question should really be interpreted in this way: if one considers it from this point of view, the work of Robbe-Grillet appears rather perhaps as an effort to constitute a narrative (a *story*) almost exclusively by means of descriptions imperceptibly modified from one page to the next, which can be regarded both as a spectacular promotion of the descriptive function and as a striking confirmation of its irreducible narrative finality.

Lastly, it should be noted that all the differences which separate description and narration are differences of content, which, strictly speaking, have no semiological existence: narration is concerned with actions or events considered as pure processes, and by that very fact it stresses the temporal, dramatic aspect of the narrative; description, on the other hand, because it lingers on objects and beings considered in their simultaneity, and because it considers the processes themselves as spectacles, seems to suspend the course of time and to contribute to spreading the narrative in space. These two types of discourse may, then, appear to express two antithetical attitudes to the world and to existence, one more active, the other more contemplative, and therefore, following a traditional equivalence, more "poetic." But from the point of view of modes of representation, to recount an event and to describe an object are two similar operations, which bring into play the same resources of language. The most significant difference might be that narration restores, in the temporal succession of its discourse, the equally temporal succession of events, whereas description must modulate, in discursive succession, the representation of objects that are simultaneous and juxtaposed in space: narrative language, then, would appear to be distinguished by a sort of temporal coincidence with its object, of which descriptive language would, on the contrary, be irremediably deprived. But this opposition loses much of its force in written literature, where nothing prevents the reader from going back and considering the text, in its spatial simultaneity, as an *analogon* of the spectacle that it describes: Apollinaire's calligrams or the graphic dispositions of Mallarmé's *Coup de dés* simply push to the limit the exploitation of certain resources latent in written expression. Furthermore, no narration, not even that of broadcast reporting, is strictly synchronic with the events that it relates, and the variety of the relations which can exist between the time of the story and that of the narrative have the effect of reducing the specificity of narrative representation. Aristotle already observed that one of the advantages of narrative over theatrical representation was that it could deal with several simultaneous actions;[8] but it has to deal with them successively, and from then on its situation, its resources, and its limits are similar to those of descriptive language.

It would appear then that description, as a mode of literary representation, does not distinguish itself sufficiently clearly from narration, either by the autonomy of its ends, or by the originality of its means, for it to be necessary to break the narrative-descriptive (chiefly narrative) unity that Plato and Aristotle have called narrative. If description marks one of the frontiers of narrative, it is certainly an internal frontier, and really a rather vague one: it will do no harm, therefore, if we embrace within the notion of narrative all forms of literary representation and consider description not as one of its modes (which would imply a specificity of language), but, more modestly, as one of its aspects—if, from a certain point of view, the most attractive.

NARRATIVE AND DISCOURSE

Reading the *Republic* and the *Poetics*, it would seem that, from the outset, Plato and Aristotle implicitly reduce the field of literature to the particular domain of representative literature: *poiesis = mimesis*. If one considers everything that is excluded from the poetic by this decision, we see the emergence of a last frontier of narrative that might be the most important and most significant. This frontier concerns nothing less than lyric, satirical, and didactic poetry: namely, to confine ourselves to a few of the names that would be known to a fifth- or fourth-century Greek, Pindar, Alcaeus, Sappho, Archilochos, and Hesiod. Thus, for Aristotle, Empedocles is not a poet, even though he uses the same meter as Homer: "Hence the proper term for the one is 'poet,' for the other 'science-writer' rather than 'poet.'"[9] But certainly Archilochos, Sappho, and Pindar cannot be called scientists: what all those excluded from the *Poetics* have in common is that their work does not consist in the imitation, by narrative or theatrical representation, of an action, real or pretended, external to the person and speech of the poet, but simply in a discourse spoken by him directly and in his own name. Pindar sings the merits of the winner at the Olympics,

Archilochos inveighs against his political enemies, Hesiod gives advice to farmers, Empedocles or Parmenides expounds his theory of the universe: no representation, no fiction is involved here, simply speech that is invested directly in the discourse of the work. The same could be said of Latin elegiac poetry and of everything that makes use of eloquence, moral and philosophical reflection,[10] scientific or parascientific exposition, the essay, correspondence, the journal, etc. All this vast domain of direct expression, whatever the modes, peculiarities, forms, eludes the consideration of the *Poetics* in that it neglects the representative function of poetry. We have here a new division, of very wide scope, since it divides into two parts of roughly equal importance the whole of what we now call literature.

This division corresponds more or less to the distinction proposed by Émile Benveniste between *narrative* (or *story*) and *discourse*,[11] except that Benveniste includes in the category of discourse everything that Aristotle called direct imitation, and which actually consists, at least as far as its verbal part is concerned, of discourse attributed by the poet or narrator to one of his characters. Benveniste shows that certain grammatical forms, like the pronoun "I" (and its implicit reference "you"), the pronominal (certain demonstratives), or adverbial indicators (like "here," "now," "yesterday," "today," "tomorrow," etc.) and—at least in French—certain tenses of the verb, like the present, the present anterior, or the future, are confined to discourse, whereas narrative in its strict form is marked by the exclusive use of the third person and such forms as the aorist (past definite) and the pluperfect. Whatever the details and variations from one idiom to another, all these differences amount clearly to an opposition between the objectivity of narrative and the subjectivity of discourse; but it should be pointed out that such objectivity and subjectivity are defined by criteria of a strictly linguistic order: "subjective" discourse is that in which, explicitly or not, the presence of (or reference to) *I* is marked, but this is not defined in any other way except as the person who is speaking this discourse, just as the present, which is the tense *par excellence* of the discursive mode, is not defined other than as the moment when the discourse is being spoken, its use marking "the coincidence of the event described with the instance of discourse that describes it."[12] Conversely, the objectivity of narrative is defined by the absence of any reference to the narrator: "As a matter of fact, there is then no longer even a narrator. The events are set forth chronologically, as they occur. No one speaks here; the events seem to narrate themselves."[13]

We have here, no doubt, a perfect description of what is, in its essence and in its radical opposition to any form of personal expression on the part of the speaker, narrative in the pure state, as it may be conceived ideally and as it may in fact be grasped in a few privileged examples, like those borrowed by Benveniste himself from the historian Glotz and from Balzac. Let us reproduce here the extract from the latter's *Gambara*, which we will have to consider with some attention:

After a walk round the gallery, the young man looked in turn at the sky and at his watch, made a gesture of impatience, entered a tobacconist's, lit a cigar, placed himself in front of a mirror, and examined his clothes, which were somewhat richer than the laws of taste allow in France. He adjusted his collar and black velvet waistcoat over which was crossed several times one of those thick gold chains made in Genoa; then, after flinging his velvet-lined overcoat over his left shoulder, draping it elegantly, in a single movement, he resumed his walk without allowing himself to be distracted by the bourgeois glances cast in his direction. When the shops began to light up and the night seemed dark enough, he walked towards the Place du Palais-Royal like a man who was fearful of being recognized, for he skirted the square as far as the fountain, before reaching, under cover of the cabs, the end of the Rue Froidmanteau.

At this degree of purity, the diction proper to the narrative is in some sense the absolute transitivity of the text, the complete absence (if we ignore a few exceptions to which we will return shortly), not only of the narrator, but also of the narration itself, by the rigorous expunging of any reference to the instance of discourse that constitutes it. The text is there, before our eyes, without being proffered by anyone, and none (or almost none) of the information it contains needs, in order to be understood or appreciated, to be related to its source, judged by its distance from or its relation to the speaker or to the utterance. If we compare such a statement to a sentence like "I was waiting to write to you that

I had definitely decided to stay. At last I have made up my mind: I shall spend the winter here,"[14] one appreciates to what extent the autonomy of narrative is opposed to the dependence of discourse, the essential determinations of which (who is "I," who is "you," what place is referred to by "here"?) can be deciphered only in relation to the situation in which it was produced. In discourse, someone speaks, and his situation in the very act of speaking is the focus of the most important significations; in narrative, as Benveniste forcefully puts it, *no one speaks*, in the sense that at no moment do we ask ourselves *who is speaking, where, when*, and so forth, in order to receive the full signification of the text.

But it should be added at once that these essences of narrative and discourse so defined are almost never to be found in their pure state in any text: there is almost always a certain proportion of narrative in discourse, a certain amount of discourse in narrative. In fact, the symmetry stops here, for it is as if both types of expression were very differently affected by the contamination: the insertion of narrative elements in the level of discourse is not enough to emancipate discourse, for they generally remain linked to the reference by the speaker, who remains implicitly present in the background, and who may intervene again at any moment without this return being experienced as an "intrusion." Thus, we read in Chateaubriand's *Mémoires d'outre-tombe* this apparently objective passage:

> When the sea was high and it was stormy, the waves, beating at the foot of the castle, along the great shore, spouted up as far as the great towers. Twenty feet above the base of one of these towers was a granite parapet, narrow and gleaming, sloping outwards, from which one communicated with the ravelin that defended the moat: we would seize the moment between two waves, and cross the perilous place before the flow broke again and covered the tower.[15]

But we know that the narrator, who has momentarily effaced himself during this passage, is not very far away, and we are neither surprised nor embarrassed when he speaks again, adding: "Not one of *us* refused the adventure, but *I* have seen children pale before attempting it." The narration had not really emerged from the order of discourse in the first person, which had absorbed it without effort or distortion, and without ceasing to be itself. On the contrary, any intervention of discursive elements within a narrative is felt as a relaxation of the rigor of the narrative part. The same goes for the brief reflection inserted by Balzac mentioned above: "his clothes, which were *somewhat richer than the laws of taste allow in France.*" The same can be said for the demonstrative expression *"one of those thick gold chains made at Genoa,"* which obviously contains the beginnings of a passage ("made" corresponds not to *which were made,* but *which are made*) and of a direct address to the reader, who is implicitly taken as a witness. Again, the same could be said of the adjective in *"bourgeois* glances" and of the adverb *"elegantly,"* which imply a judgment the source of which is here quite obviously the narrator; the relative expression *"like a man who was fearful,"* which Latin would mark with a subjunctive for the personal appraisal that it involves; and lastly of the conjunction *"for* he skirted," which introduces an explanation offered by the narrator. It is obvious that narrative does not integrate these discursive enclaves, rightly called by Georges Blin "authorial intrusions," as easily as discourse receives the narrative enclaves: narrative inserted into discourse is transformed into an element of discourse, discourse inserted into narrative remains discourse and forms a sort of cyst that is very easy to recognize and to locate. The purity of narrative, one might say, is more manifest than that of discourse.

Though the reason for this dissymmetry is very simple, it indicates for us a decisive character of narrative: in fact, discourse has no purity to preserve, for it is the broadest and most universal "natural" mode of language, welcoming by definition all other forms; narrative, on the other hand, is a particular mode, marked, defined by a number of exclusions and restrictive conditions (refusal of the present, the first person, and so forth). Discourse can "recount" without ceasing to be discourse, narrative cannot "discourse" without emerging from itself. Nor can it abstain from it completely, however, without falling into aridity and poverty: this is why narrative exists nowhere, so to speak, in its strict form. The slightest general observation, the slightest adjective that is little more than descriptive, the most discreet comparison, the most modest "perhaps," the most inoffensive of logical articulations introduces into its web a type of speech that is alien to it, refractory as it were. In order to study the detail of these sometimes microscopic accidents, we would need innumerable, meticulous analyses of texts. One of the objects of this study would be to list and classify the means by which narrative literature (and in particular the novel) has tried to organize in an acceptable way, within its own *lexis*, the delicate relations maintained within it between the requirements of narrative and the needs of discourse.

We know in fact that the novel has never succeeded in resolving in a convincing and definitive way the problem posed by these relations. Sometimes, as was the case in the classical period, with a Cervantes, a Scarron, a Fielding, the author-narrator, happily assuming his own discourse, intervenes in the narrative with ironically labored indiscretion, addressing his reader in a familiar, conversational tone; sometimes, on the other hand, as we also see in the same period, he transfers all responsibility for the discourse to a principal character who will *speak*, that is to say, both recount events and comment on them in the first person: this is the case of the picaresque novels, from *Lazarillo de Tormes* to *Gil Blas*, and other fictively autobiographical works, such as *Manon Lescaut* and *La Vie de Marianne*; sometimes, again, being unable to make up his mind whether to speak in his own name or to entrust this task to a single character, he distributes discourse between the various actors, either in the form of letters, as was often the case in the eighteenth-century novel (*La Nouvelle Héloïse, Les Liaisons dangereuses*) or, in the more supple and subtle manner of a Joyce or a Faulkner, by letting his principal characters assume the narrative successively through their interior discourse. The only moment when the balance between narrative and discourse seems to have been assumed with a perfectly good conscience, without either scruple or ostentation, is obviously in the nineteenth century, the classical age of objective narration, from Balzac to Tolstoy; we see, on the contrary, how the modern period has stressed awareness of difficulty to the extent of making certain types of elocution almost physically impossible for the most lucid and rigorous of writers.

We know, for example, how the effort to bring narrative to its highest degree of purity led certain American writers, such as Hammett or Hemingway, to exclude any exposition of psychological motives, which are always difficult to carry off without recourse to general considerations of a discursive kind, qualifications implying a personal judgment on the part of the narrator, logical links, and the like, to the point of reducing fictional diction to that jerky succession of short sentences without articulations, which Sartre recognized in 1943 in Camus' *L'Étranger*, and which were to turn up again ten years later in Robbe-Grillet. What has often been interpreted as an application to literature of behaviorist theories may have been no more than the effect of a particularly acute sensitivity to certain incompatibilities of language. All the fluctuations of contemporary fictional writing could no doubt be analyzed from this point of view, and particularly the tendency today, perhaps the reverse of the earlier one, and quite overt in a Phillipe Sollers of a Jean Thibaudeau, for example, to absorb the narrative in the present discourse of the writer in the process of writing, in what Michel Foucault calls "discourse bound up with the act of writing, contemporary with its unfolding and enclosed within it."[16] It is as if literature had exhausted or overflowed the resources of its representative mode, and wanted to fold back into the indefinite murmur of its own discourse. Perhaps the novel, after poetry, is about to emerge definitively from the age of representation. Perhaps narrative, in the negative singularity that we have just attributed to it, is already for us, as art was for Hegel, *a thing of the past*, which we must hurry to consider as it retreats, before it has completely disappeared from our horizon.

[1966]

NOTES

1. Aristotle, *Poetics*, 1448a; *Poetics*, Gerald F. Else, tr. (Ann Arbor: University of Michigan Press, 1967), p. 17.
2. Plato, *Republic*, 393a; *Republic*, D. Lee, tr. 2d. rev. ed., (Harmondsworth: Penguin, 1974), p. 150.

3. Homer, *Iliad*, Book I, lines 12–16; *Iliad*, E. V. Rieu, tr. (Harmondsworth: Penguin, 1953), p. 23.
4. Plato, *Republic*, 393e; *Repub.*, p. 151.
5. Aristotle *Poetics*, 1460a; *Poet.*, p. 65.
6. It is to be found however in Boileau on the subject of the epic:

> Soyez vif et pressé dans vos narrations;
> Soyez riche et pompeux dans vos descriptions.
> (*Art Poétique*, III, 257–58)

7. At least as interpreted and imitated by the classical tradition. It should be noted however that description here tends to become animated and therefore to turn itself into narrative.
8. Aristotle, *Poetics*, 1459b; *Poet.*, p. 64.
9. Aristotle, *Poetics*, 1447b; *Poet.*, p. 17.
10. Since it is the diction that counts here, and not what is said, we will exclude from this list, as does Aristotle (*Poetics* 1447b; *Poet.*, p. 17), Plato's Socratic dialogues, and all expositions in dramatic form, which belong to imitation in prose.
11. Émile Benveniste, "Les relations de temps dans le verbe français," *Problèmes de linguistique générale*, pp. 237–50; "The Correlations of Tense in the French Verb," *Problems in General Linguistics*, M. E. Meek, tr. (Coral Cables, Florida: University of Miami Press, 1971), pp. 205–15.
12. Émile Benveniste, "De la subjectivité dans le langage" in *Problèmes*, p. 262; "Subjectivity in Language" in *Problems*, p. 227.
13. Benveniste, "Les relations des temps," p. 241; *Problems*, p. 208.
14. Senancour, *Obermann*, Lettre v.
15. F. R. de Chateaubriand, *Mémoires d'Outre-tombe*, Book I, ch. 5.
16. "L'Arrière-fable," *L'Arc* (1965), 29:6.

PART II

8

"STENDHAL"

"The genuine *melomaniac*, a farcical character who is rarely to be met with in France, where his obsession is usually no more than a snobbish affectation, is to be encountered with every step in Italy. When I was garrisoned in Brescia, I was introduced to a certain gentleman of the neighborhood, who was a really extreme case of excessive musical sensibility. He was exceedingly well-educated, and by nature very gentle; but whenever he sat at a concert, there would come a point when in sheer delight at the music, he would proceed quite unconsciously to remove his shoes. Then he would sit quietly, shoeless, until the coming of some really *superb* passage, at which, unfailingly, he would fling both shoes over his shoulders into the crowd of spectators grouped behind him."[1]

In *Beylism*, in the *Stendhal-Club*, and in other manifestations—especially marked in the case of Stendhal—of the fetishism of the author, there is at least one good thing: they save us, or divert us, from another sort of idolatry, which is no less serious, and today more dangerous, namely, the fetishism of the work—conceived of as a closed, complete, absolute object.

But, on the other hand, nothing could be more pointless than to seek in Stendhal's writings, or in the evidence of his contemporaries, the trace of a defined, substantial being who might legitimately, in accordance wth legal status, be called Henri Beyle. How much more preferable in its excess is the reserve of Mérimée, entitling with a laconic *H.B.* a sort of clandestine necrology, and maintaining that the dead man never wrote a letter without signing it with some made-up name or dating it from whatever place happened to take his fancy, that he gave all his friends pseudonyms, and that "no one knew exactly whom he saw, what books he had written, what journeys he had made." The discoveries of scholarship since then have done little more than deepen the mystery by piling up further evidence.

The two caryatids of traditional literary studies were called, one may remember, the *life* and the *work*. The exemplary value of the Stendhal phenomenon derives from the way in which he shatters these two notions by altering their symmetry, blurring their difference, and reversing their relations. In that "pseudonym" which is Stendhal, the "person" of Henri Beyle and his "work" come together, intersect, and ceaselessly abolish one another, since if, for every Stendhalian, the work of Stendhal constantly designates Henri Beyle, Henri Beyle really exists only through the work of Stendhal. Nothing is more improbable, nothing more ghostlike, than the Beyle of the memoirs, eyewitnesses, documents, the Beyle "recalled by those who saw him," the Beyle whom Sainte-Beuve wished to discover by questioning Mérimée, Ampère, Jacquemont, "those, in a word, who saw him much and knew him in his first form." Beyle's first form, the Beyle before Stendhal whom Saint-Beuve was seeking, is merely a biographical illusion: the true form of Beyle is essentially *secondary*. For us Beyle is legitimately only one of Stendhal's characters.

◇

He says of himself that "the true occupation of the animal is to write novels in a barn," which Balzac or Flaubert or any novelist might equally well have said—except that the very fact of having to say it designates the singularity of a "writer," of whom it could have been said, unlike most of his fellow-writers, that "he always preferred himself to his works,"[2] and who, far from sacrificing himself to them, seems above all to have wanted to place them at the service of what he himself called, with a word imported for the occasion, his "egotism."

But if the "presence of the author" is, in this *oeuvre*, generally regarded as fairly cumbersome, we should note its constantly ambiguous, almost problematic character. In this case, the pseudonymic mania assumes the value of a symbol: in his novels and in his correspondence, in his essays and in his memoirs, Beyle is always present, but almost always masked or in disguise, and it is not without significance that his most directly "autobiographical" work has as its title a name that is neither that of the author, nor that of the hero: Stendhal covers Henri Brulard, who covers Henri Beyle—who in turn imperceptibly displaces the Henri Beyle of legal status, who is not at all to be confused with the other three, and forever eludes us.

◇

The paradox of egotism is more or less this: to speak of oneself, in the most indiscreet and most unrestrained way, may be the best way of concealing oneself. Egotism is, in every sense of the term, a parade.

The most effective demonstration of this is no doubt Brulard's highly disconcerting Oedipal admission:

> My mother, Madame Henriette Gagnon, was a charming woman, and I was in love with her. . . . I wanted to cover my mother with kisses, and for her to have no clothes on. She loved me passionately and often kissed me; I returned her kisses with such ardour that she was often obliged to go away. I abhorred my father when he came and interrupted our kisses. . . . One evening, when by some chance I had been put to sleep on the floor of her room, on a mattress, this woman, as light and agile as a deer, bounded over my mattress to reach her bed more quickly.[3]

For specialists, such a text ought to be something of a scandal: what does it leave to interpret? One imagines Oedipus, as the curtain rises, declaring without preamble to the Theban people: "Good people, I have killed my father Laius and given my mother Jocasta four children: two boys and two girls. Don't look any further: all the evil comes from this." Tiresias' head. (Sophocles' head.)

It is a scandal, in the etymological sense: *scandalon* means "trap," and to announce the unsayable is an infinite trap. Thanks to the *Vie de Henry Brulard*, a psychoanalysis of Stendhal is still cruelly lacking—which gives a sort of comic truth to Alain's declaration: "Stendhal is as remote as one would like from our Freudians."

◇

In the margin of the manuscript of *Lucien Leuwen*, on the subject of a character trait of the hero, Stendhal wrote in English: "Model: Dominique himself.—Ah! Dominique himself!"[4]

This strange designation of self is typically Stendhalian, as a whole and in its parts. "Dominique," we know, was for a long time his most private nickname, one that he reserved, almost exclusively, for his own use: it was what he called *himself*. A sort of pidgin English was also one of his favorite cryptographical methods, in the notes intended only for his own use. But the convergence of both codes on the same object, which happens in this case to be precisely the *subject*, is striking in its effect. The Stendhalian "ego" is not exactly detestable: it is strictly (and profoundly) *unnameable*. Language cannot approach it without disintegrating into a multitude of substitutions, displacements, and deviations that are at once redundant and elusive. *Dominique*—an Italianizing Christian name, possibly borrowed, by way of homage, from the author of the *Matrimonio Segreto* (Domenico Cimarosa); *himself*—the English "reflexive," the distorted idiomaticism of which excuses, by throwing it into a vaguely ridiculous eccentricity, the unbearable relation with oneself. "Ah! Dominique himself!" Can one affirm more clearly the decentering of the subject, the otherness, the alien origin of the ego?

Or again in English, repeated several times in the *Journal*: "Mr. (or M.) Myself."

An Oedipal refusal of the patronymic, no doubt. But what is the meaning, in the first place, of the effacement or alteration of the

Christian name (an ordinary enough practice, of course) and, more unusually, of the taboo placed here on the *mother tongue*? (Unless one should say *father tongue* (*sermo patrius*), the original language, on the Gagnon side, being—mythically—Italian.)

❖

The pseudonymic proliferation affects not only Beyle himself (there are over a hundred pseudonyms in the *Correspondence* and private papers,[5] two literary psuedonyms, not to mention the various assumed names in *Rome, Naples et Florence* or *De l'amour*), and his closest friends (Mérimée becomes "Clara," Mme Dembowsky "Léonore," Alberthe de Rubempré "Mme Azur" or "Sanscrit"), and familiar places (Milan is written "1,000 ans," Rome is "Omar" or "Omer," Grenoble "Cularo," Civita-Vecchia "Abeille"; and Milan is sometimes designated, gloriously, "Napoleon.") It also affects the titles of certain works. Thus *De l'amour* is constantly referred to as *Love*, and *Le Rouge et le noir* as *Julien*. We know that Stendhal hesitated, for *Lucien Leuwen*, between *Leuwen*, *L'Orange de Malte*, *Le Télégraphe*, *Le Chasseur vert*, *Les Bois de Prémol*, *L'Amaranthe et le noir*, *Le Rouge et le blanc:* but, rather than any real indecision being the cause, it might be said that it was due to a sort of chain reaction, as if the first title adopted immediately suggested a pseudonymic substitution, which, once it had become stabilized into a proper name, in turn suggested another substitution, and so on. This perpetual flight of denominations is a characteristic of slang, the principle of which is perhaps the wish, constantly frustrated and constantly revived, of naming otherwise what is already named. And pseudonymism, like other techniques of encoding dear to Stendhal (abbreviations, anagrams, Anglicisms, etc.) proceeds from this metalinguistic frenzy. The Stendhalian cryptographies no doubt reveal less an obsession with detection than a certain fascination with language, which is expressed in flight and self-emulation.

If Mérimée is to be believed, the French consul at Civita-Vecchia was quite capable of sending to his Minister of Foreign Affairs a coded letter, with the code enclosed in the same envelope.

Mérimée explains this fact by absent-mindedness, but if one wishes to interpret absent-mindedness itself, it is tempting to see in this parapraxis an admission that the encoding is there only for the pleasure of it. And the pleasure of codes is at the same time to divide language, and to speak *twice*.

◇

Mocenigo. What exactly does this Venetian name that haunts the *Journal* between 1811 and 1814 mean? A projected work, named after its hero? "I will be able to work to Mocenigo," Stendhal writes in (near) English. A certain social or psychological role or type? "*The* trade *of* Mocenigo *makes bashfull* by giving inner delights that one is very glad not to disturb with anything." Beyle himself? "Angélique Delaporte, now sixteen years and ten months old, and who is being judged as I write this, seems to me a being worthy of all the attention of Mocenigo." The dramatic genre, as Martineau believes? "We must understand by this word the art of the theater in which he always thought he would make his mark." More generally, "the knowledge of the human heart" and all literature of analysis? "The Memoirs written with truth. . . . True mines *for the* Mocenigo." Or, again, the *Journal* itself? "I was planning today to write the part *di* Mocenigo for yesterday. But I came back tired at midnight and had the strength only to jot down what happened today."[6] It would seem that, in the present state of Stendhalian studies, all these questions remain unanswered, and perhaps they will remain so forever. But the fact that "Mocenigo" can appear equally well, on different occasions, as the name of a character, the title of a work, a pseudonym, or as the designation of some broader literary entity, this very polyvalence is revealing and, in a way, exemplary. "Mocenigo": neither the "man" nor the "works," but something like the reciprocal, or reversible, labor that unites them and provides each with its foundations. To do "Mocenigo," to be "Mocenigo" is all one.

Similarly, perhaps, in the years 1818–20, Beyle readily uses the name *Bombet*, with which he has signed them, to designate the *Vies de Haydn, Mozart et métastase,* and by *Stendhal,* the first version of *Rome, Naples et Florence:* "Instead of writing an article on Stendhal, say something on Bombet. . . . The 158 Stendhals will have enough to say for themselves."[7] This name of Stendhal is still for him only that of a book. He is to become Stendhal himself by metonymy, by identifying himself with this book and its problematic author.

◇

The magnificent town-house built by Peter Wanghen occupies the northern end of the Friedrichgasse, the fine Königsberg street, which strangers find so remarkable for the large number of short flights of seven or eight steps that project into the street and lead up to the main entrances of the houses. The railings of these little flights of steps, which are kept sparklingly clean, are of cast iron made in Berlin, I think, and display all the rather bizarre elaboration of German design. Taken as a whole these twisted ornaments are not unpleasant, they have the advantage of novelty and match very well those of the windows of the best apartment which, at Königsberg, is on this ground floor raised four or five feet above the level of the street. The windows are provided in their lower parts with movable frames covered with wire gauze that produce a rather odd effect. These gleaming veils, so convenient for the curiosity of the ladies, are impenetrable for the eye of the passer-by, dazzled by the tiny reflections that spring off the metal material. The gentlemen can see nothing of the inside of the apartments, while the ladies who work near the windows have a perfect view of the passers-by.

This kind of sedentary pleasure and promenade, if I may be permitted so bold a phrase, forms one of the principal features of social life in Prussia. From noon to four in the afternoon, if one wishes to go riding and make a little noise with one's horse, one is sure to see all the pretty women of a town working right up against the lower pane of their casement. There is even a kind of toilette, which has a special name and which is indicated by the fashion for appearing in this way behind the window, which, in well maintained houses, is a sheet of highly transparent mirror.

The curiosity of the ladies is assisted by an additional expedient: in all the better houses one sees, on both sides of the ground-floor windows, raised four feet above the level of the street, mirrors a foot high, borne on a small iron arm and slightly inclined inwards. By means of these inclined mirrors the ladies see the passers-by arrive from the end of the street, while, as I have already said, the curious eyes of these gentlemen cannot penetrate into the apartment, through the metal gauzes that blind the lower parts of the window. But although they do not see, they know that they are being seen and this certainly gives a particular liveliness to all the little novels that animate the society of Berlin and Königsberg. A man is sure of being seen several times every morning by the woman of his choice; what is more, it is not absolutely impossible for the frame of wire gauze to be sometimes disturbed quite by chance and to enable the passer-by to perceive the pretty hand of the lady trying to put it back into place. It has even been said that the position of these frames may have a language of its own. Who would understand it or take offense at it?[8]

Indirect communication is one of the privileged situations of the Stendhalian topics. Rousseau's condemnation of the mediating function of language is well known and, for him, writing is doubly mediating: Stendhal, on the other hand, seems to reject, or at least to put aside, this relation of transparency in which "soul speaks directly to soul." The decisive moments of communication (avowals, ruptures, declarations of war) are with him usually expressed in writing: this is the case of the correspondence between Lucien Leuwen and Mme de Chasteller, which transposes into the mode of true passion the formidable technique of epistolary seduction borrowed from Laclos (of which the episode of the letters recopied for Mme de Fervaques, in the *Rouge,* constitutes, on the contrary, a sort of parody), or of the exchange of letters between Julien and Mathilde in chapters 13 and 14 of the second part of the *Rouge.* The mode of transmission, in this last episode, is also characteristic of him: Julien and Mathilde live under the same roof and meet every day, but the avowal that Mathilde has to make goes beyond words: " 'You will receive a letter from me this evening,' she said to him in a voice so faltering that he could scarcely hear her. . . . An hour later a footman handed Julien a letter; it was purely and simply a declaration of love." Julien entrusts this compromising letter to the care of his friend Fouqué, not without taking hyperbolic precautions: it is concealed in the binding of an enormous Bible bought specially at a Protestant bookshop. Then he writes a prudent reply, which he hands over personally. "He thought it his duty to speak to her; he could not have found a more convenient occasion, anyhow, but Mademoiselle de la Môle would not listen to him, and disappeared. Julien was delighted by this; he had not known what to say to her." A second letter arrives from Mathilde: "Mademoiselle de la Môle appeared on the threshold of the library door, flung him a letter and rushed away. It seems this is going to be a novel in letter-form, he said as he picked this one up." Then a third letter: "It was thrown to him through the library door. Mademoiselle de la Môle rushed off again. What a mania for writing, he said to himself with a laugh, when it's so easy for us to talk!"[9] Julien can now talk about it quite happily: he is no longer in love. For Mathilde, not only does she not find it "easy" to say what she has to say, she can only with great difficulty hold and carry what she has written, which seems to burn her hand: she has her letters carried by others, or throws them from afar like grenades.

Writing, then, is quickly duplicated, as mediation, by an act or means of transmission that aggravates its indirect and deferred character. Lucien rides six leagues to post his letters at Darney, on the Nancy to Paris road. Mme de Chasteller replies to him at the supposed address of his servant. Messengers cross and fold into one another, a postal misunderstanding at the service of crystallization. Octave and Armance entrust their letters, true and false, to the box of an orange-tree. In *Ernestine ou la naissance de l'amour*,[10] Philippe Aztézan's letters are attached to the knots of bunches of flowers laid in the hollow of a great oak-tree at the lakeside. It is also in a bunch of flowers fixed on the end of a series of rush canes that Jules Branciforte, in *L'Abbesse de Castro,* hoists his first letter up to the window of Hélène de Campireali; the favorable response is to be the dispatch of a handkerchief.

Stendhalian love is among other things a system and an exchange of signs. In such a system, the cipher is not only an auxiliary of passion: feeling tends naturally to cryptography, so to speak, as if by a sort of profound superstition. Amorous communication is carried out, then, willingly, sometimes with the help of accommodating retreats (convents, prisons, family confinements), through telegraphic codes the ingeniousness of which simulates that of desire rather well. In *Suora Scolastica*, Gennaro uses the manual alphabet of the deaf and dumb, which was well known, it seems, among Neapolitan girls, to get the following message to Rosalinda: "Since I no longer see you, I am unhappy. Are you happy in the convent? Are you free to come often to the belvedere? Do you still like flowers?" In the Farnese tower, Clelia communicates with Fabrizio while accompanying herself on the piano, pretending to sing a recitative from some fashionable opera. Fabrizio responds by tracing letters in charcoal on his hand: it is to ask for pencil and paper. The girl in turn,

> hurriedly began to trace large letters in ink on pages which she tore out of a book, and Fabrizio was beside himself with joy on seeing at length established, after three months of effort, this method of correspondence for which he had so vainly begged. He was careful not to abandon the little ruse which had proved so successful. His aim was to begin a correspondence with her, and he kept on pretending not to catch the sense of the words, the letters of which Clelia was holding up in turn before his eyes.

The connection (of substitution) between the exchange of writing and the love relationship is here almost too obvious. Fabrizio is later to receive "a fair-sized loaf of bread, marked on every side with little crosses traced with a pen. Fabrizio covered them with kisses," then messages written in the margins of a breviary, the pages of which he tore out to make an alphabet, and this mode of correspondence was to last until his escape. With Gina, he communicates first of all through light signals: one for A, two for B, etc.

> But anyone might see and interpret them; so that very night they began to arrange a system of abbreviations. Three flashes

in very quick succession would stand for the Duchessa; four, the Prince: two, Conte Mosca; two quick flashes followed by two slow ones would signify "escape." They agreed to use in future the old alphabet *alla Monaca*, which, so as to baffle inquisitive observers, changes the usual sequence of the letters and gives them another, arbitrary, order. A, for instance, is represented by 10, B by 3; that is to say, three consecutive intermissions of the light mean B, ten consecutive intermissions A, and so on. A short interval of darkness marks the separation of the words.[11]

But certainly none of these alphabets surpasses either in charm or in usefulness the mysterious language of the frames of Königsberg, which no one can understand, and at which no one can take offense.

◇

I walked this morning with a handsome, highly-educated and quite delightful young man. He was writing his confessions, and with so much elegance that his confessor has forbidden him to go on. "You enjoy your sins a second time by writing about them in this way. Tell them to me aloud."[12]

◇

All Stendhalians know the strange habit of commemorative inscription that leads Beyle, for example, to trace in the dust of Albano the initials of the women who had variously occupied him in the course of his life, or to write on the inside of his belt, on October 16, 1832, "Je vais avoir la cinquantaine, ainsi abrégé pour n'être pas compris: J. Vaisa voirla 5" (I will soon be fifty, abbreviated so as not to be understood to . . .).[13] Twenty years earlier, secretly celebrating the second anniversary or his "victory" over Angela Pietragua, he noted in his journal the following, which illustrates in a very odd way the *scripta manent:* "I see on my braces that it was on September 21, 1811, at half-past eleven in the morning."[14]

We do not know, when dealing with these private graffiti, if we should concern ourselves rather with the message, the code, or perhaps the nature of the support. Valéry, who was already irritated by the papers sewn into Pascal's linings, expressed surprise (concerning the second example) at "this uncommon action" and asks a pertinent question: "What is the point of the second act of noting it?"[15] There is in fact, in the *Journal* and in *Brulard*, a duplication of the inscription that compounds this eccentricity. A secondary question, no doubt, but one no less irritating: between the Beyle who writes in dust, on his belt, on his braces, and the Stendhal who writes on paper, at what point does literature begin?

This epigraphic fetishism also affects at least two other Stendhalian heroes, with whom, we will note in passing, it is accompanied by a certain physical impotence (in the case of Octave) or emotional impotence (in the case of Fabrizio before he meets Clelia). Octave consigns to a small notebook secretly hidden in his desk: "14th December 182. . . : Pleasant effect of two m.—Redoubling of friendships—Envy in Ar.—End.—I shall be greater than he is.—Saint-Gobain mirrors."[16] Stendhal transcribes this note without elucidation or commentary, as if its obscurity served him as a light. As for Fabrizio, he engraves on the face of his watch, in abbreviated signs, this important resolution: "When I write to the D[uchess] never say: *When I was a prelate, when I was in the Church*; that annoys her."[17]

◆

For the reader of *Brulard*, the first surprise comes from the importance of the sketches in relation to the text. The habit of drawing in the margin or between the lines of his manuscript is a constant one with Stendhal, but here the graphism proliferates and invades the page. It is not content to illustrate what is said, it is often indispensable to its understanding, and the numerous references to the sketches make the idea of an edition of *Brulard* without them impossible or absurd. Or rather, the drawing here becomes part of the text: it extends the writing by a natural movement that confirms how much Stendhal, even in haste and improvisation, and even if he occasionally dictated certain of his pages, remains very far from any declaimed, murmured, or confessed "oral" literature. His very acts of negligence are bound up with the act of writing: ellipses, gaps, breaks. It is a style of notes, abbreviations, impatiences, and boldnesses proper to writing. *Oratio soluta*.

The presence of the sketches strangles any temptation to eloquence, and sometimes exerts strange effects on the language: "On that day I saw the first bloodshed of the French Revolution. It was an unfortunate journeyman S who was wounded to death by the stab of a bayonet S' in the small of his back."[18]

◇

We also know that the margins of books that belonged to Stendhal, and particularly copies of his own works, are full of private notes, generally encoded and almost illegible, which Stendhalian scholars have striven to decipher and translate for us. This material in particular makes up the two small volumes of *Marginalia et mélanges intimes*, the sanctuary of devout Beylism. When these notes occupy the margins of a manuscript, as in the case of *Lucien Leuwen*, the role of the posthumous editor is obviously of crucial importance: it is up to him to decide between what belongs to the *work* in the strict sense, what to the *notes* permitted at the foot of the page, and what to the *margins* banished to a critical appendix with variants, outlines, plans, sketches, erasures, etc. Thus, for *Leuwen*, Henri Martineau left as footnotes such reflections as "It is a Republican who is talking," or "That is the opinion of the hero, who is mad and who will correct himself," the Beylist sincerity of which is open to question, and which are therefore to be attached to the comedy of the work: it is not Beyle who is talking, it is the "author." But can the same be said for that other footnote, which responds with some brutality to Mme de Chasteller, who, suddenly tempted to kiss Lucien's hand, wonders whence such horrors can come to her: "From the vagina, my girl!" And in that case, why not admit on the same grounds the "Model: Dominique *himself*" or "With Métilde, Dominique has talked too much," or the "Letters sent al giardino per la cameriera. And 16 years *after I write upon!* If Méti had known,"[19] which, in the spirit of the true Stendhalian, have every right to be part of the text of *Leuwen*. The Stendhalian text, margins and braces included, is *one*. Nothing allows us to isolate some preciously elaborated super-text in it that would qualify, *ne varietur*, as Stendhal's *oeuvre*. Whatever is traced by Beyle's pen (or his cane, or his penknife, or God knows what) is Stendhal, without either distinction or hierarchy.

He himself knew this very well, no doubt, or some already Beylist printer's foreman, who let through into the printed text of *Le Rouge et le noir*, the *Chartreuse de Parme* or *Promenades dans Rome* such notes as: "Esprit per.pré.gui.II.A.30," meaning "Esprit perd préfecture, Guizot, 11 août 1830" (Spirit loses prefecture, Guizot, 11 August 1830—an allusion to Beyle's greatest professional disappointment); "Para v. P. y E. 15 X 38," meaning "Pour vous Paquita et Eugénie: dédience de Waterloo aux demoiselles de Montijo" (For you Paquita and Eugenie: dedication of Waterloo to the young ladies of Montijo); "The day of paq. 1829, nopr. by lov," meaning "Le jour de Pâques 1829, pas d'epreuves corrigées, par amour" (Easter Sunday 1829, no proofs corrected, out of love):[20] *cryptological asides* (Georges Blin's expression), which, no doubt, are not exactly addressed to us. But does one ever know exactly whom Stendhal is addressing?

◇

Many people will disagree with what I have to say now, but I shall confine myself to those who have been, shall I say, unhappy enough to love passionately for many years, unrequitedly and against hopeless odds.

The sight of anything extremely beautiful, in Nature or the arts, makes you think instantly of your beloved. This is because, on the principle of the bejewelled bough in the Salzburg mine, everything sublime and beautiful becomes a part of your beloved's beauty and the unexpected reminder of happiness fills your eyes with tears on the instant. In this way a love of the beautiful, and love itself, inspire each other.

One of life's misfortunes is that one cannot remember distinctly the happiness of seeing and speaking to the beloved. Apparently you become too emotionally upset to notice the causes or the circumstances. You are aware only of your own sensations. Perhaps it is because you cannot wear out these pleasures by deliberate recollection that they are so strongly renewed by anything which diverts you from the sacred inner contemplation of your beloved and recalls her more vividly by some new relevance.*

A dried-up old architect used to meet Léonore evening after evening in society. In the course of the conversation, and without paying much attention to what I was saying,† I one day waxed eloquent in his praise. She laughed at me, and I was too cowardly to tell her it was because he saw *her* every evening.

This feeling is so powerful that it extends even to an old enemy of mine who is often with Léonore. Whenever I see this other woman, however much I want to hate her, I cannot, because she recalls Léonore so strongly to my mind.

You might say that by some strange quirk of the heart, your beloved communicates more charm to her surroundings than she herself possesses. The picture of a distant town‡ where you once glimpsed her for a moment throws you into a deeper and sweeter reverie than even her actual presence would evoke. This is because of the hardships you have suffered.[21]

Where does the work begin? Or end? Even if one wished to regard as pathological (but is the most pathological the most significant?) the extreme cases just mentioned, every reader of Stendhal who has not stopped at the five or six canonical "masterpieces" knows very well that an unbreakable continuity has been established from the *Correspondence* to the *Journal*, from the *Journal* to the essays, from the essays to the stories. The "novelistic" work

---

* Scents.

† It is for the sake of *brevity*, and in order to depict experience from the inside, that the author, by using the first person singular, brings together a number of feelings quite alien to him. He has none of his own that are worth mentioning.

‡ . . . Nessum maggior dolore
  Che ricordarsi del tempo felice
  Nella miseria.
           Dante, *Francesca*

enjoys no definable authority in relation to the writings as a whole. *L'Histoire de la peinture, De l'amour, Rome, Naples et Florence*, the *Promenades dans Rome*, the *Mémoires d'un touriste* contain dozens of more or less developed anecdotes, which fully belong, and sometimes with quite special vividness, to the empire of Stendhalian narrative. The frontier between the Italian essays and the *Journal* of 1811, on the one hand, and the *Chroniques* and the *Chartreuse* on the other, is indiscernible. The first pages of the *Chartreuse* come from the *Mémoires sur Napoléon*. The first idea for the *Rouge* was consigned to the *Promenades*. And what reader of *Leuwen* could not find the essence of the book in these few lines from *Racine et Shakspeare*:

> So it is that a young man, to whom heaven has given some delicacy of soul, made a second-lieutenant by chance and thrown into a garrison, where he sees the successes of his comrades and the nature of their pleasures, believes in good faith, when he finds himself in the company of certain women, that he is incapable of love. Then at last, one day, chance presents him with a simple, natural, honest woman, worth loving, and he feels that he has a heart.[22]

◇

None of the great Stendhalian novels, even the complete ones, is absolutely closed upon itself, autonomous in its genesis and signification. Neither Julien nor Fabrizio quite manage to break the cord that ties them to the Antoine Berthet of the *Gazette des Tribunaux* and to the Alexandre Farnese of the *Chronique*. The *Rouge* is again decentered in another respect by the existence of the draft of an article that Stendhal was going to write for Count Salvagnoli,[23] which is not only a commentary on the novel, of crucial importance in many respects, but also, in a more disturbing way, a summary, and therefore a duplication of the narrative that both challenges it and confirms it, and certainly displaces it, not without a curious effect of "shift" in the comparison of the two texts. Such a duplication also accompanies the *Chartreuse*, namely, the famous article by Balzac; but this is rather in the nature of a translation: a transposition, which is also disturbing, of the Stendhalian universe into the Balzacian register. The counter-text for *Leuwen* is missing, but we are at least aware of its existence, since we know this novel is in principle, at least as far as the first part is concerned, merely a sort of rewriting, a correction of the manuscript of *Le Lieutenant* handed over to Stendhal by his friend Mme Jules Gaulthier. We also know that *Armance* originated in a sort of competition with Mme de Duras and Henri de Latouche on the theme of impotence; and above all this novel constitutes the perhaps unique example in all literature of a work with a secret, the key to which is to be found *elsewhere:* namely, in a letter to Mérimée and in a note written in the margin of one of his own copies, which formally asserts Octave's impotence.[24] It is an extreme case of decentering, since here the center is outside: one has only to imagine a detective novel in which the murderer would be indicated solely by some posthumous comment left by the author. Indeed, he finds himself in an almost less paradoxical, but more subtle situation, neither quite inside nor quite outside. Stendhal had indeed thought of entitling his novel, like those of his competitors, *Olivier*, which in 1826 could not have failed to "give the game away." This was to be the case of *Ulysses*, except that Octave's infirmity is much more essential to the signification of the Stendhalian narrative than the reference to the *Odyssey* is to Joyce's novel. And certainly the reader himself may very well "guess" this infirmity: but in that case it remains a hypothesis, an interpretation. The fact that this interpretation is then corroborated in a marginal note radically alters, one has to admit, its status in relation to the work, and in particular it alone authorizes the use of the verb *to guess:* for one can only guess what is, and to say "Octave *is* impotent" signifies nothing more than "Stendhal says that Octave is impotent." He says so, but he says so elsewhere, and that is the whole point.

Similarly, the reader of the *Chartreuse*, especially if he is familiar with the Beylist theme of illegitimacy as a refusal of the father, will certainly be able to entertain some "suspicions" as to Fabrizio's "true" heredity. But this is different from finding these suspicions attributed to Milanese public opinion, as in the corrections entertained by Stendhal in the Chaper copy: "In time he was even thought to be the son of that handsome lieutenant Robert."[25] For

Armance, the *hors-texte* (or rather the *extra-text*, the text from the outside) resolves the mystery; for the *Chartreuse*, it helps rather to create it; but in both cases the transcendence of the work—the opening of the text on to the extra-text—dismisses the notion of an "immanent" reading.

◇

As for the *Chroniques italiennes*, everyone knows, or thinks he knows, that they are mostly made up of translation and adaptation. But, without reference to the original texts, who can assess the amount of Stendhalian "creation" involved in them? (And who cares how much there is?)

This other extreme case reminds us in time that many of Stendhal's works, from the *Vie de Haydn* to the *Promenades dans Rome*, do not entirely and unquestionably belong to him. The degree of plagiarism, borrowing, pastiche, and the apocryphal is almost impossible to determine where Stendhal is concerned. Mérimée, it will be remembered, said in 1850 that nobody knew exactly what books Beyle had written, and in 1933 Martineau, prefacing his edition of the *Mélanges de littérature*, admitted that he could not say for sure what pages were authentically Stendhal's and added: "It is very likely that not everything from his pen has yet been brought to light."[26] No one can yet, and no doubt no one ever will, mark the limits of the Stendhalian corpus.

◇

Uncompleted work forms an enormous part of Stendhal's *oeuvre*. Works as important as *Henry Brulard, Lucien Leuwen, Lamiel,* and the *Souvenirs d'égotisme* were abandoned in midstream and lost, as was *Napoléon*, the sketch for a novel called *Une poisiton sociale*, and several essays and novellas, including *Le Rose et le Vert* which, taking up once again the themes of *Mina de Vanghel*, was intended to be turned into a proper novel. If one adds the obviously hasty ending of the *Chartreuse* and the interrupted or abbreviated publication of the *Histoire de la peinture*, and the *Mémoires d'un touriste*, it is not too much to say that a destiny of mutilation weighs on most of this *oeuvre*. The sketches and rough drafts that he left do not prevent his reader from dreaming about the hypothetical continuation of *Leuwen* and of *Lamiel* or of imagining what would have become of a *Brulard* that rejoined the *Journal,* taking in and going beyond the *Souvenirs d'égotisme* and advancing to that bank of Lake Albano where the "Sleeping Baron" traces in dust the sad litany of his past loves. Or, again, from observing that the *Chartreuse* begins, more or less, where *Brulard* breaks off, with the arrival of the French in Milan: linking without break fiction to autobiography, the destiny of Lieutenant Robert to that of Second-Lieutenant Beyle—with all the consequences that follow.

◇

The aporia of Stendhalism. It might be formulated more or less as follows: what one calls Stendhal's *oeuvre* is a fragmented, elliptical, repetitive, yet infinite, or at least indefinite, text, no part of which, however, may be separated from the whole. Whoever pulls a single thread must take the whole cloth, with its holes and lack of edges. To read Stendhal is to read the whole of Stendhal, but to read all of Stendhal is impossible, for the very good reason, among others, that the whole of Stendhal has not yet been published or deciphered, or discovered, or even written: I repeat, all the Stendhalian *text,* because the gaps, the interruptions of the text are not mere absences, a pure non-text: they are a lack, active and perceptible as lack, as non-writing, as non-written text.

Against all expectations, this aporia does not kill Stendhalism, which on the contrary lives only upon it, just as every passion feeds on its impossibilities.

◇

The ambiguous status of Stendhal's Italy: exotic, eccentric, a constant alibi of eccentricity and difference, the "Italian soul" covers and justifies the most flagrant offences against the implicit code of common psychology; a locus of problematic feelings and unpredictable acts, locus of a fiction delivered from the constraints of vulgar verisimilitude. At the same time, a central, primary locus, intimately bound up with the maternal link and the negation of the father. For the exclusive descendent of the Gagnons (Guadagnis, Guadaniamos), the departure for Italy is a return to one's origins, a return to the mother's breast. The "French character," dominated by concern for money and by vanity, is no longer, for the former disciple of Helvetius and Destutt de Tracy, anything more than an external reference, a foil. The heart of the true Stendhalian debate is in Italy: a debate between energy (Rome, Ariosto) and tenderness (Milan, Tasso). Italy is the paradoxical center of the Beylist decentering, the fatherland (motherland?) of the expatriate, the locus of the unlocated, of the non-locus: an intimate utopia.

◇

Pesaro, 24 May 1817. —Here people don't spend their lives *judging* their happiness. *Mi piace*, or *non mi piace*, is the great way of settling everything. The true fatherland is where one meets the most people like oneself. I fear that in France I always find a basic coldness wherever I go. In this country, I feel a charm that I cannot account for: it's like love and yet I'm in love with no one. The shadow of the beautiful trees, the beauty of the sky at night, the view of the sea, everything has a charm for me, a vividness that reminds me of a feeling I had quite forgotten, which I had felt, at sixteen, during my first campaign. I see that I am unable to convey my thoughts: all the circumstances I employ to depict them are feeble.

The whole of nature is more touching for me here; it seems new to me: I see nothing that is flat and insipid. Often at two in the morning, returning home, in Bologna, past those great porticos, my soul obsessed by the beautiful eyes I had just seen, walking in front of those palaces which, with its great shadows, the moon drew for me, I would stop, weighed down with happiness, and say to myself: How beautiful it is! Contemplating those hills, covered with trees that advance to the edge of the city, lit by that silent light in the midst of that glittering sky, I would begin to shake; tears would come into my eyes. —I would say to myself, for no particular reason: My God! What a good thing I came to Italy![27]

The (fragmented) unity of the Stendhalian text, the absence of autonomy in any of his works, the constant perfusion of meaning that circulates from one to the other, appear best by contrast if one compares this situation to that, for example, of *La Comédie humaine*. Each of Balzac's novels is an enclosed, completed narrative, separated from the others by the uncrossable barriers of the dramatic construction, and we know that it needed the device, adopted at a later stage, of the return of characters to give some unity, somewhat after the event, to the Balzacian world.

The Stendhalian universe is based on quite different presuppositions. There is no unity of place or time, no recurrence of characters, no trace of that wish to compete with the legal status by creating an autonomous, complete, and coherent society; a few erratic novels, devoid of any linking principle, scattered throughout a heterogeneous *oeuvre*, of which they are far from constituting the main body, at least in quantity: like Rousseau, or Barrès, or Gide, Stendhal is quite obviously an impure novelist. For all that, though, the unity of Stendhalian fiction is unquestionable, but it is not one of cohesion, still less of continuity. It stems entirely from a sort of strictly *thematic* constancy: a unity of repetition and variation, which relates, rather than links, these novels to one another.

Gilbert Durand has brought out the most important of these recurrent themes.[28] The solitude of the hero and the reinforcement of his destiny by the duplication (or uncertainty) of his birth and oracular overdetermination; testing trials and temptations; feminine duality and symbolic opposition between the two types of the Amazon (or "sublime whore"—Mathilde, Vanina, Mina de Vanghel, Mme de Hocquincourt, la Sanseverina) and the tender woman, guardian of the heart's secrets (Mme de Rênal, Mme de Chasteller, Clelia Conti); the conversion of the hero and the passage from the epic register to that of tender intimacy (symbolized at least twice, in *Le Rouge et le noir* and the *Chartreuse*, by the paradoxical motif of the happy prison), which defines precisely the *moment* of Stendhalian fiction: even, it seems to me, contrary to the view expressed by Durand, in the first part of *Leuwen*, where we see a hero originally convinced, like Fabrizio, of being incapable of love, and forewarned against this feeling by political prejudice ("What! while all the youth of France has joined the fray, and so much is at stake, I am to spend my whole life gazing into a pair of beautiful eyes!"—"Since 1830," as the *Mémoires d'un touriste* comments, "Love seems to be the worst of dishonors for a young man"),[29] discover "that he has a heart" and become converted to his passion.

This fundamental theme of the *Rücksicht*, of the abandonment to female tenderness as a return to the mother, reinforced still more by the typically maternal appearance and function of the triumphant heroine (including Clélia, who is more maternal, despite her age and kinship, than the conquering Sanseverina), lies therefore at the basis of what is most essential in Stendhal's fictional creation, which scarcely alters, from one work to another, except in rhythm and tonality. The reader is thus led to make endless comparisons between situations, characters, feelings, actions, instinctively bringing out correspondences by superimposition and change of perspective. A network of interferences is thus set up between Julien, Fabrizio, and Lucien, between Mathilde and Gina, Mme de Rênal, Mme de Chasteller, and Clelia, between François Leuwen, M. de la Môle, and Conte Mosca, Chélan and Blanès, Sansfin and Du Poirier, Frilair and Rassi, the suspect paternities of Julien and Fabrizio, their common devotion to Napoleon, between the Farnese tower and Besançon prison, between the seminary, the garrison at Nancy, and the battlefield of Waterloo, etc. More than any other, no doubt, Stendhal's *oeuvre* invites a *paradigmatic* reading, in which the consideration of narrative links fades before the evidence of relations of homology: a harmonic, or vertical, reading, then, a reading on two or several registers, for the reader for whom the true text begins with the duplication of the text.

◈

Some months ago a married woman of Melito, renowned as much for her ardent piety as for her rare beauty, had the weakness to grant her lover an assignation in a mountain forest, two leagues from the village. The lover was happy. After this moment of delight, however, the enormity of her sin oppressed the soul of the guilty woman: she remained plunged into gloomy silence. "Why are you so cold to me?" asks the lover. "I was thinking how we would see each other tomorrow; that abandoned hut, in the dark wood, is the most convenient place." The lover leaves her; the unhappy woman did not come back to the village, but spent the night in the forest, busy, as she admitted, praying and digging two ditches. The next morning the lover arrives and is killed at the hands of this woman whom he believed adored him. This unhappy victim of remorse buries her lover with the greatest care, comes back to the village, where she confesses to the priest and embraces her children. She returns to the forest, where she is found dead, lying in the ditch dug next to that of her lover.[30]

◇

This brief anecdote is a fairly representative example of what one might call, without exaggerating its specificity, *Stendhalian narrative*. We will not dwell on the (striking) illustration of the "Italian soul," a mandatory element in Beylist verisimilitude, but take a closer look at the characteristic elements of the narrative treatment by which this "little true fact" becomes a text by Stendhal.

The first of these features is no doubt the almost systematic displacement of the narrative in relation to the action, which results both in the elision of the principal events and the accentuation of the incidental circumstances. The act of adultery is designated three times by a sort of narrative metonymy: the assignation given to the lover; the lover's "happiness" (a banal figure, revivified here by the conciseness of the statement); the "moment of delight," qualified retrospectively on the basis of the virtuous state of conscience that follows. Not by itself, therefore, but by the events that lead up to it, accompany it, or follow it. The murder of the lover is subtly relegated, by an academic periphrasis, to a subordinate proposition the main stress of which is elsewhere. Lastly, and above all, the suicide of the young woman undergoes a complete ellipsis between her return to the forest and the moment when she is found dead; an ellipsis reinforced still further by the temporal ambiguity of the narrative present, and the absence of any adverb of time, which make the two verbs apparently simultaneous, thus eliminating the entire duration that separates the two actions.

This elision of the strong tenses is one of the features of Stendhalian narrative. In the *Chartreuse,* the first embrace of Fabrizio and Clelia, in the Farnese tower, is so discreet that it generally passes unnoticed ("She was so beautiful, with her gown half torn off, and stirred to such a pitch of passion, that Fabrizio could not refrain from following an almost unconscious impulse. No resistance was offered him"), and Gina's "sacrifice" with Ernesto-Ranuccio V disappears between two sentences: "He had the temerity to reappear, trembling all over and extremely miserable, at three minutes to ten. At half past ten the Duchessa stepped into her carriage and set off for Bologna." Fabrizio's death is implied rather than mentioned, on the last page: "She [Gina] lived for a very short time only after Fabrizio, whom she adored, and who spent but one year in his Charterhouse."[31] In this case one may blame the forced mutilation of this epilogue, but in the *Rouge,* the execution of Julien, so long expected and prepared for, is eclipsed at the last moment: "Never had that head such poetic beauty than at the moment when it was about to fall. The sweetest moments he had known in the past in the woods of Vergy came thronging back into his mind with the most eager insistence.

"Everything passed off simply and decently, with no trace of affectation on his part." There follows a flashback (a method, on the contrary, very little used by Stendhal, who tends, seemingly, to accelerate duration rather than retard it), which contributes still more to this effacement of the death by resuscitating Julien for the space of half a page.[32] Jean Prévost remarked quite rightly of these silent and nearly disguised deaths that they constitute a sort of "literary euthanasia."[33]

This discretion concerning the cardinal functions of the narrative contrasts, obviously, with the importance given to incidental and almost technical details: the precise location of the forest, the abandoned hut, the digging of the two ditches. This "attention to small things," which Stendhal praised in Mérimée, is even more characteristic of his own manner: we have already met with some of the effects of this. Stendhal himself carries Mérimée's precision still further: "'He helped her down from her horse on some pretext,' Clara would say. Dominque says: 'He helped her down from her horse on the pretext that he had seen that the horse was losing one of its shoes and he wanted to fix it with a nail.'"[34] But it should be noted above all that this attention to objects and circumstances—which is accompanied, however, as we know, with great disdain for description—almost always serves to mediate the evocation of important actions or situations by allowing various kinds of material substitutes to speak in their place. In the last scene of *Vanina Vanini*, the "cold, sharp chains" that hold Missirilli and separate him from Vanina's embraces, the "diamonds" and "little files," the traditional tools of escape, that she gives him and which in the end he throws to her "as much as his chains allow him," all these details shine with such intensity of presence, despite the dryness of their expression, that they eclipse the dialogue between the two lovers: they bear the meaning far more than the words exchanged.[35]

Another form of ellipsis and perhaps an even more specific one might be called the ellipsis of intentions. It consists in reporting the actions of a character without informing the reader of their purpose, which will appear only after the event. The second meeting arranged for the following day in the abandoned hut misleads the reader as much as it did the lover, and if the digging of two graves hardly leaves any doubt as to what will follow, the fact remains that the narrative is deliberately silent about the purpose that gives meaning to a series of actions (coming back to the village, confessing, embracing her children), leaving us the task of filling this gap retroactively. Thus, in *L'Abbesse de Castro*, Stendhal tells us that Vanina notices her father's anger against Branciforte. "She went at once," he adds, "and threw a little powder on the wood of the five magnificent arquebuses that her father had hanging next to his bed. She also covered with a light layer of dust his daggers and swords." The connection between the father's anger and the fact of throwing dust on his weapons is not obvious, and the function of this action remains obscure until the moment we read that "visiting her father's weapons that evening, she saw that two arquebuses had been loaded and that almost all the daggers had been handled":[36] she had spread the dust in order to know what preparations her father was making, but the narrative carefully concealed this motivation from us. The most famous example of this Stendhalian habit is obviously the end of chapter 35 of the second part of *Le Rouge et le noir,* when we see Julien leave Mathilde, dash off in a post-chaise to Verrières, buy a brace of pocket-pistols from the gunsmith and enter the church, without our being informed of his intentions other than by their fulfillment in the line: "He fired a shot at her with one pistol and missed her. He fired a second shot; she fell."[37]

We must stress here the necessarily deliberate character of the method: if the Stendhalian method were, like the later manner of Hemingway, a purely "objective" relation of the actions performed, with no incursion into the consciousness of the characters, the ellipsis of intentions would conform to the overall attitude, and therefore would be much less marked. But we know that Stendhal never confined himself to this "behaviorist" prejudice, and even that recourse to interior monologue is one of his innovations and one of his most constant habits. Here, he in no way refrains from informing the reader that "the enormity of her crime oppressed the soul of the guilty woman" and if Stendhal does not let the reader know more about his heroine's intentions it is obviously by voluntary omission. Similarly, when Vanina hears Missirilli announce that with the next defeat, he will abandon the cause of Carbonarism, Stendhal simply adds, that this word "threw a fatal light into her mind. She said to herself: 'The Carbonari have received several thousand sequins from me. No one can doubt my devotion to the conspiracy.'"[38] This interior monologue is as misleading as the narrative of the criminal-narrator in *The Murder of Roger Ackroyd,* for Stendhal, pretending to relate Vanina's thoughts at this point, is careful to conceal the most important thing, which is more or less, as we learn some pages later: "So I can denounce the sale without Pietro suspecting." The incidental, here again, is substituted for the essential, just as in the story about Melito the details concerning the abandoned hut conceal, for both the future victim and the reader, the planned murder.[39]

This type of ellipsis implies great freedom in the choice of narrative point of view. Stendhal, as we know, inaugurates the technique of the "restrictions of field,"[40] which consists in reducing the narrative field to the perceptions and thoughts of a single character. But he alters this choice, on the one hand, as we have just seen, by keeping from him some of his thoughts, often the most important ones; but also by frequently changing the focal character: even in a novel as centered on the character of the hero as the *Rouge*, the narration sometimes adopts the point of view of another character, such as Mme de Rênal, or Mathilde, or even M. de Rênal. Here, the focal point is almost constantly the heroine, but the narrative makes at least one incursion, and a retrospective one at that, into the consciousness of the lover ("this woman whom he believed adored him"). Lastly, and above all, the focusing of the narrative is disturbed, as it almost always is in Stendhal, by the practice of what Georges Blin has called "the intrusion of the author," and which it would no doubt be better to call intervention of the *narrator*, making a distinction, particularly necessary in the case of Stendhal, between the identity of these two roles.

Nothing, in fact, is more difficult than to determine at each moment what the virtual source of the Stendhalian discourse is, the only two constants being that this source is highly variable and that it is rarely identical with the person of Stendhal. We know his almost hysterical taste for travesty, and we know for example that the supposed traveller of the *Mémoires d'un touriste* is a certain M. L. . . , a commercial traveller in hardware, whose opinions do not always coincide with those of Beyle. In the novels and novellas, the situation of the narrator is generally indeterminate. The *Rouge* and *Lamiel* begin with a chronicle told by a narrator-witness who belongs to the diegetic world: that of the *Rouge* is an anonymous inhabitant of Verrières who has often observed the valley of the Doubs from the promenade widened by M. de Rênal, and who praises the Mayor, "though he is on the extreme right, and I am a Liberal." The narrator of *Lamiel,* who is more precisely identified, is the son and grandson of Messrs. Lagier, notaries at Carville. The first slips away after a few pages without his disappearance being noticed by anyone, the second announces his departure with more fuss in these terms: "All these adventures . . . concern the young Lamiel girl. . . . And I have taken it into my head to write them down so that I may become a man of letters. So, O benevolent reader, farewell, you will hear no more of me."[41] As for the *Chartreuse,* Stendhal certainly acknowledges, in antedating it, the writing of this "novella," but not without placing most of the responsibility for it on the shoulders of a supposed canon of Padua, whose memoirs he seems merely to have adapted. Which of the two assumes the "I" that appears three or four times at least,[42] and always in an unexpected way, in the course of a chronicle that in principle is quite impersonal?

The situation of the *Chroniques italiennes,* and in particular *L'Abbesse de Castro,* is both clearer and more subtle, for Stendhal claims to be acting only as a translator, but an indiscreet and active translator, who does not deny himself the pleasure of commenting on the action ("Candor and uncouthness, the natural results of the liberty suffered by republics, and the habit of passions openly expressed, and not yet contained by the morals of monarchy, are revealed for all to see in the person of the Signior di Campireali as soon as he takes a step"), or of authenticating his sources ("Now, my sad task will be limited to providing a necessarily dry extract of the trial at the end of which Elena met her death. This trial, the report of which I read in a library, whose name I must not reveal, comprises no less than eight volumes in-folio"), or of judging the text that he is supposed to be recopying ("That evening, Elena wrote to her lover a naive and in my opinion very moving letter"), or even of practicing on several occasions a rather insolent censorship: "I think I ought to pass over in silence many circumstances which, in turn, depict the morals of that period, but which seem to me sad to relate. The author of the Roman manuscript took inifinite pains to arrive at the exact date of these details which I am suppressing."[43]

It is often as if Stendhal had transported this *marginal* situation in relation to a text of which he is not supposed to be the author and for which he appears to accept no responsibility, from the *Chroniques* and the anecdotes collected in the first Italian essays, into his great works of fiction: Blin has shown the quite natural passage that leads from the supposed cuts of *L'Abbesse de Castro* to the famous etc.'s which, in the novels, cut short so many tirades supposedly regarded as too flat or boring.[44] But what is true of censorship is equally so of the other forms of commentary and intervention. It is as if Stendhal, having got into the habit of annotating the texts of others, continues to gloss his own without seeing the difference. We know in particular how he burdens his young heroes with judgements, admonitions, and advice, but critics have also noticed the dubious sincerity of those paraphrases in which Stendhal sometimes seems to separate himself hypocritically from his favorite characters, to present as a defect or blunder what in actual fact he regards as sympathetic or admirable characteristics. "Why," he says in the sixth chapter of the *Chartreuse*,

> why should the chronicler who follows faithfully all the most trivial details of the story that has been told him be held up to blame? Is it his fault if his characters, led astray by passions which he, most *unfortunately* for himself, in no way shares, descend to actions that are profoundly immoral? It is true that things of this sort are no longer done in a country where the sole passion that has outlived all the rest is lust for money, that gives vanity its chance.[45]

It is almost impossible in such examples to distinguish between the ironic intervention of the author and the supposed intervention of a narrator distinct from him whose style and opinion Stendhal is playing at counterfeiting. Antiphrasis, satirical parody, the *style indirect libre,* pastiche ("This Minister, in spite of his light-hearted air and his lively manners, did not possess a soul of the French type; he could not *forget* the things that grieved him. When there was a thorn in his pillow, he was obliged to break it off and to blunt its point while getting many a prick from it in his trembling limbs. (I must apologize for this extract, which is translated from the Italian)"[46]) follow one another and sometimes overlay one another in a counterpoint of which the opening pages of the *Chartreuse* form a characteristic example, mingling the epic bombast of the victory announcements published by the revolutionaries, the bitter or furious recriminations of the despotic party, the irony of the Voltairian observer, popular enthusiasm, the cautious expressions of administrative language, etc. With Stendhal, then, the image of the narrator is essentially problematic, and when the Stendhalian narrative gives way, however little, to discourse, it is often very difficult and sometimes impossible to answer the apparently quite simple question: *who is speaking?*

From this point of view, our text of reference is distinguished first of all by its sobriety of discourse, the absence of any explicit comment (this is what Stendhal calls "recounting narratively"). This absence is not insignificant: on the contrary, it has a great value, indeed, for any reader who is at all familiar with Stendhal's Italy, an obvious one. The silence of the narrative emphasizes most eloquently the grandeur and beauty of the action: it contributes therefore to describing it. It is a zero degree commentary, precisely the one that classical rhetoric recommended for *sublime* moments, when the event speaks for itself better than any sort of speech could; and we know that the sublime is not for Stendhal an academic category, but one of the most active terms in his system of values.

Discourse is not, however, totally absent from this narrative—such an exclusion is indeed only an academic hypothesis, almost impossible in narrative practice. Here, we should note first the initial temporal indicator "some months ago," which situates the event in relation to the instance of discourse constituted by the narration itself, in a relative time that emphasizes and authenticates the situation of the narrator—a single chronological point of reference. Also there is the testimonial formula "as she admitted," which connects, according to Roman Jakobson's categories, the process of the statement (the action), the process of the enunciation (the narrative), and "a process of stated enunciation": the evidence, or more specifically in this case the avowal, which it seems could only have been received during the confession mentioned below, a confession thus designated in an oblique way as the source of most of the narrative, and in particular of everything concerning the motivations of the action. These two "shifters" place the narrator therefore in the situation of a historian, in the etymological sense, that is to say, as investigator-reporter. Such a situation is quite normal in an ethnographical text like *Rome, Naples et Florence* (or the *Promenades,* or the *Mémoires d'un touriste*), but as we have seen Stendhal, perhaps simply out of habit, maintains certain signs of it even in his great works of "fiction"; hence such strange precautions as that "I think" which crops up quite naturally, it seems, in the middle of a chronicle in the page mentioned above from *Le Rose et le vert*, but which reappears more surprisingly in a sentence like the following from *Leuwen* (it concerns Mlle Berchu's dress): "It was made of a material from Algiers, and had very wide stripes, brown, I think, and pale yellow," or from the *Chartreuse*: "The Contessa smiled—as a measure of precaution, I fancy."[47]

The case of the demonstrative ("That unfortunate woman . . ."), of which Stendhal makes a very marked use, is rather more subtle, for it consists essentially (apart from its stylistic value as—perhaps Italianate—emphasis) of an anaphoric reference by the narrative back to itself (the unfortunate woman already mentioned): this reference back necessarily passing through the instance of discourse and therefore by the relay of the narrator, and consequently of the reader, who imperceptibly finds himself called upon as a witness. The same goes for the intensive "so," also typically Stendhalian, and which again implies a return of the text upon itself. Indeed the two turns of phrase are often frequently found together: "that woman so tender. . . ."

As for expressions implying a measure of judgment, they remain, despite their discretion, difficult to assign. "The unfortunate woman," "unfortunate victim of remorse" may express Stendhal's sympathetic opinion, but "gave in," "sin," "guilty," and even "delight" involve a moral judgment that it would be very imprudent to attribute to him. These moralizing terms stem rather from the heroine herself, with a slight inflection of indirect discourse, though they may reflect the common opinion of the village, the vehicle of the anecdote, whose judgments Stendhal would not hesitate to reproduce without necessarily agreeing with them, as when he reports in italics certain expressions borrowed from vulgar speech for which he refuses to take responsibility himself—too anxious to preserve a dignity that he lets us perceive without allowing us to judge it; faithful to his policy, which is to be always present, and always out of reach.

◇

An equivocal relation between the "author" and his "work"; the difficulty of separating the "literary" text from the other functions of writing and graphism; borrowings of subjects, plagiarisms, translations, pastiches; an almost invariable failure to complete works, a proliferation of sketches, variants, corrections, marginal notes, a decentering of the *text* in relation to the "work"; a strong thematic relation between one work and another, which compromises the autonomy and therefore even the existence of each of them; a confusion of the discursive and the narrative; a displacement of the narrative in relation to the action; an ambiguity of narrative focus; an indetermination of the narrator, or, to be more precise, of the source of the narrative discourse: everywhere, at every level, in every direction, the essential mark of the Stendhalian activity is to be found—a constant and exemplary transgression of the limits, rules, and functions that apparently make up the literary game. It is characteristic that, beyond his admiration for Tasso, Pascal, Saint-Simon, Montesquieu, or Fielding, his true models were musicians, Mozart or Cimarosa, and a painter, Correggio, and that his dearest ambition was to restore through writing the scarcely definable qualities (lightness, grace, limpidity, gaiety, sensousness, tender reverie, the magic of distant places) that he found in their works. Always *in the margin,* a little to one side, beneath or beyond words, moving in the direction of that mythical horizon that he designates by the terms "music" and "tender painting," his art constantly exceeds and perhaps rejects, the very idea of literature.

◇

Ave Maria (twilight), in Italy the hour for tenderness, for the pleasures of the soul and for melancholy: sensation enhanced by the sound of those lovely bells.

Hours for pleasure unrelated to the sense except through memories.[48]

◇

The particular quality of Stendhalian discourse is not clarity; still less is it obscurity (of which he had a horror, and which he regarded as the accomplice of stupidity and "hypocrisy"); but something like an enigmatic transparency, which always, here or there, disconcerts some resource or habit of the mind. Thus he writes for the "happy few" and offends or, as he himself said,[49] "Stendhalizes" all the others (pronounced "st*a*ndhalizes").

◇

(*On the steamer, in Toulon bay*) I was amused by the gallantry of a bashful (?) sailor toward a very pretty woman of comfortably well-off family, who had been driven from the room below, with one of her companions, by the heat. He covered her with a sail to shelter her a little, she and her child, but the violent wind swelled up the sail and moved it; he tickled the beautiful traveller and uncovered her while pretending to cover her. There was much gaiety, naturalness and even grace in this action, which lasted for an hour. It took place a foot and a half away from me. The woman's friend, who had not been treated to such gallantry, was paying attention to me and said to me: "This gentleman is sticking his neck out." I ought to have talked to her; she was a fine creature; but the sight of the graceful action before me gave me more pleasure. The beautiful woman warned the sailor when she could. To one of his first gallantries, which was a phrase with a double meaning, she replied in the most lively fashion: *Merde.*[50]

[1968]

NOTES

1. Stendhal, *Vie de Rossini* (Divan), i:30–31; *Life of Rossini*, Richard N. Coe, tr. (Seattle: University of Washington Press, 1970), p. 24. [The reference *Divan* refers here to the edition in 79 volumes (1927–37); *Divan critique* refers to the critical editions, edited by Henri Martineau, for the Divan collection—Tr.]
2. Jean Pouillon, "La création chez Stendhal," *Les Temps modernes* (1951), no. 69.
3. *Vie de Henry Brulard* (Divan critique), i:41–42, 45; *The Life of Henry Brulard*, Catherine A. Phillips, tr. (London, 1925), pp. 27–28.
4. Stendhal, *Lucien Leuwen*, Henri Martineau, ed. (Paris: Hazan), p. 671.
5. Cf. Jean Starobinski, "Stendhal pseudonyme," *L'Oeil vivant* (Paris: Gallimard, 1961), pp. 193–244.
6. *Journal* (Divan), v:258, 94, 85; Henri Martineau, *Le Coeur de Stendhal* (Paris: Albin Michel, 1952–53), p. 361; *Journal*, iv:254, v:153. [Italicized words in English in the original—Tr.]
7. *Correspondance* (Divan), v:108–9.
8. *Le Rose et le vert* in *Romans et nouvelles* (Divan), i:17.
9. *Le Rouge et le noir*, Henri Martineau, ed. (Paris: Garnier, 1973), pp. 306–7, 315–16; *Scarlet and Black*, Margaret R. B. Shaw, tr. (Harmondsworth: Penguin, 1955), pp. 333, 341–42.
10. *De l'Amour* (Divan critique), pp. 320–43; *Love*, Gilbert and Suzanne Sale, tr. (Harmondsworth: Penguin, 1975), pp. 293–315.
11. *L'Abbesse de Castro* in *Chroniques italiennes* (Divan), i:33–37; *Suora Scolastica* (Divan), ii:236; *La Chartreuse de Parme*, Henri Martineau, ed. (Paris: Garnier, 1973), pp. 352, 355, 363; *The Charterhouse of Parma*, Margaret R. B. Shaw, tr. (Harmondsworth: Penguin, 1958), pp. 327, 328, 330, 337–38.
12. *Mémoires d'un touriste* (Paris: Calmann-Levy), ii:140.
13. *Vie de Henry Brulard*, i:15; *H.B.*, p. 6.
14. *Journal*, v:211.
15. Paul Valéry, *Oeuvres*, Pléiade (Paris: Gallimard, 1957), i:567; "Stendhal" in Valéry, *Masters and Friends*, Martin Turnell, ed. (Princeton: Princeton University Press, 1968), p. 192–93.
16. *Armance*, Henri Martineau, ed. (Paris: Garnier, 1950), p. 27; *Armance*, Gilbert and Suzanne Sale, tr. (London, 1960), p. 27.
17. *La Chartreuse de Parme*, p. 231; *Charterhouse*, p. 220.
18. *Vie de Henry Brulard*, i:68; *H.B.*, p. 43.
19. Martineau, *Le Coeur*, pp. 257, 671, 680, 675 [italicized words in English in the original—Tr.]
20. *Le Rouge et le noir*, p. 311; *La Chartreuse de Parme*, p. 56; *Promenades dans Rome* (Divan), iii:237; *A Roman Journal*, Haakon Chevalier, tr. (New York: Orion Press, 1957), p. 250.

21. *De l'Amour*, p. 33; *Love*, pp. 62–63.
22. *Racine et Shakspeare* (Divan), p. 112. A similarity indicated by Martineau, *Lucien Leuwen*, p. xi.
23. *Le Rouge et le noir*, pp. 708–26.
24. *Armance*, pp. 249–53, 261; *Armance*, pp. 166–69, 174.
25. *La Chartreuse de Parme*, p. 614.
26. *Mélanges de littérature* (Divan), p. 1.
27. *Rome, Naples et Florence en 1817* (Divan critique), pp. 118–19.
28. Gilbert Durand, *Le Décor mythique de la Chartreuse de Parme* (Paris: J. Corti, 1961).
29. *Lucien Leuwen*, p. 145. (Cf. p. 146: "Any moment the voice of the fatherland may be heard; I may be called. . . . And that's the moment I choose to make myself the slave of some little provincial reactionary!"); *Mémoires d'un touriste*, I:59.
30. Stendhal, *Rome, Naples et Florence*, Pléiade, p. 554.
31. *La Chartreuse de Parme*, pp. 472, 508, 537; *Charterhouse*, pp. 433–34, 463–64, 488.
32. *Le Rouge et le noir*, p. 487; *Scarlet and Black*, p. 510.
33. Jean Prévost, *La Création chez Stendhal* (Paris: Mercure de France, 1951), p. 260.
34. *Marginalia*, II:96.
35. *Chroniques italiennes* (Divan), II:125.
36. *Chroniques italiennes*, I:39–40.
37. *Le Rouge et le noir*, p. 432; *Scarlet and Black*, p. 456.
38. *Chroniques italiennes* (Divan), II:103.
39. Here is another example of this ellipsis of intentions, accompanied by another, very beautiful effect of silence:

"The priest was not old; the servant girl was pretty; there was gossip, which did not prevent a young man from the next village from courting the servant girl. One day, he hid the tongs from the kitchen fire in the girl's bed. When he came back a week later, the girl said to him: 'Whatever did you do with my tongs? I've been looking everywhere for them since you went. It really isn't funny.'

The lover kissed her, tears in his eyes, and left." *Voyage dans le Midi* (Divan), p. 115.

40. Georges Blin, *Stendhal et les problèmes du roman* (Paris: J. Corti, 1954).
41. *Lamiel* (Divan), p. 43.
42. *La Chartreuse de Parme*, pp. 1, 2, 156; *Charterhouse*, pp. 17, 18, 154.
43. *Chroniques italiennes*, pp. 31, 157, 107, 154.
44. Blin, *Stendhal*, p. 235.
45. *La Chartreuse de Parme*, p. 118; *Charterhouse*, p. 119.
46. *La Chartreuse de Parme*, p. 107; *Charterhouse*, p. 109.

47. *Lucien Leuwen*, p. 117; *La Chartreuse de Parme*, p. 87; *Charterhouse*, p. 92.

48. *De l'Amour*, p. 233; *Love*, p. 230.

49. "Vous allez encore vous *Stendhaliser*" (to Mareste, January 3, 1818), *Correspondance*, v:92.

50. *Voyage dans le Midi*, pp. 284–85.

9

FLAUBERT'S SILENCES

A coach-and-four had been whirling them along for a week, towards a new world from which she would never return. On and on they drove, their arms entwined, in silence. Often from a mountain height they would suddenly catch sight of a splendid city below them, with domes, ships, bridges, forests of orange-trees, cathedrals of white marble with storks' nests on their spiky steeples. They slowed down to a foot-pace over the big flagstones, and by the wayside were bunches of flowers, proffered you by women in red bodices. You heard bells chime and mules bray. You heard guitars murmuring and fountains splashing, their spray flying up to freshen the fruits standing in pyramids at the feet of white statues that smiled beneath the squirting jets of water. And then one night they came to a fishing village with brown nets drying in the wind all along the huts and under the cliff. Here they would stay, in a little low house with a flat roof and a palm-tree shading it, at the head of a gulf by the sea. They would swing in a hammock or drift in a gondola[1]

One will no doubt have recognized the famous passage from *Madame Bovary* in which Flaubert conveys Emma's reveries when, having become Rodolphe's mistress and thinking she is about to leave Yonville with him, she imagines, lying in her room at night, beside her sleeping husband Charles, their future life of romantic travel and love. Albert Thibaudet remarks that with the exception of some conditionals (and, incidentally, he does not seem to see that they have no modal value and simply express, as in "he told me that he would come," the future of an indirect discourse in the past), all the sentences in this passage have their verbs in the imperfect—the imperfect, here, of indirect style, which is equivalent to a present indicative and which marks the intensity of an imagination for which "everything is given as having taken place."[2] In what follows, the return to reality is marked by no temporal break, which, Thibaudet rightly says, is a way of making this dream as present as the noises in the room:

> The vision hovered on the horizon, infinite and harmonious, in a haze of blue, in a wash of sunshine. . . . Then the baby started coughing in its cradle, or Bovary snored more loudly, and Emma didn't get to sleep until morning, as dawn was whitening the window-panes and young Justin already taking down the chemist's shutters across the square.

Thibaudet's remark on the use of tenses can be complemented and corroborated by another, which concerns the content and character of the description by which Flaubert wishes to restore—or bring about—Emma's reverie. It is, it should be made quite clear, not a dream, but a daydream; Flaubert says, curiously enough, that, while Charles dozed off beside her, Emma "was awake in a very different dreamland." In view of this, one cannot fail to be surprised by the clarity and precision of certain details, like the storks' nests on the spiky steeples, the flagstones that slowed them down to a foot-pace, the red bodices, the spray from the fountains, the pyramids of fruits, the brown nets, etc. The earlier version, preserved by the Pommier-Leleu edition,[3] provides more effects of this kind that were cut by Flaubert in his final version: the women have black tresses; to the sounds of the bells, mules, and fountains is added the rustling of the monks' cassocks; and, above all, this very characteristic sentence: "The sun beat down on the leather hood and the dust, which rose up like smoke, struck them in their gums." The fact that a character is able, in the vagueness of a daydream, to perceive these details with such sharpness obviously goes beyond general verisimilitude. Thibaudet's commentary, which recalls La Fontaine's *Perrette et le pot au lait* ("Quand je l'eus!") and sees in this power of illusion a specifically feminine feature, is rather questionable. One could, equally well, attribute to Flaubert some intention of a psychological order concerning Emma's particular personality: perhaps he wished, by this strange profusion of details, to show the hallucinatory character of her daydreams, which could be seen as one of the aspects of Emma's pathology. There is no doubt some truth in this interpretation, but it is not entirely satisfying. A little later, when Emma, having become really ill after Rodolphe's betrayal, sinks into an attack of mystical devotion, Flaubert will present her *visions* in a much more objective—and more traditional—manner when he writes:

> Then she let her head drop down on to the pillow, seeming to hear through space the harps of the seraphs playing, and to see, seated upon a thrown of gold in an azure Heaven with His Saints around Him bearing branches of green palm, God the Father, resplendent in majesty, at whose command angels with wings of flame descended to Earth to carry her up in their arms.[4]

Through the vagueness of the details, their quite conventional character, and the "seeming to hear" (compared with the earlier "whirling them along") that places them unequivocally on the plane of the unreal, we see very clearly that hallucination, or apparition, is given to us here with a force of illusion very inferior to that which Flaubert accorded to a mere daydream. A psychological interpretation would seem to be rather weak therefore. In any case, one finds effects of a similar kind in the case of Frédéric in *L'Éducation sentimentale* who, though close to Emma in his tendency to daydream, is far from sharing her capacity for illusion. Frédéric is not a Bovaryst: he may be an impulsive dreamer, but, in the end, he is a lucid one. Yet it is of him that Flaubert writes:

> When he went to the Jardin des Plantes, the sight of a palm-tree carried him off to distant lands. They travelled together on the backs of dromedaries, under the awnings of elephants, in the calm of a yacht among blue archipelagoes, or side by side on a couple of mules with bells on their harness, which stumbled over broken pillars in the grass.[5]

Here again, the precision of the details—the last, in particular—

exceeds the verisimilitude of the pretext. The rest of the passage shows us Frédéric's imagination sustained, this time, by the presence of an external representation:

> Sometimes he stopped in front of old pictures in the Louvre; and, his love embracing her even in vanished ages, he substituted her for the figure in the paintings. Wearing a wimple, she prayed on her knees behind a leaded casement. A lady of Castille or Flanders, she sat dressed in a starched ruff and boned bodice with puffed sleeves. Or she came down some great porphyry staircase, under a canopy of ostrich feathers, surrounded by senators and wearing a gown of brocade.

The visual details—ruff, boned bodice with puffed sleeves, porphyry, ostrich feathers, brocade—are provided here by the picture, Frédéric having simply to substitute Mme Arnoux for the characters represented; but the tone of the description has not changed, and in the last sentence—"At other times he dreamt of her in yellow silk trousers on the cushions of a harem"—there is nothing to show whether the reverie has reassumed its autonomy or whether it is continuing to paraphrase a museum painting: the vision is the same. Whether Frédéric is looking at a picture or imagining some fantastic scene, the mode and degree of presence are identical. Similarly, in the scene from *Madame Bovary* quoted at the beginning, the passage from dream to reality is carried out without change of narrative register and without substantial discontinuity. The Pommier-Leleu version said: "Then *suddenly* the baby started coughing in its cradle, or Bovary snored more loudly, *or the lamp, which was about to go out, flickered for a few minutes longer in its bowl of oil.*" The elimination of "suddenly" obviously reinforced the effect of continuity (and proves no doubt that this effect was aimed at), but one may regret the detail of the lamp: it harmonized perfectly with the murmuring guitars and the splashing of the imaginary fountains. It is a dissonant chord, if one considers the emotional significations, between the perceptions of the (unreal) fictional journey and those of (real) prosaic life, but the important thing is that the dissonance can *take place*, that is to say, that the two series of perceptions can vibrate here in the same way, in the same space; and if one wishes to consider only the intensity of its perceptible presence, this lamp sputtering in its bowl of oil would in no way mar the setting of Emma's reverie.

This excess of material presence in pictures that are in principle quite subjective, in which verisimilitude would on the contrary call for vague, diffuse, elusive evocations, is one of the most marked aspects of Flaubert's writing, and it is to be found in many another page of *Bovary* or *L'Éducation*. Here is one of Frédéric's memories, the paradoxical precision of which Flaubert stresses in advance and by that very fact excuses:

> The whole of his journey on the boat came back to his mind, so clearly that he could now remember fresh details, more intimate particulars: her foot, in a brown silk boot, peeping out under the lowest flounce of her dress, the drill awning forming a wide canopy over her head, and the little red tassels on the fringe trembling perpetually in the breeze.[6]

But here it is quite clear that the psychological motivation in no way diminishes, for the reader, the strangeness of such a picture—or rather the irrepressible feeling of objective reality that he experiences before a vision the purely subjective character of which the author has nevertheless been at pains to assert.

In the cinema, a memory sequence is never (unless artifices of writing, such as the dissolve, the speed up or the slow down, and so on, which have in any case been abandoned now, intervene and mark it with its heavy imprint) felt as such by the spectator during its entire duration: the idea that "the character is remembering" functions as a link with the preceding shots, the memory-sequence then being received as a flashback, without any diminution of the sense of reality, that is to say, as a simple manipulation of chronology, as when Balzac or Dumas tells us, "Some years previously, our hero, etc." This is because the unchallengeable presence of the image opposes any subjectifying interpretation: the tree that I see on the screen is a tree, it cannot be a memory—and still less a phantasy of a tree. Flaubert's style often seems as resistant to interiorization as the cinematographic image. More so, perhaps; for the cinema has only visual image and sound, but Flaubert's writing plays, across the screen of verbal representation, on all the sense-perceptible modes (tactile in particular) of material presence. This brown silk boot, these little red tassles trembling *perpetually* in the breeze—we may be forewarned and solicited by Flaubert, but we cannot, like Frédéric, receive them as facts of memory: they are real, present objects for the reader—and that is why this passage, in reading, does not act as a memory, but as a true flashback. Thus Emma's imaginary journeys are for us neither more nor less imaginary than her real life at Yonville l'Abbaye: Emma descends from her gondola or her hammock and finds herself in her room, where the lamp is sputtering out in its bowl of oil. And if that is possible, it is because Flaubert perceived, or imagined, both, in the same way and to the same degree; it is also, no doubt, because in a sense the gondola, the hammock, the room, the lamp, the bowl, Emma Bovary herself are, in the same way and to the same degree, merely words printed on paper.

But let us leave these evocations of memories or phantasies to consider a more ambiguous order of representation, in which the role of the character seems less important and, consequently, that of the author more so. Here are two brief descriptions that do not entirely belong either to the order of the subjective or to that of the objective, but rather to a sort of hypothetical objectivity. The first occurs in the Pommier-Leleu version of *Madame Bovary*. Emma is at the theater in Rouen with Charles. She has just sat down in her box and taken her place "with the assurance of a marquise, of a lady of the manor, as if she had had her carriage and horses awaiting her in the street and behind her a footman in a gold-laced coat carrying on his arm an ermine stole."[7] The evocation—brief, but here again surprisingly clear—of the marquise's accessories is introduced by a comparative-conditional locution that is frankly unreal in suggestion: *as if she had had;* but the footman with the gold-laced coat and the ermine stole appear with as much precision as if Emma's box had been occupied by a real marquise. Is the hypothesis in Emma's mind? No doubt; she is luxuriating in the pleasure and vanity of her first visit to the theater, and obviously she is playing the marquise; the details are involved with the idea that she has of the life of a lady of the manor. But it is quite clear that the evocation is not purely subjective: the *as if* stresses Emma's mimicry not without an ironic touch suggesting childish affectation, and the definitive version was to preserve this suggestion in a concentrated form: "Elle se cambra la taille avec une désinvolture de duchesse" (She drew herself up in her seat as if to the manner born).[8] Thus Flaubert is not entirely absent from this sentence, and the vision of the footman with the ermine stole is as much his as Emma's. In the other example the subjective motivation has become still more perceptibly weakened: during the celebrations at Rosanette's, a girl spits blood in front of Frédéric and, despite his entreaties, she refuses to go home to be looked after:

> "Oh, what's the use? If it wasn't this, it would be something else. Life isn't much fun."
> He shivered, seized with an icy melancholy, as if he had caught a glimpse of whole worlds of misery and despair, a charcoal stove beside a trestle-bed, and the corpses at the mortuary in their leather aprons, with the cold tap-water running over their hair.[9]

Again we find the *as if* that introduces a hypothetical vision, but this time nothing leads one to think that the term of comparison or the vision itself is to be found in the character's mind: *as if he had caught a glimpse,* but he probably sees nothing; it is Flaubert who compares his shiver with that of someone who has seen a charcoal stove beside a trestle-bed, corpses in their leather aprons, and that cold tap-water running—the present indicative (*qui coule*), in a sentence in the past conditional!—over their hair. This macabre close-up obviously belongs only to Flaubert. The impression of freezing poverty experienced by Frédéric has led him far from his hero, far from his novel, into a vision of the morgue, which, for a moment, is to absorb him entirely in a sort of horrified fascination, of morbid ecstasy; and the comparison here has no other effect—no other aim, perhaps—than to break and to *suspend* for that moment, the course of the narrative.

> Often, for a mere trifle, a drop of water, a shell, a hair, you have stopped in your tracks, motionless, your eye fixed, your heart open.

> The object that you contemplated seemed to encroach upon you, as you bent over it, and links were forged; you pressed against one another, you touched one another through innumerable, subtle adhesions. . . . You penetrated one another to an equal depth and a subtle current ran from you into matter, while the life of the elements slowly invaded you, like rising sap; a degree more and you became nature or nature became you.[10]

Thus speaks the Devil, addressing St. Anthony, in the Spinozist episode of the first version of the *La Tentation de Saint Antoine,* and the hermit recognizes at once the truth of this analysis: "It is true, often I have felt something larger than myself mingle with my being; little by little I would enter the verdure of the meadows and the current of the rivers that I watched pass me by; and I no longer knew where my soul was, it was so diffused, universal, expanded!"

All Flaubert specialists agree that this passage expresses something of Flaubert's own dispositions. He attributes to himself a "peculiar faculty of perception."[11] He experiences "almost voluptuous sensations gazing at nothing, but how well [he gazes]." To Louise Colet, he recommends a *deep view,* a *penetration of the objective,* "for external reality must enter into us, almost to the point of making us cry out . . . ," and in a sentence very close to that given to the Devil in *La Tentation,* he writes: "Sometimes by dint of looking at a pebble, an animal, a picture, I have felt myself enter into them. Communications between human beings are not more intense."[12] The youthful works provide abundant evidence of these moments of ecstasy experienced by Flaubert at the sight of nature and particularly of the sea in sunlight or moonlight. There is direct evidence in the *Voyage en Corse* of 1840:

> Everything inside you palpitates with joy and beats its wings with the elements, one clings to them, one breathes with them, the essence of animated nature seems to have passed into you in an exquisite Hymen;

and in *Par les champs et par les grèves:*

> Our minds wallowed in the profusion of these splendors, we feasted our eyes upon them, we parted our nostrils over them,

we opened our ears to them. . . . By penetrating into them, entering them, we also became nature, we became diffused in her, she took us again, we felt her invading us and a boundless joy swept through us; we would have liked to have lost ourselves in her, be taken by her or carry her off within us.[13]

There is transposed evidence in *Smarh*:

Everything that sang, flew, palpitated, radiated, the birds in the woods, the leaves trembling in the wind, the rivers flowing through the enamelled meadows, barren rocks, tempests, storms, foaming waves, embalming sand, autumn leaves falling, snow on graves, sunlight, moonlight, all songs, all voices, all scents, all the things that form the vast harmony one calls nature, poetry, God, resounded in his soul, vibrated in it in long interior songs that emerged in scattered words, torn from him,[14]

and in *Novembre*:

I longed to be absorbed into the sun's light and lose myself in that azure immensity along with the salt smell that rose from the crests of the waves. And then I was seized by a lunatic joy and began to walk as if all the joys of heaven had entered my soul. . . . I thought that Nature was as beautiful as some perfect harmony audible to ecstasy alone. . . . I felt that I was dwelling in it, happy and noble as the eagle that gazes on the sun and mounts his beams.[15]

Flaubert generally interprets this ecstatic contemplation, which sometimes assumes the form of extreme concentration ("By dint of gazing at a pebble . . . I have felt myself enter into them"), sometimes that of infinite expansion ("I no longer knew where my soul was, it was so diffused, universal, expanded!"), like the Devil in *La Tentation*, in a "pantheistic" sense, as the sign of universal harmony and interconnectedness: "Are we not made up of the emanations of the Universe? The light that shines in my eye might have been taken from the core of some still unknown planet."[16] But sometimes, rather like Proust, he sees it as the trace of a lost memory: "Anyone who looks at things with some attention *rediscovers* more than he finds. A thousand notions that one had within one in seed form, grow and become clearer, like a memory revived."[17] But what is one to say when this impression of reminiscence seizes you before some absolutely new sight, which brings you, according to the *Voyage en Corse*, something "like a memory of things I had not seen"?[18] Perhaps then the origin of this memory is to be found not in past experience, but in that silent reserve of experiences which cannot be situated and which make up one's dream past. "One dreams before contemplating," Bachelard was to say. "Before being a conscious spectacle, every landscape is a dream experience. One observes with esthetic passion only landscapes that one has first seen in dreams."[19] Flaubert was strongly aware that the real spectacle is preceded by the dream vision, and the journey to the East, for example, was for him often only a return to the places that he had long dreamt of during his adolescence, like the hero of *Novembre* or that of the first *Éducation sentimentale*. "It is often," he writes from Egypt to his mother, "as if I were suddenly rediscovering old forgotten dreams."[20] But many other places, on which this preliminary work of the imagination had not worked in so conscious a way, seem to have immediately assumed, in Flaubert's vision, a depth and a resonance that suggest a whole background of inner contemplation: one has only to consider, for example, the fantastic intensity he gives to the site of Quimperlé.[21] The whole town appears as if it were bathed, covered, seen transparently through the "smooth surface" of its two rivers, "where tall, slender grasses leaned above it in a mass." Flaubert did not forget these details; they are to be found again in *Madame Bovary*.[22]

The abundance of the descriptions does not correspond in Flaubert, then, as it does for example in Balzac, to needs of a dramatic kind, but primarily to what he himself calls "the love of contemplation."[23] One certainly finds in his *oeuvre* a number of descriptive tableaus, like that of Yonville at the beginning of the second part of *Madame Bovary*, the presence of which is justified by the need to give to the action and to the character's feelings a sort of explanatory framework: one has to know the setting of Yonville in order to understand what Emma's life in it is to be. But more often description is elaborated for its own sake, at the expense of the action, which it does not attempt to elucidate, it might be said, so much as to suspend or distance. *Salammbô* is the best known example of a narrative crushed as it were by the sumptuous proliferation of its own setting. But, simply because it is less overwhelming, this effect of immobilization is perhaps more noticeable in a work like *Bovary*, where a nevertheless very powerful dramatic tension is constantly thwarted by descriptive interruptions of admirable gratuitousness.

Maxime du Camp recounts how Louis Brouilhet (already responsible for the interment of the first *Tentation* in 1849) persuaded Flaubert to sacrifice "many parasitical sentences" and "hors d'oeuvre that slowed up the action";[24] he quotes the example of the toy given by Charles to the Homais children, the description of which took up, according to him, no less than ten pages. In the Pommier-Leleu version, it scarcely takes up a single page,[25] and it is difficult to see in what way the elimination of this satirico-picturesque piece, which Thibaudet (who had not read it) rightly compared with the descriptions of Charles' cap and the set-piece of the Bertaux's wedding, rendered Flaubert, as du Camp claims, an "inestimable service." It is true that what we have may be only an already reduced version of that "hors d'oeuvre," but how can one not regret those ten pages of which du Camp speaks, and which seem to have been necessary "to explain that complicated machine, which depicted, I think, the court of the king of Siam?" The docility with which Flaubert, while protesting, gave in to Brouilhet's censorship is rather odd, and the effects of that castrating influence are impossible for us today to estimate in full. At least a comparison of the versions of *Madame Bovary* enables us to imagine what that novel would have been if Flaubert had dared to abandon himself to his deeper tendencies. It would be tedious to list all the moments of ecstasy (in the double sense of contemplative delight and suspension of narrative movement) cut from the definitive edition, and which the publication of the sketchbooks has restored to us, but we should at least note a page with which Flaubert himself, unusually for him, had at first expressed his satisfaction. It was not unworthy of him. It occurs during the visit to the Château de la Vaubyessard, during the morning that follows the ball. Emma is walking in the park and enters a pavilion the window of which has glass of several different colors. She looks at the countryside through these panes of glass: the blue, then the green, then the red, then the white. These multicoloured landscapes give her in turn varying emotions, and finally plunge her into a deep reverie from which she is suddenly awoken by the passing of a flight of crows. Charles, meanwhile, was being shown round the tillage and learning about the income of the estate.[26] This last note integrates the episode into the novel as a whole by bringing out the opposition of the two characters; but here again the development goes beyond its diegetic function and blossoms for its own sake, in an immobile fascination to which Flaubert lends himself even more perhaps then his heroine. "Do you know how I spent the whole afternoon the day before yesterday? Looking at the countryside through panes of different colored glass; I needed it for a page of my *Bovary*. And it will not, I think, be one of the worst."[27]

One of the marks of these moments when the narrative seems to fall silent and become frozen under what Sartre was to call "the great petrifying gaze of things" is precisely the arrest of all conversation, the suspension of all human speech. I have already drawn attention to the phrase "they drove . . . *in silence*" in the passage from *Madame Bovary* quoted at the beginning of this study. Even such frivolous or crude individuals as Léon, Rodolphe, and Charles himself, abandon themselves to these magical silences. Here is a scene between Emma and Charles before their marriage:

> Having said goodbye, *they would speak no further*. . . . She turned back at the door and went to fetch her parasol. She opened it out; it was of shot silk, and the sun shining through it cast flickering lights over the white skin of her face. She smiled in the moist warmth beneath it, and they heard the drops of water dripping on to the taut silk one by one.[28]

Another, with Rodolphe, during one of their nights of love, in the moonlight:

> *They did not speak,* caught as they were in the rush of their reverie. . . . Now and again a ripe peach could be heard softly dropping from the tree.[29]

A third, at Rouen with Léon:

> They heard eight o'clock strike from the various clocks in the Beauvoisine quarter, which is full of boarding-schools, churches, and big derelict mansions. *They had stopped talking,* but as they looked at one another they felt a humming in their heads, as though some vibrant message had passed between their gazing eyes. They had joined hands; and past and future, memory and dream, all mingled together in the sweetness of their esctasy.[30]

And in *L'Éducation sentimentale*, between Louise and Frédéric:

> Then *there was a silence.* They could hear nothing but the crunch of the sand under their feet and the murmur of the weir.[31]

Between Frédéric and Rosanette:

> The solemnity of the forest took hold of them; *and there were hours of silence* when, abandoning themselves to the gentle rocking of the springs, they lay sunk in a calm intoxication.[32]

And again:

> They would lie face to face in the grass, gazing deep into each other's eyes, slaking the constant thirst they had for one another, and then *remaining silent* with half-closed eyelids.[33]

Moments which, as we see, are doubly silent: because the characters have stopped talking in order to listen to the world and to their dreams, and because this interruption of dialogue and action suspends the very speech of the novel and absorbs it, for a time, in a sort of unspoken interrogation. Proust placed above everything else, in *L'Éducation sentimentale* the "unprepared change of gear" that opens the penultimate chapter: not for the technique, but for the way in which Flaubert, unlike Balzac, frees these narrative means from their *active or documentary character,* "frees them from the parasitism of anecdotes and the dross of history. He is the first to set them to music."[34] Thus it is possible to prefer above everything else, not only in *L'Éducation sentimentale* but also in *Madame Bovary,* those musical moments when the narrative is lost and forgets itself in the ecstasy of an infinite contemplation.

The extratemporal character of such interruptions is frequently emphasised by a sudden transition to the present. We saw an example of this in Frédéric's macabre vision at Rosanette's. Proust cites another:

> It was a low-built, single-storied house, with a garden full of box-trees and a double avenue of chestnuts stretching up to the top of the hill, from which there was a view of the sea (d'où l'on découvre la mer).[35]

The present is obviously justified here, as Proust says, by the more "durable," and also more universal, character of the spectacle of the sea: the transition to the present is in some sense made necessary by the transition to the indefinite, as in this other passage from *L'Éducation sentimentale*:

> Then they crossed mountainous clearings. . . . (Rocks) became more and more numerous, finally filling up the whole landscape . . . like the monstrous, unrecognizable ruins of some vanished city. But the frenzied chaos in which they lay conjured up (*fait . . . rêver*) thoughts of volcanoes, floods, great unknown cataclysms.[36]

But it is quite clear that these grammatical justifications do not exhaust the effect of such changes of tense, which are also changes of register. A single word is enough to carry us from the space of the "action" (Mme Arnoux's retreat in Brittany, Frédéric and Rosanette's walk in the forest) to that of fascination or reverie. This microscopic effect, if examined closely, can be seen as alone capable, like a well-placed grain of sand, of stopping a whole fictional movement. To conclude, let us quote an example that occurs in chapter 1 of the third part of *Madame Bovary*, in the famous episode of the coach, one of the least defensible bravura pieces in the whole of realistic literature. The coach, occupied as we know by Emma and Léon, rushes through the city in every direction at top speed. In the midst of this "fury of locomotion," Flaubert has placed the following:

> Immediately it moved off again, past St. Sever, the Quai des Curandiers, the Quai aux Meules, back over the bridge, across the Drill Square and behind the workhouse gardens, where old men in black jackets *are to be seen strolling in the sunshine along the ivy-mantled terrace.* It drove along the Boulevard Bouvreuil.[37]

One wonders whether Emma or Léon, at this speed and in these circumstances, had the leisure to contemplate an "ivy-mantled terrace," and in any case the blinds were lowered. Their unfortunate coachman, overworked and dying of thirst, had other things to worry about. Thus, from the point of view of the rules of realistic narration, this description, however brief, but here again extended indefinitely by its verb in the present, is as little "in situation," as unjustified, dramatically and psychologically, as possible. This motionless close-up in the middle of a frantic drive is clumsiness itself. In reality, such an inadvertance could hardly mean more than this: this mobile love-making does not interest Flaubert very much, and suddenly, passing the hospital gardens, he thinks of something else. Memories of his childhood come back to him. He sees again "those old men in black jackets, swaying on their crutches, warming themselves in the sun, along a cracked terrace, built on the old city walls,"[38] and he could not help devoting a line or two to them. The rest could wait. For us—need it be said?—this second of inattention saves the whole scene, because in it we see the author forgetting the curve of his narrative and *going off on a tangent.*

Valéry found Flaubert (in *La Tentation de Saint Antoine*) "carried away by accessories at the expense of the main point."[39] If the "main point," in a novel, consists of the action, the characters, the psychology, the *mores*, the story, it is clear how this judgement can be applied to his novels, how his taste for detail, and not only for useful, significant detail, as with Balzac, but for gratuitous and insignificant detail, could compromise in his work the efficacy of the narrative. Roland Barthes observes that it requires only a few unmotivated descriptions to obliterate the whole signification of a novel like Robbe-Grillet's *Les Gommes:* "Every novel is an intelligible organism of an infinite sensibility: the least point of opacity, the least (mute) resistance to the desire which animates and sustains any reading, constitutes an *astonishment* which affects the entire work. Thus Robbe-Grillet's objects engage the anecdote itself, and the characters which the anecdote collects, in a kind of silence of signification."[40]

Although Flaubert's descriptive style, so profoundly substantial, steeped in radiating materiality, is as far as possible from Robbe-Grillet's, these remarks may be relevant to certain aspects of his work. There is that final sentence of *Hérodiade* ("Comme elle etait très lourde, ils la portaient alternativement") in which the whole story of the execution of St. John the Baptist dashes itself against that impenetrable adverb, so powerfully insignificant a phrase that it is enough to freeze the entire meaning of the narrative. Proust perceived very well this peculiar rhythm of Flaubert's diction, made heavier rather than lighter by his symmetrical cuts, that monotonous scansion, which, at each step, lets the sentence fall and fall again, with all its weight, on the consistent opacity of some useless, arbitrary, unexpected detail: "The Celts [missed] three rough stones, under a rainy sky, at the end of a gulf full of islets";[41] and he knew, admirably, how to recreate it in a few sentences of his pastiche, the finest, perhaps, that each of them ever wrote: or rather, in that exceptional encounter, the one *by* the other:

> They met one another with her, in the country, to the end of their days, in a wooden house painted entirely in white, on the sad edge of a broad river. They would have known the cry of the petrel, the rising of the fogs, the bobbing of the boats, the movement of the clouds and would have stayed for hours with her body on their knees, watching the tide rise and the moorings strike against one another, from their terrace, in a wicker chair, under a blue striped awning, between metal balls. And in the end all they could see were two clumps of violet flowers, descending to the rapid water, which they almost touched, in the harsh light of a sunless afternoon, along a reddish, crumbling wall.[42]

Valéry could not accept the element of the *incidental,* and therefore of the arbitrary, that there is in the sentence, "The marquise went out at five o'clock," and that is why the art of the novelist was for him "almost inconceivable." Flaubert, however, becomes absorbed (and with him, his novel) in the incidental. He forgets the marquise, her walk, her love affairs, and becomes fascinated by some material circumstance: a door, behind her, that bangs to and vibrates, *interminably.* And this vibration that is interposed between a network of signs and a universe of meaning unmakes a language and installs a silence.

This frustrated transcendence, this *escape* of meaning into the indefinite trembling of things, is what is most specific in Flaubert's writing, and it is perhaps this, after the verbose facility of his first works, that he had most difficulty in mastering. The *Correspondance* and the early works show this clearly enough: Flaubert was choking with things to say, enthusiasms, rancors, loves, hates, contempts, dreams, memories. . . . But, one day, as if that were not enough, he conceived the project of *saying nothing;* that refusal of expression inaugurates the modern literary experience. Jean Prévost saw in Flaubert's style "the strangest petrifying fountain of our literature"; Malraux speaks of his "fine paralyzed novels": these images express what remains the most striking effect of his writing and his vision. He did not write (and no one will write) the "book about nothing," the "book without subject," but he cast over all the subjects with which his genius abounded that heavy density of petrified language, that "moving sidewalk," as Proust calls it, made up of imperfects and adverbs that alone would *reduce them to silence.* His project—as he said more than once—was to die to the world in order to enter literature. But language itself becomes literature only at the price of its own death, since it has to lose its meaning in order to accede to the silence of the work. Flaubert was, of course, the first to undertake this turning round, this sending of discourse back to its silent underside, which is, for us, today, the very essence of literature—but this undertaking was, on his part, almost always unconscious or accompanied by shame. His literary consciousness was not and could not be at the level of his work and experience. The *Correspondance* is an irreplaceable document for the light it throws on one of the most acute cases of the *passion* for writing (in both senses of the word passion), on literature experienced both as a necessity and an impossibility, that is to say, as a sort of *forbidden vocation:* in this respect one can only compare it with Kafka's *Journal*. But Flaubert does not provide us with a true theory of his practice, the boldness of which he was unaware of. He himself found L'*Éducation sentimentale* an esthetic failure, on account of its lack of action, perspective, construction. He could not see that this book was the first to effect that *dedramatization*, one would almost like to say *denovelization*, of the novel with which the whole of modern literature seems to have begun,[43] or rather he felt as a defect what is for us his major quality. From *Bovary* to *Pécuchet*, Flaubert continued to write novels while *refusing*—without knowing it,[44] but with the whole of his being—the demands of fictional discourse. It is this refusal that is important to us, and the involuntary, almost imperceptible trace of boredom, indifference, lack of attention, forgetfulness, that he leaves over an *oeuvre* apparently aspiring to a useless perfection, and which remains for us admirably imperfect and as it were absent from itself.

[1965]

NOTES

1. *Madame Bovary*, in Gustave Flaubert, *Oeuvres complètes*, Collection "Intégrale," (Paris: Seuil, 1964), 1:640 (unless otherwise indicated the following notes will refer to this edition); *Madame Bovary*, Alan Russell, tr. (Harmondsworth: Penguin, 1950), p. 208.

2. Albert Thibaudet, *Gustave Flaubert* (Paris: Plon, 1922), p. 252. [The point about Flaubert's use of the imperfect is lost in the translation, which uses the English past simple. A closer rendering of the French verbs would have necessitated the use of the English imperfect "would" form, which the translator uses only once: "they *would* suddenly catch sight. . . ." However, the translator is surely right to avoid what would otherwise have proved to be clumsy and repetitious—TR.]

3. *Madame Bovary*, new version based on the Rouen manuscripts by Jean Pommier and Gabrielle Leleu (Paris: J. Corti, 1949), p. 431.

4. *Madame Bovary*, 1:646; *Mme B.*, p. 255. [Again, the translation weakens

Genette's point. In the original, the use of the verb *croire* (to think, to believe) in "croyant entendre" contrasts neatly with that of *être* (to be) in the earlier "elle était emportée"—TR.]

5. *L'Éducation sentimentale*, II:33; *Sentimental Education*, Robert Baldick, tr. (Harmondsworth: Penguin, 1964), p. 78.

6. *L'Éducation sentimentale*, II:11; *S.E.*, 22.

7. *Madame Bovary* (Pommier/Leleu version), p. 467.

8. *Madame Bovary*, I:649; *Mme B.*, p. 233. [It will be noted that Flaubert's attribution of rank (*duchesse*), actually a promotion from the earlier version (*marquise*), is sacrificed in the translation to fluency—TR.]

9. *L'Éducation sentimentale*, II:53; *S.E.*, pp. 130–31.

10. *La Tentation de Saint Antoine*, I:444.

11. *Correspondance*, (Paris: Conard, 1926–33), III:270.

12. *Extraits de la correspondance*, Geneviève Bollème, ed. (Paris: Seuil, 1963), pp. 33, 134, 121.

13. *Par les champs et par les grèves*, II:443, 502.

14. *Smarh*, I:215.

15. *Novembre*, I:256–57; *November*, Frank Jellinek, tr. (London: Michael Joseph, 1966), pp. 53–54.

16. *Extraits de la correspondance*, p. 121.

17. *Correspondance*, II:149.

18. *Voyage en Corse*, II:452.

19. Gaston Bachelard, *L'Eau et les rêves* (Paris: J. Corti, 1942), p. 6.

20. *Correspondance*, II:147.

21. *Par les champs et par les grèves*, II:507.

22. *Madame Bovary*, I:606; *Mme B.*, p. 107.

23. *Extraits de la correspondance*, p. 190.

24. *Souvenirs littéraires*, I:29.

25. *Madame Bovary* (Pommier/Leleu version), p. 458.

26. *Madame Bovary* (Pommier/Leleu version), pp. 215–17.

27. *Extraits de la correspondance*, p. 74.

28. *Madame Bovary*, I:580; *Mme B.*, p. 30.

29. *Madame Bovary*, I:641; *Mme B.*, p. 210.

30. *Madame Bovary*, I:654; *Mme B.*, p. 247.

31. *L'Éducation sentimentale*, II:99; *S.E.*, p. 249.

32. *L'Éducation sentimentale*, II:127; *S.E.*, p. 324.

33. *L'Éducation sentimentale*, II:127; *S.E.*, p. 325 (I have italicized the indications of silence).

34. Marcel Proust, *Chroniques* (Paris: Gallimard, 1927), pp. 205–206.

35. *L'Éducation sentimentale*, II:160; *S.E.*, p. 413. Quoted by Proust, *Chroniques*, p. 199.

36. *L'Éducation sentimentale*, II:127; *S.E.*, p. 323. [The translation evidently misses the feature that Genette points out—M.-R.L.]

37. *Madame Bovary*, 1:657; *Mme B.*, p. 256 (my italics).
38. Variant given by Pommier and Leleu, p. 499.
39. Paul Valéry, *Oeuvres*, Pléiade (Paris: Gallimard, 1957), 1:618; "The Temptation of (St.) Flaubert" in Valéry, *Masters and Friends*, Martin Turnell, tr. (Princeton: Princeton University Press, 1968), p. 229.
40. Roland Barthes, *Essais critiques* (Paris: Seuil, 1964), p. 200; *Critical Essays*, Richard Howard, tr. (Evanston, Ill: Northwestern University Press, 1972), p. 199. [Translation modified—M.-R.L.]
41. *Salammbô*, 1:763.
42. Marcel Proust, *Pastiches et Mélanges* (Paris: Gallimard, 1919), p. 22.
43. "In *L'Éducation sentimentale*, he had to show in advance what was only to exist much later, the unfictionalized novel, sad, vague, mysterious like life itself, content with dénouements that are all the more terrible in that they are not materially dramatic"—Banville, May 17, 1880, republished in *Critiques*, (Paris: Fasquelle, 1917).
"The finest things in his novel, what makes it unlike the usual fiction, are those great vacant spaces; not the events, which are contracted under Flaubert's hand, but what lies between the events, those stagnant expanses where all movement ceases. . . . Flaubert is the great novelist of inaction, of boredom, of immobility"—Jean Rousset, "Madame Bovary ou le Livre sur rien," *Forme et Signification* (Paris: J. Corti, 1962), p. 133.
44. Again he writes to Louise Colet, about the ball scene in *Madame Bovary:* "I had to write a narration; now narrative is something I find very tiresome" (*Extraits de la correspondance*, p. 72). A crucial aspect of literary modernity appears with this disgust with narrative. Flaubert is the first to challenge, in a profound, but quiet way, *narrative function*, hitherto regarded as essential to the novel. It is an almost imperceptible, but decisive jolt.

10

PROUST PALIMPSEST

In the Proustian theory of style, which to begin with is a theory of the Proustian style, there is a difficulty, perhaps an impossibility, the examination of which might throw light on all the other difficulties. This difficulty concerns the fundamental question, that of the role of metaphor.

For Proust, as we know, there is no "well wrought style" without metaphor, and "metaphor alone can give style a sort of eternity."[1] This is not, for him, a mere formal requirement, an esthetic point of honor, as it was for the practitioners of the "style artiste" and, more generally, for those naive dilettantes for whom "beauty of imagery" constitutes the supreme value of literary writing. According to Proust, style is "a question not of technique but of vision,"[2] and metaphor is the privileged expression of a profound vision: a vision that goes beyond appearances and penetrates to the "essence" of things. If he rejects "so-called realistic" art, the "literature of description," which "contents itself with 'describing things,' with giving of them merely a miserable abstract of lines and surfaces,"[3] it is because, for him, this kind of literature ignores true reality, which is to be found in essences:

He can describe a scene by describing one after another the innumerable objects which at a given moment were present at a particular place, but truth will be attained by him only when he takes two different objects, states the connection between them . . . and encloses them in the necessary links of a well wrought style; truth—and life too—can be attained by us only when, by comparing a quality common to two sensations, we succeed in abstracting their common essence and in reuniting them to each other, liberated from the contingencies of time, with a metaphor.[4]

Thus metaphor is not an ornament, but the necessary instrument for a recovery, through style, of the vision of essences, because it is the stylistic equivalent of the psychological experience of involuntary memory, which alone, by bringing together two sensations separated in time, is able to release their *common essence* through the *miracle of an analogy*—though metaphor has an added advantage over reminiscence, in that the latter is a fleeting contemplation of eternity, while the former enjoys the permanence of the work of art. "To this contemplation of the essence of things I had decided therefore that in future I must attach myself, so as somehow to immobilize it. But how, by what means, was I to do this?"[5] The answer comes, unequivocally, three pages later: "This method, this apparently sole method, what was it but the creation of a work of art?"[6]

At this point we should be clear as to what the nature of this vision of essences is and why it is so important to Proust. For him it is a crucial experience: the search for essences orients the development of his work as strongly as does the search for *lost time*;[7] in fact the search is only its means, and the world of essences is his true Lost Paradise: if the "true self" can only live "outside time," this is because eternity is the only "medium" in which it can "enjoy the essence of things."[8] There alone it finds "its sustenance and delight," it "is awakened and reanimated as it receives the celestial nourishment that is brought to it."[9] These terms, with their characteristically mystical overtones, are enough to show the importance of what is at issue; they also show under what species Proust represents the essence of things to himself: he takes delight in it, feeds on it, takes it into himself; it is not an abstraction, but a profound material, a substance. Deprived of this beneficent grounding in essences, abandoned to intermittency, to evanescence, things become arid and wilt, and—near them, but separated from them—the self languishes, loses its taste for the world, and forgets itself.

It was in this way, as substantial unities, that the young narrator imagines the cities, monuments, and landscapes that he would like to visit: the magic of their Names presents him with an *essentially different* image of each of them, "a confused picture, which draws from the names, from the brightness or darkness of their sound, the colour in which it is uniformly painted, like one of those posters, entirely blue or entirely red, in which . . . are blue or red not only the sky and the sea, but the ships and the church and the people in the streets."[10] Thus the whole of Parma was necessarily "compact and glossy, violet-tinted, soft," Florence "miraculously embalmed, and flower-like," and Balbec, like an "old piece of Norman pottery that keeps the colour of the earth from which it was fashioned." It is only later that contact with "reality" disintegrates these unique, simplified images, showing for example that Balbec-Ville and Balbec-Plage have no common substance and that the sea cannot "unleash itself at the foot of the church" because they were several kilometers apart, and teaching the Narrator that reality is always, inevitably, disappointing because "impressions such as those to which [he] wished to give permanence could not but vanish at the touch of a direct enjoyment which had been powerless to engender them."[11] From then on the narrator divorces himself from a reality that is unfaithful to its own essence, of which it offers only a pale, dull reflection like the shadows in Plato's Cave. From then on, too, "it was scarcely ever except in my dreams, while I was asleep, that a place could lie spread before me wrought in that pure matter which is entirely distinct from the matter of the common things that we see and touch but of which, when I had imagined these common things without ever having seen them they too had seemed to me to be composed."[12] The work projected as an artificial equivalent of the dream will, therefore, be an attempt to restore to objects, places, monuments their essence or lost substance: "I should have to execute the successive parts of my work in . . . a new and distinct material, of a transparency and a sonority that were special."[13]

This idea of a substance-style, restoring simply by virtue of its high degree of fusion the material unity of things, is one that Proust often expressed in almost identical terms. In a letter to Lucien Daudet, he speaks of those few marvelous sentences "in which the supreme miracle, the transubstantiation of the irrational qualities of matter and life into human words is achieved."[14] In *Contre Sainte-Beuve*, he says that he has found this quality in Flaubert:

"All the elements of reality are rendered down into one unanimous substance, with wide, unvaryingly polished surfaces. No flaw remains in it. It has been rubbed down to looking-glass smoothness. Everything is shown there, but only by reflection, without affecting its consistent substance. Everything at variance with it has been made over and absorbed."[15] In a letter to the Comtesse de Noailles he attributes the same merit to La Fontaine's fables and Molière's comedies, and this diversity of attribution shows that he was trying to define through the "great authors" an ideal of style that was his own: "a kind of cast, of transparent unity . . . without a single word that remains outside, that has remained resistant to this assimilation. . . . I suppose it is what is called the Varnish of the Masters."[16] This "varnish" is not a superficial glaze, but a diaphanous depth of color itself. It is the varnish of Vermeer, "the precious substance of the tiny patch of yellow wall," which the dying Bergotte contemplates, and which provides him with his last lesson in style: "'That is how I ought to have written,' he said. 'My last books are too dry, I ought to have gone over them with several coats of paint, made my language exquisite in itself.'"[17] Again the exquisite sentence, the well wrought style are not for Proust an ideal in themselves: but the sentence must be given a weight equal to that of the objects represented, a density in which can reside that "hidden essence" which eludes perception, but which one must feel in the transparent *"impasto* of the text."

But in what sense do these effects of *transubstantiation* require a recourse to metaphor? What could be less analogical, what could be more enclosed in immanence than the art of Vermeer, referred to here, or that of Chardin, the subject of a posthumous article, which have no other merit, it seems (but a crucial merit nonetheless) than to know how to make "beautiful to the eye" by making "beautiful to paint,"[18] those simple objects, those familiar scenes, "those peaceful moments when it is as if things are surrounded by the beauty that there is in being"?[19] And if one regards Flaubert's descriptive style (and this is apparently Proust's very thought) as the equivalent in literature of the still lifes of the great masters, what could be less metaphorical (in the Proustian sense) than a body of work which, Proust declares, perhaps does not contain "a single beautiful metaphor"?[20]

It would in fact seem that Proust's ideal of the "well-wrought style" contains something like two degrees, of which the "miracle" of the substantial style (despite the qualification "supreme" used in the letter to Lucien Daudet) is only the first, the second being that other miracle of which *Le Temps retrouvé* speaks, that of analogy. To the beauty which there is in being is added another, more mysterious, more transcendent beauty, the appearance of which is marked specifically in the passage from Chardin to Rembrandt: the former "has proclaimed the divine equality of all things under the light which beautifies them and to the mind which reflects on them. . . . With Rembrandt, even reality will be left behind. We shall learn that beauty does not lie in objects, since then it would certainly be not so unsearchable and so mysterious."[21] This passage from Chardin to Rembrandt, or perhaps from Chardin to Elstir (which Proust suggests when he says that "as Elstir had found with Chardin—you can make a new version of what you love only by first renouncing it,"[22] that is, by going beyond it), is also, of course, the passage from Flaubert to Proust himself. No doubt this new, secondary beauty, which is no longer simply a question of being, but of suggesting something other than what is, or of being both what is and something other, the paving stones of the Guermantes' courtyard and those of the baptistry of St. Mark's, is for Proust actually just an indirect but necessary way of reaching primary beauty (or truth, the two terms being for him equivalent), the beauty of being. The discovery of this inevitable diversion would then appear to merge into the fundamental experience of the inaccessibility of reality, of its evanescence in contact with direct enjoyment, of our powerlessness (revealed by the twin or synonymous disappointments in love and travel) "to realize ourselves in material enjoyment or in effective action,"[23] and the necessity, if we are to attain reality in its essence, of abandoning the direct use of our senses and of borrowing the link provided by imagination, "which was the only organ that I possessed for the enjoyment of beauty."[24] The passage from the ontological to the analogical, from the substantial style to the metaphorical style, would appear to mark therefore a progress not so much in the quality of esthetic achievement as in the awareness of the difficulties, or at least of the conditions, or such an achievement. So the success of Chardin or Flaubert (in attaining the essence through a perception or a direct representation) no longer seems to be inferior to that of Elstir or Proust, but rather to be too *miraculous*, too easy not to be improbable, illusory, or at the very least inaccessible to Proust by virtue of some weakness peculiar to himself. Metaphor, then, like reminiscence, would seem to be merely an indispensable expedient.

Whether expedient or supreme miracle, the use of metaphor is nevertheless given a profound justification by Proust. But it is precisely in this justification that the difficulty resides. How, in fact, can we say that a metaphor, that is to say, a displacement, a transfer of sensations from one object to another, can lead us to the essence of this object? How can we admit that the "profound truth" of a thing, that particular, "distinct" truth sought by Proust, can be revealed in a figure that brings out its properties only by transposing them, that is to say, by making them strange? What reminiscence reveals is a "common essence" of the sensations and, through them, of the objects that awaken them in us; it is the writer's task to "present the relationship" between these objects in a metaphor. But what is a *common* essence, if not an abstraction—that is to say, what Proust wants to avoid at all costs—and how can a description based on the "relationship" between two objects avoid destroying the essence of each? If in every metaphor there is the simultaneous operation of both a resemblance and a difference, an attempt at "assimilation" and a resistance to this assimilation, without which there would be a sterile tautology, is not the essence to be found more on the side that differs and resists, on the irreducible and *refractory* side of things?[25]

This is certainly what Proust himself shows, perhaps without intending to, in the passage from *La Fugitive* where he compares Venice and Combray, and where the particular essence of Venice is revealed, precisely through the opposition that it manifests within resemblance itself: "I was receiving there impressions analogous to those which I had felt so often in the past at Combray, but transposed into a wholly different and far richer key."[26] As at Combray, the windows of his room open on to a church tower, but instead of the slates of Saint-Hilaire, it is the golden angel of the campanile of St. Mark's. As at Combray on Sunday morning, the streets are in holiday mood, but these streets are canals. As at Combray, there are rows of houses, but these houses are Gothic or Renaissance palaces, etc. Venice is another Combray, but a Combray that is quite *other*: aquatic, precious, exotic, and it is this difference, of course, that is essential to him.

It is true that the "relationship" considered by Proust in Le Temps retrouvé is the analogy between a present sensation and a past sensation and that the abstraction effected here consists in the effacement of the temporal distances necessary to the blossoming of a "minute freed from the order of time." The present object, then, is merely a pretext, an occasion: it vanishes as soon as it has fulfilled its mnemonic function. Moreover it is not a question here of metaphor in the true sense, since one of the terms would appear to be purely incidental. The "common essence" is reduced in fact to the earlier sensation of which the later one is merely the vehicle: "a profound azure intoxicated my eyes, impressions of coolness, of dazzling light, swirled round me."[27] This takes place "in" the Guermantes' courtyard, but the Guermantes' courtyard has totally disappeared, just as the present madeleine disappears, effaced by the memory of the past madeleine with, around it, the houses and gardens of Combray.

But very often Proust lingers over purely spatial transpositions that involve no "freeing from the order of time," and which, in fact, have nothing in common with the phenomenon of reminiscence. It is these transpositions that are the Proustian metaphors in the true sense: the Paris Opéra transformed into an underwater crypt during a gala performance given by the Princesse de Parme, the sea turned into a mountainous landscape on waking that first morning at Balbec. The latter provides a particularly characteristic version of Proustian metaphor. The key to it is to be found later when, analyzing Elstir's art in his picture of the harbor of Carquethuit, Proust observes that by "a sort of metamorphosis of the things represented in it, analogous to what in poetry we call metaphor," the painter had employed "for the little town, only marine terms, and urban terms for the sea."[28] Similarly, when describing the sea seen from his window at the Grand Hôtel, Marcel uses only what might be called Alpine terms: "vast amphitheatre, dazzling, mountainous;" "snowy crests"; "steep fronts"; "mountain-chains"; "glaciers"; "hills"; "undulations" (*vallonnements*); "pastures"; "craggy sides"; "peaks"; "crests"; "avalanches."[29] What we have here is an implicit, developed comparison, "tacitly and untiringly repeated,"[30] the landscape referred to never being directly named, but constantly suggested by a vocabulary the allusive value of which is obvious. But we do not see that this dazzling counterpoint of sea and mountain leads us to the "essence" of either. We are presented with a paradoxical landscape in which mountain and sea have exchanged their qualities and, as it were, their substances, in which the mountain has become sea and the sea mountain, and nothing is further removed from this sort of vertigo than the feeling of stable assurance that the true vision of essences ought to inspire in us. Similarly, in Elstir's picture, the terrestrial parts seem more marine than the marine parts, and the marine more terrestrial than the terrestrial, and each of the elements resembles the other more than it resembles itself. The sailors in their boats seem to be perched on jaunting-cars, "racing over sunlit fields into shadowy places, dashing down into the troughs of waves"; the women among the rocks, on the other hand, had the appearance "of being in a marine grotto overhung by ships and waves, open yet unharmed in the path of a miraculously averted tide."[31] A little later Proust adds this revealing comment:

At one time [Elstir] had painted what were almost mirages, in which a castle crowned with a tower appeared as a perfect circle of castle prolonged by a tower at its summit, and at its foot by an inverted tower, whether because the exceptional purity of the atmosphere on a fine day gave the shadow reflected in the water the hardness and the brightness of the stone, or because the morning mists rendered the stone as vaporous as the shadow.[32]

Thus, in his seascapes of Carquethuit, the "reflexions had almost more solidity and reality than the floating hulls, vaporized by an effect of the sunlight." Mirages, misleading perspectives, reflections more solid than the objects reflected, a systematic inversion of space: we are very close to the usual themes of Baroque description, which cultivates through them a whole esthetic of paradox—but by the same token we are very far from the essentialist intentions of the Proustian esthetic. No doubt this is an extreme case and, anyway, it might be objected that Proust's art is not necessarily a replica of Elstir's art. But Proust himself answers this objection by invoking "illusions" of the same order, and declaring: "The rare moments in which we see nature as she is, with poetic vision, it was from those that Elstir's work was taken"—and this is a perfect formulation of the Proustian enterprise. We have to admit, then, that Elstir's style corresponds faithfully to Proust's idea of his own style and, consequently, of his own vision.

In fact, the most characteristic feature of Proustian representation is no doubt, together with the intensity of their material presence, that superimposition of objects perceived simultaneously which has been called "surimpressionism."[33] We know of the fascination exercised over Marcel by the effect of "transverberation" that was produced by the magic lantern at Combray,[34] projecting its immaterial, yet visible images over the various objects of his bedroom: Golo's red cloak and pale face molding themselves over the folds of the curtain, over the swelling surface of the door-handle, two spaces, the real and the fictional, combining without merging. In the room of the Grand Hôtel at Balbec, it is not a projection, but a reflection throwing across the glass doors of the low bookcases "a frieze of sea-scapes, interrupted only by the polished mahogany of the actual shelves":[35] the natural landscape thus takes on, through the artifice of a particularly unexpected *mise-en-scène*, the appearance of a work of art: reality becomes the object of its own representation. These sophisticated spectacles are a typical expression of Proust's taste for indirect vision, or rather of his marked incapacity for direct vision. Was not nature herself, he writes, "a beginning of art, she who, often, had allowed me to become aware of the beauty of one thing only in another thing, of the beauty, for instance, of noon at Combray in the sound of its bells, of that of the mornings at Doncières in the hiccups of our central heating?"[36]

But this indirect perception is necessarily a multilated perception, so that it is often impossible to discern whether it results from an unfortunate evanescence (reality lost), or from a beneficent reduction of the essential (reality regained): for it obliterates not only the object perceived through transparency—Combray transposed into the sound of its bells, Doncières filtered through the hiccups of the central heating—it alters even more the object on which it imposes the transitory role, and as it were the transitive state of a mere signal. This sound of bells apparently swollen with a presence that goes beyond it and enriches it can be opened up to this new meaning only by impoverishing itself in another respect, only by exhausting itself, almost to the point of disappearing as a perceptible event. One cannot at one and the same time hear the village in the sound of its bells and hear the sound of the bells in its sonorous plenitude; one can only gain one by losing the other. Proust knows this better than anyone: he himself writes, concerning the "text" from the Goncourts' *Journal* that has just revealed to him in the Verdurin drawing-room realities of which he was previously unaware: "The apparent, copiable charm of things and people escaped me, because I had not the ability to stop short there—I was like a surgeon who beneath the smooth surface of a woman's belly sees the internal disease which is devouring it. If I went to a dinner-party I did not see the guests: when I thought I was looking at them, I was in fact examining them with X-rays."[37] The superimposition results here from an excess of penetration on the part of the gaze, which is unable to stop at appearances and perceives "in the middle distance, behind actual appearances, in a plane that was rather more withdrawn." At the same time, it is received rather favorably: through the different states of the Verdurin drawing-room, it makes it possible to uncover its identity "in various places and at various times." On other occasions a phenomenon of the same order is experienced as a painful servitude: "If we seek to portray what is relatively unchanging in [a character], we see it present in succession different aspects (implying that it cannot remain still but keeps moving) to the disconcerted artist."[38] Time metamorphoses not only characters, then, but faces, bodies, even places, and its effects are sedimented in space (what Proust calls "Temps incorporé," or "integral time")[39] to form a blurred image the lines of which overlap in a sometimes illegible, almost always equivocal palimpsest, like Gilberte's signature, which Marcel is to take for Albertine's, like the face of Odette de Forcheville, which contains in suspension the memory of the Lady in Pink, Elstir's portrait of Miss Sacripant, the triumphant photographs of Madame Swann, the "quite simple little old daguerreotype" kept by her husband, and many other successive "proofs," plus an obscure resemblance to Botticelli's Zephora.

This palimpsest of time and space, these discordant views, ceaselessly contradicted and ceaselessly brought together by an untiring movement of painful dissociation and impossible synthesis—this, no doubt, is the Proustian vision. In the train taking him to Balbec for the first time, Marcel sees through the window a ravishing sunrise: over a small black wood, "some ragged clouds whose fleecy edges were of a fixed, dead pink, not liable to change, like the colour that dyes the wing which has grown to wear it, or the sketch upon which the artist's fancy has washed it." But the course of the line alters and the landscape presents to the eye its nocturnal face: "a nocturnal village, its roofs still blue with moonlight, its pond encrusted with the opalescent nacre of night, beneath a firmament still powdered with all its stars."[40] Each of these pictures summarizes and concentrates a page of Flaubert or Chateaubriand at their most substantial, most intensely penetrated by the freshness and plenitude of reality; but instead of exalting one another they combat one another in painful alternation: with Proust, two euphoric visions can come together to form a tormented vision: "so that I spent my time running from one window to the other to reassemble, to collect on a single canvas the intermittent, antipodean fragments of my fine, scarlet, ever-changing morning, and to obtain a comprehensive view of it and a continuous picture." If the movement that presents them successively accelerates, the compensatory movement "from one window to the other" will no longer be possible: one will have to submit first to intermittence, then to confusion, and finally to the mutual effacement of the two pictures. But is not this precisely what occurs in Elstir's "mirages" and in Proust's metaphors?

Thus, between its conscious intentions and its real execution, Proust's writing falls prey to a singular reversal: having set out to locate essences, it ends up constituting, or reconstituting, mirages; intended to reach, through the substantial depth of the text, the profound substance of things, it culminates in an effect of phantasmagoric superimposition in which the depths cancel each other out, and the substances devour one another. It certainly goes beyond the "superficial" level of a description of appearances, but it does not reach that of a higher realism (the realism of essences), since on the contrary it discovers a level of the real in which reality, by virtue of its plenitude, annihilates *itself*.

This destructive movement, which ceaselessly involves a sensible presence in equivocation and dispute (of which each moment, taken by itself, seems unalterable) this movement so characteristic of Proust's writing, is obviously the actual method of the *Recherche du temps perdu*. Just as each fragment of his "versatile" landscapes might be one of Chateaubriand's descriptions, except that the whole forms a "disconcerted" vision that belongs only to him, so each appearance of his characters, each "state" of his society, each episode of his narrative could provide material for a page of Balzac or La Bruyère, were it not that all these traditional elements are swept away by an irresistible force of erosion. It might be said of Proust what was said of Courbet,[41] that his vision is more modern than his theory; it might also be said that the work as a whole is more Proustian than each of its details.

At first sight the characters of the *Recherche* scarcely differ either in their physical appearance or in their social and psychological characteristics from the characters of the traditional novel: at most one might detect, in the depiction of a Bloch, a Legrandin, a Cottard, the Guermantes or the Verdurins, certain rather over-stressed features, certain elements of pastiche bordering on parody, which might push the portrait over into caricature and the novel into satire. But such a tendency is not contrary to the traditions of the novel; it represents rather a permanent temptation of the genre, perhaps a condition of its exercise: it is the price that has to be paid if a character is to escape the inconsistency of life and attain a fictional existence, which is a hyper-existence.

But for the Proustian character this state is merely an initial one, which is soon contradicted by a second, a third, sometimes by a whole series of versions, all equally exaggerated, which are superimposed on each other to form a figure on several planes the eventual incoherence of which is merely a sum of partial excessive coherences;[42] thus there are several Saint-Loups, several Rachels, several Albertines, all incompatible and mutually destructive. "Albertine's face" is a striking illustration of this: just as the narrator, during his first stay at Balbec, discovers in turn a young-urchin-Albertine, a naive-schoolgirl-Albertine, a young-lady-of-good-family-Albertine, a perverse-innocent-Albertine, so Albertine's face alters from one day to the next, not only in its expression, but also in its very form and material:

> On certain days, slim, with grey cheeks, a sullen air, a violet transparency falling obliquely from her. . . . On other days her face, more sleek, caught and glued my desires to its varnished surface . . . sometimes, instinctively, when one looked at her face punctuated with tiny brown marks among which floated what were simply two large, bluer stains, it was like looking at the egg of a goldfinch—or often like an opalescent agate.[43]

As one looks at it, each successive "face" is richly endowed with the attributes of material existence: a matte or glossy surface, a violet transparency, a pink glaze, blue stains, but the total effect, as in the picture of Balzac's *Chef-d'oeuvre inconnu*, of which this page, and several others, seem to be intended as a kind of literary reply, is not a transparent depth, but an overloading, a textual plethora in which the face becomes bogged down, engulfed, and finally disappears. This is more or less the experience of the Narrator in the celebrated description of kissing Albertine:

> In this brief passage of my lips towards her cheek it was ten Albertines that I saw; this single girl being like a goddess with several heads, that which I had last seen, if I tried to approach it, gave place to another. . . . Suddenly my eyes ceased to see; next, my nose, crushed by the collision, no longer perceived any fragrance, and . . . I learned, from these unpleasant signs, that at last I was in the act of kissing Albertine's cheek.[44]

With the exception of the Narrator's own family, which embodies, among other values, a sort of nostalgia for stability, almost all the characters of the *Recherche* are just as protean, and the reader might say of them what Marcel, some days after their first meeting, thinks of Saint-Loup: "I was taken in by a mirage; but I have corrected the first only to fall into a second."[45] It is the effects of Time, of course, that change the proud Charlus into a pitiful wreck, the grotesque Biche into the celebrated Elstir, Madame Verdurin into the Princesse de Guermantes, and which lead Odette from the *demi-monde* to the *grand monde*, or Rachel from the brothel to the Faubourg Saint-Germain. But time is not the only, or even the principal worker of the Proustian metamorphoses; often it merely reveals after the event sudden changes for which it is not itself responsible: certainly we see Swann gradually detach himself from his love for Odette, but what progress, what duration can explain their subsequent marriage? As Georges Poulet has shown,[46] Proustian time is not a flow, like Bergson's duration, but a succession of isolated moments; similarly, the characters (and groups) do not evolve: one fine day, they find that they have changed, as if time confined itself to bringing forth a plurality that they contained *in potentia* from all eternity. Indeed, many of the characters assume the most contradictory roles *simultaneously*: Vinteuil, the ridiculous neighbor and the famous composer: Saint-Loup, Rachel's passionate lover and Morel's admirer; Charlus, prince of the Faubourg Saint-Germain and Jupien's accomplice; Swann, the intimate of the Prince of Wales and the butt of Madame Verdurin's jokes. All simulate and dissimulate, lie or lie to themselves, all have a secret life, a vice, a passion, a virtue, a hidden genius, all are Dr. Jekyll and Mr. Hyde, lending themselves from one day to the next to the most spectacular revelations. Certain historical events (the Dreyfus affair, the War), certain social facts (Sodom and Gomorrha) seem to take place only to provide further surprises: this ladies' man cared only for waiters, this violent anti-Semite was a Dreyfusard, this hero was a coward, this man was a woman, etc. The caprices of heredity, the confusion of memory, secret influences effect mysterious transformations: the elderly Bloch becomes Monsieur Bloch *père*, a dulled Gilberte becomes Odette, Gilberte and Albertine, Swann and Marcel are "telescoped," and in the midst of the universal movement even certain stabilities become paradoxical: thus Odette, incomprehensibly intact among a hundred unrecognizable old people, represents, at the last of the Guermantes' afternoon parties, the strangest anachronism.

Just as individuals are unaware of duration, society is unaware of history, but each event determines a massive and almost instantaneous modification of what Proust calls, very revealingly, the *social kaleidoscope*.[47] In Proust one does not find those slow upsurges that manifest, in the work of Balzac or Zola, the progressive renewal of the "social body," the rise of "new strata," that subterranean but irresistible movement which Zola compares to that of germination. Moreover, we know that Proust represents not society, in the broad sense, but Society, in the narrow sense (the *Monde*, or rather *Mondanité*, which is embodied in several *Mondes*: aristocracy, bourgeois bohemia, the provinces, domesticity), that is to say, the formal side of society, which is governed not by the social laws dear to the nineteenth century, but by those *decrees* of Opinion of which Oriane's caprices, Aunt Léonie's gossip, Françoise's fads, the vetoes of Madame Verdurin or the "Marquise" des Champs-Elysées represent the most characteristic forms. The succession of these decrees does not proceed from history, that is to say, from a meaningful evolution. It is based above all on Fashion, the only fixed value of which is, at each stage, a radical novelty with no memory: "Oriane's latest" effaces the last but one, and all the preceding ones; hence that feverish haste to get to the news, to keep "up to date." For this tradition provides a whole range of attitudes and feelings of which only the object is renewed, since snobbery, a recurrent form, is indifferent to its content. Similarly, the Dreyfus Affair or the War structure and restructure Society around new values (anti-Semitism, Germanophobia), the rearrangement of which is enough to hoist some petty-bourgeois woman suddenly to the top, or to hurl some Highness down to the bottom of a hierarchy that is preserved only by constantly overthrowing its criteria: a rigid but unstable protocol, a closed world compensating and preserving its enclosure by ceaseless permutation, Proust's society is confirmed in a perpetual denial.

The very movement of the work seems to oppose the security of the fictional material with a sort of obscure, negative will. Certainly Proust is neither Joyce nor even Woolf, and his narrative technique is in no sense revolutionary. In detail, his masters seem to be the great traditional writers he himself quotes, Balzac, Dostoevsky, George Eliot, Dickens, or Hardy, to which are added a few models that might be termed pre-fictional: Sévigné and Saint-Simon in narration, Chateaubriand and Ruskin in description, Ruskin again and perhaps Bergson in the essay, not to mention the contribution of the minor genres that Proust had himself practiced at the outset of his literary career, such as the society columns of *Le Figaro*, nearly all of which are to be found, almost intact, in his work. Thus the *Recherche du temps perdu* might be seen as an agreeable succession of scenes, tableaus, portraits, digressions of all kinds, skillfully linked together by the unsurprising thread of a *"roman de formation,"* or *Bildungsroman*: childhood loves, entry into Society, first love affair, literary discoveries, and so on—the novel departing from its own tradition only to the benefit of even more traditional genres. But this is only a first impression, one that can be sustained only by the most selective kind of reading of the *Recherche*—a reading obviously contrary to the wishes of the author, who constantly claimed for his work the benefit of patience, attention, the ability to perceive distant relationships ("My work is not microscopic, it is telescopic,")[48] in fact, a structuring reading.

Now the paradox of this work is that its structure devours its substance. We know that what Proust admired more than anything else in *L'Education sentimentale* was that "hole" of several years which follows the days of June 1848. Lacunae of this kind, like the indeterminate time that separates the chapters on the War from the last afternoon party given by the Guermantes, and other less visible ones in which chronology is lost, and with it the material of the narrative, occur constantly in his work. We have seen what a gap is introduced between *Un amour de Swann* and the resurgence of the character as Odette's husband; later, Swann is to die as he married, by ellipsis. The second event is more expected than the first, it is even prepared for at length, only to vanish the more completely—in actual fact, Swann does not *die*, he has no right to a true death, as does Bergotte or the Narrator's grandmother; he disappears between two pages: he fades away (his necrology is to be retrospective). Saniette, on the other hand, dies twice. Albertine revives (but it is a mistake). The age of the Narrator and that of the other characters are often inconsistent with one another, as if time did not pass for all of them at the same speed, and one sometimes has the sense of an inexplicable overlap of generations. The material incompleteness of the *Recherche* is doubtless responsible for some of these effects, but it merely accentuates a tendency that is already there: the contradictions of the manuscript can be interpreted not as insignificant oversights, but on the contrary as *parapraxes* in the Freudian sense, all the more revealing in that they are involuntary.

Marcel's childhood is not quite an origin, since it is, essentially, resuscitated by the little madeleine, and it is more a dreamed childhood than a real childhood: "chronologically" anterior to the revelation of *Le Temps retrouvé*, it is psychologically posterior to it, and this ambiguity of situation cannot but alter it. The childhood loves are not quite an initiation, since Swann's love affair has already more than outlined their course. Marcel is later to say that it is difficult for him to distinguish between his own experiences and those of Swann: just as the phrase heard by Swann in Vinteuil's sonata is recognized by Marcel in the septet, the feelings, memories, and even things forgotten slip from one character to another, and these transfers disturb the time of the work by introducing into it an incipient repetition.

The spatial framework is hardly more stable than the temporal dimension: the settings of the *Recherche* are apparently well isolated, by their substantial individuality even more than by their distance;[49] between Balbec, bathed in its marine atmosphere, impregnated with salt and foam, and Combray, with its confined, old-world atmosphere, where the sweet scent of home-made preserves hangs in the air, no relationship seems possible; no journey ought to be able to link such heterogeneous materials: Marcel is amazed at the idea that a train can take him in one night from Paris to Balbec or from Florence to Venice. Yet, even without recourse to this mechanical expedient, the Proustian narrative passes effortlessly, and as if without perceptible movement, from one place to another: this is the privilege of memory or of day-dreaming, but it is also, above all, the sovereign ubiquity of the narrative, by which places are dematerialized and slide over one another. All novels, of course, move their action from one setting to another in this way; but generally these settings are neutral, they remain in their place and do not adhere to the narrative. With Proust, on the other hand, places are active, they become attached to the characters,[50] penetrate the texture of the novel, which they follow from page to page, ceaselessly recalled, reintegrated, reinvested, always present all at once (a reading of the entries under Balbec, Combray, or Venice in the index of the Pléiade edition is instructive in this regard) and therefore made absent by their very omnipresence: having emerged from a cup of tea, Combray finds itself enclosed in a Paris bedroom, Oriane carries with her, in the midst of the Faubourg Saint-Germain, the landscape of Guermantes with the Vivonne and its water-lilies, just as Albertine takes with her Balbec, with its jetty and its beach. The "two ways" of Combray, the opposition and incommunicability of which, "one of those distances of the mind which time serves only to lengthen, which separate things irremediably from one another, keeping them for ever upon different planes,"[51] were the very foundation of Marcel's view of the world (and of the construction of the work), are revealed in the opening pages of *Le Temps retrouvé* to be singularly close and in no way irreconcilable, and are symbolically joined together in the person of Mademoiselle de Saint-Loup, daughter of a Swann and a Guermantes. Thus the reader undergoes in the time and space of the work the motionless journey of the sleeper mentioned in the first pages of *Du Côté de chez Swann*: "The magic chair will carry him at full speed through time and space, and when he opens his eyes again he will imagine that he went to sleep months earlier and in some far distant country."[52] And in the end it is the entire material of the novel, all its characters and events, that come together, in the mind of the reader as well as in that of Marcel observing Mademoiselle de Saint-Loup, "interlacing their threads" in a single point—manifesting by their inconceivable encounter the unreality of their hitherto separated existences.

There is also, at the heart of the work, another place where its impossibility is in some sense concentrated: this is the pastiche of the Goncourts. That the Narrator, opening the Goncourts' journal, should find there an account of a dinner at the Verdurins', that the Verdurins, and Elstir, and Cottard, and Brichot, and consequently, by degrees, all the characters and the Narrator himself should thus escape from the fiction and slide into the gossip column, this is no doubt a plausible adventure at the level of the fiction, since this fiction offers itself as a gossip column and its characters as real persons whom the Goncourts might have met, but it is impossible at the level of the work as it exists for a reader, who knows very well that he must regard it as a pure fiction, from which its characters can no more emerge than the brothers Goncourt, or he himself, can enter it. Yet this is precisely what is persistently suggested by this strange episode, which serves as a door in the work, leading to something other than the work, something that it cannot know without destroying itself, a door that is there and which nevertheless can be neither opened nor closed.

Maurice Blanchot, considering the relations between *Jean Santeuil* and the *Recherche du temps perdu*,[53] observes that, by the involuntary trick of an apparently inexplicable postponement, which no doubt corresponded to the profound necessity of his work, Proust gradually moved away from his initial purpose, which was to write a "novel of poetic moments" (the privileged moments of reminiscence): these moments declined into scenes, the appearances into portraits and descriptions, thus diverting the execution of the whole from the poetic to the fictional; but he also shows that this "fictionality" is in turn diverted towards something else, insofar as the work turns around, folds back upon itself, taking up all its eposides in "a slow, relentless movement," in "the moving density of spherical time." Here indeed is the most disturbing paradox of the *Recherche*: it is offered simultaneously as a work and as an approach to the work, as fulfillment and as genesis, as search for lost time and as an offering of time regained. This ambivalence gives it the openness, the critical dimension, which Proust saw as the essential mark of the great works of the nineteenth century (and which is even more so of those of the twentieth), works that are still "marvelously incomplete," in which the writers, "watching themselves at work as though they were at once author and critic, have derived from this self-contemplation a novel beauty, exterior and superior to the work itself";[54] such an ambivalence also gives the work a double time and a double space, a "double life" like that of its heroes, a double foundation, or rather, the absence of a foundation, through which the work is constantly seeping away, escaping from itself. "We never know," says Blanchot, "to what time the event described belongs, whether it is taking place only in the world of the narrative, or whether it is taking place to facilitate the arrival of the moment in the narrative from which what has taken place becomes reality and truth." In fact each moment of the work appears in a sense twice over: first in the *Recherche* as the birth of a vocation and second in the *Recherche* as the exercise of this vocation; but these two occasions are not given together, and it is the lot of the reader—informed *in extremis* that the book which he has just read remains to be written and that this book that is to be written is more or less (but only more or less) the one which he has just read—to go back to those distant pages, to the childhood at Combray, the evening at the Guermantes, the death of Albertine, which he had first read as safely deposited, gloriously embalmed in a finished work, and which he must now read again, almost identical but a little different, as if in abeyance, still unburied, stretching anxiously towards an as yet unwritten work; and conversely, forever. Thus, not only is the *Recherche du temps perdu*, as Blanchot says, a "completed-uncompleted" work, but its very reading is completed in incompletion, forever in suspense, forever "to be taken up again," since the object of that reading is constantly thrown into a dizzy rotation. "The literary object is a peculiar top which exists only in movement," writes Sartre.[55] This is particularly true of Proust's work, which is more unstable, more *mobile* than those of Calder, since a single glance is enough to set off a circulation that nothing can then stop.

A reading of *Jean Santeuil* or *Contre Sainte-Beuve* can only enhance this sense of dizziness. In these "works," which are, like the earlier texts collected in *Mélanges* or *Chroniques*, no more than sketches for the *Recherche du temps perdu*, we witness the appearance of a whole series of first drafts of certain episodes, settings, themes, or characters of the "definitive" work. To the multiple images of the Baron de Charlus is added the figure of the Marquis de Quercy, who, in *Contre Sainte-Beuve*, is obviously a first sketch of him, just as Bertrand de Réveillon in *Jean Santeuil* foreshadows Robert de Saint-Loup, or Marie Kossichef, Gilberte Swann. At first Bergotte was the name of a painter. To our surprise, we find Albertine's kiss on the lips of Oriane. Charlus is strangely enriched for having first been merged with Monsieur de Norpois. Between Illiers and Combray, in a strange intermediary zone that does not yet belong to the work, but no longer quite belongs to life, is interposed the Etreuilles of *Jean Santeuil*. In the same way Ernestine is placed between Félicie and Françoise, and Jean himself between Proust and Marcel—but also between Proust and Swann, for if Jean Santeuil is a sketch of the Narrator, his composite love affairs prefigure several others: Marie Kossichef at the Champs-Elysées is Gilberte, Charlotte Clissette refusing a kiss is Albertine; but the scene of the lighted window, with Madame S., the sonata by Saint-Saëns, with Françoise, already suggest Odette.

A rather disturbing perspective is thus set up between life and the work, which gives an unusual piquancy to the search for "sources" and "models." Albert Le Cuziat seems to have had something of Albertine and much of Jupien. Madame de Chevigné had the face and the voice of Oriane, Madame Strauss her wit; Charles Haas, Swann's red moustache, Charles Ephrussi, his culture. Balbec is Trouville, Dieppe, Cabourg, Évian. The garden at Combray is the garden at Illiers, but it is also Uncle Weil's at Auteuil. . . . All these transformations, these substitutions, these unpredictable splittings and fusions, not to mention what still lies hidden in the unpublished notebooks, add to the Proustian palimpsest almost unfathomable depths. One dreams of a monstrous edition in which, around the *Recherche du temps perdu*, would be gathered all the preparations and successive modifications which—as work in progress—culminated in that final state, which as we know was the result not of an act of completion, but of a sudden interruption, outside the profound law of this work, which was to go on growing ceaselessly and never to reach its end.

Similarly no page of the *Recherche* can be regarded as truly definitive, none of its variants can be absolutely rejected. Starting from *Les Plaisirs et les Jours*, Proust's work exists and did not cease to move until November 18, 1922. This growth, this ceaseless metamorphosis, is not only a circumstance of its elaboration, which one might ignore, considering only its "result," it is integral to the work itself, it belongs to it as one of its dimensions. The work itself stands on that "giddy summit" of "years past but not separated from us"; it too must be taken as "having the length not of [its] body but of [its] years," weighed with its "incorporated time," described as "occupying a place, a very considerable place—for simultaneously . . . they touch epochs that are immensely far apart, separated by the slow accretion of many, many days—in the dimension of Time."[56]

If one considers only the "theoretical" pages of the *Recherche du temps perdu*, there can be no doubt that Proust had conceived of his work according to the unambiguous scheme of a spiritual experience, a completed spiritual experience, the culmination of which was known, as *Contre Sainte-Beuve* shows, well before the publication of *Du Côté de chez Swann*. The movement of this experience is in some sense analogous with that of the great Judeo-Christian myths. There is a Lost Paradise, which is the distant time of childhood daydreams, when the world appeared as an immediate spectacle, an unlimited possession; there is a Fall into Time, which is the negative experience of life "as lived": the evanescence of reality, the intermittences of the self, impossible love (there is even the sketch, valuable perhaps for psychoanalysts, of an explanation by means of Original Sin, namely the scene of the maternal Kiss interpreted as an abdication and an irreversible moral lapse); there is a long promise of Salvation, with its portents (the hawthorns at Tansonville, the steeples at Martinville, the trees at Hudimesnil), its prophets (Bergotte, Elstir, Vinteuil), its Precursor (Swann); there is the final ecstasy of Reminiscence, the fleeting contemplation of eternity and the certainty of embodying in a work what Proust himself calls Perpetual Adoration. Whatever might be said of these (perhaps purely formal) analogies, which Proust stresses in his vocabulary with a satisfaction no doubt tinged with humor, what concerns us here in that experience is its movement, its univocal orientation, summed up in the word Vocation, which it imprints on the existence of the Narrator, and consequently on the work itself, which receives from it the value of a message, even of a revelation.[57] Whatever precautions were taken to save appearances ("a work in which there are theories is like an object which still has the ticket that shows its price,"[58] the *Recherche du temps perdu* was to be the illustration of a doctrine, the demonstration, or at least the gradual unveiling, of a Truth.

Can we say that the work, in its execution, remains faithful to this manifest intention? Yes, since its apparent structure still corresponds to the course, for so long thwarted but never forgotten, of the truth that emerges in the Narrator's consciousness, and culminates in the illumination that gives it order and meaning. No, since the negative experience that was to be no more than a stage in the overall progress of the work sweeps it up whole and entire into a movement that is the reverse of the one proposed, and since its point of arrival finds it carried off on a new trajectory, which it is no longer in its power to terminate. The relationship between the work and the system that engenders it is therefore ambiguous: the Proustian ideology is not a "superstructure," a useless excrescence that one could quickly dismiss in order to approach Proust's work independently of it and in a "healthier" spirit; on the contrary, it represents an inevitable reference and even, in a sense, the only possible reference for the reading and understanding of the work. But at the same time the positive meaning that it is intended to give to the work is, if not betrayed, reversed and finally *absorbed* by a counterpoint of contrary movements: that which carries a message in plain language and that which accompanies this message to the point that it becomes obscure and gives way to the question that has no answer. One of Proust's successes is in having undertaken and carried out a spiritual experience; but how little this success matters to us beside that other success, of having succeeded in the failure of his undertaking, and of having left us the perfect spectacle of that failure, namely, his work. Directed entirely toward the revelation of Essences, it never ceases to move away from them, and it is out of this failed truth, this dispossessed possession, that the possibility of a work is born, and its true power of possession. Like Proust's writing, Proust's work is a palimpsest in which several figures and several meanings are merged and entangled together, all present together at all times, and which can only be deciphered together, in their inextricable totality.[59]

[1961]

NOTES

[References to Proust's *À la Recherche du temps perdu* are to the three-volume Pléiade edition (Paris: Gallimard, 1955–56) and to the seven-volume translation by C. K. Scott Moncrieff and Andreas Mayor (vol. 7), published by Vintage Books (New York: Random House, 1970)—Tr.]

1. *Essais et articles*, Pléiade (Paris: Gallimard, 1971), p. 586.
2. *A la Recherche du temps perdu*, iii:895; *Remembrance of Things Past*, 7:152.
3. iii:885; 7:144.
4. iii:889; 7:147.
5. iii:876; 7:136.
6. iii:879; 7:139.
7. For Proust, lost time is not, as is widely but mistakenly believed, "past" time, but *time in its pure state*, which is really to say, through the fusion of a present moment and a past moment, the contrary of passing time: *the extra-temporal, eternity.*
8. iii:871; 7:133. "As if," as a passage from *Jean Santeuil* (Pléiade—Paris: Gallimard, 1971, pp. 401–2), makes even more clear, "our true nature were outside time, created to taste the eternal."
9. iii:873; 7:134.
10. i:388; 1:296.
11. iii:877; 7:137.
12. iii:876; 7:137.
13. iii:871; 7:132.
14. Letter of November 27, 1913, *Choix de lettres*, Philip Kolb, ed. (Paris:

Plon, 1965), p. 195. Elsewhere (on the subject of Flaubert), he speaks of those pages in which "intelligence . . . seeks to become the vibration of a steamboat, the color of mosses, a tiny island in a bay. . . . It is transformed intelligence, which has become incorporated in matter" (*Essais et articles*, p. 612).

15. *Contre Sainte-Beuve*, Pléiade (Paris: Gallimard, 1971), p. 269; *On Art and Literature 1896–1919*, Sylvia Townsend Warner, tr. (New York: Meridian, 1958), p. 170.
16. *Correspondance générale* (Paris: Plon, 1930–36), II:86.
17. III:187; 5:129.
18. *Essais et articles*, p. 373; *Art and Literature*, p. 325.
19. *Jean Santeuil*, p. 320.
20. *Essais et articles*, p. 586.
21. *Essais et articles*, p. 380; *Art and Literature*, p. 334. [Translation modified: Warner has "quality" where the French text reads *égalité*—M.-R. L.]
22. III:1043; 7:268.
23. III:877; 7:138.
24. III:872; 7:133.
25. Cf. I:387; 1:296—". . . more special, and in consequence more real."
26. III:623; 6:149.
27. III:867; 7:129.
28. I:835–36; 2:301.
29. I:672–73; 2:182–83.
30. I:836; 2:301.
31. I:837; 2:301.
32. I:839; 1:296.
33. Benjamin Crémieux, quoted by André Maurois, *A la Recherche de Marcel Proust* (Paris: Hachette, 1949), p. 201; *Proust: Portrait of a Genius*, Gerard Hopkins, tr. (New York: Harper, 1950), p. 188.
34. The Pléiade edition (I:10) has *transvertébration*. [Scott Moncrieff (1:8) has "transubstantiation"—Tr.]
35. I:383; 1:293.
36. III:889; 7:147.
37. III:718–19; 7:18.
38. III:327; 5:228.
39. The Pléiade edition has here (III:1046) *temps évaporé*, which is obviously a mistake. Earlier editions gave *incorporé*, a reading confirmed by the context. [Scott Moncrieff follows the later editions and has "evaporated," 7:270—Tr.]
40. I:654–55; 2:169.
41. Pierre Francastel, *Art et technique* (Paris: Minuit, 1956), p. 146.
42. Proust himself points out these effects of superimposition in relation to Albertine and Oriane. See Georges Poulet, *L'Espace proustien* (Paris:

Gallimard, 1963), p. 113; *Proustian Space*, Elliott Coleman, tr. (Baltimore: Johns Hopkins University Press, 1977), p. 92.

43. I:946; 2:380.
44. II:365; 3:263.
45. I:732; 2:226.
46. Georges Poulet, *Etudes sur le temps humain* (Paris: Plon, 1950), pp. 396–97; *Studies in Human Time*, Elliott Coleman, tr. (Baltimore: Johns Hopkins University Press, 1959), p. 293.
47. II:190; 3:135.
48. Maurois, *Proust*, p. 271;
49. Poulet, *L'Espace proustien*, pp. 47–51; pp. 31–33.
50. Poulet, *L'Espace proustien*, pp. 36–39; pp. 24–26.
51. I:135; 1:103–104.
52. I:5; 1:5.
53. Maurice Blanchot, *Le Livre à venir* (Paris: Gallimard, 1959), pp. 18–34.
54. III:160; 5:110.
55. Jean-Paul Sartre, *Situations II* (Paris: Gallimard, 1948), p. 91; *What is Literature?* Bernard Frechtman, tr. (New York: Harper and Row, 1949) p. 34.
56. III:1046–48; 7:270–72.
57. "At last I have found a reader who has *guessed* that my book is a work of dogmatics and a construction!" (Letter to Jacques Rivière, February 7, 1914, Kolb, *Choix*, p. 197).
58. III:882; 7:141.
59. The image of the palimpsest appears at least twice in Proust (I:132, 1:101; and II:109, 3:76), but in a very modest way. On the other hand, it is given a particularly high (and very Proustian) value in this page from Baudelaire's *Paradis artificiels*, translated from the *Suspiria de Profundis*: "What is the human brain, if not an immense natural palimpsest? My brain is a palimpsest, as yours is too, reader. Innumerable layers of ideas and feelings have fallen one after another on your brain, as gently as light. It seemed as if each were swallowing up the previous one. But in reality none has perished. . . . Forgetting is only momentary therefore; and in such solemn circumstances, in death perhaps, and generally in the intense excitement generated by opium, the whole immense, complicated palimpsest of memory unfolds in an instant, with all its superimposed layers of dead feelings, mysteriously embalmed in what we call oblivion. . . . Just as every action, thrown into the whirlwind of universal action, is in itself irrevocable and irreparable, an abstraction of its possible results, so each thought is ineffaceable. The palimpsest of memory is indestructible."

11

PROUST AND INDIRECT LANGUAGE

The function and the task of a writer are those of a translator.
(À la recherche du temps perdu III:890; 7:148).

Proust's interest in the "facts of language" is well known,[1] and indeed obvious enough to any reader, even a careless one, of *À la recherche du temps perdu*. We know something of the success— and sometimes trouble—that his exceptional gift for observation and verbal imitation brought him in society, and of how this mimicry, the obsessive, almost "intoxicating" power of which he himself remarks on, was both exercised and exorcised in relation to Flaubert's style in that series of pastiches, the *Affaire Lemoine*.[2] It is also obvious how much the existence of certain characters, whether central ones like Charlus or incidental ones like the manager of the Grand Hotel at Balbec, owes to this linguistic sensitivity. In the essentially verbal universe of the *Recherche*, certain individuals are represented almost entirely as stylistic models (Norpois, Legrandin, Bloch) or as collections of linguistic accidents (the hotel manager already mentioned, the lift-boy, Françoise). The professional career of a Cottard is obliterated behind the story of his differences with the language—and is medicine, which "has made some slight advance in knowledge since Molière's days, but none in its vocabulary,"[3] really anything more for Proust than an activity of language?

> The doctor, who was called in at once, declared that he "preferred" the "severity," the "virulence" of the rush of fever which accompanied my congestion of the lungs, and would be no more than "a fire of straw," to other forms, more "insidious" and "septic"; . . . the docile Cottard had said to the Mistress: "Upset yourself like that, and tomorrow you will *give me* a temperature of 102,"as he might have said to the cook: "Tomorrow you will give me a *ris de veau.*" Medicine, when it fails to cure the sick, busies itself with changing the sense of verbs and pronouns.[4]

Proust even goes so far as to observe and transcribe, as does Balzac for a Schmucke or a Nucingen, the defects of pronunciation of the Marquis de Bréauté, for example ("Ma ière duiesse"), or a Princess Sherbatoff ("Oui, j'aime ce petit celcle intelligent, agléable . . . où l'on a de l'esplit jusqu'au bout des ongles"[5]). Characters like Octave (in his Balbec period) or Mme Poussin are so closely identified with their principal linguistic tics that these become their nicknames ("Dans les choux," "Tu m'en diras des nouvelles"); Mme Poussin's brief appearance in the *Recherche* (one page of *Sodome et Gomorrhe*) is indeed purely linguistic, since it is reduced to the habit that gave rise to this nickname and to her mania for softening the pronunciation of certain words. More or less the same could be said of the footman "Périgot, Joseph," whose existence has no other justification than the unforgettable letter that he carelessly leaves one day on Marcel's desk:

> "As you are aware, Madame's mother has passed away amid unspeakable sufferings which fairly exhausted her as she saw as many as three doctors. The day of her interment was a great day for all Monsieur's relations came in crowds as well as several Ministers. It took them more than two hours to get to the cemetery, which will make you all open your eyes pretty wide in your village for they certainly won't do as much for mother Michu. So all my life to come can be but one long sob. I am amusing myself enormously with the motorcycle of which I have recently learnt."[6]

Marcel might never have joined the "little band" at Balbec were it not for the power of fascination exercised over him by Gisèle's words: "C'pauvre vieux, i m'fait d'la peine, il a l'air à moitié crevé,"[7] and if Albertine later becomes his mistress, it is because she has annexed to her vocabulary such expressions as "distingué," "sélection," "laps de temps," "j'estime que," a clear indication of an emancipation that seemed to promise more intense pleasures, and even more for the (strictly aphrodisiac) appearance of the word "mousme": "What made me finally decide," Marcel comments, "was another philological discovery."[8] The power of words, of *connotation*.

It is significant that several characters of the *Recherche* have difficulty in using language—and no less significant is the meticulousness with which Proust observes the slightest accidents of their linguistic behavior. These accidents occur not only in learning a foreign language, as when Bloch, out of a hyper-Englishness, thinks the word "lift" is pronounced "lighft" and Venice "Venighce," or when Prince von Faffenheim says "arsheologist" instead of "archeologist," or "periphery" for "proximity,"[9] or in the speech of the uneducated, such as Françoise or the lift-boy at Balbec; but also, and in a perhaps more remarkable way, in men as educated as Dr. Cottard, or with the social background of the Duc de Guermantes. These solecisms may be "mispronunciations," like "lighft" or "arsheologist"; slight deformations like *september* for *septembre* or *estoppeuse* for *stoppeuse* (mender);[10] substitutions (*parenthèse* for *parenté*, Camembert for Cambremer);[11] or the incorrect use of words: *rester* for *demeurer, en thèse générale*;[12] and almost all the "bricks" dropped by the Balbec hotel manager, who "would also adorn his business conversation with choice expressions, to which, as a rule, he gave a wrong meaning."[13]

These "mistakes" are diverse not only in their origin and nature, but also in their psychological or social significance and in their esthetic value. Those of the cosmopolitan hotel manager connote a certain ill-advised pretentiousness even more than his "Rumanian *originality*"; those of Basin, "who had never succeeded in learning the exact meaning of certain phrases,"[14] together with his affected, ridiculous vulgarisms,[15] his involuntary squawks,[16] and his sudden blushes, are all part of the somewhat maladjusted personality of Charlus' brother, whose dottiness seemed at times to verge on a kind of drunkenness; perhaps, too, they indicate that there was something cosmopolitan, though in a different way from the Monégasque hotel manager, in that half-Bavarian dynasty, whose fiefs and claims (not to mention alliances) stretched across Europe.[17] Oriane, on the other hand, with her peasant accent ("bête comme eun' oie") and her provincial vocabulary carefully preserved like old furniture or family heirlooms, embody the "vieille France" side; in this respect, her archaisms are related to Françoise's mistakes and the similarity is noted by Proust himself.[18]

For the language of the old peasant woman, with all its solecisms, represents for him, as that of the carriers at the Port au Foin had for Malherbe, "the genius of language in a living state, the future and past of French":[19] the deep-seated authenticity of a language, which the vulgar affectation of Parisian slang, as practiced by Françoise's own daughter, adulterates no less than Mme de Crécy's would-be fashionable Anglicisms, Saint-Loup's cliquish jargon, or Bloch's studentish style. But just as bad money chases out good, Françoise gradually yields to her daughter's influence and fondly believes that she has advanced in Parisian elegance because she has learned to say: "Je vais me cavaler, et presto" (I'll get a move on). This "decadence of Françoise's speech, which I had known in its golden period"[20] is one of the more evident signs of the general decline that has affected everything in the last sections of the *Recherche du temps perdu*.

In spite of this diversity of value, some general laws do govern the genesis and persistence of these linguistic errors. The first, and most important, concerns an apparently universal desire, which will be found at work elsewhere, to motivate the sign; linguists have often observed it in connection with what used to be called "popular etymology": it consists of a tendency to reduce any new form to a better-known related form. Thus Françoise says "Julien" for "Jupien" and "Algiers" for "Angers," or there is the pronunciation of the English word "lift," already mentioned, or the substitution of "Camembert" for "Cambremer." Concerning the first instance, Proust himself notes that Françoise "readily assimilated new names to those with which she was already familiar," and in the case of the second, that "it was quite natural that he should have heard her say a name which he already knew"; the "syllables" (of the old name), he continues, "familiar and full of meaning, came to the young employee's rescue when he was embarrassed by this difficult name and were immediately preferred and readopted by him, not by any means from laziness or as old and ineradicable usage, but because of the need for logic and clarity which they satisfied."[21] What Proust means by "logic" and "clarity" are obviously the need for simplification and motivation (syllables "full of meaning") which is opposed to the arbitrary proliferation of forms. If Françoise says "Nev' York ham," it is because she believes the language "to be less rich than it actually was," and because she feels it to be "hardly conceivable that the dictionary could be so prodigal as to include at once a 'York' and a 'New York.'"[22]

The second law, which stems from the first, explains not the origin of the mistakes, but their resistance to all correction: the persistence in error and the obstinate refusal of the ear to perceive the "correct" form rejected by the mind. "It is curious," says Marcel, "that anybody who heard people, fifty times a day, calling for the lift [*ascenseur*] should never himself call it anything but a 'left' [*accenseur*]"; but the lift-boy hears only what he can hear, and Marcel's surprise is no more justified here than when he hears the name of a fish (sole) pronounced like the name of a tree (*saule*, willow) by "a man who must have ordered so many in his life."[23] He is later to learn that where a language, and indeed everything else, is concerned, "the evidence of the senses is also an operation of the mind in which conviction creates the evidence."[24]

This sort of linguistic deafness is particularly evident in the way in which Françoise, imitating as best she can the voice of Mme de Villeparisis and believing that she is repeating her exact words, "whereas she was really corrupting them no less than Plato corrupts the words of Socrates or St. John the words of Jesus," conveys from her to the Narrator and his grandmother this message, unconsciously translated into the only language she practised, and was therefore capable of hearing: "You'll be sure and bid them good day."[25] It is true that to this natural obstinacy may be added in certain cases a sort of voluntary and so to speak demonstrative persistence, as when the Narrator's butler, duly informed by his master how to pronounce the word "envergure," repeats "enverjure" with an insistence intended both to show that he does not have to accept orders outside his work and that the Revolution was not in vain, and to demonstrate "that this pronunciation was the result not of ignorance but of an act of will following upon ripe reflection."[26] If Bloch's arrogance had not hidden a deep sense of inferiority, he might, in the same spirit of independence and self-justification, have decided to impose his pronunciation of the word "lighft," and one may suppose that ignorance of the language is maintained on Basin's part by the proud feeling that a Guermantes "does not have to" bend himself to so common a norm as usage. Thus, with perhaps the same measure of bad conscience and bad faith, working-class self-assertion and aristocratic arrogance meet. But account should also be taken here of a third law, which is applied to at least three characters as different as the butler, the hotel manager at Balbec, and Prince von Faffenheim. We see, in effect, that even in the absence of any opposition, and therefore of any obligation dictated by *amour-propre*, the first says *"pistière"* (for *pissotière*), "incorrectly, but constantly"; just as "although" is a misunderstood "because," this "but" is a mistaken "thus"; of the hotel manager, Proust writes more neutrally that "he enjoyed using the words that he pronounced wrongly"; and, lastly, the Prince inspired the following remark in which Proustian causality is put back on its feet once more: "Not knowing how to pronounce the word archeologist . . . [he] never missed an opportunity of using it."[27] "Proust's law" on this point might therefore be stated thus: error, conscious or not, tends not only to persist, but to increase in frequency. Perhaps we should not—though Proust sometimes seems to tend in this direction—seek the explanation of the fact in deliberate stubbornness or in a sort of sensuality immanent in error itself, but rather in the necessarily compulsive character of everything (error, moral defect, secret vice, inferiority, etc.) that the mind censors and would like to repress: we will see other examples elsewhere.

However, the absolute imperfectibility that seems to be implied by these laws is not quite without exception in the world of the *Recherche*. After all, the way in which Françoise finally adopts the slang used by her daughter is a kind of apprenticeship, rather like the gradual maturing of Albertine's vocabulary. But the most interesting case is that of Cottard. To begin with, as we meet him in *Un amour de Swann*, the future Professor is, in relation to the language of society, in a situation of marked *incompetence*, which is manifested at first by what Proust calls his "naivety," that is to say, his inability to distinguish in the speech of others between what is "serious" and what is ironical or polite, his tendency to "take everything literally": if someone does him a great favor and adds that it is nothing, he feels obliged to confirm that indeed it is nothing, and even that it upsets him; the other element of the "Cottard complex" is his ignorance of the meaning of, and therefore of the appropriate occasion to use, such clichés as "sang blue" (blue blood); "vie de bâton de chaise" (a life of pleasure). "carte blanche," etc. The common feature of these two infirmities is obviously a sort of rhetorical insufficiency (in the sense in which he himself would speak of hepatic insufficiency), which constantly prevents him from crossing the literal meaning and reaching the figurative, and no doubt even of conceiving the existence of the figurative. But instead of remaining like others, happy in his ignorance, Cottard displays from the beginning a desire for improvement that is finally rewarded: he learns puns by heart and never misses an opportunity of learning something new on the subject of idioms: this "linguist's zeal"[28] constitutes for a long time the sole theme of his role in the *Recherche du temps perdu*—of his social role, of course, for the character of the infallible medical practitioner is utterly distinct in him from that of the stupid guest, or rather these two roles are united only by a relation of paradox: "and we realized that this imbecile was a clinical genius."[29] As almost always in Proust, the end of the process appears suddenly, with all its intermediary steps dispensed with, when, collapsing breathless into his seat on the little local train, the Professor exclaims, "That's what they call arriving in the nick of time!" and winks, "not so much to inquire whether the expression were apt, for he was now overflowing with assurance, but to express his satisfaction." Indeed, his mastery is now confirmed by Mme de Cambremer: "Now, there's a man who can always say the appropriate thing." He now has such a mastery of clichés, he can distinguish so well between the appropriate and the inappropriate, that he can give himself the pleasure of criticizing their use by others: "Why 'stupid as a cabbage'?" he asks M. de Cambremer. "Do you suppose cabbages are stupider than anything else?"[30] Of course, this triumphant aggressiveness still has something disturbing about it: the Professor is in no way cured of his linguistic neurosis, it has simply changed its sign, inverted its symptom.

And it would seem that Proust himself never quite escaped this fascination either. At least he attributes it to the Narrator of the *Recherche*, in a particular form and at a particular point in his development. The object of his choice is, as we know, what Proust calls the Name, that is to say, the proper noun. The difference between the Name and the Word (common noun) is explained in a famous passage from the third part of *Swann* where Proust describes his hero's daydreaming around the names of certain places where he hopes to spend the Easter holidays:

> Words present to us little pictures of things, lucid and normal, like the pictures that are hung on the walls of schoolrooms to give children an illustration of what is meant by a carpenter's bench, a bird, an ant-hill; things chosen as typical of everything else of the same sort. But names present to us—of persons and of towns which they accustom us to regard as individual, as unique, like persons—a confused picture, which draws from the names, from the brightness or darkness of their sound, the colour in which it is uniformly painted.[31]

We see here that the traditional (and questionable) opposition between the individuality of the proper noun and the generality of the common noun is accompanied by another, apparently secondary, difference, but one that in fact sums up the whole semantic theory of the name according to Proust: the "picture" that the common noun presents of the thing is "lucid and normal," it is neutral, transparent, inactive, and in no way affects the mental represention, the concept of bird, carpenter's bench, or ant-hill; on the other hand, the picture presented by the proper noun is "confused" in that it derives its unique color from the substantial reality (the "sound") of this name: it is confused, therefore, in the sense of *indistinct*, by unity, or rather, unicity of tone; but it is also confused in the sense of *complex*, by the confusion that is set up in it between the elements that derive from the signifier and those that derive from the signified: the extra-linguistic representation of the person or town which, as we will see, in fact always coexists with, and often exists prior to, suggestions presented by the name. Let us agree, therefore, that Proust reserves to proper nouns this active relation between signifier and signified that defines the *poetic state of language*, and which others—a Mallarmé, a Claudel, for example—apply also to common nouns, or to any other kind of words.[32] Such a restriction may come as a surprise in the case of a writer so obviously familiar with the metaphoric relation; the reason for this is the predominance, so marked in his case, of the spatial, or rather, geographical, sensibility: for the proper nouns that crystallize the Narrator's daydreams are in fact almost always (and not only in the chapter that bears this name) names of places—or names of aristocratic families, which derive most of their imaginative value from the fact that they are "always names of places."[33] The unicity, the individuality of places is one of the young Marcel's articles of faith, as it is also of the Narrator of *Jean Santeuil* and, despite the later denials of experience, he is to retain a trace of them at least in his dreams, since he can still write of the landscape of Guermantes that "sometimes, at night, in my dreams, [its individuality] binds me with a power that is almost fantastic."[34] The supposed singularity of the proper noun corresponds to the mythical singularity of the place, and reinforces it: "[Names] magnified the idea that I formed of certain points on the earth's surface, making them more special, and in consequence more real.... How much more individual still was the character that they assumed from being designated by names, names that were only for themselves, proper names such as people have."[35] However, we should not succumb to this linguistic laziness, which seems here to be making the "person" the very model of individuality ("towns . . . as individual, as unique, as people"); however mythical it may be, the individuality of places is in fact much more marked, in Proust, than that of people. From their first appearances a Saint-Loup, a Charlus, an Odette, an Albertine manifest their elusive multiplicity and the network of confused kinships and resemblances that attach them to many other people, who are as little "unique" as they are themselves; moreover, their names, as will become clearer later, are not really fixed, and do not belong to them in any very substantial way: Odette changes hers several times, Saint-Loup and Charlus have several, even Albertine's or Gilberte's Christian names are calculated in such a way that one day they will become confused, etc. In appearance, at least, places are much more "people" than people themselves,[36] moreover, they *hold on* to their names a great deal more.

We should now specify the nature of this "active relation" between signifier and signified in which we saw the essence of Proust's nominal imagination. If we referred to the theoretical statement already quoted, one might conclude that it was a unilateral relation, in which the "picture" of the place drew all its content from the "sound" of the name. The real relation, insofar as it can be analyzed from the various examples that appear in the *Recherche*, is more complex and more dialectical. But we must first draw a distinction between those names invented by Proust for fictitious places, such as Balbec, and the (real) names of real places such as Florence or Quimperlé—it being understood, of course, that this distinction is relevant only to the (real) work of the author, and not to the fictitious daydreams of its hero, for whom Florence and Balbec are situated on the same level of "reality."[37] According to a remark made by Roland Barthes, the role of the narrator here is that of a decoding ("to decipher in the names that are given to him a sort of natural affinity between signifier and signified"); the role of the novelist, on the other hand, is an encoding: "Having to invent some place at once Norman, Gothic, and windswept, one seeks in the general tablature of phonemes certain sounds that accord with the combination of these signifieds."[38] But this remark can be valid only for the invented names, such as Balbec, of which

Barthes is obviously thinking here, that is to say, for a very small proportion of the place names that give rise in the *Recherche* to a "linguistic" daydream. As far as the real names are concerned, the situation of the hero and that of the novelist are no longer symmetrical and inverse, but parallel: Proust attributes to Marcel an interpretation of nominal form that is necessarily invented, and therefore (the two activities being equivalent, as it happens) one that he himself has experienced. However, one cannot say that these two situations are absolutely identical, for on one point at least the experience of the hero does not coincide with that of the writer: when he thinks of Venice or of Bénodet, young Marcel has not yet been to either of these places, but when he wrote that page, *Proust* already knew them and perhaps was not totally disregarding his own memories—of his real experience—when he attributes to his hero daydreams of which the only two starting-points are in principle the names of these places and some knowledge gained through books or hearsay.

Indeed, a fairly attentive reading reveals that none of these images is determined solely by the form of the name, and that on the contrary each of them is the result of a reciprocal action between this form and some notion, true or false, but in any case independent of the name and originating elsewhere. When Marcel says that the name of Parma appeared to him "compact and glossy, violet-tinted, soft," it is obvious that at least the color specified has more to do with the violets of that town than with the sound of the name, and this is confirmed some lines later: "I could imagine it" (the house in Parma where he dreams of staying for a few days) "only by the aid of that heavy syllable of the name of Parma, in which no breath of air stirred, and of all that I had made it *assume* of Stendhalian sweetness and the reflected hue of violets."[39] The semantic analysis, then, is provided for us here by Proust himself, who clearly attributes the qualities of compactness and undoubtedly of glossiness to the influence of the name, the mauve color to knowledge by hearsay of the violets, and sweetness to his memory of the *Chartreuse de Parme*: the signifier certainly acts on the signified to make Marcel imagine a town in which everything is glossy and compact, but the signified also acts on the signifier to make him perceive the "name" of this town as violet-tinted and soft.[40] Similarly, Florence owes its image ("miraculously embalmed, and flower-like") as much to the red lily of its emblem and to its cathedral, Our Lady of the Flowers, as to the floral allusion of its first syllable, content and expression no longer being here in a relation of complementarity and exchange, but of redundancy, since in this case the name happens to have been motivated. Balbec derives its archaic image ("old piece of Norman pottery," "long abolished custom," "feudal right," "former condition of some place," "obsolete way of pronouncing the language") from the "incongrous syllables" of its name, but we know very well that the fundamental theme of "waves surging round a church built in the Persian manner" contaminates, without any reference to the name, two suggestions made by Swann and Legrandin; here, the verbal suggestion and the extralinguistic notion have not combined entirely successfully, for if the Norman essence of the place and even the pseudo-Persian style of its church are "reflected" in the sound of the name *Balbec*,[41] it is more difficult to find in it an echo of the storms referred to by Legrandin.[42] Subsequent references provide more effective realizations, as in the case of *Parma*, of the reciprocal contagion of the name by the idea and of the idea by the name that constitutes the imaginary motivation of the linguistic sign: thus, Bayeux cathedral, "so lofty in its noble coronet of rusty lace," catches at its highest point "the light of the old gold of its second syllable"; the old windows (*vitrage*) of its house justify the name of Vitré, the acute accent of which (one should note here the action not only of the sound of the word, but of its graphic form), the diagonal movement of which "a lozenge of dark wood" in turn suggests the old façades of the town; the "final consonants" of Coutances soften the "tower of butter" of its cathedral; the clear streams that already fascinated the Flaubert of *Par les champs et par les grèves* correspond to the transparent *perlé* (pearled) of the last part of the name *Quimperlé*, etc.

The same interaction animates other daydreams about names distributed throughout the early volumes of the *Recherche*, like the one concerning that most magic of all names, Guermantes, which suggests "a dungeon keep without mass, no more indeed than a band of orange light":[43] the dungeon obviously belongs to the castle that is the supposed cradle of this feudal family, the orange light "emanates" from the last syllable of the name.[44] It is, indeed, a less direct termination than one might at first have supposed, for the very name of Guermantes is given elsewhere an amaranthine color,[45] which is scarcely compatible with orange, the resonance of which derives from the Guermantes' golden hair: these two indications, contradictory from the viewpoint of the "colored hearing" dear to the theoreticians of phonic expressivity, derive therefore not from a spontaneous synesthesia,[46] but more probably from a *lexical association*, that is to say, from the common presence of the sound *an* in the name Guermantes and in the names of the colors "orange" and "amaranthine," just as the acidity of the Christian names of Gilberte, "pungent and cool as the drops which fell from the green watering-pipe,"[47] derives no doubt less from the direct action of its sounds than from the assonance *Gilberte-verte*: the ways of motivation are often less direct than one imagines. A final example: if the name *Faffenheim* suggested, in its boldness of attack and "the stammering repetition" that scanned its first syllables, "the impulse, the mannered simplicity, the heady delicacies of the Teutonic race," and in the "dark blue enamel" of the last, "the mystic light of a Rhenish window behind the pale and finely wrought gildings of the German eighteenth century," it was not only on account of its sounds, but also because it was the name of the Prince Elector:[48] the boldness and the repetition are certainly inscribed in the *Faffen* but their specifically Teutonic nuance comes from the signified and even more from the memory, which the first version of the same passage in *Contre Sainte-Beuve* recalls,[49] of the "colored sweets eaten in a small grocery shop on the old German square"; the colored hearing of the final *heim* may suggest the transparency of a dark blue enamel, but the Rhenishness of this window and the rococo gildings that served as its setting do not spring fully armed from what the earlier version called the "variegated sound of the last syllable." These predisposed, controlled interpretations are like a particular kind of program music in which the "expressive" leitmotifs, which, Proust observes, "paint in splendid colours the glow of fire, the rush of water, the peace of fields and woods, to audiences who, having first let their eyes run over the programme, have their imagination trained in the right direction."[50] The expressiveness of a vocable often derives from the content that it is supposed to suggest; if this collusion on the part of the signified is lacking, the vocable "expresses" nothing or something quite different. In the little railway that takes him from Balbec-en-Terre to Balbec-Plage, Marcel is struck by the strangeness of the names of the villages on the way, Incarville, Marcouville, Arambouville, Maineville, "dreary names, made up of sand, of space too airy and empty and of salt, out of which the termination 'ville' always escaped, as the 'fly' seems to spring out from the end of the word 'butterfly,'" in short, names the connotations of which strike him as typically marine, though he seems unaware of their resemblance to other, familiar names, such as Roussainville or Martinville, whose "sombre charm" derives on the contrary from a flavor of "preserves" or the smell of the log fire associated with the childhood world at Combray; the forms are certainly similar, but the unbridgeable distance of the contents invested prevents him from even perceiving their similarity: thus, "to the trained ear two musical airs, consisting each of so many notes, several of which are common to them both, will present no similarity whatever if they differ in the colour of their harmony and orchestration."[51]

One finds at work, therefore, in Marcel's poetic daydreams that same tendency to the motivation of language that already inspired the solecisms committed by Françoise or the lift-boy at Balbec: but instead of acting on the material of an unknown signifier in order to bring it to a "familiar and meaningful" form, and being by that very fact justified, it operates, more subtly, both on the form of this signifier (the way in which its "substance," phonic or otherwise, is perceived, actualized, and interpreted) and on that of its signified (the "picture" of the place) to make them compatible, harmonious, each suggestive of the other. We have seen how very illusory this harmony of "sound" and "sense" is—and particularly in the role attributed to the first by the imagination—and we will see later how in the *Recherche* the awareness and the critique of this illusion is expressed. But another mirage affects meaning itself:

Barthes insists quite rightly on the imaginary character of the semic complexes evoked by the daydreaming on names and how wrong it would be, here as elsewhere, to confuse the signified with the *referent*, that is to say, the real object; but this error is precisely the one committed by Marcel: its correction is one of the essential aspects of the painful apprenticeship constituted by the action of the novel. The daydreaming on names has the effect, says Proust, of making the image of these places more beautiful, "but at the same time more different from anything that the towns of Normandy or Tuscany could in reality be, and, by increasing the arbitrary delights of my imagination, aggravated the disenchantment that was in store for me when I set out upon my travels."[52] We know, for example, how bitterly disillusioned Marcel is when he discovers that the composite image of Balbec that he had formed for himself (a church of Persian style battered by waves) had only a distant resemblance to the real Balbec, the church and beach of which were separated by several kilometers.[53] The same disappointment occurs shortly afterward, at the spectacle of the Duc and Duchesse de Guermantes "withdrawn from that name Guermantes in which long ago I had imagined them leading an unimaginable life," or before the Princesse de Parme, a small woman dressed in black (not violet), more concerned with pious works than with Stendhalian sweetness, or before the Prince d'Agrigente, "as independent of his name ('a transparent sheet of coloured glass through which I beheld, struck, on the shore of the violet sea, by the slanting rays of a golden sun, the rosy marble cubes of an ancient city') as of any work of art that he might have owned without bearing upon his person any trace of its beauty, without, perhaps, ever having stopped to examine it," and even before Prince von Faffenheim-Munsterburg-Weinigen, Rheingraf and Elector Palatine, who uses the income and prostitutes the prestige of his Wagnerian fief in the maintenance of "five Charron motorcars, a house in Paris and one in London, a box on Mondays at The Opéra, and another for the "Tuesdays' at the 'Français,'" and whose only ambition in life is to be elected a Corresponding Member of the Academy of Moral and Political Sciences.[54]

Thus, when Proust declares that names, "whimsical draughtsmen,"[55] are responsible for the illusion in which his hero is imprisoned, we must not understand by "name" simply the vocable, but the sign as a whole, the unity constituted, according to the Hjelmslevian formula, through the relation of interdependence set up between the form of the content and the form of the expression:[56] it is not the succession of sounds or letters that creates of the name *Parma* the poetic myth of a compact, violet-tinted and soft town, it is the "interdependence" (another Hjelmslevian term) gradually established between a compact signifier and a soft, violet-tinted signified. The "name" is not therefore the cause of the illusion, but it is very precisely its *locus*, in which it is concentrated and crystallized. The apparent indissolubility of sound and sense, the *density* of the sign, encourage the childish belief in the unity and individuality of the place designated by it. We have seen how the arrival at Balbec dissipates the first; the motorcar rides with Albertine, in *Sodome et Gomorrhe*, dispose in turn of the second. Indeed, contrary to the train journey which, in Proust, is a sudden passage (a suddenness enhanced by the traveler's sleep between two stations) from one essence to another, essences materialized by the sign-board which bears in each station the individual, distinct name of a new place,[57] in a car, the uninterrupted progression brings out the continuity of the landscape, the interconnectedness of the places, and this discovery abolishes the myth of their separation and respective individualities,[58] just as Gilberte, at the beginning of *Temps retrouvé*, will abolish the cardinal opposition of the "two ways" simply by saying to Marcel: "If you like, we might go out one afternoon and then we can go to Guermantes, taking the road by Méséglise, it is the nicest walk."[59]

Thus ruined in contact with geographical reality, the prestige of names is subjected to another attack when the narrator, listening to the Duc de Guermantes' self-satisfied genealogical explanations, discovers the continuous network of alliances and inheritances that unite so many aristocratic names—names of places—that he had hitherto believed to be as irreconcilable, as radically dissociated by "one of those distances in the mind that not only distance, but separate and place on another plane," as those of Guermantes and Méséglise, Balbec and Combray. We know with what surprise, despite Saint-Loup's previous explanations, he had learnt at Mme de Villeparisis' that M. de Charlus was the brother of the Duc de Guermantes; when the Duc revealed to him, for example, that a Norpois, under Louis XIV, married a Mortemart, that "M. de Bréauté's mother had been a Choiseul and his grandmother a Lucinge," or that "M. d'Ornessan's great-grandmother had been the sister of Marie de Castille Montjeu, the wife of Timoléon de Lorraine, and consequently Oriane's aunt," all these names "sprang to take their places by the side of others from which I should have supposed them to be remote. . . . Each name displaced by the attraction of another, with which I had never suspected it of having any affinity,"[60] he is confronted again with distances that are abolished, divisions that collapse, incompatible raw essences that become merged and by that very fact disappear. The life of names is revealed as being a succession of transmissions and usurpations that deprive onomastic daydreaming of any foundation: that of Guermantes will finally fall into the possession of the all-too-common *'Patronne,'* ex-Verdurin (via Duras); Odette is successively Crécy, Swann, Forcheville; Gilberte is Swann, Forcheville, and Saint-Loup; the death of a parent makes the Prince des Laumes a Duc de Guermantes, and the Baron de Charlus is "also Duc de Brabant, Damoiseau de Montargis, Prince d'Oléron, de Carency, de Viareggio and des Dunes."[61] In a more laborious, but no less significant way Legrandin becomes Comte de Méséglise. There is certainly very little in a name.

Again Marcel was able to feel a sort of dizziness that was not entirely devoid of poetry before the onomastic ballet of the *Côté de Guermantes*;[62] the same cannot be said of one last experience, purely linguistic this time, which is to reveal to him, without any esthetic compensation, the vanity of his daydreamings on the names of places: it concerns the etymologies of Brichot in the last part of *Sodome et Gomorrhe*.[63] Much has been said about the function of such etymologies in the novel, and J. Vendryès, who saw in these tirades a satire on academic pedantry, added that they also revealed a sort of fascination. This ambivalence is not in doubt, but the "etymological passion" probably does not have the meaning attributed to it by Vendryès when he declares that "Proust believed in etymology as a rational means of penetrating the hidden meaning of names and consequently obtaining information about the essence of things. This is a conception that goes back to Plato, but which no scholar would defend today."[64] To do so is to link without hesitation the etymologies of Brichot to those of Socrates in the first part of the *Cratylus* and to place them at the service of Marcel's "Cratylian consciousness,"[65] whereas for Marcel, as we have seen, "the essence of things" is to be found in the *hidden meaning* of their names.

Now, if one examines these etymologies and their effect on the hero's mind a little more closely, one becomes convinced easily enough that their function is exactly the reverse. Whatever their real scientific value, it is obvious that they are presented and received as so many corrections of the errors of common sense (or of the amateur linguist as represented by the parish priest of Combray), popular or naive etymologies, the spontaneous interpretations of the imagination. Against all this, and therefore against the instinctive "Cratylism" of the Narrator, who is convinced of the existence of an immediate relation between the *present* form of the name and the non-temporal essence of the thing, Brichot re-establishes the deceptive truth of historical filiation, of phonetic erosion, in short, of the diachronic dimension of the language. Not all etymologies are necessarily of *realist* inspiration: those of Socrates (which, anyway, make no claim to scientific truth) are realist because they try to establish by arbitrary analyses a conformity between sound and sense that does not appear sufficiently obvious in the overall form of the name: *Dionysos* is broken down into *Didous oïnon* (wine-giving), *Apollo* into *Aei ballon* (unavoidable), etc. Brichot's, on the other hand, are almost systematically anti-realist. If, by way of an exception, *Chantepie* does happen to be the forest in which the magpie sings, the queen (*reine*) who sings at *Chantereine* is a vulgar frog (*rana*), with all due deference to M. de Cambremer; Loctudy is not the "barbarous name" that it is thought to be by the parish priest of Combray, but the very Latin *Locus Tudeni*; Fervaches, whatever Princess Sherbatoff thinks, means "warm waters" (*fervidae aquae*); Pont-à-Couleuvre shelters no snake, it is a corruption of *pont à qui l'ouvre*, a toll-bridge; Charlus has his oak tree at Saint-Martin du Chêne, but no yews at Saint-Pierre des Ifs (a corruption of *aqua*); in Thorpehomme, "*homme* does not in the least mean what you are naturally led to suppose, Baron," but is a corruption of *holm*, which means a "small island"; lastly, Balbec itself has nothing Gothic, or tempestuous, let alone Persian about it: it is a corruption of Dalbec, from *dal* (valley) and *bec* (stream); and even Balbec-en-Terre does not mean "Balbec on land," by reference to the distance that separates it from the coast and its storms, but "Balbec of the continent," in opposition to the barony of Dover of which it was once a dependency, "for which reason it was often styled Balbec d'Outre-mer." "Anyhow," M. Verdurin remarks ironically, "when you go back to Balbec, you will know what Balbec means";[66] but his irony does not reach only its intended target (the pedant Brichot), for it is certainly true that Marcel has long thought that he knew what Balbec meant, and if he is so delighted by Brichot's revelations, it is because they succeed in destroying his old beliefs and induce in him the salubrious disenchantment of truth. Thus he must no longer be charmed by the "flower" that ends such names as Honfleur (it is a corruption of "fiord," meaning "harbor") or be amused by the "boeuf" in Briqueboeuf (a corruption of "budh," "a hut"); so, too, he will discover that names are no more individual than the places they designate, and that to the continuity (or contiguity) of those on the "ground" corresponds the kinship of the others and their organization into a paradigm in the system of the language:

> What had appeared to me a particular instance became general, Bricqueboeuf took its place by the side of Elbeuf, and indeed in a name that was at first sight as individual as the place itself, like the name Pennedepie, in which the obscurities most impossible for the mind to elucidate seemed to me to have been amalgamated from time immemorial in a word as coarse, savoury and hard as a certain Norman cheese, I was disappointed to find the Gallic *pen* which means mountain and is as recognizable in Pennemarck as in the Appennines.[67]

Like experience of the "visible world," linguistic apprenticeship depoeticizes and demystifies: the names of places are "half-stripped of a mystery which etymology had replaced by reason."[68] The fact is that after this lesson, daydreaming about names disappears completely from the text of the *Recherche*: Brichot has made them strictly speaking *impossible*.

So we should not, without some reservations, attribute to Proust himself the "optimism of the signifier"[69] examplified by his young hero: belief in the truth of names is an ambiguous privilege of childhood, one of those "illusions to be destroyed" of which the hero must divest himself one after another in order to accede to the state of absolute disenchantment that precedes and lays the way for the final revelation. We know from a letter to Louis de Robert that Proust had considered calling the three parts of the *Recherche* planned in 1913 The Age of Names, The Age of Words, The Age of Things.[70] Whatever interpretation might be given to the last two, the first formula designates unambiguously the passion for names as a transitory stage, or rather as a point of departure. The age of names is what the *Côté de chez Swann* more cruelly calls "the age in which one believes that one gives a thing real existence by giving it a name."[71] The remark arises because Bloch has asked Marcel to call him "cher maître," and it is to be understood here in its most naively realist sense: the illusion of realism is a belief that what one names is *as one names it*.

One can find a sort of anticipated mockery of the deceptive "magic" of proper names in *Un amour de Swann*, in the jokes of doubtful taste exchanged at the Sainte-Euverte party between Charles and Oriane concerning Cambremer's name—certainly one of the vulnerable points of the Proustian onomastics—puns and parodies of Cratylian etymology about which one would like to consult the illustrious Brichot:

> "These Cambremers have rather a startling name. It ends just in time, but it ends badly!" she said with a laugh.
> "It begins no better." Swann took the point.
> "Yes; that double abbreviation!"
> "Someone very angry and very proper who didn't dare to finish the first word."
> "But since he could stop himself beginning the second, he'd

have done better to have finished the first and be done with it."[72]

It is not always a good thing to open (or break), without taking due precautions, what *Contre Sainte-Beuve* calls the "urn of unknowabilities."[73]

In the *Recherche du temps perdu*, therefore, there is not only a mass of very precise evidence concerning what I would like to call the *poetics of language*, but also a critique, sometimes explicit, but always severe, of that form of imagination, doubly denounced as the realist illusion: first, as the belief in the identity of the signified (the "image") and referent (the place), it is what we would now call the *referential illusion*, and, second, as the belief in a natural relation between the signified and the signifier, it is what might very properly be called the *semantic illusion*. If, on occasion, this critique resembles or anticipates certain themes to be found in modern linguistic thinking, it is nevertheless closely allied in Proust to the movement and perspective of a body of personal experience, which is the apprenticeship to (Proustian) truth by the hero-narrator. This apprenticeship is concerned among other things with the value and function of language, and the succession of the two formulas already referred to—the age of names, the age of words—shows quite clearly the direction it takes. However, we must avoid, in the case of the second, a misunderstanding that might find an apparent justification in the opposition, already encountered, between the Name (the proper noun) and the Word understood as a common noun ("work-bench," "bird," "ant-hill"). If the title envisaged in 1913 for the second part of the *Recherche* referred to this opposition, its relevance would appear to be rather doubtful—and it is easy to imagine that it was precisely for this reason that it was abandoned, but the question would then arise as to how Proust could have thought about it long enough to submit it for the approval of Louis de Robert. It would seem more likely, then, that "word" is not to be understood here in the sense of the common noun, which, as we already know, is the object of no experience or thought of any importance in the *Recherche*. The only relevant meaning that we can give it refers not to what might be called the solitary use of language, which is that of childhood daydreams, but on the contrary to the social, inter-individual experience of speech: not to the fascinating dialogue of the imagination with verbal forms considered as poetic objects, but to the relationship with others as it is formed in the real practice of linguistic communication. If this were the case, "word" would seem to have here more or less the sense in which one speaks of "words of character," in Molière or Balzac, for example, the *revelatory* word, the feature or accident of language in which is expressed, sometimes voluntarily, more usually involuntarily, and even unknown to the individual offering it, an aspect of his personality or situation. The discovery of this new dimension of language would appear to be, therefore, a new stage in the hero's apprenticeship, a stage that is at once negative, in that it reveals to him the essentially deceptive character of relationships with others, and positive, in that any truth, however "distressing," is to be welcomed: the experience of "words" thus becomes identified with the (painful) emergence from the verbal solipsism of childhood, with the discovery of the speech of the Other, and of one's own speech as an element in the relationship of otherness.

The *age of words*, then, would seem to be that of the apprenticeship to human truth—and human lies. The importance accorded here to this formula and the use of such an expression as "revelatory word" should not for a moment lead one to suppose that Proust attributes to speech a power of truth comparable, for example, with that presupposed by the practice of the Platonic dialectic, or by the transparent dialogue of souls in Rousseau's *La Nouvelle Héloïse*. The veracity of the logos is no more established in the age of words than in the age of names: this new experience is on the contrary a new stage in the critique of language—that is to say, in the critique of the illusions that the hero (and man, in general) is able to sustain with regard to language. A revelatory word can only exist against the background of an essentially untruthful speech, and the truth of speech is the object of a conquest that passes necessarily through the experience of lying: the truth of speech is to be found *in* lying.

In effect, we must distinguish between the revelatory word and the simply truthful word, which may sometimes exist. When Orgon says to Cléante that under Tartuffe's influence he has freed his soul from all affections, and that he would see "his brother, children, mother, and wife die" without the slightest concern, no one would think of calling this statement "revelatory": Orgon simply states where his latest craze has brought him, and what he says appears here simply as the transparent expression of his thought. On the other hand, the words "and Tartuffe?" in the previous scene are revelatory, for they express the truth without Orgon wanting them to, perhaps without his knowing, and in a form that must be interpreted. In this case the word says more than what it means, and it is precisely in this that it reveals, or, to put it another way, betrays. We see immediately that such statements pose a semiological problem that "truthful" statements (that is to say, those received as such) do not; whereas the truthful message is univocal, the revelatory message is ambiguous, and it is received as revelatory only because it is ambiguous: what it says is distinct from what it means, and is not said in the same way. Orgon means that we should feel sorry for Tartuffe, and in the way he says it, inopportunely and compulsively, says in turn that Orgon is "Tartuffed": his word denotes Tartuffe's (imaginary) asceticism and connotes Orgon's (real) passion. In the revelatory statement, the organ of revelation—of truth—it is this connotation, this indirect language that is conveyed, as Proust remarks, not through what the speaker says, but through the *manner* in which he says it.[74] At the end of *Sodome et Gomorrhe*, it will be remembered, it is a few words of Albertine's informing him that she has been intimate with Mlle Vinteuil, that "reveal" to Marcel his friend's lesbianism. Yet we should not regard these words as a revelatory statement, since they connote nothing, they lend themselves to no interpretation, and if they assume such importance for Marcel, it is because an earlier experience, outside this statement, gave a disturbing value to *what it said*. Albertine's words are not ambiguous, they carry only one signified (intimacy with Mlle Vinteuil), and it is this signified itself that in turn signifies Albertine's lesbianism for Marcel: the interpretation does not concern the words, therefore, but the facts; we are not in the hermeneutics of the revelatory word, but simply in a speculation, outside any question of language, concerning the necessary relation between two facts. On the other hand, in Albertine's same words, a parenthesis like, "Oh! Not at all the kind of woman you might think!" immediately sets the work of interpretation into motion: the eagerness with which Albertine combats a hypothesis that has not yet been formulated is obviously suspect, and bears a signification contrary to that borne by the negation itself: the connotation refutes the denotation, the "manner" in which it is said says more than what is said.

When Swann arrives one evening at Mme Verdurin's, his hostess points to the roses that he had sent to her that morning and remarks quickly, "I am furious with you!" and, without more ado, sends him to the place kept for him, by Odette's side.[75] This polite antiphrasis ("I am furious with you!" = "Thank you"), which is effective here only by virtue of the economy of what is known among the Guermantes as her "way of talking," is more or less what classical rhetoric called *asteism*: "delicate, ingenious banter, by means of which one praises or flatters while appearing to blame or reproach."[76] It goes without saying that the figures of polite rhetoric, like all figures, are overt forms of the lie, which are offered as such and await decipherment according to a code recognized by both parties. If Swann had taken it into his head to reply to Mme Verdurin with something like, "You're furious with me when I send you flowers—that's not very nice of you, I won't send you any more," he would prove both his ignorance of polite practice and what Proust would call his naivety. This weakness, as we have already seen, is exemplified preeminently in Cottard (first manner), who takes everything literally and, as Mme Verdurin quite rightly complains, "accepts everything we say as gospel."[77] The other typical innocent of Proustian society is the blunderer Bloch who, when Mme de Guermantes declares that "Society isn't my strong point," replies in all simplicity, imagining that it was meant sincerely, "Indeed; I thought it was just the other way,"[78] or when, during the war, Saint-Loup, while "moving heaven and earth" to get enlisted, declared that he did not want to return to the front "quite simply from *fear*," called Saint-Loup to his face a "privileged dandy" and a shirker, incapable as he is of conceiving of a "reticent" heroism, let alone one concealed behind an apparent "admission" of cowardice, which is precisely what the true coward would never do: we know that one point shared both by the "Guermantes spirit" and the "Combray spirit" is precisely the principle that one must not express "sentiments that lie too deep within them and that seem to them quite natural";[79] but for the literalism of a Bloch or a Cottard, what is not said—let alone what is denied—cannot be, and conversely what is said cannot but be. Both could subscribe to Jean Santeuil's words, which are the emblematic statement of all naivety: "I have proof to the contrary, she has told me that it isn't so."[80] Similarly, when a fellow guest tells Odette that he is not interested in money, she says of him: "Why, he's an adorable creature; so sensitive! I had no idea!" while she remains quite insensitive to Swann's inconspicuous generosity: "What appealed to her imagination," Proust adds, "was not the practice of disinterestedness, but its vocabulary."[81]

We see that the "innocents" are more numerous than one might think. On occasion, Proust is even capable, in a moment of humor, of embracing the whole of society under that definition, saying of M. de Bréauté for example that "his hatred of snobs was a derivative of his snobbishness, but made the simpletons (in other words, everyone) believe that he was immune from snobbishness."[82] But this generalization obviously goes beyond his thinking, and in the precise case of Bréauté, for example, the reader must not be an innocent in turn, and take literally Oriane's protestations ("A snob! Babal! But, my poor friend, you must be mad, it's just the opposite. He loathes smart people."): let him wait until the Princess's final party to find, again from Oriane's mouth, this brief funeral oration: "Bréauté was a snob."[83] In fact social life is for Proust a veritable school of interpretation, and no one could make a career out of it (were it not for events like the Dreyfus Affair or the War, which overthrew all the norms) without at least learning its rudiments. The hero's interpretation depends precisely on the rapidity with which he assimilates the lessons of polite hermeneutics. When, having arrived at the Duc de Guermantes', hoping to learn from him whether the invitation that he has received from the Princess is genuine, he comes up against the Guermantes' well-known dislike of this kind of favor, and when Basin pours out a series of more or less contradictory arguments to justify his refusal, he is able to understand, not only that he has been taken in by "the little farce" which M. de Guermantes has performed for his benefit, but also that he must act as if he has been taken in.[84] So he pays a visit to "Marie-Gilbert" without becoming any the wiser, and when, all danger passed, Oriane says to him, "Do you suppose that I should be unable to get you an invitation to my cousin's house?" he is not so innocent as to believe her, or to reproach himself with his own shyness: "I was beginning to learn the exact value of the language, spoken or mute, of aristocratic affability . . . that one should discern the fictitious character of this affability was what they [the Guermantes] called being well-bred; to suppose it to be genuine, a sign of ill-breeding." We see why Bloch embodies in this world both innocence and coarseness: it is the same thing. And in Marcel's gradual initiation into polite ritual, one can regard as a qualifying, even glorifying proof, the little scene that takes place shortly afterward, during an afternoon party at the Duchesse de Montmorency's: invited with broad gestures by the Duc de Guermantes, who is supporting the arm of the Queen of England, to come over and be presented to her, Marcel, who is "becoming word-perfect in the language of the court," makes a deep bow, without smiling, and moves off. "Had I written a masterpiece, the Guermantes would have given me less credit for it than I earned by that bow." The Duchesse, meeting the Narrator's mother, compliments him on it, saying that "it would have been impossible for anyone to put more into it"; in fact, what it had in it was the one thing it was important to put in it, the importance of which could be measured by the care with which one avoided referring to it: "They never ceased to find in that bow every possible merit, without however mentioning that which had seemed the most priceless of all, to wit that it had been discreet, nor did they cease either to pay me compliments which I understood to be even less a reward for the past than a hint for the future."[85] The lesson of the incident is obviously, as Cottard would say if he had been capable both of understanding it and of formulating it in that language of clichés that he had not yet mastered, "Hail to the good listener!"

A contra-proof: when M. de Cambremer offers his seat to Charlus, the latter pretends to take this gesture as respect shown to his rank and, believing quite rightly that "he could not establish his right to this precedence better than by declining it," bursts out into vehement protest, bringing his hands down with all his strength on the shoulders of his social inferior, who had shown no sign of getting to his feet, as if to force him to sit down again.

> "You reminded me, when you offered me your chair, of a gentleman from whom I received a letter this morning addressed: 'To His Highness, the Baron de Charlus,' and beginning: 'Monseigneur.'" "To be sure, your correspondent was slightly exaggerating," replied M. de Cambremer, giving way to a discreet show of mirth. M. de Charlus had provoked this; he did not partake in it. "Well, if it comes to that, my dear fellow," he said, "I may observe that, heraldically speaking, he was entirely in the right."[86]

One can never make oneself too clear in the provinces.

Life in polite society, then, as in diplomacy, requires skill in deciphering and the habit of immediate translation. Just as the use, in a speech addressed to France by the Tsar, of the world "ally" instead of the word "friend" announces, for the initiated, that in the next war Russia will send five million men to the assistance of France, one word said in place of another by the Duc de Réveillon signifies whether he will or will not invite his interlocutor to his next ball. Moreover, the Duc gives to his language the same care as a head of state, and precisely calibrates the civilities he addresses to his holiday acquaintances, using four "texts" the relative values of which are perfectly clear for anyone who "knows how to live," in other words, *knows how to read*: "I hope to have the pleasure of seeing you again in Paris at my home/in Paris/of seeing you again/ of seeing you again here [at the waters]." The first is an invitation, the last is a condemnation without appeal, the other two are left to the interpretation, whether perspicacious or naive, of the recipient; this last possibility is still covered: "Even the most innocent did not take it into their heads to reply: 'Certainly I shall come and see you,' for the Duc de Réveillon's face was eloquent and one could in a sense read on it what he would have replied in different cases. In this case one could already hear in advance the chilly, 'You are too kind,' followed by the sudden suppression of the handshake that would have diverted the unfortunate forever from pursuing so insensate a project."[87] The mute expression of the face served here, then, as a gloss or handbook to any possible Cottard or Cambremer of the watering place.

This cryptographical aspect of polite conversation explains how, when certain interests are involved, professional diplomats, experienced in such exercises of transcoding, are able to perform wonders, even when they are as utterly stupid as M. de Norpois. The finest scene of polite negotiation, entirely played out on a double register between two actors each of whom instantly translates the coded discourse of the other, is that in which the same Norpois is pitted against Prince von Faffenheim in the *Côté de Guermantes*.[88] It concerns—a revealing situation if ever there was one—a candidature: the prince's application to become a member of the Academy of Moral and Political Sciences. But in order to appreciate it, one must be aware of Norpois' attitude with regard to an earlier candidature, that of Marcel's father. Norpois' influence (he has at his disposal two-thirds of the votes), his "proverbial" obligingness, his marked friendship for the candidate apparently leave no doubt as to his position and Marcel, entrusted with the task of "putting in a word" on his father's behalf, is treated to a quite unexpectedly savage reply, of the most warmly discouraging kind, a subtle variation on the theme of obligation: your father has better things to do, all my colleagues are fossils, he *must not* stand, it would be a false move, and if he made it I would carry my affection for him to the point of refusing to vote, so he must expect people to come and beg him not to. . . . All this leads up to the grand conclusion: "I should prefer to see your father triumphantly elected in ten or fifteen years' time."[89] Being the bearer of a simple request, and having nothing to propose, Marcel has no alternative but to swallow this refusal: this is an instance of the simple candidature. More productive (textually) is the negotiable candidature, in which the applicant can offer something equivalent in exchange for what he is asking for. Moreover, this *quid pro quo* must correspond to the wishes, arrived at by a tacit hypothesis, of the solicited party. The story of von Faffenheim's candidature becomes, therefore, that of a series of attempts to find the "right key." The first offers, the laudatory quotations, or Russian decorations, lead only to various inconsequential courtesies and such responses as: "Ah! I should be most happy!" (To see you in the Academy), which could have taken in only "a simpleton, a Dr. Cottard" (still a standard of naivety), who would say to himself: "Well . . . he tells me that he would be happy to see me in the Academy; words do have some meaning after all, damn it!" But, contrary to Cottard's belief, words do not have a meaning: rather, they have several. "Trained in the same school," the Prince knows this as well as his partner. Both know what may be contained in "some piece of official wording which is, for all practical purposes, meaningless," and that the fate of the world will be announced not by the appearance of the words "war" or "peace," but signified "by some other, apparently commonplace word, a word of terror or blessing, which the diplomat, by the aid of his cipher, would immediately read . . . and so, in a private matter like this nomination for election to the Institute, the Prince had employed the same system of induction which had served him in his public career, the same methods of reading beneath superimposed symbols." He arranges for Norpois to receive the Cordon of Saint Andrew, but his reward is no more than a speech like the one already summarized above. He writes a long, flattering article about Norpois in the *Revue des Deux Mondes* and the ambassador replies that he does not know "how to express his gratitude." Reading in these words, as in an open book, his new failure, and drawing from his feeling of urgency a saving inspiration, von Faffenheim replies apparently as

Cottard would have done: "I am going to be so indelicate as to take you at your word." But this case of taking someone at his word is not here, as it would be if Cottard had been speaking, a question of taking himself literally. It is still an asteism, since the "request" that the Prince is about to make is in reality an offer—and this time, as its antiphrastic form leads one to foresee, a sign of certainty and anticipation of success, this offer is the right one: it is a question of making it possible for Mme de Villeparisis (who was linked for many years in a quasi-conjugal way with Norpois) to come and dine with the Queen of England. Success is now so sure that the Prince can pretend to withdraw his candidature; it is the Ambassador who restrains him: "You must on no account give up the Academy; tomorrow fortnight, as it happens, I shall be having luncheon before going on with him to an important meeting, at Leroy-Beaulieu's."

More crudely—but this very crudity has the merit of bringing out the *double* character of polite discourse—a scene from *Jean Santeuil* sets side by side for us the words spoken in a drawing-room and their "translation."[90] Jean has been invited as the fourteenth guest to Mme Marmet's; the hostess feels obliged to justify his socially inauspicious presence to the other guests. Hence such statements as: "Your father wasn't angry that we took you away just as you were about to go into dinner?" (Translation: "You must all understand that it was so that there would not be thirteen of us—it was all arranged at the last minute."); "Come now, Julien, have you introduced your friend to these gentlemen?" (Translation: "Don't think he's one of my acquaintances—he's one of my son's schoolfriends"); "It is so good of your father to recommend Julien whenever he takes an examination at the Ministry of Foreign Affairs" (Translation: "I know what I'm doing inviting him—he's useful to Julien"). The same process takes place at the end of the evening: Mme Scheffler: "How beautiful the Princess is! I like her because they say she is very intelligent, but I don't know her, though we have the same friends" (Translation: "Come now, introduce me"). Mme Marmet: "Oh! She's delightful. But won't you have some tea, don't you want anything, my dear?" Need one translate?

Trained in the art of translation by statement of this kind, the duplicity of which is more or less overt, and given that it is as it were obligatory, if one is to live in polite society, to know how to interpret, the Proustian hero is now ready[91] to confront forms of statements that are closer to what I have called revelatory speech, those the real meaning of which can be attained only in spite of (and generally unknown to) the person who is making them.

In the world of the *Recherche*, language is one of the great revealers of snobbery, that is to say, both of the hierarchization of society into social and intellectual castes and of the incessant movement of borrowings and exchanges that constantly alter and modify the structure of this hierarchy. The circulation of modes of expression, of linguistic features and tics characterizes this social life as least as much as that of the names and titles of the nobility, and certainly more than that of wealth and fortunes. Stylistic stability is as exceptional there as social or psychological stability and, in the same way, it seems to be the rather miraculous privilege of the Narrator's family, especially the mother and grandmother, enclosed as they are in the inviolable refuge of classical good taste and Sévigné-speech. Another miracle, but this time one rather of balance than of purity, protects Oriane's style, a subtle synthesis of a provincial, almost peasant inheritance and an ultra-Parisian dandyism that she shares with her friend Swann (and which is imitated clumsily by the whole of the Guermantes coterie), composed of litotes, an affectation of frivolity, and disdain for "serious" subjects, a detached way of speaking expressions thought to be pretentious or Prudhommesque as if they were in italics or in inverted commas. Norpois and Brichot will remain faithful to their styles to the end, a solemn succession of clichés in the case of the diplomat, a mixture of pedantry and demagogic familiarity in the case of the "scholar" ("the witticisms of a fifth-form schoolmaster unbending among his prize pupils on Saint Charlemagne's holiday"),[92] but these two forms of language will eventually come together, in their articles of war, in the same paroxysm of official rhetoric—so much so that the Pléiade editors suspect a confusion of persons.[93] Charlus's aging is noted, at the beginning of *La Prisonnière*, by a sudden feminization, expressed not only in the tone of voice, but also in the choice of words, hitherto corsetted in powerful rhetoric, and by the "extraordinary frequency in his conversation of certain expressions that had taken root in it and used now to crop up at any moment (for instance: 'the chain of circumstances') upon which the Baron's speech leaned in sentence after sentence as upon a necessary prop":[94] an invasion of style by the stereotype that carries Charlus over to the side of Norpois (we should remember that at the time of *Contre Sainte-Beuve* the two characters were still one), or to that of his own brother, Basin, whose verbal clumsiness takes comfort at regular intervals in such expletive expressions as: "what more can I say?"[95] Even Swann's elegance does not protect him from the pretentious petty-bourgeois circle forced on him by his marriage to Odette. He is even heard to say of a Permanent Secretary: "It appears that he has immense capacity, a man quite of the first rank, a most distinguished individual. He's an officer of the Legion of Honour"—words that sound quite idiotic in the mouth of a friend of the Guermantes, a pillar of the Jockey Club, but which have become inevitable in the mouth of Odette's husband.[96]

No one, or almost no one, then, is spared this movement of social language, and the adoption of a turn of phrase might be the infallible sign of decline or promotion, or of a pretentiousness which usually precedes the next step of a career in polite society. Then there is promotion in the hierarchy of age groups: we have seen what conclusion Marcel could draw from the appearance of certain words in Albertine's vocabulary, but he had already observed at Balbec that the daughters of lower-middle-class families acquired at certain special moments the right to use certain expressions that their parents keep for them in reserve as a kind of usufruct: Andrée is still too young to be allowed to say of a certain painter: "It appears, *the man* is quite charming!"—this will come in due course, when she's allowed to go to the Palais-Royal; for her first communion, Albertine had been given as a present the right to say, "I'm sure I should find that simply terrible!"[97] Above all, there is social promotion. Marcel discovers in Swann's drawing-room the almost sensual elegance of pronouncing "Comment allez-vous?" without the *t*, and "odieux" with an open *o*, and hastens to take these precious pledges of elegance home with him. We know how, from the outset, Odette's patient career was adorned with a choice collection of Anglicisms; when she becomes Mme Swann, she borrows from the Guermantes circle, through her husband, words and expressions that she, too, will repeat *ad nauseam*, "the expressions which we have borrowed from other people being those which, for a time at least, we are fondest of using."[98] The privilege of being able to call such august persons as the Prince d'Agrigente, M. de Bréauté (Hannibal), M. de Charlus (Palamède) or Mme de Pommeraye by their nicknames, "Grigri," "Babal," "Mémé," "La Pomme," is an outward sign of aristocracy that no beginner would fail to exhibit, and one remembers that Mlle Legrandin married a Cambremer in order to be able to say one day, if not like other married women of higher degree, "ma tante d'Uzai" (Uzès) or "mon onk de Rouan" (Rohan), at least, according to Féterne usage, "mon cousin de Ch'nouville" (Chenouville)— the prestige, modest enough, of the alliance being enhanced by the exclusivity of pronunciation.[99]

And as aristocracy is "a relative thing" and snobbery a universal attitude (the conversation of the "Marquise" at the little pavilion on the Champs-Élysées is "typical of the Guermantes, or the Verdurins and their little circle"),[100] we see the lift-boy at the Grand Hotel seeking, as a modern proletarian, "to efface from [his] language every trace of the rule of domesticity," carefully replacing "livery" with "tunic" and "wages" with "salary," referring to the hall-porter or the coachman as his "chiefs" in order to conceal under this hierarchy among "colleagues" the old and humiliating opposition between masters and servants that his real function perpetuates in spite of himself: thus he refers to Françoise as "that *lady* who has just gone out" and to the chauffeur as the "*gentleman* you went out with," an unexpected designation which reveals to Marcel "that a working man is just as much a gentleman as a man about town." "A lesson in the use of words only," he adds. "For in point of fact I had never made any distinction between the classes." This is certainly a very dubious distinction, a denial all the more suspect when one remembers the same Marcel asserting that "the title of 'employee' is, like the wearing of a moustache among waiters, a sop to their self-esteem given to servants."[101] When "words" are ladened with such heavy connotations, the lesson of words is certainly a lesson of things.

But social ambition and the prestige of the upper classes are not the only way by which snobbery acts upon language. Proust himself mentions as a "law of language" the fact that we express ourselves "like others of our mental category and not of our caste":[102] a new explanation of the Duc de Guermantes' vulgarisms, and a perfect definition of the "intellectual jargon," which Saint-Loup took from Rachel, and by which the young blasé aristocrat becomes spiritually integrated into a new caste, socially inferior to his own, and whose intellectual superiority over a Swann or a Charlus is far from obvious, but which possesses in his eyes all the charms of exoticism, and the imitation of which gives him the excitement of an initiation. So, when he hears his uncle declare that there is more truth in a single tragedy by Racine than in all the plays of Victor Hugo, he hastens to whisper to Marcel: "Preferring Racine to Victor, you may say what you like, it's epoch-making!" The narrator adds, "he was genuinely distressed by his uncle's words, but the satisfaction of saying 'you may say what you like' and, better still, 'epoch-making' consoled him."[103] One "law of language," which Proust illustrates in several ways, though he does not define it, seems to be that any language which is highly characteristic, whether in vocabulary, syntax, phraseology, pronunciation, or for any other reason, whether it be an author's style (as in the contagious power of Bergotte's style), an intellectual jargon, a way of speaking confined to one group, or a patois, exercises over those who encounter it, in speech or writing, a fascination and attraction proportional, not so much to the social or intellectual prestige of those who speak or write it, as to the degree to which it departs from normal usage and to the coherence of its system. At Doncières barracks, the young arts graduate strives to imitate the slang and faulty grammar of his illiterate companions, "pedantically displaying the new forms of speech which he had only recently acquired and with which he took a pride in garnishing his conversation."[104] Similarly, during the war, though patriotism has little to do with it, a whole society, from the duchess to the butler, tried to talk the language of the day ("G.H.Q.," "blue-penciled," "bowler-hatted") with as much, indeed the same pleasure, as that procured some years earlier by the use of "Babal" and "Mémé"; and it is perhaps even more by verbal contagion than out of a wish to make oneself important that Mme Verdurin says *"We* demand of the King of Greece that he should withdraw from the Peloponnese, etc.; *we* send him, etc.," and Odette says, "No, I do not think that they will take Warsaw" or "The worst thing that could happen is a patched-up peace"; in any case, is not her admiration for "our loyal allies" the exaltation of her former linguistic Anglomania, and does she not project this onto Saint-Loup when she announces with unfortunate pride that her "son-in-law Saint-Loup has learned the slang of all the brave 'tommies'"?[105] For all of them in effect—except perhaps for those who "make" it, not as Clemenceau "makes it," but in suffering it—the war, like so many other historical situations, is above all a "slang."

These elementary forms of social comedy do not seem to involve any ambiguity and present no semiological difficulty, since one feature of language is overtly proposed in it as connoting a quality to which it is bound by quite transparent semiosis; Anglicism = "distinction," the use of the diminutive = "familiarity with the aristocratic milieu," etc. However, it should be observed that the apparent simplicity of the relation of signification covers at least two types of very different relation, depending on the attitude adopted by the addressee of the message. The first type, which, in the Proustian vocabulary, can be termed "naive," and which is obviously the one intended by the addresser, and which is postulated in his discourse, consists of interpreting the connoter as an *index,* in the current sense of the term, that is to say, as an effect signifying its cause: "This young woman says 'Grigri' *because* she is a close friend of the Prince d'Agrigente." The second attitude, on the other hand, consists in receiving the connoter as an intentional index, and therefore in reading a relation of finality in what was presented as a relation of causality: "This young woman says 'Grigri' *in order* to show that she is a close friend of the Prince d'Agrigente." But one sees immediately that this modification of the semiotic relation involves a modification of the signified itself: for if the connoter received as an index signifies what it is supposed to signify, this same connoter *reduced* to the state of an index can no longer signify anything but the signifying *intention* and therefore the *exhibition* of the connoted attribute. Now, in the system of Proustian values, an exhibited attribute is inevitably depreciated (for example, "distinction," too obviously displayed, becomes affectation) and, moreover, almost inevitably denied by virtue of that law, by which one never feels a need to exhibit what one possesses, and possession of it is, by definition, of no importance to you: thus as long as Swann was in love with Odette, he looked forward to the day when he could show her that he no longer cared for her, but when he finally became capable of it he was careful not to do so; on the contrary, he took great pains to conceal his infidelities from her. With his love, says Proust, he lost the desire to show that he no longer had love; from the point of view that concerns us here, one would say rather that in acquiring the advantage that indifference brings he lost the desire to display it.[106] When Charlus, on his first appearance at Balbec, wants to keep his "countenance" in order to divert the suspicions of Marcel, who has caught him staring at him, he pulls out his watch, looks into the distance, makes "the perfunctory gesture of annoyance by which people mean to show that they have waited long enough, *although they never make it when they are really waiting.*"[107] This incompatibility of being and appearing already foreshadows as fatal the failure of the signifier, whether verbal or gestural. Marcel, certain at last of being introduced by Elstir to the "little band" of girls, prepares to wear "that sort of challenging expression *which betokens not surprise but the wish to appear as though one were surprised.*" "So far is everyone of us a bad actor," he adds, "or everyone else a good thought-reader."[108] Thus the exhibiting message is immediately deciphered as a simulating message and the proposition "She says 'Grigri' *in order to show* that. . . ." is transformed into "She says 'Grigri' in order *to make people think* that. . . ." and thus the reduced index comes to indicate almost infallibly the opposite of what it is supposed to indicate, the relation of causality being inverted *in extremis* to the detriment of the signifying intention: she says "Grigri" because she does not know the Prince d'Agrigente, Charlus is not waiting for anybody since he looks at his watch, Marcel looks surprised and therefore isn't. The failure of "deceptive" signification is thus sanctioned not by the mere absence of the intended signified, but by the production of the contrary signified, which is found to be precisely the "truth": it is in this ruse of signification that relevatory language consists, this relevatory language being essentially an indirect language, a language that "betokens" what is not said, and precisely because it does not say it. "The truth," says Proust, "has no need to be uttered to be made apparent";[109] but it would hardly be to traduce his meaning to translate it as: truth can be made apparent only when it is not said. To the well-known maxim, according to which language was given to man in order to conceal his thoughts, one should add that it is in concealing them that he reveals them. *Falsum index sui, et veri*.

Proust seems to pay particular attention—and later we will see why—to occasions when (dis)simulating speech is contradicted by facial expression or gesture. Here are three very clear examples, again at the expense of the Guermantes couple. *Oriane*: "At these tidings the Duchess's features breathed contentment and her speech boredom. 'Oh, good heavens, more princes!'" *Basin*: "I couldn't place him at all; you know I never can remember names, it's such a nuisance,' he added, in a tone of satisfaction." *Basin* again, in a rather more developed form: "'I, who have not the honour to belong to the Ministry of Education,' replied the Duke with a feigned humility but with a vanity so intense that his lips could not refrain from curving in a smile, nor his eyes from casting round his audience a glance sparkling with joy."[110] The *feint* is obviously in each case in the verbal discourse, since it is the "features," the "tone," the "lips" and the "eyes" that "cannot refrain" from expressing the *deep* feeling. It is, of course, possible that unawareness or the will to dissimulate are not very marked here in the case of Basin, who really makes no mystery of the fact that he despises other people in general and the civil servants at the Ministry of Education in particular; and therefore that "could not refrain" signifies here "could not deprive himself" of the pleasure of showing it. According to this hypothesis, we would still, with these last two examples, be in the world of open rhetoric—except that it would no longer be a rhetoric of politeness, but one of insolence, the importance of which should not be underestimated in the Guermantes circle. But this interpretation obviously does not apply in the case of the Duchess, who can in no way wish, or even bear, that anyone should learn (supposing that she admits it even to herself) exactly how much she enjoys the company of princes. Still less would one imagine that the artistic snobbery of Mme de Cambremer would wish to admit her own ignorance of *Pelléas*, which she has just declared to be a masterpiece, when, to a more precise reference from Marcel, she replies, "Of course I do!" This was what she said, "but 'I haven't the faintest idea' was the message proclaimed by her voice and features which did not mould themselves to the shape of any recollection and by a smile that floated without support, in the air."[111] Here, we find the same elements of mimicry (face, smile) already encountered in the cases of Basin and Oriane, but we should note the appearance of another revealer, the *voice*, separated from verbal expression, of which it is nevertheless the instrument—but a rebellious, unfaithful instrument. In fact, with Proust, it is as if the *body* and all the manifestations directly linked to corporeal existence—gestures, mimicry, look, vocal emission—escape more easily the control of the consciousness and will, and are the *first to betray*, even when the verbal discourse still remains under the conscious control of the speaker. Marcel speaks of signs "traced as though in invisible ink," in Albertine's features and gestures, and, earlier, denouncing himself, recognizes that he has often said "things in which there was no vestige of truth, while I made the real truth plain by all manner of involuntary confidences expressed by my body and in my actions (which were at once interpreted by Françoise)":[112] there is, therefore, more wisdom than naivety in the way in which Françoise (just as she checks in the newspaper, which she cannot read, the information given her by the butler) looks at Marcel's face in order to assure herself that he is not lying "as though she had been able to see whether the report was really there";[113] it is really there, and she sees perfectly this "invisible ink."

From the autonomy of the body derives the fact that gestural expression is more difficult to master than verbal language: Odette is quite capable of lying in words, but she is unable to suppress, perhaps because she is not even aware of it, that stricken, desperate look that is depicted each time on her face. And since lying has become second nature to her, perhaps she is unaware not only of the mimicry that betrays it, but of the lie itself: only her body is still able to distinguish between the true and the false, or rather, sticking physically and as if substantially to the truth, it can tell only the truth. There can be nothing more imprudent, therefore, than to try to lie through gesture: we have seen this with Charlus and Marcel at Balbec—no one is a sufficiently good actor for that. When Swann questions her about her relationship with Mme Verdurin, Odette thinks that she is able to deny this relationship with a single gesture: alas, this sign (shaking her head, while pursing her lips), which she thought she could control, had been chosen by her body, with the infallible clearsightedness of the automaton, in the repertoire not of denials, but of rejections, as if it had to reply not to a question, but to a proposition. Wishing to show that she has "never done" anything with Mme Verdurin, she can obtain from her body only the mimicry by which it has sometimes managed, and rather out of "personal convenience" than out of "any moral impossibility," to reject her advances. This denial, then, is worth a semi-confession: "When he saw Odette *thus* make him a sign that the insinuation was false, he realized that it was quite *possibly* true."[114] The two words that I have italicized have their full meaning here: it is the *way* in which Odette denies the fact that confesses its *possibility*, and it goes without saying that this possibility (that is to say, the certainty of Odette's lesbianism) is enough to make Swann despair. In less serious circumstances, we see the Princesse de Parme, perhaps a better actress than Mme de Cambremer, impose on her features the appropriate mimicry when Oriane talks to her of a painting by Gustave Moreau, a painter she has never heard of, shaking her head and smiling with all the ardor of her supposed admiration; but the listlessness of the gaze, the last refuge of truth tracked down, is enough to give the lie to all this facial gesticulation: "The intensity of her mimicry could not fill the place of that light which is absent from our eyes so long as we do not understand what people are trying to tell us."[115]

These apparently marginal situations, in which discourse finds itself refuted from the outside by the attitude of the speaker, have in reality for Proust a quite exemplary value, for it is on them that is modeled, as it were, at least ideally, the technique of reading that will enable the Narrator to locate and interpret not the external features, this time, but the internal features of language, by which discourse betrays and refutes itself. Such linguistic events (an unusual turn of phrase, one word replacing another, an unexpected stress, an apparently superfluous repetition, etc.) have "no meaning save in the second degree" and yield that meaning only on condition, says Proust, that "they could be interpreted in the same way as a sudden rush of blood to the cheek of a person who is embarrassed, or, what is even more telling, a sudden silence,"[116] that is, as we see, like a physical accident external to the words spoken. This interpretation of verbal language regarded as nonverbal language has some relation—and that is why I have called it *reading*—with the decipherment of ideographical writing or, more precisely, in the middle of a text in phonetic writing and for a reader used to the type of reading that it calls for, of a suddenly aberrant character, incapable of functioning in the same way as those around it, and which would reveal its meaning only on condition that it is read not as a phonogram, but as an ideogram or pictogram, not as the sign of a sound, but as the sign of an idea or image of a thing.[117] Confronted by such statements, the listener obviously finds himself in a situation symmetrical with that of the reader of a rebus, who must take the image of an object as standing for a syllable, or that of the hypothetical first man, who would have had to use an ideogram for purely phonetic ends. So Marcel compares his hermeneutic apprenticeship to a walk "in the opposite direction to those races which make use of phonetic writing only after regarding the letters of the alphabet as a set of symbols." Thus speech becomes writing. And verbal discourse, abandoning its univocal linearity, a text that is not only polysemic but, if one can use the term in this sense, *polygraphic*, that is to say, combining several systems of writing—phonetic, ideographic, sometimes anagrammatic: "Sometimes the script from which I deciphered Albertine's falsehoods, without being ideographic needed simply to be read backwards"; thus a sentence like "I don't want to go the Verdurins' tomorrow" is then understood as "a childish anagram of the admission: 'I shall go tomorrow to the Verdurins', it is absolutely certain, for I attach the utmost importance to the visit,'"[118] the extreme importance being precisely connoted by the negation, as a message written backwards proves simply by this cryptographic effort, however elementary it may be, that it is not quite innocent.

Of those accidents of language that are to be interpreted as so many signs of an extra-linguistic kind, as it were, one will find a first state in what might be called *involuntary allusion*. We know that allusion—which is a figure duly listed in rhetoric, and which Fontanier places among the figures of expression (tropes in several words) by *reflection*, in which the ideas stated suggest indirectly other unstated ideas—is one of the first forms of indirect language encountered by Marcel, since it animates, at Combray, the discourse of the two great-aunts, Céline and Flora ("M. Vinteuil is not the only one who has nice neighbours" = "Thank you for sending us a case of Asti wine.")[119] Fontanier defines allusion as consisting in "conveying the relation of a thing one says with something else that one does not say."[120] The locus of this relation could very well be reduced to a single word (in which case the allusion belongs to the category of tropes in the strict sense). When it might have an offensive signification, the involuntary allusion is a form of social blunder. A simple example is when M. Verdurin, wishing to convey to Charlus that he includes him among the intellectual élite delares: "Dès les premiers mots que nous avons échangés, j'ai compris que vous en étiez," or when his wife, irritated by the volubility of the same Charlus, points to him and exclaims: "Ah! quelle tapette!"[121] But these incidents have no more than a fairly weak value, since they derive only from ignorance and coincidence; indeed, M. and Mme Verdurin are in no way aware of the effect of their words on the Baron. More serious is the situation of M. de Guermantes when, wishing simply to remind his brother of his early passion for travel, says to him in public: "Ah! You were a peculiar type, for I can honestly say that never in anything did you have the same tastes as other people," a statement in which the proximity of the words "taste" and "peculiar" even more than the affirmation of an essential originality, dangerously suggests Charlus' "peculiar tastes."[122] It is more serious, first because, being "aware of his brother's reputation, if not of his actual habits," he may fear that his brother may be attributing to him quite wrongly an offensive intention: so he immediately blushes, which is even more accusatory than the two unfortunate words; but it is serious above all because in his case the allusion incurs the very strong risk of being neither voluntary (as he fears it might appear) or really fortuitous (like those of the Verdurins), but, in the strong sense, involuntary, that is to say, determined by the thrust of a repressed, compressed thought, which has become for that very reason explosive. This is the well-known mechanism of the blunder by prevention, which Proust himself refers to in a passage of *Jean Santeuil*, in which the hero, visiting Mme Lawrence, whom he knows to be a snob and an adulteress, is disturbed "as if he were going to see a person suffering from a particular disease, to which he must be careful not to refer and from the first words they exchange, he watches over his words like someone who is walking with a blind man takes care not to bump into him. And for a whole hour he had expelled from his brain the three words 'snob,' 'bad conduct,' 'M. de Ribeaumont.'"[123] This "expulsion" gives rise to fears of "the return of the repressed," which would inevitably have taken the form of a blunder, had not Jean been saved in the middle of it by the eagerness that led Mme Lawrence herself to speak—in a roundabout way which will be further examined subsequently—of snobism, adultery, and M. de Ribeaumont. All obsessive thought is a constant threat to the security and integrity of discourse, "for the most dangerous of all forms of concealment is that of the crime itself in the mind of the guilty party" of the crime,[124] or of any thought rejected by voluntary language, and which lies in wait for the opportunity of *expressing itself* through its faults. One remembers how Swann, finding it impossible to confide his love for Odette, grasps the hint involuntarily held out to him by Froberville, who had just spoken the words "killed by savages," in order to refer to Dumont d'Urville, then to La Pérouse—a metonymic allusion (and how!) to the beloved object, who lives in the Rue de la Pérouse.[125] Of Mme Desroches' allusive speech Proust writes in *Jean Santeuil*, enigmatically and decisively, "an unconscious force stirred up her words and drove her to reveal what she said she wanted to hide."[126] One can see that allusion belongs not only to the repertoire of drawing-room comedy: with it, we enter the domain of what Baudelaire would allow us perhaps to call *deep rhetoric*.

In its more canonical form, allusion consists in the borrowing of one or several elements of the allusive discourse from the material (for example, the vocabulary) of the situation alluded to: forms which, strictly speaking, betray their origin, just as, in the well-known description of the sea at Balbec, the appearance of such words as "slopes," "summits," "avalanches," and so on, reveals the implicit comparison between the landscape of sea and mountain; this is obviously the case, for example, of the adjective "peculiar" in what Basin says to his brother. When Marcel, having finally succeeded in meeting Albertine's aunt, announces this encounter to Andrée as if it were some unpleasant duty:

> "I have never doubted it for a single instant," exclaimed Andrée in a bitter tone, while her eyes, enlarged and altered by her annoyance, focused themselves upon some invisible object. These words of Andrée's were not the most reasoned statement of thought which might be expressed thus: "I know that you are in love with Albertine, and that you are working day and night to get in touch with her people." But they were the shapeless fragments, easily pieced together again by me, of such thought that I had exploded by striking it, through the shield of Andrée's self-control.[127]

By insisting on the exploded, shapeless, and disordered character of Andrée's discourse, Proust's commentary runs the risk of concealing what appears to be its essential feature: "I have never doubted it for a single instant," says Andrée, apparently about Elstir's invitation, which will enable Marcel to meet Mme Bontemps; but this sentence in fact relates to Marcel's determination, and therefore to his love for Albertine—denouncing at the same time his duplicity, Andrée's awareness of it, and no doubt, too, her jealousy with regard to Albertine and therefore her love for Marcel (unless one should rather say: her jealousy with regard to Marcel, and therefore her love for Albertine). Rather than a shapeless statement, it is again, as with Basin, a *displaced* statement.

It is in the same category, it seems to me, that we should place two other obviously disturbed and apparently insignificant statements, of which Proust himself, in any case, offers no interpretation. We owe the first, once again, to the Duc de Guermantes: blackballed from the presidency of the Jockey Club by a cabal that has succeeded in using against him his Dreyfusard opinions and Oriane's Jewish acquaintances, the Duc manages to put a good face on it and to show his just contempt for a post so far below his social rank.

> Actually, his anger never cooled. One curious thing was that nobody had ever before heard the Duc de Guermantes make use of the quite commonplace expression "out and out"; but ever since the Jockey election, whenever anybody referred to the Dreyfus case, pat would come "out and out." "Dreyfus case, Dreyfus case, that's soon said, and it's a misuse of the term. It is not a question of religion, it's *out and out* a political matter." Five years might go by without your hearing him say "out and out" again, if during that time nobody mentioned the Dreyfus case, but if, at the end of five years, the name Dreyfus cropped up, "out and out" would at once follow automatically.[128]

It would obviously be unwise to hazard an "interpretation" for an example that may have been conceived arbitrarily by Proust (though this is hardly likely), but one cannot help thinking that the "out and out" (*bel et bien*), mechanically linked in Basin's speech with the Dreyfus case, is linked in his thinking with a consequence, for him not a negligible one, of that case, namely, his own failure at the Jockey Club, where a prince of the first rank was beaten *out and out* as if he were some vulgar provincial landowner: a failure all the more obsessive in that self-esteem prevents him from directly expressing his resentment, which is thus forced to express itself in a lateral way, by a metonymy from the effect to the cause. The other example is taken from smaller fry: Françoise comes into Marcel's bedroom while Albertine was "completely naked in my arms," and Albertine suddenly blurts out: "Good heavens, here's beautiful Françoise!"[129] This phrase was so "unprecedented" that it was "in itself enough to betray its origin" and Françoise "had no need to look to understand what was happening; she went out muttering in her dialect the word *poutana*." It should be noted here that the "anomaly" of the statement was in itself enough for Françoise to infer Albertine's guilt but it does not follow that this anomaly should be regarded as equally arbitrary in its form as Proust seems to indicate when he writes that Françoise sensed that "the words had been snatched at random by emotion." Chance obviously plays no part in this kind of "snatching," and if the detail of the mechanism eludes us, with the particular motifs that Albertine's past might introduce into it, the link between the girl's present situation and the "beauty" that her phrase attributes to the old servant is obvious enough, and therefore, once more, the way in which the surface statement borrows from the deep statement certain elements which, to say the least, disturb the "normality" of the first, and sometimes even make it possible to reconstitute the second. It is no doubt to the same type of mechanism that two perfectly parallel accidents of pronunciation should be related: that of ex-Mlle Bloch, who is suddenly asked what her maiden name was, and who, taken by surprise, replies "Bloch," pronouncing it in the German way, and that of Gilberte, who in the same circumstances, replies "Swann," also in the German way: both, no doubt, projecting into the very statement of their names the pejorative attitude of the anti-Semitic milieu of which they have become, as far as possible, part.[130] The allusive borrowing here concerns only a single phoneme, producing in the discourse a simple metaplasm, but one in which it holds, as we see, more things than in "a long speech."[131]

Although all these cases (except, or course, the last two) are more extended productions of language, it is easy to see the similarity between these involuntary allusions and the parapraxes studied by Freud. In both, there is a contamination, of variable extent, of the surface statement by the censored deep statement. One can regard the presence of the adjective "beautiful" in "here's beautiful Françoise" as the equivalent of that of *dig* in *begleitdigen*, an *amalgam* of *begleiten* (accompany),[132] which is what the speaker wanted to say and the *beleidigen* (insult), which obsesses his unconscious.[133] The "alterations in speech" which concerned Proust so much can,[134] therefore, in their form as well as in their origin, be regarded as examples of Freudian parapraxis, however different the two theories may otherwise be; Freud's formula can be applied to both:

The speaker decides not to put it [the repressed intention] into words, and after that the slip of the tongue occurs: after that, that is to say, the purpose which has been forced back is put into words against the speaker's will, either by altering the expression of the intention which he has permitted, or by mingling with it, or by actually taking its place.[135]

To both, too, I will apply this formula of Proust's, more rigorous perhaps in its very ambiguity: "That portentous language, so unlike the language we habitually speak, in which emotion deflects what we had intended to say and causes to emerge in its place an entirely different phrase, issued from *an unknown lake wherein dwell these expressions alien to our thoughts which by virtue of that very fact reveal them.*"[136]

A variant of the allusion to which Proust pays particular attention is the presence in the statement of a term that is not borrowed from the obsessive situation, but indicating in an abstract, in some sense *empty* way the reference to a situation that is not the one to which this statement explicitly refers. The typical example of this category, a privileged instrument of the blunder (and not only in Proust), is the adverb "justement" (precisely), which Proust cites (precisely!) in the page analyzed above to illustrate his theory of "ideographical" interpretation: M. de Cambremer, thinking that Marcel is a writer, says to him, about a party given at the Verdurins'

"Il y avait *justement* de Borelli" (translated as "Why, Borelli was there!"), this adverb, the relevance of which in the statement itself is obviously non-existent, actually functions as a gesture, as an act of turning to one of his listeners in particular, in order to say to him, "this concerns you": it serves only to show, without specifying it, the existence of a relation between the situation to which the statement refers and that in which it is proffered, and, through this role of index of enunciation in the statement, it belongs to the category of what Roman Jakobson calls *shifters*. Of such a word Proust says, "bursting into flames at the unintended, sometimes perilous contact of two ideas which the speaker has not expressed, but which, by applying the appropriate methods of analysis or electrolysis, I was able to abstract from it."[137] The two ideas that are telescoped here are obviously the (referential) idea of Borelli's status as a writer and the (situational) idea of Marcel's status as a writer: an analogical or metaphorical relation. On the other hand, the relation revealed, through the same accident, when Andrée says to Marcel, "J'ai *justement* vue la tante à Albertine" ("Oh, guess who I've just seen—Albertine's aunt") is metonymic.[138] The "translation" of the adverb is given by Proust himself: "I could see through your casual remarks all right that the one thing you were really thinking of was how you could make friends with Albertine's aunt." Let us note in passing that the adverb unmasks here, like the "I have never doubted it for a single instant" mentioned earlier, two insincerities at once, Andrée's (she had until now pretended that she had been taken in by it) and Marcel's; but above all let us examine the commentary by which, once more, Proust compares these accidents of speech and the mute confidences of the body: "[the word *justement*] was of a kind with certain glances, certain gestures which, for all that they have not a form that is logical, rational, deliberately calculated to match the listener's intelligence, reach him nevertheless in their true significance, just as human speech, converted into electricity in the telephone, is turned into speech again when it strikes the ear." What we have here is, again, the principle of "ideographical" interpretation: such words cannot be directly absorbed (understood) by the intelligence of the listener, for whom, in the linear continuity of discourse, they are meaningless; they must first be converted into gestures or looks, read as a gesture or a look, and again translated into words.

This first type of involuntary revelation proceeds, then, by the insertion into the proferred discourse of a fragment borrowed from the repressed discourse ("out and out," "beautiful Françoise"), or of a term that can be explained only by reference to the repressed discourse (*justement*). A second type comprises statements in which the repressed truth is expressed in an attenuated way, as it were, either through a quantitative diminution, or by an alteration which, by snatching it from its authentic circumstances, makes it less virulent and more bearable. A typical example of quantitative attenuation, in the discourse of Aunt Léonie, and by contagion in the discourse of Combray in general, one of the dogmas of which is the perpetual insomnia of the habitual invalid, is the use of such terms as "to be quiet" or "to rest," which indicate in a more acceptable way that Léonie was asleep.[139]

When Saint-Loup, who has constantly been pestered by Marcel to introduce him to Oriane, finds that he must at last give an account of his mission, he begins by saying that he has not until now had an opportunity of bringing up the matter. This is simply a lie; but he cannot keep to it, and thinks he has to add: "She's not being at all nice just now, Oriane isn't. . . . She's not my old Oriane any longer, they've gone and changed her. I assure you it's not worth while bothering your head about her." This addition is obviously intended by Saint-Loup to put an end to Marcel's petitions by deflecting his desire, and in fact he immediately offers him another object in the person of his cousin Poictiers; but the choice of pretext ("She's not being at all nice") is a trace (in the chemical sense of the term: a very weak, non-measurable quantity) of the truth, namely, that Oriane has refused, or even that, knowing that she would refuse, Robert has not even tried to get her to meet Marcel; thus Marcel understands that in speaking in this way Saint-Loup had acted with "innocent self-betrayal."[140]

But the most characteristic example of this homeopathic use of the truth in lying is the speech in which Bloch, whose spectacular

Jewishness is well known, speaks of "the share (not that it is more than a very tiny share) [of his feelings], which may be ascribed to my Jewish origin," or of "a rather Jewish side of my nature . . . coming out," "contracting his pupils as though he had to prepare for the microscope and infinitesimal quantity of 'Jewish blood.'" He considers it both courageous and witty to tell the truth, which, at the same time, however, "he managed to water down to a remarkable extent, like misers who decide to pay their debts but have not the courage to pay more than half."[141] In this attenuated admission there is still, of course, an element of conscious maneuver, which consists (very naively here) in attempting to set aside any suspicion on the part of his interlocutor by getting him to concentrate on the small part of the truth that is being offered, rather as Odette sometimes adds to her lies some true and harmless detail that Swann will be able to check without damage to her. But the very example of Odette shows that this ruse is not the essential reason for the presence of a truth-witness in lying discourse; the reason is once more the obsessive presence of the true, which seeks by every means to make a path for itself and to erupt in the midst of the untrue: "As soon as she found herself face to face with the man to whom she was obliged to lie, she became uneasy, all her ideas melted like wax before a flame, her inventive and her reasoning faculties were paralysed, she might ransack her brain but would find only a void; still, she must say something, and there lay within her reach precisely the fact which she had wished to conceal, which, being the truth, was the one thing that had remained."[142] And, as we will see later, one can infer from the other forms that Bloch's involuntary admission of his Jewishness takes, that it is also for him a speech that is certainly not unknown, but refused, repressed, and for this very reason irrepressible.

If these quantitative attentuations belong to what rhetoric would regard as a descending synecdoche (that is to say, part of the truth for the whole), others can proceed on the contrary by ascending synecdoche: these are generalizations by which the particular truth is diluted as it were in a discourse that is more vague, apparently theoretical, universal, or potential, as when Joas says "thinking exclusively of Athalie," but in the form of a general maxim,

Le bonheur des méchants comme un torrent s'écoule
(The happiness of the wicked runs out like a mountain stream).[143]

Thus the Princesse de Guermantes, who is in love with Charlus, manages to express this love through such remarks as: "I feel that any woman who fell in love with a man of such priceless worth as Palamède ought to have sufficient breadth of mind, enough devotion, etc."[144]

The last mode of attenuation, by modification of circumstances, proceeds rather by metonymic sliding: wishing to exhibit in general his relationship with Morel and to hide in particular that he has met him in the afternoon, Charlus declares that he saw him in the morning, which is neither more nor less innocent; but "between these two incidents, the only difference is that one is false and the other true."[145] In fact, only the circumstances differ, the truth is spoken in essentials. The need to lie and the muted desire to confess combine here as two forces pulling, not in opposite, but in different directions, to produce a deviation: a strange mixture of avowal and *alibi*.

The third and last form of involuntary avowal also corresponds to a principle enunciated, some years later by Freud: "The content of a repressed image or idea can make its way into consciousness, on condition that it is *negated*. Negation is a way of taking cognizance of what is repressed; indeed it is already a lifting of repression, though not, of course, an acceptance of what is repressed."[146] This intrusion of the repressed content into discourse, in a negative form, which Freud calls *Verneinung* (negation) and which, following Jacques Lacan, we generally translate into French as *dénégation* (denial),[147] obviously corresponds to the rhetorical form of antiphrasis.[148] Proust cites at least two, very closely related examples of statements that so to speak necessarily take the form of a denial, and which are never uttered except to conceal (from oneself) a reality that is precisely the opposite. The first ("Not that it is of the slightest importance") is made by Bloch when he learns that his pronunciation of the word "lift" (as "lighft") is incorrect: it is certainly a futile occasion, but this sentence, Proust observes, is "the same in all men whose self-esteem is great, in the gravest circumstances as well as in the most trivial, betraying there as clearly as on this occasion how important the thing in question seems to him, declares that is of no importance."[149] The second ("After all, what do we care?") is the sentence repeated every couple of minutes, in front of Jupien's house of pleasure by a young potential customer manifestly paralyzed by "extreme fright," and who cannot make up his mind to go in.[150] We know how many denials are produced, in the *Recherche* by those two great "vices," snobbery and homosexuality, both obsessive and both unavowable, as is evidenced, for example, in the speech of Legrandin and Charlus respectively. But it should be noted at once that the anti-snobbish discourse of the snob and the anti-homosexual discourse of the homosexual already represent a more complex condition of the statement-as-denial than those just mentioned: what we have here, in short, to continue our borrowing of the vocabulary of psychoanalysis, is an amalgam of denial and *projection*, an amalgam that makes it possible at one and the same time to expel the guilty passion far from oneself and to speak of it constantly where others are concerned. In actual fact, denial is presented here only as the implicit, and as it were presupposed, condition: Legrandin never says "I am not a snob," but this denial is the virtual signified of his incessant inveighing against snobbery; Charlus does not need to say, "I am not a homosexual," but he certainly expects such a conclusion to emerge from his expatiations on the homosexuality of others. The projective avowal is, then, a particularly economic form, and it is no doubt to this fact that one must attribute what Proust calls "the bad habit . . . of denouncing in other people defects precisely analogous to one's own . . . as though it were a way of speaking about oneself, indirectly, which added to the pleasure of absolution that of confession."[151] Bloch provides an example of this, verging on caricature, in a passage from *Les Jeunes filles en fleur* that would lose much if not quoted in its crushing obviousness:

> One day when we were sitting on the sands, Saint-Loup and I, we heard issuing from a canvas tent against which we were leaning a torrent of imprecation against the swarm of Israelites

that infested Balbec. "You can't go a yard without meeting them," said the voice. "I am not in principle irremediably hostile to the Jewish nation, but here there is a plethora of them. You hear nothing but, "I thay, Apraham, I've chust theen Chacop." You would think that you were in the Rue d'Aboukir." The man who thus inveighed against Israel emerged at last from the tent; we raised our eyes to behold this antisemite. It was my old friend Bloch.[152]

We see that in Bloch's case involuntary avowal takes alternatively the forms of synecdoche ("my Jewish side") and a somewhat hyperbolic antiphrasis. In a way both more dissociated (since it concerns two different "vices") and more synthetic (since in the same discourse), Mme Lawrence uses both figures to exculpate herself from—while actually confessing to them—her snobbery (and also her frivolity), which she attributes to Mme Marmet, and her affair with M. de Ribeaumont, which she accepts by passing it off as pure friendship.

Projective denial obviously finds in the love relationship a privileged terrain, since the guilty party designated happens to be at the same time the intimate enemy. Thus the suffering, reciprocally inflicted, is accompanied almost constantly by a reciprocal rejection of guilt on to the victim: a rejection whose archytypal statement, as we know, is the "filthy creature" to which Françoise, at Combray, treats the chicken that refuses to die.[153] Odette's lies are often no more than a response to Swann's,[154] and the two letters that Marcel writes to Albertine after her flight say a great deal about the hero's ability to simulate.[155] Moreover, it is not out of the question to regard Swann's jealousy, if not Marcel's, as a vast projection of his own infidelity. But, conversely, the desire, the hopeless quest for the other, lend themselves equally well to this kind of transfer as the immortal Bélise in Molière's *Les Femmes savantes* shows. Charlus himself sometimes toys with these "chimera." Thus one sees him claim, several years after their break, that Morel regrets the past and would like to make it up with him, adding that in any case it is not up to him, Charlus, to take the first steps—without realizing, as Marcel immediately remarks, that the mere fact of saying this is precisely a first step:[156] an exemplary situation in that the act of enunciation (*énonciation*), in itself, refutes and ridicules the statement (*énoncé*) as when a child declares loudly and intelligibly, "I am mute."

In this table of the discourse of denial, a place should be made for the emblematic Legrandin. The semiotics of his supposed anti-snobbery is indeed more diverse, richer, and stylistically more accomplished than any other. It begins with his dress, in which the short, single-breasted jacket and the loosely knotted Lavallière necktie,[157] contrasted item by item with the frock-coat and flowing tie of the man of fashion, and suiting the juvenile innocence of his face, signify in a very effective way the simplicity and independence of the unworldly, rustic poet. Of this dress he himself gives, as he should, a quite pragmatic justification when he meets Marcel in a Paris street: "Ah! So it's you, a man of fashion, and in a frock-coat too! That is a livery in which my independent spirit would be ill at ease. It is true that you are a man of the world, I suppose, and go out paying calls! To go and dream, as I do, before some half ruined tomb, my flowing tie and jacket are not out of place." (It is like reading one of those pages from fashion magazines analyzed by Barthes, in which the symbolic value of an item of clothing is disguised as suitability: for autumn weekends, a roll-neck Shetland sweater; to go and dream before some half ruined tomb, a single-breasted jacket and a flowing tie.) The semiological effectiveness of this costume can be gauged on at least two occasions. The first is when the Narrator's father meets Legrandin walking by the side of a lady who owns a country house in the neighborhood and, receiving no acknowledgment of his wave, makes the following comment on the incident: "I should be all the more sorry to feel that he was angry with us, because among all those people in their Sunday clothes there is something about him, with his little cut-away coat and his soft neckties, so little dressed-up, so genuinely simple; an air of innocence, almost, which is really attractive"; but when a second meeting has confirmed his rudeness and therefore his snobbery, the Narrator's grandmother still refuses to recognize the obvious for the following reasons: "You admit yourself that he appears at church there, quite simply dressed, and all that; he hardly looks like a man of fashion." Thus, in any circumstances, even the most compromising the single-breasted jacket continues to protest against "a detested splendor," and the spotted necktie continues to float in front of Legrandin, "like the standard of his proud isolation, of his noble independence."

The art of mimicry and silent expression is also more developed in the case of Legrandin than in that of more ordinary mortals. Taken aback by a direct question like "Do you know the lady of Guermantes?" it is true that he is unable to conceal "a little brown dimple" that appeared in the middle of each of his blue eyes, the drooping of his "fringed eyelids," the "bitter lines" around the mouth, which signified very clearly for his interlocutor, "Alas, no!" but he is at least capable of mitigating his confession, not only by a discourse of denial ("No, I do not know them; I have never wished to know them; I have always made a point of preserving complete independence; at heart, as you know, I am a bit of a Radical, etc.") but also and above all by a resumption of control, so to speak, of his features, which might have made a less perceptive spectator hesitate: the stiffened mouth turned into a smile, the wounded pupil reacted by secreting "the azure overflow." To an unwelcome question, which he prefers not to hear, he still knows how to return the gaze of his interlocutor, "with an air . . . of not being afraid to look him in the face," as if behind that face, which the intensity of his gaze had suddenly made transparent, he saw in the distance "a brightly coloured cloud, which provided him with a mental alibi." His masterpiece in this kind is no doubt the way in which he managed, on the occasion of a second meeting in aristocratic company, to give Marcel and his father a look of deep affection that would not, however, be perceived by his companion, "lighting up for us, and for us alone, with a secret and languid flame invisible by the great lady upon his other side, an enamoured pupil in a countenance of ice."[158]

But it is obviously in verbal expression that Legrandin's art achieves its greatest success. The Narrator's grandmother criticizes him for speaking "a little too well, a little too much like a book,"[159] of lacking in his language the simplicity of his dress, and it may indeed appear, on a superficial reading, that his anti-snobbery and literary speech are, as so often in those composite beings that are Proust's "characters," two features quite independent of each other and juxtaposed to some extent by chance. Nothing could be further from the truth: textual production (which, in any case, is not only oral, since Legrandin is also a writer) is in his case in a very close functional relationship with the claim to anti-snobbery, the denial of his social failures, and the discouragement of intruders who might compromise his difficult career. The most elaborate speeches, the apparently most purely decorative examples of what can be regarded as a complex pastiche of the Chateaubrianesque stylistic inheritance of the late nineteenth century, make up in fact the proliferating signifier of an almost single signified, which is sometimes "I am not a snob," sometimes "Don't come and spoil for me the few connections I have." And if these very simple signifieds may assume so sumptuous a literary form, it is thanks to the relay of an intermediary signified-signifier that is more or less: I'm not interested in people, but only in things; "a few churches, books—two or three pictures—rather more, perhaps, and the light of the moon";

> "Perhaps it is a castle which you encounter upon the cliff's edge; standing there at the roadside, where it has halted to contemplate its sorrows before an evening sky, still rosy, through which a golden moon is climbing; while the fishing-boats, homeward bound, creasing the watered silk of the Channel, hoist its penant at their mastheads and carry its colours. Or perhaps it is a simple dwelling-house that stands alone, ugly, if anything, timid-seeming but full of romance, hiding from every eye some imperishable secret of happiness and disenchantment."[160]

This "Romantic" music is certainly a language, but what it speaks of is not what it names: and we know that later, when he has become Comte de Méséglise, a frequent visitor at the Guermantes' parties, an ally of Baron de Charlus, associated with high society, homosexuality having entirely supplanted snobbery, Legrandin will lose all his eloquence.[161] Proust attributes his verbal decay to old age, but one cannot help thinking that with snobbery it is the very inspiration, the source of the "well-wrought style" that has dried up. Legrandin's stylistic *etymon* is the proliferating efflorescence of a wholly antiphrastic discourse, which ceaselessly speaks of nature, landscape, bunches of flowers, sunsets, rosy moonlight in violet skies, because it never ceases to think of Society, parties, castles, duchesses. With reference to him, Proust refers to that "learned swindler" who put all his labor and all of his skill into producing "false palimpsests," which he sold for true ones: this is certainly Legrandin's function, except that his is a true palimpsest, that is to say, more than a form of speech, a *text*, written over several layers, which has to be read at several levels: that of the Romantic signifier, that of the signified suggested ("I do not belong to Society"), that of the real, repressed, and obsessive signified: "I am only a snob." Marcel's grandmother did not quite know how well she put it when she said that Legrandin spoke "like a book." These ambiguous words, several times folded back upon themselves, which say what they do not say and avow what they deny, is first of all one of the finest examples of Proustian indirect language; but are they not also, in a way, the image of all literature?

They are at least, perhaps, the image of the *Recherche du temps perdu* itself, which, in order to present itself both as a tireless quest and as a message of truth, cannot but appear, at the same time, as an immense text, at once allusive, metonymic, synecdochic, (metaphoric, of course) and disavowing, of involutary avowal, in which are revealed, but by concealment and disguise in innumerable transformations, a small number of simple statements concerning its author, his origins, his ambitions, his morals, everything he shares secretly with Bloch, with Legrandin, with Charlus, and of which he has carefully exempted his hero, the colorless, yet idealized image of himself. We know with what perhaps naive severity André Gide judged such trickery; to which Proust replied that one can say anything so long as one does not say "I." By "can," of course, Proust meant "has the right"; but perhaps the verb should be given a stronger meaning: perhaps there is no truthful language, in language as elsewhere, outside indirect language.[162] Perhaps, here too, the truth has as its condition, in the double sense of a necessary clause and a way of being, that is to say, as *locus*, the lie:[163] inhabiting the work, as it inhabits all speech, not insofar as it shows itself in it, but insofar as it hides itself in it.

It is legitimate, therefore, to relate the Proustian "theory" of language, as it occurs explicitly or as it can be extracted from the principal episodes in which it is illustrated, to a critique of the realist illusion, which consists of seeking in language a faithful image, a direct expression of reality: the Cratylian utopia (whether ignorant or "poetic") of a motivation of the sign, of a natural relation between the name and the place, the word and the thing (what Proust called the *age of names*), gradually ruined by contact with reality (travel, participation in Society) and by linguistic knowledge (Brichot's etymologies); the "naivety" of a Bloch or a Cottard, which imagines that truth is expressed "literally" in discourse, but disproved by the constant, obsessive, universal experience of the lie, of bad faith, and of the unconscious, in which is manifested in a startling way the decentering of speech, however "sincere" it may be, in relation to the inner "truth," and the inability of language to reveal that truth other than in a concealed, disguised, inverted, always indirect and, as it were, secondary way: the *age of words*.[164]

The provisional title that was for a time given to the last part, to the future *Temps retrouvé*, a synthesis and spiritual culmination of the whole Proustian experience, the *age of things*, might lead one to believe in a sort of "last illusion to be lost," which would not have been lost, in a final falling back into the realistic utopia of a relation both direct and authentic with the world. This is obviously not the case, and already a passage in *Les Jeunes filles en fleurs* put the reader on his guard against this error by contrasting the "visible world" with the "true world," and by criticizing that other mirage, perception through the "senses," as the nominal illusion.[165] For Proust, the only authentic reality, as we know, is that which is given in the experience of reminiscence and perpetuated in the exercise of metaphor—the presence of one sensation in another, the "mirroring" of memory, analogical and differential depth, the ambiguous transparency of the text, the palimpsest of writing. Far from bringing us back to some immediacy of the perceived, the *Temps retrouvé* will plunge us irrevocably into what James called the "splendour of the indirect," into the infinite mediation of language.

In this sense, "linguistic" theory—a critique of "naive" conceptions, the privileged position accorded to secondary language as revelation, the reference from immediate discourse to indirect speech, and therefore from discourse to writing (to discourse as writing)—all this does not occupy a marginal place in Proust's work: it is, on the contrary, theoretically and practically, its necessary, and almost sufficient, condition: the work, for Proust, like the "line" for Mallarmé, "makes up for what is lacking in languages." If words were the image of things, says Mallarmé, everybody would be a poet, and there would be no such thing as poetry; poetry is *born* from what is lacking in (for lack of) languages. Proust's lesson is more or less parallel: if "primary" language were truthful, secondary language would not be necessary. It is the conflict between language and truth that *produces*, as we have seen, indirect language; and indirect language is, above all, writing—the work.

[1968]

NOTES

[References to *À la recherche du temps perdu* are to the three-volume Pléiade edition, (Paris: Gallimard, 1955–56), each volume being represented by a roman numeral, and to the seven-volume English translation by Scott Moncrieff and (volume 7) Andreas Mayor, published by Vintage Books (New York: Random House, 1970), each volume being represented by an arabic numeral—Tr.]

1. Cf. R. Le Bidois, "Le langage parlé des personnages de Proust," *Le Français moderne* (June–July 1939); J. Vendryès, "Proust et les noms propres," *Mélanges Huguet*, (Paris: Boivin, 1940); Roland Barthes, "Proust et les noms," *To Honor Roman Jakobson* (The Hague: Mouton, 1967); and on Proustian semiotics in general, Gilles Deleuze, *Marcel Proust et les signes* (Paris: P.U.F., 1964); *Proust and Signs*, Richard Howard, tr. (New York: George Braziller, 1972).

2. Proust, *Chroniques* (Paris: Gallimard, 1927), p. 204.
3. II:641; 4:33.
4. I:496; 2:51; II:900; 4:214.
5. III:41; 5:26; II:893; 4:209. Or again, the enthusiastic hissings of Mme de Cambremer and the accent of Prince von Faffenheim. "There are times," says Proust, "when, to paint a complete portrait of someone, we should have to add a phonetic imitation to our verbal description" (II:942; 4:243).
6. II:771; 4:124; II:566; 3:403-4.
7. I:792; 2:270. [Rewritten in correct French, the sentence would read: "Ce pauvre vieux, il me fait de la peine, etc." Scott Moncrieff makes no attempt to convey the speaker's idiom, but simply translates thus: "Oh, the poor old man; he makes me sick; he looks half dead."—TR.]
8. II:357; 3:257.
9. I:739; 2:232; II:526-27; 3:376; II:510; 3:365.
10. II:392; 3:283; II:736-37; 4:99.
11. I:154; 1:118; II:805, 825, 857; 4:141, 161-62, 184.
12. III:515; 6:72; II:720; 4:87.
13. I:663; 1:175.
14. II:239; 3:171; cf. II:725; 4:91: "his incapacity to assimilate exactly the niceties of the French language."
15. "La dèche" (on the rocks) II:826; 4:162, "à la revoyure" ('till we meet again) II:724; 4:90, "votre pelure" (your skin) II:547; 3:390, "je m'enfous" (not that I care a damn), "ma bourgeoise" (my good woman) II:580; 3:413.
16. "He dragged me across to Mamma saying: 'Will you do me the great honour of presenting me to your *mother*?' letting go a little as he came to the last word" (II:338; 3:242).
17. One should mention however another explanation, according to which Basin owes his bad French, like a whole "generation of noblemen" to the education of Msgr. Dupanloup (II:720; 4:87).
18. III:34; 5:21.
19. II:736; 4:99.
20. III:154; 5:106.
21. II:19, 825, 857; 3:11; 4:161-62, 184.
22. I:445; 2:114.
23. II:791, 765; 4:138, 120.
24. III:190; 5:131. And a few lines later: "But error is more obstinate than faith and does not examine the grounds of its belief." Already, at Combray, "one of Eulalie's most rooted beliefs, and one that the formidable list of corrections which her experience must have compiled was powerless to eradicate, was that Mme Sazerat's name was really Mme Sazerin" (I:70). Françoise makes the same mistake, III:573; 6:113.
25. I:697; 2:201.
26. III:842; 7:111.

27. III:750; 7:42; II:778; 4:129; II:526; 3:376.
28. I:217; 1:166.
29. I:499; 2:53.
30. II:869, 1094, 923; 4:192, 352, 229.
31. I:387–88; 1:296.
32. As far as I am aware, Proust's only remark concerning the form of a common noun (and it does not amount to much!) concerns the word *mousmé*: "The mere sound of it makes one's teeth ache as they do when one has put too large a spoonful of ice in one's mouth" (II:357; 3:257); but is is obvious that this is merely the description of a sensation, without the slightest semantic motivation.
33. *Contre Sainte-Beuve* (Paris: Gallimard, 1954), p. 274. Cf. the passage in *Sodome et Gomorrohe* in which Marcel receives an invitation to a funeral signed by a host of names of the Norman nobility ending in *-ville, -court,* and *-tot*: "Garbed in the roof-tiles of their castle or in the roughcast of their parish church, their nodding heads barely reaching above the vault of the nave or banqueting hall, and then only to cap themselves with the Norman lantern or the dovecot of the pepperpot turret, they gave the impression of having sounded the rallying call to all the charming villages straggling or scattered over a radius of fifty leagues." (II:786; 4:135).
34. *Jean Santeuil*, Pléiade (Paris: Gallimard, 1971), p. 570; I:185; 1:142. [The only available English translation of *Jean Santeuil* diverges so widely in arrangement from the later Pléiade edition that I have not referred to it here—Tr.]
35. I:387; 1:296.
36. *Jean Santeuil*, pp. 534–35.
37. An intermediary case is that of names borrowed from reality and given a fictional locus, like *Guermantes*: there the freedom of the novelist lies not in the combination of the phonemes, but in the overall choice of an appropriate vocable.
38. Barthes, "Proust et les noms," p. 154.
39. My italics. [The word *assume* in the French text is *absorber*; Genette's point is obscured by the translation.—M.-R.L.] This word, which indicates very clearly the action of the signified on the signifier, was already to be found at the beginning of this passage carrying the same value: "If their names thus permanently absorbed the image that I had formed of these towns it was only by transforming that image, by subordinating its reappearance in me to their own special laws" (I:387; 1:296). The reciprocity is highly marked here.
40. I:388; 1:296; cf. II:426; 3:307: "Its compact and almost cloying name."
41. The Norman essence, by analogy with Bolbec, Caudebec, etc. The Persian style of the name (I:658; 2:172: "The name—almost Persian in style—of Balbec") derives no doubt from its homophony with such names

as Usbeck from Montesquieu's *Les Lettres persanes*, not to mention the Lebanese Baalbeck.

42. Unless, as Barthes suggests, one passes through the "conceptual relay of the word *rugueux* (rugged)," which would enable him to evoke "a complex of high-crested waves, sheer cliffs and spiky architecture" (Barthes, "Proust et les noms," p. 155).

43. II:13; 3:6.

44. I:171; 1:132: "the orange light which glowed from the resounding syllable 'antes.'"

45. II:209; 3:149: "That amaranthine colour of the closing syllable of her name."

46. As is, on the other hand, it seems, the association i = purple, attested at least twice (I:42; 1:32; and *Contre Sainte-Beuve*, p. 168. Noted by Barthes, "Proust et les noms," p. 155).

47. I:142; 1:109.

48. II:256; 3:183. Cf. J. Pommier, *La Mystique de Marcel Proust* (Paris: Droz, 1939), p. 50.

49. In which the name, curiously enough, was analyzed without being quoted, which might lead one to suppose (but it is hardly likely) that it was invented after the event (*Contre Saint-Beuve*, p. 277).

50. I:684; 2:191.

51. I:661; 2:174.

52. I:387; 1:296.

53. I:658; 2:172.

54. II:524, 432–33, 257; 3:374, 311, 184.

55. I:548; 2:90.

56. Louis Hjelmslev, *Prolegomena to a Theory of Language*, F. J. Whitfield, tr. 2d rev. ed. (Madison: University of Wisconsin Press, 1961), p. 60.

57. I:644; 2:161.

58. II:1005; 4:363.

59. III:693; 6:193.

60. II:536, 539, 540–42; 3:382, 384–85, 387.

61. II:942; 4:243. Saint-Loup, at Balbec, had already warned (Marcel of this instability: "In that family they change their names as you'ld change your shirt" (I:755; 2:243).

62. "The name Guermantes itself received from all the beautiful names—extinct, and so all the more glowingly rekindled—with which I learned only now that it was connected, a new sense and purpose, purely poetical" (II:542–43; 3:387).

63. The functional relation between these etymologies and Basin's genealogies is clearly indicated by Proust: nobles are "the etymologists of the language not of words but of names" (II:532–33; 3:380). But Brichot, too, clings to the etymology of names (and places). We should remember

that his etymologies are dispersed between pp. 888 and 938 of vol. II of the Pléiade edition (or between pp. 205 and 241 of vol. 5 of the English translation). Before that there had been a few etymologies provided by the parish-priest of Combray (I:104–6; 1:79–81), but again these are lacking in critical value, and will indeed be often refuted by Brichot. As for the link between their genealogies and etymologies, one may note what is in some sense a hybrid "revelation" when Marcel learns that the name Surgis-le-Duc derives not from a ducal connection, but from a misalliance with a rich manufacturer called Leduc (II:706; 4:78).

64. Vendryès, "Proust et les noms propres."
65. Barthes, "Proust et les noms," p. 158.
66. II:1100, 936, 950; 4:355, 239, 248.
67. II:1098; 4:355.
68. II:1109; 4:362.
69. This is the term by which Jean-Pierre Richard designates Chateaubriand's belief in an "immediate expressiveness of signs"—*Paysage de Chateaubriand*, (Paris: Seuil, 1967) p. 162.
70. André Maurois, *À la recherche de Marcel Proust* (Paris: Hachette, 1949), p. 270.
71. I:91; 1:69.
72. I:341; 1:262.
73. *Contre Sainte-Beuve*, p. 278.
74. I:587; 2:119.
75. I:218; 1:167.
76. Pierre Fontanier, *Les Figures du discours*, new ed. (Paris: Flammarion, 1968), p. 150.
77. I:201; 1:154.
78. II:244; 3:174. Another of Bloch's literalisms appears on II:222; 3:158.
79. III:378–40, 742; 5:264–66, 7:36–37. It is Charlus, at Balbec, who gives Marcel, who had just declared that he "adores" his grandmother, this double lesson, which would be equally applicable to Bloch: "You are still young; you should profit by your youth to learn two things; first, to refrain from expressing sentiments that are too natural not to be taken for granted; and secondly not to dash into speech to reply to things that are said to you before you have penetrated their meaning" (I:767; 2:251–52).
80. *Jean Santeuil*, p. 736.
81. I:245; 1:188.
82. II:504; 3:361.
83. II:451; 3:325; III:1007.
84. II:577; 3:411.
85. II:662–63; 4:48.
86. II:943–44, 946; 4:244, 246.
87. *Jean Santeuil*, pp. 708–11.

88. ɪɪ:257–63; 3:183–88.
89. ɪɪ:226; 3:161.
90. *Jean Santeuil*, pp. 668–73.
91. This should not however lead one to think in terms of a true chronological succession: the two forms of apprenticeship, in the *Recherche*, are in fact simultaneous.
92. ɪɪɪ:711; 7:13.
93. ɪɪɪ:1248 (index entry under "Norpois").
94. ɪɪɪ:212; 7:147.
95. ɪɪ:530; 3:378. Proust adds: "They were for him, among other things, almost a question of prosody," which is curiously reminiscent of Michelet's "Shall I say," in which he sees "not a scholar's precaution but a musician's cadence" (ɪɪɪ:161; 5:110).
96. ɪ:512–13; 2:63; "It was not thus that Swann used to talk in days gone by," Marcel comments.
97. ɪ:909–10; 2:353.
98. ɪ:504, 511, 510; 2:57, 62.
99. ɪɪ:819; 4:157.
100. ɪɪ:312; 3:222.
101. ɪ:799; 2:275; ɪɪ:855; 4:183; ɪɪ:790; 4:138; ɪ:800; 2:276; ɪɪ:1026; 4:302; ɪ:800; 2:276.
102. ɪɪ:236; 3:168.
103. ɪ:763; 2:249.
104. ɪɪ:94; 1:64.
105. ɪɪɪ:729, 733, 788, 789; 7:27, 29, 72.
106. ɪ:525; 2:73. The same observation concerning Marcel after his break with Gilberte, ɪɪ:713; 4:83.
107. ɪ:752; 2:241 (my italics). Some lines later; "He emitted the loud panting breath that people who are not feeling too hot but would like it to be thought that they were."
108. ɪ:855; 2:315 (my italics). It should be noted that *Jean Santeuil* (ɪɪɪ:30) said exactly the opposite: "Our interlocutors attribute to what we say so absent-minded or so indifferent attention, that we are thought to be absent-minded when we are most attentive, and the facial expressions, the blunders, the marks of contempt, which we think must have been so obvious, almost always pass unnoticed." It would certainly be pointless to attempt to *reduce* this contradiction by reference to some difference of context or "evolution" in Proust's thinking: the two "truths" coexist without meeting, by *turning their backs to one another*.
109. ɪɪ:66; 3:44.
110. ɪɪ:586, 231, 237; 3:417, 165, 169.
111. ɪɪ:822; 4:160.
112. ɪɪɪ:423–24; 6:6; ɪɪ:66; 3:45.

113. III:467; 6:38. Indeed, she is quite capable, and in a voluntary way, of expressing herself in silent language; condemned as she is by the tyranny of her masters to speak "like Tiresias," in figures and riddles," she managed to embody everything that she could not express directly in a sentence for which we could not find fault with her without accusing ourselves, indeed in less than a sentence, in a silence, in a way in which she placed a thing in a room" (II:359; 3:259).

114. I:362; 1:277.

115. II:520; 3:372.

116. I:929; 2:367; III:88.

117. For example, and very commonly, in such statements as "Il se tient comme un i" ("He stands like an *i*"), which, even in oral communication, imply a detour through writing.

118. III:88, 90–91; 7:59, 61. Cf. I:860; 2:318, and II:1023; 4:30: "*The inverse signs* whereby we express our sentiments by their opposites."

119. I:25; 1:19.

120. Fontanier, *Les Figures du discours*, p. 125.

121. II:941; 4:242; III:278; 5:193. [The full impact of the Verdurins' remarks is inevitably weakened in translation. The phrase *"en être"* (to be one of them) is the commonest euphemism in use in French for "to be a homosexual." Similarly *"tapette,"* which is translated here as "rattle," as well as being slang for "tongue," is more usually used to mean "queen" or "fairy."—TR.]

122. Which immediately reconstitutes the latent syntagm (II:718; 2:86).

123. *Jean Santeuil*, p. 735.

124. II:715; 4:84.

125. I:343; 1:263.

126. *Jean Santeuil*, p. 779.

127. I:928–29; 2:367.

128. III:40; 5:25.

129. III:822–23; 7:96.

130. III:823; 7:96, and III:585; 6:121–22. In the second case, Proust explains the distortion by the wish "to mitigate the crudity of what she had to say" in order to make the confession less painful: this explanation does not exclude the other one, of course—the parapraxis is overdetermined here or, to put it another way, determined at the same time by several aspects of the complex of denial.

131. One last example of this kind is the sentence of the lift-boy: "*You know*, I couldn't find her" (Albertine) (II:794; 4:140): in fact, he knows very well that Marcel learns this by the words themselves, and he is afraid of being reprimanded for this failed mission; "and so he said 'You know' to ward off the terror which menaced him as he uttered the words that were to bring me the knowledge." Here an element of the surface statement

is borrowed from the situation desired deep down, and which is realized in a utopian way in the discourse.

132. The word [*amalgam*] is Proust's own, III:89.

133. Sigmund Freud, *The Psychopathology of Everyday Life* (1901) in *Standard Edition* (London: Hogarth Press, 1953–66), 6:68.

134. II:794; 4:140.

135. Freud, *A General Introduction to Psychoanalysis* (1916–17) in *Standard Edition*, 15:65,

136. III:822; 7:96 (my italics). Is there a better definition of the unconscious?

137. III:89–90; 5:59.

138. I:928; 2:366. Another example, III:178. An adverb, Proust adds, "akin to an expression dear to Mme Cottard: 'in the nick of time.'"

139. I:51; 1:39.

140. II:146; 3:103.

141. I:746; 2:237.

142. I:278; 1:213.

143. Quoted I:108; 1:82, on Françoise's oblique recriminations.

144. II:715; 4:84.

145. III:213; 7:148.

146. Freud, "Negation" (1925) in *Standard Edition*, 19:235–36.

147. In fact the expression is to be found in Proust: "It is moreover the property of love to make us at once more distrustful and more credulous, to make us suspect, more readily than we should suspect anyone else, her whom we love, and be convinced more easily by her denials" (II:833; 4:167).

148. We have already seen that Proust metaphorically qualifies Albertine's denials as *anagrams*, because they must be read inside out.

149. I:740; 2:232.

150. III:822; 7:96. On this cliché of disavowal, cf. II:960; 4:255.

151. I:743; 2:234.

152. I:738; 2:230–31.

153. I:122; 1:193; cf. I:285; 1:219.

154. I:360; 1:276.

155. III:454; 469; 7:29, 39.

156. III:803; 7:82.

157. I:68, 120, 125, 126; 1:51, 91, 95, 96; II:154; 4:108.

158. I:127, 131, 125–26; 1:97, 100, 96.

159. I:68; 1:51.

160. I:128, 132; 1:98, 101.

161. III:934; 7:182.

162. As in every rule, especially in Proust, room must be made for the exception. This role is carried out, twice, by the indefatigable Bloch. During the Villeparisis' afternoon party, as the Duc de Châtellerault refuses

to talk to him about the Dreyfus case, arguing that it is a subject "which, on principle, I never mention except to Japhetics," Bloch, always ready to joke about his "Jewish origin," is taken aback and can only mutter, all defenses down: "But how on earth did you know? Who told you?" (II:247; 3:177). A little later, at the same Mme de Villeparisis', learning that an old lady with whom he has just been scarcely polite is none other than Mme Alphonse de Rothschild, he cries out in her presence: "If only I'd known!" a proof, Proust adds, "that sometimes in this life, under the stress of an exceptional emotion, people do say what is in their minds" (II:506; 3:362).

163. As I have already had occasion to remark, the "lie" in Proust is almost never a fully conscious and deliberate act. Whoever lies, also lies to himself, like Legrandin, who, though he "was not altogether truthful," was no less "sincere" when he inveighed against snobs, for "it is only with the passions of others that we are ever really familiar" (I:129; 1:99). Swann, for example, delivers long speeches that are full of lies: thus, on the magnanimity of the Verdurins, when they encourage his meetings with Odette (I:249; 1:191); on the baseness of the same Verdurins, after the break (I:286–88; 1:220–21); on his wish to go and visit Pierrefonds precisely when Odette happens to be there (I:293; 1:225–26); and above all when, while sending money to Odette, he protests within himself against her reputation as a "kept woman," the unfortunate meeting of these two ideas being avoided by one of those attacks of mental blindness that he inherited from his father, a typical example of censorship by "scotomization": "His mind fumbled, for a moment, in the darkness, he took off his spectacles, wiped the glasses, passed his hands over his eyes, and saw no light until he found himself face to face with a wholly different idea, the realization that he must endeavour, in the coming months, to send Odette six or seven thousand-franc notes instead of five, simply as a surprise for her to give her pleasure" (I:268–69; 1:206). Marcel is not safe from this kind of internal bad faith (see his comments after Albertine's departure, III:421–22, 6:4–5), and he says himself that the lies he tells Françoise, for example, are so automatic that he is not aware of them (II:66; 3:44). When a snob like Legrandin or M. Bloch *père* says of a person outside his reach "I have no wish to know him," the *intellectual sense* (the truth, for the "perspicacious" interlocutor) is "I have no means knowing him," but "the emotional sense is indeed, 'I have no wish to know him.'" The speaker knows that it is not true, but he does not, all the same, say it simply to deceive; he says it because it is what he feels most (I:771; 2:254). With Proust, then, a lie is much more than merely a lie: it is so to speak the very being of what elsewhere is called "consciousness."

164. To this critique of speech, one ought, of course, to link Proust's severe judgment on what we know about friendship (I:736; 1:229, and II:394; 3:284), considered as pure conversation, superficial dialogue, without moral authenticity or intellectual value.

165. "Names are, no doubt, but whimsical draughtsmen, giving us of people as well as of places sketches so little like the reality that we often experience a kind of stupor when we have before our eyes, in place of the imagined, the visible world (which, for that matter, is not the true world, our senses being little more endowed than our imagination with the art of portraiture, so little, indeed, that the final and approximately lifelike pictures which we manage to obtain of reality are at least as different from the visible world as that was from the imagined)" (1:548; 2:90).

INDEX

Allegory, 45; *see also* Figures
Alliteration, 55
Allusion, 269–76; *see also* Figures
Anagram, 151, 269, 293*n*148
Analogy, 8, 30, 89, 94, 125*n*38, 203–4, 206–9, 225, 275, 285, 288*n*41; figures of, 107–21
Antiphrasis, *see under* Figures
Antonomasis, 106, 115; *see also* Figures
Apollinaire, Guillaume, 76, 136
Apostrophe, 56; *see also* Figures
Arbitrariness, *see under* Sign
Aristotle, 17, 22, 55, 67, 104, 124*n*29, 136; *Poetics*, 128–33, 137–38; *Rhetoric*, 103
Augustine, St., 22, 76
Authorship, *see under* Writing

Bachelard, Gaston, 17, 27–28, 65, 72, 92, 114, 120, 192
Bally, Charles, 49, 78, 88–90, 100*n*46
Balzac, Honoré de, 87, 135, 139–42, 148, 162–63, 167, 187, 192, 195, 198, 214–15, 217–18, 230, 250
Baroque, the, 21, 72, 77, 84–85, 125*n*39, 135, 211
Barthes, Roland, 4, 27–44, 58, 72, 78, 92, 98*n*8, 104, 126*n*41, 198, 238–39, 243, 281; *see also* Sign; Writing
Bary, René, 51, 60*n*7
Bataille, Georges, 67
Baudelaire, Charles, 35, 73, 81–83, 88, 96, 101*n*51, 119, 228*n*59, 271

Benda, Julien, 61
Benveniste, Émile, 67–68, 71, 138–40; *see also* Discourse
Bergson, Henri, 216, 218; Bergsonianism, 62, 67
Blair, Hugh, 56
Blanchot, Maurice, 4, 18, 65, 69, 73, 221–22
Blin, Georges, 141, 173, 175
Boas, Franz, 6
Boileau, Nicolas, 19, 46, 67, 85, 135, 144*n*6
Book, the (Mallarmé), 22, 64, 68, 199; *see also* Text
Borges, Jorge Luis, 17–18, 21, 45, 73, 103
Bréal, Michel, 105
Brecht, Bertolt, 21, 27, 37
Breton, André, 45–46, 98*n*18, 118, 120
Bricolage, 3–6
Brunetière, Ferdinand, 19, 62–64, 67

Cassirer, Ernst, 11
Catachresis, *see under* Figures
Chateaubriand, François, 140, 213–14, 218, 283, 290*n*69
Cicero, 51, 104
Cinema, 21, 27, 34, 187
Classicism, 20–21, 54, 57, 60*n*7, 79–90, 125*n*39, 135; *see also* Rhetoric
Classification: *see* Literary function; Literary history; Rhetoric

Claudel, Paul, 21, 69, 82, 92, 98*n*18, 100*nn*37, 41, 237
Cliché, *see under* Usage
Code, 7, 9, 29–30, 32, 34–35, 42*n*12, 48, 54, 58, 90, 150–52, 156, 158–60, 165, 238, 252, 255–56
Cohen, Jean, 77–91, 97–101, 110, 113
Connotation: *see under* Figurative meaning; Ideology
Contiguity, 53–54, 94, 107–9, 115, 122*n*15, 123*n*17, 247
Copenhagen School, *see* Linguistics, structural
Corneille, Pierre, 14, 79, 81, 84–85
Cratylism, 92, 120, 246, 248, 285

Decentering, 60, 162–63, 178, 285
Deguy, Michel, 103, 113, 115–17, 124*n*35
Denotation, *see under* Literal meaning
Derrida, Jacques, 69
Description, 10, 68, 133–37, 171, 186, 192–93, 197–98, 203, 206, 214; descriptive epithets, 80–81; figure of, 52–53
Diegesis, *see under* Narrative
Dilthey, Wilhelm, 13
Discourse (*discours*), 67–68, 137–43, 176–78
Dispositio, *see* Rhetoric, parts of
Domairon, 46–48, 52, 60*n*7
Du Bos, Charles, 61–62
Dumarsais, César, 48, 50–51, 56, 60*n*7, 104–6, 108, 122*n*7, 125*n*38
Dumézil, Georges, 23*n*20
Durand, Gilbert, 17, 24*n*31, 167–68

Écriture (writing), *see under* Writing
Écrivain (writer), *see under* Writing
Eichenbaum, Boris, 23*n*10, 107
Ellipsis, *see under* Figures
Elocutio, *see* Rhetoric, parts of
Elocution, 142; figure of, 55
Éluard, Paul, 46, 95–96, 110, 118
Empson, William, 10
Epithet: *see under* Description; Figures
Essence, 29, 65–72, 116, 168, 172, 199, 222, 226, 238, 245–46, 288*n*41; of poetic language, 10, 64, 67, 78–79, 95–96; Proustian, 203–214
Étiemble, René, 8
Euphemism, 106; *see also* Figures

Figurative meaning (*or* signification), 51–52, 56–57, 60*n*6, 86–87, 94, 99*n*31, 116, 125*n*36; connotation, 31–33, 43*n*49, 57–58, 83, 87, 89–90, 99*n*31, 105, 231, 235, 242, 251–52, 262–65; *see also* Figure; Literal meaning
Figure (*or* trope), 9, 12, 45–60, 75, 86–90, 94, 98*n*14, 99*nn*27, 31, 103–26, 169, 208, 226, 252, 269, 280, 292*n*113; of meaning (*or* signification), 9, 32–33, 105, 107; of the sublime, 48, 176; of thought, 54–55, 105; translatability as criterion of, 46, 51–53, 56, 60*n*6, 90; *see also* Form; Literary function; Rhetoric; Space; Synonymy; Text
Figures: abruption, 53, 55; aethopoeia, *see* Description; allegory, 45; allusion, 269–76; anatanaclasis, 117; antiphrasis, 106–7, 122*n*15, 175, 252, 278, 280, 284; antonomasis, 106, 115; apostrophe, 56; asteism, 252; catachresis, 50–51; 60*n*7, 105; commination, 53; communication, 121*n*4; distribution, 56; dubitation, 53–54; ellipsis, 56, 165, 169–73, 181*n*39, 218; epanorthosis, 56; epithet, 55, 82, 86, 98*n*14 (*see also* Description); euphemism, 106; hypallage, 98*n*14, 106, 115; hyperbaton, 56; hyperbole, 57, 107, 280; hypotyposis, *see* Description; irony, 106–8; litotes, 49, 57, 107, 259; metalepsis, 106, 115; metaphor, 9, 19, 45, 51, 56–57, 60*n*7, 83, 86–87, 89, 94, 98*n*14, 103, 106–21, 122*n*14, 123*n*20, 124*nn*27, 35, 125*nn*36, 38, 275, 284, obsessive, 5, Proustian, 72, 203–13, 237, 285–86 (*see also* Analogy); metonymy, 9, 51, 55, 94, 98*n*14, 103, 106–10, 113–19, 123*n*16, 125*nn*35, 38, 271, 273, 275, 278, 284,

Index

narrative, 169 (*see also* Contiguity); onomatopoeia, 93, 106; periphrasis, 106; polyptotis, 117; prosographia, *see* Description; repetition, 56; syllepsis, 116–17; synecdoche, 32–33, 49, 51, 57, 94, 98*n*14, 106–10, 115–18, 123*n*16, 125*n*35, 237, 280, 294; topographia, *see* Description; *see also* Alliteration; Analogy; Description; Elocution

Flaubert, Gustave, 35, 148, 183–202, 205–8, 213, 218, 229

Fontanier, Pierre de, 46–54, 60*n*7, 86, 105–8, 115–17, 122*n*7, 125*n*38, 269

Form, 6, 8, 12, 20, 24*n*30, 32, 36, 38–39, 67–68, 72, 92, 94, 242, 244, 251, 259, 269; figure as, 47, 49–50, 55; literary, 10–11, 70, 75, 138, 283; and substance in language, 70–71, 76–77

Formalism, 29, 39, 71; Russian, 6–9, 11, 20–21, 22*n*6, 71, 99*n*34, 107; *see also* Thematic criticism

Foucault, Michel, 143

Freud, Sigmund, 28, 108, 119, 122*n*15, 125*n*37, 150, 219, 274, 278; *see also* Parapraxis

Frontier: *see under* Genre; Narrative

Function, literary, *see* Literary function

Game, 73, 94; play, 17, 64, 110, 175

Gap (*écart*), *see* Space

Genre, 4, 73, 78, 85, 98*n*7, 129, 214, 218; as internal frontiers of literature, 67; rhetorical, 104; as structures of literary discourse, 16, 64, 67–68; traditional theory of, 17, 19, 32, 133–34, 144*n*10; *see also* Literary history; Novel; Rhetoric

Grammar, 9, 48–49, 68, 75, 80, 95–96, 101*n*50, 104, 196–97, 262; sentence, 6, 10, 39, 55, 184, 189–90, 198, 205; *see also* Sign

Grammont, Maurice, 8, 100*n*41

Graphism, *see under* Writing

Groupe μ (*or* Liège group), 103, 114, 116, 121*n*1

Guiraud, Pierre, 77, 82

Hegel, G.W.F., 143

Hemingway, Ernest, 143, 172

Hermeneutics, *see* Meaning

History, *see* Literary history

Hjelmslev, Louis, 70, 76–77, 89, 244; *see also* Linguistics, structural

Homeric poems, 19, 21, 75, 104, 110, 128–31, 134–35, 137, 163

Homology, 8

Hugo, Victor, 63–64, 79–82, 88, 98*n*7, 111, 115, 262

Hypallage, *see under* Figures

Hyperbaton, 56; *see also* Figures

Hyperbole, *see under* Figures

Ideology, 16, 27, 36, 119, 225; connotation as a mechanism of, 34; of criticism, 5, 28; rhetoric of, 40, 43*n*49; structuralism as, 11; *see also* Cratylism

Iliad, the, see Homeric poems

Imitation (*or* mimesis), 118, 128–33, 137–38; art as imitation of nature, 22; mimicry, 93, 189, 229, 262, 266–67, 282

Index, 65, 263–64

Invention, *see* Rhetoric, parts of

Irony, 106–8; *see also* Figures

Jakobson, Roman, 7–9, 21, 23*n*10, 54, 68, 93, 99*n*34, 101*n*51, 107–8, 115, 123*n*23, 124*n*27, 125*n*38, 176, 275; *see also* Shifter

James, Henry, 286

James, William, 131

Jespersen, Otto, 8, 100*n*41

Joyce, James, 67, 142, 163, 218

Kafka, Franz, 21, 40, 66, 200

Kant, Immanuel, 61*n*

Lacan, Jacques, 66, 114, 124*n*27, 278

Laclos, Choderlos de, 154; *Les liaisons dangereuses*, 142

La Fontaine, Jean de, 46, 52, 77, 85, 184, 206

La Harpe, Jean François de, 17, 22, 55, 98*n*16

Lamartine, Alphonse de, 79
Lamy, Bernard, 50, 52, 56–57, 122*nn*7, 14
Langue (language), *see under* Linguistics
Lautréamont (Isidore Ducasse), 67, 110, 113
Lemaître, Jules, 62
Lévi-Strauss, Claude, 3–6, 9, 14–15
Lexical choice, *see under* Vocabulary
Liège group, 103, 114, 116
Linguistics, 6, 10–11, 29–30, 39, 48, 68, 219; *langage*, 59; *langue* and *parole*, 18–19, 30, 50, 58; relation to semiology, 30–31; structural, 7, 10, 69–70, 76–77, 244
Literal meaning, 37, 45, 47, 50–51, 57, 60*n*6, 80, 86–87, 94, 99*nn*27, 31, 116, 235, 253, 258, 285; denotation, 31–32, 43*n*49, 57, 83, 87, 90, 99*n*31, 105, 252; *see also* Figurative meaning
Literariness (*literaturnost*), 4, 21, 22*n*6, 68
Literary (*or* poetic) function, 4, 7, 14, 20–21, 23*n*20, 66, 83, 92, 108, 172; figures classified by, 51–52, 54, 94; literature as system of, 58–59
Literary history, 4, 11, 20–21; problem of classification, 62–63, 120; relation to genre theory, 64; "Republic of Letters" (Thibaudet), 18, 62, 65; as a system, 7, 19–20, 23*n*20; *see also* Rhetoric
Literary language, *see* Poetic language
Litotes, *see under* Figures
Lyotard, Jean-François, 124*n*27

Malherbe, François de, 77, 85–86, 232
Mallarmé, Stephane, 10, 64, 67–69, 76, 78, 81–82, 84, 88, 90–93, 100*n*42, 101*nn*50, 51, 110, 114, 136, 237, 286; *see also* Book, the
Marcel, Gabriel, 62–63
Margin, 96, 100*n*50, 156, 158–59, 163, 175, 178, 268, 286
Martineau, Henri, 152, 159, 164
Maupassant, Guy de, 80
Mauron, Charles, 23*n*20

Mauss, Marcel, 108
Meaning, 4, 8–9, 13–14, 28, 33, 44*n*54, 46–50, 92, 167, 171, 197, 212, 225, 231, 245–46, 250–51; and figures, 89, 110, 115, 226; and form, 22*n*7, 39, 71, 92; hermeneutics, 13–15, 54, 252–56, 268; relation to signification, 24*n*30, 28–29, 31, 34–36, 39, 41, 44*n*52, 54, 60*n*6, 83, 244–46, 257, 268; semantics, 7, 29, 32, 40–41, 59*n*3, 77, 83, 86–87, 93–94, 96, 100*n*42, 116, 118–19, 236–39, 249; *see also* Figurative meaning; Figure; Literal meaning; Synonymy
Mérimée, Prosper, 147–48, 151–52, 163–64, 171
Merleau-Ponty, Maurice, 15
Metalepsis, 106, 115; *see also* Figures
Metaphor: *see* Analogy; Figures
Meter, 75–77, 79, 97*n*3
Metonymy, *see under* Figures
Michaux, Henri, 94, 131
Michelet, Jules, 36, 88
Mimesis, *see* Imitation
Mimicry, *see under* Imitation
Modernism, 21–22, 40, 50, 58–59, 63, 76, 79, 84, 86–87, 98*n*8, 100*nn*50, 51, 127–28, 135, 142–43, 199–200, 212*n*44, 221–22; *see also* Surrealism; Symbolism
Molière, J.B.P., 79, 84–85, 206, 229, 280; *Tartuffe*, 250–51
Motivated comparison, 111–13
Motivation, *see under* Sign

Names, *see* Vocabulary
Narrative, 10, 67–68, 137–43, 186, 189, 193–97, 218–20, 222; diegesis, 128–35, 173, 194, 202*n*44; frontiers of, 127–44; narration, 133–37; Stendhalian, 169–78; *see also under* Figures: ellipsis, metonymy
Networks, *see under* Relations
Novel, 16, 19, 68, 98*n*7, 127, 134, 142–43, 148, 161–64, 167–68, 175, 193–95, 198–200, 202*nn*43, 44, 214, 218, 220

Odyssey, the, *see* Homeric poems
Onomatopoeia, 103, 106; *see also* Figures
Ordinary language, *see* Poetic language

Palimpsest, 50, 72, 213–226, 228*n*59, 284, 286
Paradigmatic, *see under* Relations
Parapraxis, 113, 152, 219, 274, 292*n*130
Parole (speech), *see under* Linguistics
Pascal, Blaise, 49, 158, 178
Paulhan, Jean, 59, 60*n*5; *see also* "Terror"
Plato, 19, 69, 119, 144*n*10, 205, 250; *Cratylus*, 92, 132, 246, (*see also* Cratylism); *Republic*, 128–33, 137
Play, *see* Game
Pleonasm, 36–37
Poetic (*or* literary) language, 7, 9–10, 29, 31, 58–59, 75–102, 110, 118, 120, 137, 237; relation to critical language, 3–6, 28–29, 72–73; relation to social language, 40, 43*n*49; rhetoric as, 50, 57–58, 68; signified by figures, 33; structure of, 67, 88–89, 96; as system of versification, 75–76; *see also* Essence; Literary function
Poetics, 8, 78–79, 92, 98*n*14, 99*n*34, 110, 117, 121, 249; classical, 75, 77–79,; *see also* Space
Poetry: *see* Poetic language; Poetics; Relations
Ponge, Francis, 10
Poulet, Georges, 12–13, 38, 61, 216
Prévost, Jean, 170, 199
Propp, Vladimir, 10, 14
Prose, *see under* Relations
Proust, Marcel, 11, 40–41, 66–67, 70, 72–73, 110, 113–14, 123*n*23, 191, 195–96, 198–99, 203–295; *see also under* Essence; Figures (metaphor); Style

Queneau, Raymond, 19
Quevedo, Francisco de, 45, 58
Quintilian, 61, 104

Racine, Jean, 28, 36–37, 46, 77, 79, 84–85, 88, 90, 101, 116, 252; *Andromaque*, 53–54; *Athalie*, 277–78; *Phèdre*, 52, 81–82
Ramus, Petrus, 122*n*7
Ransom, John Crowe, 10
Raymond, Marcel, 72
Reading, 11, 21, 68–70, 96, 165, 218, 222, 225, 256–57, 268, 276; history of, 22, 76, 99*n*2; reader, the, 16, 32, 55, 67, 89, 96, 168, 171, 189, 221, 229
Realism, *see under* Verisimilitude
Relations: connections, 8, 24*n*30, 106, 208; networks, 12, 23*n*20, 168, 199, 238; paradigmatic and syntagmatic, 10, 30, 107, 247; poetry/prose, 20–21, 75–79, 88, 92, 96–97, 99*n*34, 100*n*50, 102*n*52, 107; of reader to text, 67; structures as systems of, 11, 20–21, 28, 70–71; *see also* Sign: Signification; Space
"Republic of Letters," *see under* Literary history
Rhetoric: classical (*or* traditional *or* ancient), 9, 16, 19, 32, 46–48, 54–56, 58, 59*n*3, 72, 89, 94, 99*n*32, 104, 109–110, 115, 117–18, 120, 121*n*7, 176, 252, 269; of figures (*or* tropes), 9, 32–33, 87, 103–26, 271, 277; Fontanier's significance for, 51–52; as genre theory, 8; "new," 10, 68, 121; parts of, 59*n*3, 104, 120*n*7; social, 235, 259–60, 266; as system (*or* classification) of figures, 48, 51, 54–58, 107; *see also* Figure; Figures; Genre; Ideology; Poetic language; Silence
Richard, Jean-Pierre, 12, 290*n*69
Richards, I. A., 111
Ricoeur, Paul, 13–15
Rimbaud, Arthur, 8, 79, 81
Robbe-Grillet, Alain, 27, 37, 43*n*47, 135, 143, 198
Romanticism, 20–21, 79–88, 120, 283–84
Rousseau, Jean-Jacques, 88, 154, 167, 250

302   *Index*

Rousset, Jean, 12, 72, 125*n*39
Russian Formalism, *see under* Formalism

Saint-Amant, M. A. G., 84, 95; *Moyse sauvé*, 135
Sainte-Beuve, C. A., 4, 148
Sartre, Jean-Paul, 27, 31, 54, 100*n*37, 143, 194, 222
Saussure, Ferdinand de, 29–31, 37–38, 51, 91, 95; *see also* Linguistics, structural
Semantics, *see under* meaning
Semiology (*or* semiotics), 10, 34–35, 37–41, 43*n*49, 56–57, 120, 136, 251, 281; of literature, 29–30, 38, 77, 121; semiological system, 33, 55, 156–57; semiotic relation, 118–19; *see also* Linguistics; Sign; Signification
Shifter (Jakobson), 176–77, 275
Shklovsky, Viktor, 20
Sign, 5–7, 27, 44, 54–55, 69, 71, 135, 199, 244; arbitrariness and motivation of, 8–9, 36–37, 57, 91–96, 100*n*46, 118, 120, 124*n*27, 198–99, 232–33, 240–42, 246, 285, 288*n*32; extralinguistic, 30–31, 34–35, 130–31, 237, 240, 264, 266–68; grammatical linearity of, 49; signifier and signified, 6, 30–36, 38–40, 43*n*49, 47–50, 54, 70–71, 77, 83, 91, 93–94, 96, 102*n*52, 116, 237–39, 241–44, 248–49, 264–65, 283–84, 288*n*39; "Signs of Literature" (Barthes), 29, 33, 58–59; "zero degree," 47–48; *see also* Cratylism; Form; Meaning; Signification; Symbol
Signification, 15, 24*n*30, 31, 33–36, 38–41, 44*n*52, 51, 55, 57, 69, 83, 91, 125*n*38, 162–63, 186, 198, 252, 255, 257, 266, 269, 281; figurative, *see* Figurative meaning; figures of, 9, 32, 55, 89; literal, *see* Literal meaning; relation of, 263–65; system of, 8, 28–30, 34–35, 37, 48, 70, 89; *see also* Form; Meaning
Silence, 38, 40, 43*n*52, 73, 96, 176, 193–200, 292*n*113; of reading, 22, 96, 97*n*3, 100*n*50; rhetoric of, 41

Similarity, *see* Analogy
Sojcher, Jacques, 103, 113, 115
Sollers, Phillipe, 69, 143
Space, 12, 18, 69, 72, 92, 187, 209, 211–13, 219–22, 237; criticism as a 38; figure and spatial relations, 108–110, 116; figure as a gap (*écart*), 46–51, 54, 57, 59, 78–83, 86–90, 96–97, 98*n*18, 99*n*34, 102*n*52, 124*n*27; literature as a, 18, 70, 72, 133, 136; *see also* Form
Spitzer, Leo, 11–13, 16, 78
Stendhal (Henri Beyle), 16, 147–182; *see also under* Narrative; Text
Structuralism, 3–25, 28
Structure: *see* Genre; Narrative; Poetic language; Relations
Sturluson, Snorri, 45
Style, 11–12, 24*n*30, 32, 47, 55, 71, 75, 78, 87–91, 96, 98*nn*7, 8, 99*n*31, 175, 177, 187, 198, 229, 232, 259–60, 262, 281–84; Proustian, 203–8; stylistics, 8, 55, 59*n*3, 78, 88, 122*n*13
Sublime, *see* Figure
Surrealism, 81, 83, 118–20, 124*n*27
Syllepsis, 116–17; *see also* Figures
Symbol: different from sign, 30; *sumbolon*, 108, 118–20
Symbolism, 79–86, 119–20
Synecdoche, *see under* Figures
Synesthesia, 8–9, 80, 93, 98*n*14, 114, 241
Synonymy, 55, 59, 80
Syntagmatic, *see under* Relations
Syntax, *see* Grammar
System: *see under* Literary function; Literary history; Poetic language; Relations; Rhetoric; Semiology; Signification

Tacitus, 104
"Terror" (Paulhan), 50, 59, 60*n*5
Text *and* textuality, 4, 10, 31, 36, 69–70, 140, 214–15, 257, 269, 283–84, 286; and figures, 53, 65; Stendhalian, 158–60, 163–65, 167–69, 177–78; *see also* Relations; Signification
Thematic criticism, 5, 11–12, 16, 24*n*30,

27, 167–68, 178, 211; relation to formalist criticism, 71–72
Thibaudet, Albert, 18, 61–68, 72–73, 183–84, 193; *see also under* Literary history
Tomachevski, Boris, 20
Topics, 16–17, 59*n*3
Trope, *see* Figure
Tynianov, Jurij, 20, 23*n*10

Usage, 51, 86–88, 124*n*27, 234, 262; cliché as an aspect of, 57, 87, 235–36, 255, 259, 293*n*150; literary and ordinary distinguished, 48–50, 82, 94, 96, 99*n*27
Utopia, 18, 40, 97, 285, 293*n*131

Valéry, Paul, 9–11, 17–18, 31, 60*n*7, 62–66, 68, 78, 82, 91–93, 97*n*2, 127, 158, 197, 199
Varga, A, Kibédi, 99*n*34, 121*n*7, 126*n*41
Vergil, 104; *Aeneid*, 53–54
Verisimilitude (*vraisemblance*), 17, 169, 184–87, 214; realism, 8, 135, 196–97, 203, 214
Verlaine, Paul, 71, 94
Verne, Jules, 134
Vigny, Alfred de, 79
Vocabulary (*and* names), 18, 75, 82, 93–95, 106, 210, 231–49, 253, 263, 279, 288*nn*33, 37, 39, 41, 289*nn*49, 63; lexical choice, 84, 102*n*51; words, 5–6, 39, 92, 100*n*42, 249–52, 262, 285–86, 288*n*32, 289*n*42
Vossius, Gerard, 106

Words, *see* Vocabulary
Writing, 3–4, 21, 33, 40–41, 46, 54, 67–70, 77, 98*n*8, 127, 136, 154–59, 165, 178, 187–88, 199–200, 214, 222, 226, 262, 268–69, 284, 286, 292*n*117; authorship, 16, 55, 58, 141–42, 147, 149, 159, 173, 175, 178, 238, 262; *écriture* (Barthes), 78; graphism, 71, 76, 158–59; writer (*écrivain*), 4–7, 21, 32, 72–73, 92, 148, 239, 275